Collective Bargaining in the Public Sector

Collective Bargaining in the Public Sector

Labor-Management Relations and Public Policy

Alan Edward Bent
University of Cincinnati

T. Zane Reeves
California State University
Dominguez Hills

The Benjamin/Cummings Publishing Company, Inc.
Menlo Park, California • Reading, Massachusetts
London • Amsterdam • Don Mills, Ontario • Sydney

The Benjamin/Cummings Publishing Company
2727 Sand Hill Road
Menlo Park, California 94025

Contents

v

About the Authors

Alan Edward Bent is Professor and Head of the Department of Political Science, McMicken College of Arts and Sciences, University of Cincinnati. He is a specialist in Public Administration, Labor-Management Relations, and Urban Politics. Dr. Bent received his PhD from Claremont Graduate School. Among his other published works are the following books:

- *Police, Criminal Justice and the Community* (with Ralph A. Rossum)
- *Urban Administration: Management, Politics and Change* (with Ralph A. Rossum)
- *The Politics of Law Enforcement: Conflict and Power in Urban Communities*
- *Escape from Anarchy: A Strategy for Urban Survival*

T. Zane Reeves is Associate Professor, Department of Public Administration, California State University, Dominguez Hills. He is a specialist in Public Policy Analysis and Educational Finance. Dr. Reeves received his PhD from the University of Southern California.

Preface

Much has already been written about the common strains affecting America's larger, older cities. The conventional literature has focused on such problems as the flight of the middle-class to the suburbs, the wholesale abandonment of tax-paying properties, and the growing concentration of poor and minority inhabitants, who require more extensive public services. To be sure, these are real and vexing problems. But the crisis of the city—and of the nation—cannot be fully appreciated without paying attention to the workers, at all levels of government, who provide the nation's public services and examining how their political strength and accelerating demands—achieved through employee groups—influence public policy.

Moreover, the activities of public employees transcend current policies adjusted to meet their demands. The fiscal plight of cities and the difficulties of governments and members of the public to match the political power wielded by many employee groups pose some essential questions about the current philosophy of government, as well as its structures and functions. Fundamentally, the contemporary phenomenon of public employee unionism—with its concomitant power manifestations—is neither merely another urban problem nor a national problem concerning the "arrival" of a new interest group in the polity; it has implications for the governability of the American regime. It is with all of these problems that the book deals. The book is written to provide a new perspective on the study of American politics and its public bureaucracies. It may be used as a basic text in public labor-management relations courses, or in Political Science, Public Administration, and Economics classes concerned with public personnel administration, public policy, urban problems, or interest groups.

Before discussing the contents of the book, a few introductory remarks about public employee unionism may be helpful: The increase in public employment at all levels of government is matched by the rising unionization of public employees. Since the 1960s, the stagnation of the labor movement in the private sector has coincided with the flourishing of the movement among public employees—the fastest growing sector of unionization in America. "The 1960s have already earned the right to go down in labor relations history as the decade of the public employee" has been the pronouncement of one scholar in labor relations. "The rise of these unions is the most significant development in the industrial relations field in the last thirty years."* This occurs at a time when the proportion of blue-collar and craft workers is diminishing and professional and subprofessional employees is growing. The spirit of unionization in public employment and the attractiveness of union membership among the white-collar employees signal an emerging self-conscious proletarianism of a new class of workers. Even employee groups that normally eschew labor organizations—teachers, social workers, nurses, engineers—now readily form and join unions.

A growing militancy in public employee organizations has paralleled their growth. Strikes—often in defiance of existing statutes and court orders forbidding strikes or work stoppages against government—occur with increasing regularity. Additionally, public labor organizations have employed highly effective political strategies to apply pressure on elected and administrative officials on behalf of their members. This has been done on two levels: one, to secure advantages internally through bilateral decisionmaking, and, two, to influence the external public policy-making process in a way that is advantageous to the membership. Both approaches converge on the objectives of bettering economic conditions, challenging the merit system, and obtaining employee participation in determining both personnel policies and the nature of public services to be rendered.

The response of government, especially some state legislatures, has been a slow, almost grudging recognition of union activities. But, there now appears to be an acceptance of employee organizations. A number of states have followed the example of the federal government in instituting statutes authorizing or requiring collective bargaining in their municipalities. Some of the larger, more industrialized states have passed laws on labor relations that surpass those of the federal government. In general, however, the government has had to play catch-up with the private sector in its knowledge about labor relations and collective bargaining procedures. Having failed to arrest the evolutionary progress of public employee unionization by claiming of state "sovereignty" and government as a "model employer" and by holding up of the merit principle as an antithesis to unions, governments at all levels of the federal system are learning to function in the new era of labor relations. Ultimately, how governments adjust to this phenomenon has an impact on the viability of the American regime.

This book describes the phenomenon of public sector unionism, its growth and its relationship to public personnel administration and civil service; the issues and tactics of collective bargaining, its economic

* Jack Stieber, Director, Michigan State University, School of Labor and Industrial Relations, quoted by David R. Jones in *New York Times* 2 April 1967.

impact and the political environment in which it operates; and strikes and impasse resolutions. Case studies are employed throughout the book to illustrate real-world occurrences and to dramatize, for the reader, the manifestations of the phenomenon. The book is descriptive in its treatment of the state of the art and practice of public sector collective bargaining. It examines the influence that public policy has had in the evolution and development of collective bargaining. It also considers public employee unions as an emerging variable in the field of public policy analysis and research.

The role of public employee unions in the political process is not analyzed solely from the institutional or legal framework. Rather, heuristic models developed in public policy studies are combined with analytic constructs to explore the profound ways by which public employee unions are reshaping contemporary political power relationships at all levels of government.

We take this opportunity to thank those who aided us in the development of this book. We are indebted to Michael McDowell, Dwight Moore, Linda Reeves, and Larry Wade for their assistance. We would also like to express our appreciation to the many officers and representatives of labor organizations, and career, appointed, and elected officials in local, state, and federal agencies for their insights and information and for permitting us to examine internal records and reports. We would like to thank the Benjamin/Cummings staff and Phoenix Publishing Services of San Francisco for their editorial guidance and assistance in the production of the book. Finally, we would like to offer our special thanks to our wives Dawn and Jean for their continued support and interest in the progress of our work.

Alan Edward Bent
T. Zane Reeves

June, 1978

Nature of
Collective Bargaining

Public sector unionism has certain characteristics unique to it, and some that are not. The development of public employee unions is a recent phenomenon activated by an emerging self-consciousness among workers and facilitated by changing attitudes in government and society-at-large. The growth of unionism in public employment has been so compelling that it poses a formidable challenge to the civil service system and the traditional public policy process. Part one of this book examines the growth of unionism, the environment in which public employee unions operate, and the principles governing collective bargaining in the public sector. Fundamentally, collective bargaining in public employment operates within both an economic and a political context, and this is emphasized throughout the book. This part concludes with a chapter on the economic characteristics of public sector collective bargaining to acquaint the reader with the importance of labor economics in the field of labor-management relations. In general, the subjects treated in this part are the fundamentals that describe the reasons for and the essence of collective bargaining in the public sector.

Development and Implications of Public Sector Unionism

1

With about three million civilian employees, the federal government is the largest single employer in the United States; its work force is larger than that of the ten largest industrial corporations combined.[1] State and municipal work forces are often the largest employers in their respective jurisdictions. In addition to size there is an occupational diversity found in no other organization.[2] All the occupational classes are represented in government service: unskilled, skilled, craftsmen, clerical and secretarial, paraprofessional, and professional. Government at all levels assumes such varied responsibilities and functions that for practically any kind of work performed in private industry one can find its counterpart in government service.[3]

A distinct majority (77 percent) of these governmental positions, at least at the federal level, are of the so-called white-collar classification; that is, they are of a professional, scientific, administrative, or supportive nature.[4] * A unique feature of government employment is that there is a much greater proportion of white-collar employment in the public service than in the private economy.[5] The remaining 23 percent of federal positions are regarded as blue-collar. Almost 85 percent of the total blue-collar employees are employed in three agencies: Defense, Post Office, and Veterans Administration.[6] Employment trends indicate that the number of governmental blue-collar jobs is declining. Indeed, the number of blue-collar workers has decreased every year except two since 1957.†

* Generally speaking, the Civil service Commission defines a "blue-collar employee" as one who earns a wage and a "white-collar employee" as one who earns a salary.
† During 1961 and 1966, when blue-collar employment showed an increase, there were definitional revisions of blue-collar occupations by the civil service commission.

Implications for Unionization

Total union membership has been steadily increasing during this century. For example, in the twenty years between 1950 and 1972, union membership increased by over five million persons to 20,838,000 —the highest total in history.[8] However, when this membership is viewed as a percentage of the total nonagricultural labor force, we find a steady reduction in the proportion of the labor force having union membership. The union movement reached a peak in 1945 with 35.5 percent of the total nonagricultural work force enrolled; membership had declined to 31.5 percent of the labor force by 1950, 31.4 percent in 1960, and 27.4 percent in 1970.[9] During this period public sector employees were joining unions in increasing numbers, but in 1972 they comprised only 11.8 percent of all union members as compared to 42.8 percent participation in manufacturing and 45.4 in nonmanufacturing[10] (see table 1-1). The implications are clear to union organizers: if union growth is to be continued and sustained, greater numbers of public employees must be added to the membership roles. Since over three-quarters of public employees work in white-collar jobs, if the union movement is to succeed in organizing the public sector, it must succeed in organizing the white-collar workers. And, it is these very white-collar occupations that historically have been the most resistant to labor union organizing.

Difficulties in Organizing

There are four factors that present problems to labor unions when they attempt to attract public sector membership. The first of these factors concerns inter-union rivalries that develop over matters of jurisdiction. Economists Neil Chamberlain and Donald Cullen explain:

> It is understandable enough that most unions seek to define their jurisdiction broadly enough to give themselves plenty of room for survival, if not expansion, and that in the process they can scarcely avoid overlapping the vague or shadowy claim of some other union also bent on survival and expansion.[11]

It is in the union's self-interest to define its membership eligibility as broadly as possible. This tendency often produces jurisdictional squabbles when an active organizing campaign arouses antipathy on the part of a rival union that feels its territory is being encroached. Willem Vosloo argues that union rivalries are generally oriented around one of two controversies: the craft union versus the industrial union dichotomy and the affiliated union versus the independent union dichotomy.[12]

TABLE 1-1: Percentage of Total Union Members in Each Sector of the Economy (Selected Years, 1956-1972)

| Year | Total | Nonmanufacturing | Manufacturing | Government | |
				Federal	State and Local
1956	5.1%	46.1%	48.8%	-	-
1958	5.8%	47.7%	46.5%	-	-
1960	5.9%	46.4%	47.6%	-	-
1962	7.0%	47.2%	45.8%	-	-
1964	8.1%	45.3%	46.6%	5.0%	3.1%
1968	10.7%	43.7%	45.6%	6.7%	4.0%
1970	11.2%	44.5%	44.3%	6.6%	4.6%
1972	11.8%	45.4%	42.8%	6.6%	5.2%

Source: U.S., Bureau of Labor Statistics *Handbook of Labor Statistics 1976*, tab. 142, p. 295; and *Handbook of Labor Statistics 1972*, Bulletin 1735 (1970), tab. 150, pp. 327-30.

The craft-industrial controversy is illustrated by some disputes involving the American Federation of State, County and Municipal Employees (AFSCME), the American Federation of Government Employees (AFGE), and some other AFL-CIO unions. Both AFSCME and AFGE can be classified as industrial unions because of the wide jurisdiction that they claim. AFSCME claims jurisdiction over any employee in the nonindustrial, noncommercial labor force with the exception of federal government employees; AFGE claims rights over all civilian employees of the federal government and the District of Columbia. Obviously, these broad claims lead these unions into frequent conflict with craft unions. Two particularly significant disputes have involved the Building Service Employees International Union and AFSCME, and AFL-CIO's Metal Trades Department and the International Association of Machinists against AFGE. These conflicts developed primarily as a result of the practice of issuing charters to any unaffiliated groups within the broad boundaries of AFSCME and AFGE that showed a desire to join their organizations. This includes groups that were also eligible to join craft unions.[13]

The rivalry between affiliated and independent unions often seems to be even more intense. An affiliated union is one formally associated with AFL-CIO; independents include professional associations, employee associations, and other unaffiliated bargaining agents. The independents like to claim that they are embarrassed by the tactics and deep-rooted conflicts within AFL-CIO. On the other hand, the affiliated unions brand the independents as company unions or dues collection agencies.[14] An example of a particularly intense organizational rivalry is that between the National Education Association (NEA), a professional association, and the affiliated American Federation of Teachers (AFT). During the 1960s AFT made significant increases in membership in a number of major metropolitan areas and among groups that had previously designated NEA as being their exclusive representative.[15]

A second factor that labor unions must contend with when attempting to organize public workers is the comparatively strong sense of job security that most government employees have. They feel protected in the civil service system; they also feel that a public job is less subject to the vagaries of the market than a comparable job in the private sector. At any rate, this attitude is a problem for union organizers; historically it has contributed to the relatively slow growth of unionism in the public sector.[16]

The third factor leading to organizing difficulties is the opposition of governmental units to public unionism. Hervey Juris and Peter Feuille note that:

> *Employer resistance to public unionization has been phrased in many ways, but it reflects the same desires among public sector employers to avoid sharing managerial authority and to keep labor costs down that are historically found in the private sector.[17]*

Allan Cartter and Ray Marshall describe a subtle intimidation employed by some employers when white-collar workers are told that the positions of trust and confidence that they occupy with management will be jeopardized by unionization.[18] Generally, the federal government has been much more accepting of collective organizing than the states or local governments. Although this is due in part to the federal Executive Orders of the early 1960s, which affirmed the right of employees to organize, it may also be attributed to beneficial experiences with collective bargaining predating these orders. For instance, a model of harmonious relations exists in the Tennessee Valley Authority, which has engaged in bargaining with its employees since the 1930s. Wilson Hart gives this glowing account:

> *The ultimate in employee-management cooperation ... is found in an agency such as the Tennessee Valley Authority where strong and active unions not only exist but are welcomed and encouraged. They are acknowledged as partners of management in every phase of decision-making which affects employees and also collaborate in personnel operations.[19]*

However, it must be remembered that this situation is the exception rather than the rule; most public employers continue to resist unionization either overtly or covertly.[20] As a result, unions may face organizational problems when trying to enroll members who feel that their job or their chances for advancement may be in jeopardy.

The fourth and final factor in describing the difficulties of organizing public employees is the prevalent anti-union bias of white-collar workers. The reasons for this phenomenon are complex but may be summarized in terms of two primary issues—status and utility.

The argument is made that clerks and other lower level white-collar employees identify with management and will not reject this identification to join a union. Extensive study by Arthur Thompson and Irwin Weinstock of government white-collar workers has produced some notable findings in this area. One of their significant conclusions was that "support of unions varied inversely with the level of education."[21] They also found unfavorable reactions among the younger employees and those with the shortest length of service.[22] These findings could very well spell trouble for organizers, given the rising educational level among white-collar employees and the declining average age of labor force participants resulting from the influx of young workers and earlier retirement.[23] Interestingly, their research into the attitudes of TVA workers, in an environment of outstanding labor-management relations in which employees are practically encouraged to join labor unions, found that almost 75 percent viewed union membership as unprofessional.[24] Albert A. Blum argues that white-collar workers regard labor unions as "dirty, noisy and lower class."[25] He notes that some studies indicate a tendency for a blue-collar worker to terminate his union membership once moving into a white-collar position.[26] Indeed, Blum feels that as white-collar work becomes functionally more and more like blue-collar work (or perhaps because of it) the clerks come to identify with and cling to middle-class values all the more vigorously.[27] On the other hand, Blum does believe that "[there] are some trends that indicate that in the long run a salaried proletariat may emerge"[28] However, this cannot occur as long as the white-collar worker continues to identify himself with management and does not evolve a working-class consciousness.[29]

In addition to the fact that the white-collar worker may be reluctant to reduce his status by joining a union, there is the pragmatic question of what is to be gained. Professionals in particular often view the union as irrelevant to their quest for higher salaries and benefits. They often feel that in the final analysis they will have to go to Congress or the appropriate legislative body to obtain pay raises and that lobbying can be done at least as well by a professional association or an employee association as by a union.[30] Leo Troy notes that, at least in the federal sector, "wages, hiring, promotion, transfer, suspension, demotion, discharge, or other disciplinary action" are all either outside the scope of collective bargaining or are so dependent on laws and regulations that bargaining is not meaningful.[31] In addition, Troy makes the point that some white-collar professionals feel that union membership would be disadvantageous to them because the union will inevitably be responsive to the needs and wishes of the majority of its membership, which may or may not coincide with those of the white-collar worker, particularly the professional. As Troy states:

> In terms of pay, the professionals feel that membership in a union representing both professionals and non-professionals, even in separate units, must eventually mean that the demands of the most numerous lower-paid members will be favored and therefore that the differential between the two groups will be reduced.[32]

Additionally, most professionals are oriented toward increasing the prerogatives of management in order to secure their needs rather than trying to limit managerial prerogatives as the union desires.[33]

We have seen, then, that union organizers face some real difficulties in terms of convincing white-collar workers that union membership would be advantageous. Jurisdictional squabbles among the unions themselves, the relative job security of the civil service system, government opposition in some quarters, and a basic antiunion bias of white-collar workers based on considerations of status and utility all combine to produce a formidable challenge to the union movement.

Interestingly enough, the union movement has been able to respond effectively to these challenges to a surprising degree. How the union movement has managed to grow and flower in the public sector despite the difficulties of organizing is the subject of the next section.

Emergence of Public Sector Unions

As was indicated in table 1-1, union memberships in the public sector have been increasing over the past two decades, albeit slowly. In the twelve years between 1956 and 1968 the percentage of affiliated governmental employees doubled, while the other sectors decreased in membership. Public unionism advanced at the tantalizingly slow pace of about .4 percent a year in the state and local levels of government between 1964 and 1970; growth seemed to have stabilized in the federal sector during this period.[34]

Table I-2 gives us some indication at the federal level of how this growth translates in terms of white-collar and blue-collar memberships. Note that a steadily increasingly number of federal employees were

TABLE 1-2: Federal Employees in Exclusive Bargaining Units or Covered by Agreements (Selected Years, 1964-1974)

| | | | Employees in Exclusive Units | | | | | | Employees Covered by Agreement | |
| | Total Employees | | Blue Collar [a] | | White Collar [b] | | | | | |
Year	Total	Percentage	Total	Percentage	Total	Percentage			Total	Percentage
1964	250,543	12	...	...	...	...			110,573	6
1965	319,724	16	...	...	...	...			241,850	12
1966	434,890	21	226,150	40	179,293	15			291,532	14
1967	629,915	29	338,660	54	291,255	21			423,052	20
1968	797,511	40	400,669	67	396,842	28			556,962	28
1969	842,823	42	426,111	72	416,712	29			559,415	28
1970	916,381	48	429,136	81	487,245	35			601,505	31
1971	1,038,288	53	437,586	84	600,702	42			707,067	36
1972	1,082,587	55	427,089	83	655,498	46			753,247	39
1973	1,086,361	56	404,955	84	681,406	47			837,410	43
1974	1,142,419	57	406,000	82	736,419	48			984,553	49

Source: U.S., Civil Service Commission, *Union Recognition in the Federal Government* (November 1974), p. 26.

Note: The figures quoted are executive branch employees excluding the U.S. Postal Service, FBI, CIA, NSA, and foreign nationals serving outside the U.S.

[a] Wage system employees.

[b] General schedule employees.

covered by agreements in the years 1964-1974.[35] We also learn that blue-collar employees in exclusive units doubled between 1966 and 1974; white-collar employees in the same period more than tripled in numbers.[36] The trends are clear. Unions continue to make gains in their traditional haven in the blue-collar sector; the surprise is in the impressive gains that unions are making in recruiting white-collar workers.[37] It appears that despite the potential difficulties for union recruiting of the white-collar workers advanced in the previous section, public unions are attracting white-collar members in impressive numbers for the first time. Four areas of analysis will be developed in order to explain this phenomenon.

One, due to the inflationary state of the economy, workers are more conscious of their financial status and are being convinced in increasing numbers that unions are effective in securing their economic gains. (A later chapter will deal with the correctness or incorrectness of this perception.) A task force organized by the nonpartisan research foundation Twentieth Century Fund supports the workers' conclusion in its 1970 report:

> It is in local government where what once may have been the advantage of being a public employee has been most seriously eroded by rising living costs, greater economic gains by private employees, and in some occupations—policeman, fireman, and teacher particularly—by increased job hazards. These conditions and the fact that unionism has become more acceptable in American society and has demonstrated its effectiveness, have led public employees to organize.[38]

Morton Godine notes that the "traditional popular hostility toward governmental bureaucracy" serves to keep the salaries of public employees at a lower level than those in the private sector because of taxpayer resistance.[39]

These tendencies are becoming increasingly obvious to the white-collar worker, who sees the gap between his salary and benefits and those of blue-collar workers steadily closing. Consider the following evidence. Between 1939 and 1955 the median annual salary paid clerical and kindred workers increased by only 172.3 percent; operative and manual workers had their wages raised 256.1 percent in the same period.[40] Between 1936 and 1971 the average weekly earnings of a production worker in manufacturing increased 661 percent, while the rate of increase in the weekly salary of a nonsupervisory worker in wholesale trade was only 542 percent.[41] Furthermore, while the weekly earnings of a blue-collar contract construction worker were increasing 62 percent between 1964-71, the earnings of a white-collar worker in the transportation and public utilities sector rose only 43 percent.[42] This trend generally holds true even when comparing the earnings of a blue-collar worker to those of a professional white-collar employee. For example, the average weekly earnings of a contract construction worker in 1971 were $213.36; the average weekly earnings of an engineer (at the lowest level of responsibility) in 1971 were $205.33, and only $172.60 for an accountant.[43] Also compare the average hourly earnings for several occupations in 1971: Blue-collar production workers in contract construction and in mining (production) earned on the average $5.72 and $4.05 per hour respectively; white-collar non-supervisory workers in services earned $2.99 per hour; in finance, insurance, and real estate, $3.28; and in transportation and public utilities, $4.21.[44] * Finally, refer to table 1-3, which illustrates the fact that both skilled and unskilled blue-collar workers are achieving larger increases in wages and salaries than low-skilled white-collar workers in terms of percentage gains.[45] Given this evidence, it is not surprising that Howard Coughlin, the president of one of the major white-collar unions (Office and Professional Employees International), perceptively remarked in 1966, "The underlying reason for organization [of white-collar employees] and subsequent collective bargaining is money. . . . We must continue to emphasize money as the initial incentive for unionization and collective bargaining. . . . "[46]

The gap between the blue and the white-collar worker is also closing in the fringe benefit area. In the 1950s some fringe benefits that in prewar days were offered only to salaried employees were finding their way into collectively bargained agreements for blue-collar workers.[47] Surveys conducted by the Bureau of Labor Statistics in the early 1960s demonstrated that by that point in time blue-collar benefits had actually surpassed white-collar fringes in some respects.[48] For example, employers paid 27.6 percent of basic pay for supplementary benefits for production workers in 1962 compared to 25 percent of basic pay for these benefits for white-collar employees in 1963.[49]

In addition to the fact that the white-collar worker increasingly finds himself at a relative disadvantage in terms of earnings and benefits, he also finds his job becoming more menial and clerical and devolving into a position more blue-collar in nature.† The culprit is automation. Blum identifies three effects of automation on the white-collar worker: his skills are reduced or disappear as his work becomes more menial, he is beginning to doubt his dreams of upward mobility in the

---

* It must be noted, however, that there were some exceptions to this trend. For example, in the years 1964-71, production workers in manufacturing increased their weekly earnings by only 38.3 percent.

† This generalization applies primarily, of course, to white-collar workers at the lower end of the scale in terms of skill and education.

TABLE 1-3 Average Weekly or Hourly Earnings, Selected Occupational Groups in Metropolitan Areas (1967 = 100)

Year	Office Clerical a	Skilled Maintenance b	Unskilled Plant b
1960	80.1	80.3	79.4
1961	82.7	83.2	82.3
1962	85.4	85.4	84.9
1963	87.9	88.1	87.7
1964	90.4	90.5	90.4
1965	92.9	92.7	93.0
1966	95.9	96.1	95.9
1967	100.0	100.0	100.0
1968	104.9	105.5	105.4
1969	111.0	112.4	111.8
1970	118.1	119.0	118.6
1971	125.5	127.9	128.1
1972	132.9	137.9	138.5
1973	139.5	146.6	147.2

Source: U.S., Bureau of Labor Statistics, *Handbook of Labor Statistics 1976*, tab. 102, p. 237.

Note: Earnings of office clerical workers relate to regular straight-time salaries that are paid for standard work weeks. Earnings of skilled maintenance and unskilled plant workers relate to hourly earnings exculding overtime.

a Men and women.

b Men.

bureaucracy, and he has less job security.[50] As Blum so aptly puts it, the white-collar workers are learning that "clerks they are and clerks they will be. . . . "[51] It is this dawning realization that may develop more of a working-class ethos on the part of these workers and reduce their identification with management.

In a recent work on the shaping of American working-class consciousness, Stanley Aronowitz discusses the proletarianization of American white-collar workers and professionals. "White-collar proletarians" are vulnerable to the appeal of collectivization through unionization. One contributing factor is a growing recognition that the "white-collar" appellation is not truly descriptive but rather a concept oftentimes perpetrated by management as a form of strike insurance because

Part I: Nature of Collective Bargaining

white-collar workers have traditionally not unionized and not struck. Another factor has been the disenchantment of white-collar workers with the decreasing challenge of their work in only being allowed to perform prescribed tasks that are mechanized, routine, and boring. Even professionals have become susceptible. Aronowitz believes that relief from various professional associations is hopeless because they have been co-opted by corporations to perpetuate the professional label despite debased (bureaucratized) skills.[52] In essence the professionals, in contrast to theoreticians, possess a body of expertise that is directly applicable in real life, i.e., engineering, teaching, nursing. They are even provided with adequate pay, status, and prestige. Yet, professional creativity and initiative are increasingly stifled by management. Hence, the proletarianized professional joins a union in order to regain his professional integrity and identity.

A second reason for the emergence of unions in the public sector has been the unions' efforts to diversify their appeal by expressing concern for a range of employee interests and needs. Although, as we have seen, economic gains are still very important to union success, there are a number of other areas of concern for both white- and blue-collar employees that unions can attempt to introduce as subjects for bargaining. For example, Garbarino describes the environment in higher education in the 1960s that led to increasing faculty unionization at some institutions.[53] The late 1950s and early 1960s were very prosperous years for faculties in higher education—more students were enrolling, governments were providing more support, budgets were higher, and salaries were competitive. By the late 1960s, however, these conditions had moderated and the faculties at some institutions, accustomed to a much higher rate of growth, felt that their positions had considerably worsened for six reasons. One, reduction in available positions limited faculty mobility; two, the rate of salary increases slowed; three, the rate of advancement through the salary range was also slowed; four, the proportion of nontenured faculty acquiring tenure declined as decreases in new positions made the administration concerned about becoming "top-heavy"; five, attacks on tenure policy and encouragement of early retirement threatened the established faculty; and six, professional employees lacking official faculty rank became very insecure.[54] Again we note that salary considerations are important, but issues relating to working conditions and job security are also clearly on the minds of the employees. This helps to explain the results that George Angell obtained in interviews with unionized faculty members in Michigan and New York:

> *Their primary reasons for organizing were low salaries, unilateral decisions by trustees and administrators, lack of communication*

*between administration and faculty, and a general feeling of being
treated as high school teachers rather than as members of a college
faculty.... Perhaps the most telling factor leading to unionism,
however, was the lack of academic freedom on some campuses.*[55]

Obviously union organizers have been able to capitalize on this job dissatisfaction and convince increasing numbers of public employees that collective bargaining can improve their working conditions.

In fact, the concept of having a formal agreement between employees and employers is one of the most basic changes that accompanies collective bargaining.[56] The advantages that this affords the member in explanation and clarification of his rights can be used as an important selling point for unionism when recruiting members.

Another recruiting device that unions have used successfully is that of launching a concentrated effort to enlist public workers who were union members prior to government employment. These workers have already been experienced with the advantages of unionism and may therefore offer a high return on recruitment efforts. This situation is usually more applicable to blue-collar occupations such as machinists, electricians, boiler-makers, and other craft-oriented occupations due to the strong presence of unions in these trades.[57]

Unions have also helped their organizing efforts by taking advantage of workers' desire to "belong" and be a part of a group. Union organizers have come to realize that, as Helen Christrup observes, "Collective bargaining . . . provides individuals with a sense of participation . . . the individual may derive a greater sense of mastery over the forces controlling him."[58] George Meany astutely realized this fact when he talked more than a decade ago about the future of the union movement and the problem of recruiting white-collar workers:

*I think the labor movement has to take on the character of a social
movement. It is dealing more and more with the problems of the
whole community and will have to enlist these people, give them a
sense of consciously participating in the great issues that will
determine the kind of society in which we are going to be living.*[59]

This view of the union as a social crusade apparently struck a harmonious note with some workers, perhaps as a concomitant reaction to other organized group activities in the 1960s that relied on tactics of confrontation to achieve their demands.

A third reason for union growth in the public sector has been the increased efforts and activities of other organizations to adopt the posture of a union while attempting to maintain their independent or professional character. This has led to an increased competition between professional and employee associations and affiliated unions, which has resulted, as previously noted, in increased lobbying activities by these groups among public employees. To date it is clear that the associations and the independent unions are winning the contest—white-collar membership in these organizations more than doubles white-collar membership in affiliated unions.[60] However, these independent associations have had to adopt many tactics and selling points from their affiliated rivals in order to stay competitive. Krislov notes, "The typical structure of an association does not differ substantially from that of a union."[61] The American Nurses' Association has advanced the idea of a so-called multipurpose organization, which would combine the best features of both unions and associations—retaining professional orientation and status while seeking exclusive recognition and bargained agreements.[62] Such innovations can greatly enhance the acceptance and respectability of collective organizations among public employees and hasten the growth of organized workers, particularly white-collar workers.

The fourth and final point in regard to the emerging growth of public sector unionism is the fact that governments are increasingly giving their support to collective bargaining in the public sector; this has a positive effect on the openness with which organizational activity can be pursued as well as on its chances for success. We have previously observed in the federal sector that major gains in recruitment at this level were correlated with a more permissive attitude toward unionism on the part of many federal employees. Garbarino argues that this is equally true for public employees at the state level:

> *Permissive state legislation is the key explanation for the burst of academic unionism in the late 1960's and early 1970's. . . . By 1972, twenty-nine states had adopted laws permitting the formation of unions of state employees.*"[63]

It is apparent, then, that a changing attitude on the part of the public employer was a significant contributor to rising public sector unionism.

To review, four reasons have been advanced to explain rising public sector unionism: public employee belief in the effectiveness of unions in securing benefits, union concern over working conditions and other job-related matters, competition with associations for membership has led to union organizational adaptiveness, and reduction in employer antagonism toward unions.

This rationale offers a theoretical framework in which to explain the rapid increases made in public employee union membership especially in the past fifteen years.

Public Sector Unions

Public employee unions are active at all levels of public policymaking. As we will observe, they apply pressure to accomplish their priorities both within the bureaucracy and the larger political environment. Historically, public sector unions have primarily organized in a particularistic rather than a universal fashion, i.e., within a single agency or a single level of government (federal, state, local, district). In 1974, there were over twenty-six different public employee organizations representing state and local public employees.[64] Of these, ten were AFL-CIO affiliated. The major labor participants in public collective bargaining are categorized as follows:

1. Federal Employees (Generic)

a. American Federation of Government Employees (AFGE)

The American Federation of Government Employees is currently the fastest growing union, private or public, in the United States. In the decade from 1962 to 1972, AFGE grew from 83,767 to 620,744 members with over 55 percent of these members classified as GS or "white-collar" workers. AFGE, affiliated with the AFL-CIO, has aggressively recruited federal employees but is also showing increasing expansion among local employees.

The union's most controversial position has been its drive begun in 1975, to organize U.S. armed forces personnel. In 1977, the AFGE membership rejected a motion, by an 80 percent to 20 percent vote, to launch a military service organizing drive. However, AFGE President Kenneth Blaylock said that the idea of a unionized military "will not be soon laid to rest." He said that the proposal failed only because AFGE members were not willing to expend substantial amounts of money and effort for the organizing effort. Despite this setback, AFGE may not have altogether abandoned organizational efforts among these two million potential union members.

To counter this threat, in September 1977 the Senate voted to prohibit labor unions in the military services. The bill (still to be acted on by the House) would impose criminal penalties on any member of the armed forces who, through joining a union, sought to negotiate with the government the terms and conditions of military service. Officers and civilian employees would be prohibited from bargaining with a labor union. Also banned would be the solicitation of union membership among military personnel.

b. National Federation of Federal Employees (NFFE)

The National Federation of Federal Employees has organized more than 130,000 federal employees as of 1975. The federation has generally assumed a more conservative stance on labor-management issues than its larger rival, AFGE. For example, AFGE and AFL-CIO enthusiastically supported an amendment to the Hatch Act, allowing public employees greater political involvement, while NFFE vigorously opposed it.

c. **National Association of Government Employees (NAGE)**
The National Association of Government Employees currently has over 115,000 members and has organized an average of 30,000 members in the three years from 1970-73.

2. Federal Employees (Departmental)

a. **National Treasury Employees Union (NTEU)**
The National Treasury Employees Union claims to include over 59,000 members as of 1975, 96 percent of whom are covered by collective bargaining contracts.[65] NTEU claims this percentage is unmatched by any other federal employee union. This remarkable growth is attributed by union president Vincent Connery to the successful negotiation of three nationwide contracts, which are significant because they:

> *go about as far as they can in terms of the scope of benefits and protections available. . . . Rather than negotiating on a local level, each of our agreements was negotiated with top agency management who are empowered to determine policy for their respective agencies.*[66]

Formerly the National Association of Internal Revenue Employees (NAIRE), the union's 1973 change to NTEU reflects an expanded scope to include other agencies within the Treasury Department. Its 1975 convention voted to revise its constitution to permit unrestricted organizing of all federal employees. NTEU has since focused on an organizing campaign within the newly created Department of Energy.

b. **Postal Clerks and Letter Carriers**
The Postal Clerks and Letter Carriers increased their memberships during the 1968-1974 period from 139,000 to 249,000 and from 168,000 to 232,000 members respectively.[67] Significantly, the Postal Clerks increase of 110,000 members occurred preceding and following the 1970 postal strike.

3. Federal Employees (Crafts)

a. **The Metal Trades Council (MTC)**
The Metal Trades Council with 46,522 members and the International Association of Machinists and Aerospace Workers (IAM-AW) are both crafts unions whose members work primarily with defense and aerospace projects. Both blue-collar unions were the only public employee unions to decline in membership in recent years.

4. Local Employee Unions (Generic and Professional)

a. American Federation of State, County and Municipal Employees (AFSCME)

Although it split from AFGE in 1936 because of what it called a diverse clientele, AFSCME remained within AFL and retained its primary focus on municipal employees. Initially, AFSCME concentrated its resources on enactment of civil service legislation rather than on collective bargaining. The union, like its federal counterpart (AFGE) grew rapidly from 234,840 in 1964 to over 648,000 members in 1972 and over 750,000 in 1977. The union's rapid growth period coincides with a 1965 policy shift. Following an internal leadership struggle, AFSCME adopted a policy that committed the union to the collective bargaining process and reaffirmed the right to strike. Perhaps the union's most militant stance occurred with the Memphis garbage collectors' strike in 1968, which is thought to have precipitated the assassination of Dr. Martin Luther King Jr.

Since its position reaffirming the public employees' right to strike (excluding law enforcement), AFSCME has concluded more than 1,200 collective bargaining contracts and has become the dominant public employee union at the municipal and county government level; it has recently become AFL-CIO's largest affiliate, either private or public.

b. Assembly of Government Employees (AGE)

This is a loose confederation somewhat akin to the AFL-CIO structure. As of 1974 it included more than 700,000 employees in both state and municipal associations. In California, over half of the municipal employees belong to independent municipal associations. Most local associations are composed of police and fire fighter associations (which are unaffiliated nationally). Many AGE associations are being threatened by absorption within nationally affiliated unions, e.g., IAFF. The national leadership "recommends" that affiliates abdicate the right to strike providing that:

(1) Management not contract to private business the performance of approved government services; and (2) specific procedures for the resolution of impasses (e.g., fact-finding, mediation, arbitration, etc.) are provided and adequately financed.[68]

c. International Association of Fire Fighters (IAFF)

The International Association of Fire Fighters, affiliated with the AFL-CIO, had a membership of approximately 167,023 members as of 1974. The union's membership primarily includes uniformed fire fighters but also allows management (officers) to join. Thus far, IAFF has focused on obtaining unit recognition as the exclusive representative with local government. Although IAFF does not advocate strikes, in a landmark case before the California Supreme Court (1974), a local in Vallejo won a decision which "held that issues which the city considered to be nonnegotiable were negotiable and arbitrable."[69] Significantly, the court took a restrictive view on the scope of management rights and relied heavily on private sector precedent.[70]

d. **Fraternal Order of Police (FOP)**

The Fraternal Order of Police includes approximately 157,000 policemen as of 1974 and does not exclude supervisors (officers). The Order's constitution forbids strikes; rather, it focuses on state and local legislation. The ban on strikes has not, however, deterred the members from striking.

e. **International Conference of Police Associations**

This association, with 200,000 members (1974), was established in 1954 from among disgruntled FOP members. It serves as a national lobbying device for criminal justice policymaking rather than as a collective bargainer at the municipal level. The association also forbids strikes, although the membership has engaged in them, as well as in "job actions."

f. **International Brotherhood of Police Officers (IBPO)**

The International Brotherhood of Police Officers has organized only 8,000 members but seeks to build power legitimacy upon AFL-CIO recognition (which it has thus far not attained).

g. **American Nursing Association (ANA)**

The American Nursing Association represents approximately 205,000 members and one-third of the nurses in both private and public hospitals. Interestingly, ANA was forced to rescind its rigid no-strike policy by a particularly militant affiliate, i.e., the California Nursing Association.

h. **Service Employees International Union (SEIU)**

The Service Employees Union included 125,000 public employees within its membership of 550,000 in 1974. By 1977, SEIU claimed to include over 600,000 members. Although most of its private sector members are maintenance and custodial employees, SEIU is presently the second largest AFL-CIO affiliate organizing public professional employees. The union scored an important organizing coup when it was elected as the representative for the Los Angeles County social workers. Its "cutting edge" role in local labor-management relations is exemplified by two SEIU-related court decisions: the Los Angeles Civil Service Commission was compelled to consult with the local before making employee layoffs;[71]

and the city of Hayward was compelled by a lower court (although later overturned) to honor an agency shop clause.[72]

i. **International Brotherhood of Teamsters (IBT)**

The Teamsters' Union includes a cross section of 70,000 (1974) professionals, skilled, and unskilled employees in municipal and county government. A mid-1977 survey conducted by the National League of Cities indicated that policemen in at least fifteen states now "pay Teamster dues and carry Teamster cards." The union also signed a "representational contract" with the San Diego Police Officers' Association for which the Teamsters represented the association in salary talks with the city. Although the Teamsters publically disavow any major effort to organize law enforcement (due to an alleged organized crime linkage to the union), substantial gains have been made in organizing major enforcement departments in Flint, Michigan, and Anchorage, Alaska.

j. **Laborers' International Union (LIU)**

The Laborers' Union, an AFL-CIO affiliate, includes 75,000 public employee members who are primarily blue-collar workers in unskilled positions.

k. **Transit and Craft Unions**

Neither transit nor craft unions include a sizeable public employee contingent nationally. Yet both types of unions have played key roles in county and municipal collective bargaining. The major transit and craft unions include:

(1) International Brotherhood of Electrical Workers (AFL-CIO) with approximately 40,000 federal and 14,000 local employees as union members.

(2) Amalgamated Transit Union (AFL-CIO) with 63,000 members in Canadian and U.S. public employment.

(3) American Association of Classified School Employees with 93,000 members (55,000 in California).

5. State Employee Associations

State employee associations are the principal organizing units within most of the fifty states; they are loosely federated together as Civil Service Employee Associations (CSEA). The two largest units include over 200,000 members alone within the California State Employees' Association and New York's Civil Service Employee Association. Generally unaffiliated and independent, CSEA's often admit supervisory personnel and maintain an "aloofness" from the other labor organizations.

Although pressured into a posture of more militancy by union competition, state employee associations generally have de-emphasized collective bargaining strategies and sought their objectives through political action and lobbying tactics. Thus far, these state employee associations have been successful in accomplishing economic objectives through the traditional pluralistic process. Their impressive size and the unified front generally demonstrated in state capitols has resulted in significantly higher benefits for state employees when compared to their local public employee counterparts.

Despite the reluctance of state employee associations to bargain collectively, state employees belonging to other unions are often more militant. For example, correctional officers in Ohio engaged in strike and/or sickouts every year from 1971-75. This included a system-wide strike in 1975 that lasted for seventeen days. Major strikes in correctional facilities also occurred during the early 1970s in New Jersey, Massachusetts, Rhode Island, and Pennsylvania.

6. Education Employee Associations

a. National Education Association (NEA)

NEA is unquestionably the largest association, with over 1.7 million members in 1977, but it is not the powerful and unanimous association of classroom teachers that it once was. This is true in part because it includes a controversial unit of supervisory employees, the American Association of School Administrators.

Thus, NEA has, in the past, viewed its role as an association of educational "professionals." It functioned most effectively in articulating the policy concerns of professional educational administrators, i.e., school administrators, university schools of education, and state departments of education.

b. The American Federation of Teachers (AFT)

An AFL-CIO affiliate, the American Federation of Teachers, has increasingly served as NEA's militant alter ego, despite an earlier era of peaceful cooperation. AFT experienced a period of rapid growth (membership increased impressively from approximately 100,000 in 1968 to 444,000 in 1974 and over 650,000 in 1977) due primarily to NEA's perceived domination by administrative interests. Many classroom teachers left NEA and turned to AFT as a vehicle for expressing their professional concerns, which were often policy issues, i.e., classroom size, equipment, teaching loads, and nonclassroom assignments. Consequently, NEA was forced to adopt a more assertive position toward strikes and collective bargaining.

The often intense rivalry between NEA and AFT focused primarily on organizing efforts, particularly in urban and post-secondary systems, as an increasing number of teachers were granted collective bargaining rights. The struggle intensified in 1972 when the NEA convention voted to make college campus organizing a top priority with a 1974 budget of one million dollars allocated for that purpose. By 1977 NEA and AFT were in a virtual dead heat with each organization representing more than two hundred institutions of the over five hundred campuses thus far unionized. However, AFT, the American Association of University Professors (AAUP), and some independent associations have achieved some important victories at NEA's expense. NEA affiliates in the New York and Pennsylvania state college system severed their ties with NEA so that AFT now represents a predominant number of four-year institutions, including several major state systems. Although NEA scored a victory in 1977 through its election as faculty bargaining agent at the University of Massachusetts, it now represents community colleges almost exclusively.

AFT and NEA: The Incentive for Cooperative Policy Strategies

As indicated, NEA and AFT have engaged in intense competition for the loyalties of classroom teachers. Each group has focused its resources on organizing teachers and winning unit recognition through massive publicity campaigns designed to impugn the other group's professional integrity. The consequences of this competition for union recognition has somewhat handicapped both organizations in obtaining common policy objectives in education.

The potential for union solidarity in achieving common objectives was demonstrated from 1946-1965 when NEA, actively supported by AFT, focused on policy objectives at the national level, particularly in securing federal aid to public education with the final passage of the Elementary and Secondary Education Act—ESEA—in 1965. In effect, the educational profession lobbied cohesively for federal-aid-to-education with a unified, well-organized voice. The NEA-AFT educational lobby operated quite effectively by interacting with the educational "subsystem of government." Specifically, by maintaining a close relationship with the bureaucracy (Office of Education) and by coalescing support from pressure groups, e.g., the National Congress of Parents and Teachers, the NEA-AFT lobby applied effective pressure on the House Education Committee.

The two educational groups remained competitive while functioning as a stimulus for common objectives. NEA had lobbied, without success, for a comprehensive federal-aid-to-education act for over twenty years. Yet compromise with parochial education groups, e.g., National Catholic Welfare Conference, was prevented because of NEA's emphatic opposition to any form of federal assistance to private schools. Significantly, AFT's pressure on NEA to reach a compromise was a crucial factor in ESEA's final passage.

> *If for no other reason, the NEA could not afford to be with the losers the year federal aid finally got enacted. Since NEA's principal reason for being was the passage of federal aid to education legislation, the rival teacher organization's (the AFL-CIO affiliated American Federation of Teachers) charges that the NEA had not been successful up to 1965 touched a sensitive chord.*[73]

AFT and NEA's cooperative focus on federal policymaking and participation in the federal subsystem of government disintegrated during the late 1960s. Since then, both NEA and AFT have increasingly converged to again express a unified voice for educational policy concerns. This convergence is currently occurring on both ideological and organizational levels.

Ideologically, NEA has legitimized the collective bargaining concept with the right of teachers to strike. Although NEA itself does not officially go "on strike," it does invoke "professional sanctions" against offending states and school districts which often include a collective refusal to teach and to sign teacher contracts. Organizationally, NEA has formed a Department of Classroom Teachers. Since 1969, mergers of NEA and AFT affiliates, particularly in urban areas, have been increasing—Los Angeles (1970), New York (1971), New Orleans (1972). Whereas AFT and NEA once waged internecine warfare, they are now more frequently addressing urban school administrators as a unified policy advocate. Undoubtedly, as NEA-AFT apply cooperative and organized pressure, the increase in collective bargaining agreements and strikes will be evident.

Public Employee Organizations: From Fragmentation to Solidarity

Recent indications of increased cooperation among public employee organizations in seeking mutual labor objectives parallel the private sector experience before the AFL-CIO merger (1935). The renewed cooperation between AFT and NEA is evidenced by an increasing number of no-raiding agreements and mergers.[74] As an example of this cooperative consciousness, AFL-CIO formed a Public Employees Division (PED) in 1974 which now includes twenty-nine unions pledged to accomplish the following objectives:

[to] help affiliates with collective bargaining, engage in research and public relations efforts "appropriate to the department" and to settle disputes among member unions.[75]

Interestingly, PED's membership includes both affiliates at all levels of public employment as well as a "consortium arrangement" with NEA, Letter Carriers, and the United Auto Workers.[76] During 1977, PED obtained the support of AFL-CIO's executive council and lobbied at the national policymaking level for public employee collective bargaining legislation.[77]

The move toward unification of all public employee unions also received substantial impetus with the recent (1973) cooperation of AFSCME, NEA, the National Treasury Employees' Union, and the American Nurses' Association within the Coalition of American Public Employees (CAPE). Although one observer termed CAPE "the largest union (in membership) in the world,"[78] it is actually more a confederation than a union. Again, the concerted effort by CAPE, the AFL-CIO's Committee on Legislation, and the AFL-CIO's Public Employee Division to obtain federal legislation for public sector collective bargaining indicates a second stage in the growth of public employee organizations. They have matured beyond the cannabalistic first stage and are now seeking solidarity on policy issues.

The Impact of Collective Bargaining on Public Personnel Administration

Fredrick Mosher dryly pointed out, "The founders of civil service did not bargain on collective bargaining."[79] As Mosher indicated, the collective services are but the latest personnel system to be grafted onto public bureaucracies, along with political appointment, professional careers, and the general civil service. Frequently, each of these career systems is found within the same public organization. The central issue is whether or not these divergent personnel systems can and will (1) coexist, (2) complement each other, or (3) destroy each other.

The political appointee system will undoubtedly continue at the elite levels of public bureaucracies as a necessary concomitant of electoral mandates for policy changes. Interestingly, current (albeit limited) efforts to exempt agency heads currently covered by civil service are gaining momentum. For example, voters in Los Angeles County have recently approved charter amendments making the heads of two county agencies appointive and exempt from civil service. The movement to make bureaucratic heads partisan appointees is frequently viewed in the bureaucratic reform literature as a technique for regaining control and accountability over autonomous department heads. Although a threat to civil service career systems, the political appointee system has never been seriously advocated for more than a few select high-level positions.

As indicated, professionals in career systems have become susceptible to unionization appeals. There is every indication that professionals, due to their proletarianization,[80] will continue to be organized into collective bargaining units. It is somewhat ironic that professionals and professional career systems should be so easily assimilated into a collective system. Philosophically, the civil service system has valued *individualism*; the individual's unique merit is the basis of job assignment and promotion. By contrast, collective bargaining requires that individual identity be submerged within a *collective effort* in order to better the condition of all workers. However, the desire of professionals to have a voice in policy matters appears to be decisive; and unions offer the basis for this kind of expression.

Can collective and civil service coexist as public personnel systems? Not surprisingly, scholars and practitioners respond with a wide range of opinions from cautious optimism that both systems might perform separate although positive functions to increased pessimism.[81] On the optimistic side, Jerry Lelchook and Herbert Lahne contend that the civil service structure is not inherently in conflict with the process of collective bargaining. In fact, the civil service system's emphasis on objective employee selection and security from partisan influences could serve as a useful supplement to collective bargaining. Although other scholars recognize the differing purposes of civil service and collective bargaining, such studies characteristically reflect a search for alternative ways to preserve the civil service system.[82] Other labor-management experts conclude either that (1) there is no consistent pattern to union approaches to collective bargaining vis à vis the merit system,[83] (2) unions will support the merit system only when it supports their supposed best interests.[84]

Despite O. Glenn Stahl's contention that "most observers do not find that merit systems have been seriously compromised by the pressures of collective agreement,"[85] such characterizations seem increasingly speculative. In fact, the debate at times resorts to both sides quoting the same author (Nigro) for support.[86] Although the debate among academicians concerning the impact of collective bargaining on merit service systems is unresolved, the empirical evidence among practitioners is more conclusive and cannot be ignored. Whether or not some restricted form of the merit system continues, the evidence indicates that the future role of civil service commissions will be severely curtailed by collective bargaining agreements.

On the local level, data collected by John Burton from forty-one cities and counties indicate that collective bargaining systems have forced many local governments to significantly change their personnel systems and deemphasize the role of civil service commissions.[87] The vulnerablity of the civil service system to the influence of collective bargaining is exemplified by the U.S. Civil Service Commission's susceptibility to covert influences.

Weakening of the U.S. Civil Service System

The attack upon the U.S. civil service system stems from a number of disparate and, in combination, overwhelming sources. The collective bargaining system is but the final blow to a civil service system that has become vulnerable on three key counts: (1) it has succumbed too often to partisan and personal patronage; (2) it has been inadequate as an instrument for "affirmative action"; and (3) it has, perhaps most fatally, become a liability to public management in the collective bargaining process.

The Judge as Defendant: Partisan and Personal Patronage in the U.S. Civil Service Commission

The repercussions of Watergate have obscured a potentially nasty political patronage scandal. Only after prodding in 1973 did the Civil Service Commission begin to "uncover" a procedure employed during the Nixon presidency to influence the merit system. In essence, the Administraiton availed itself of the "flexibilities" in the existing civil service system for the benefit of the "ins," albeit doing it within the letter of the law. The exposure of the common practice of politicizing the civil service damaged the credibility of the merit system's supposed objectivity.

Soon after taking office, Nixon gave Fredrick V. Malek, assistant director of the Office of Management and Budget (OMB), broad discretionary powers to develop a plan for obviating the supposed indifference and hostility of a "Democratic civil service."[88] The goal of manipulating the civil service system was rationalized by pointing to apparently similar expurgations during the Kennedy (conducted by Larry O'Brien) and Johnson Administrations.

Malek's comprehensive strategy to politicize the civil service is candidly described in House Committee (post office and civil service) hearings as "the federal political personnel manual" or, more commonly, as "Malek's manual."[89] The underlying thesis of the Malek manual was simply stated for partisan department heads: "You cannot achieve management, policy or program control, unless you have established *political* control.[90] The manual directs each federal department head to surreptitiously appoint a special assistant and support staff to form a departmental political personnel office whose objective was to ensure "the placement in all key positions of substantively qualified and politically reliable officials."[91] Malek's manual represented a detailed strategy for restructuring the civil service in order to produce "maximum political benefit for the President and the Party."[92]

The first task of each political personnel office was to identify key decision-making administrators within each agency. Secondly, each administrator's decision-making performance would be evaluated in terms of support for administrative policies. Whenever an administrator was rated unfavorably, administrative strategies were devised to either effect his removal or turn his responsibilities over to a politically reliable administrator. The Malek manual outlined an intricate system of harassment designed to encourage an uncooperative administrator to resign through such tactics as job transfer, downward reclassification of a position, frequent travel, etc.[93]

Each department's political personnel staff also recruited politically reliable applicants referred from Republican congressional and White House sources. Applicants were screened and classified by secret political classification systems similar to the ACTION, the voluntary action agency's "P.Q.M." (Personality, Qualifications, and Maturity) criteria.[94] In addition, agency political officers carried out campaigns similar to HEW's "Operation Talent Search," which screened and recruited applicants for specific positions. Once politically classified, both referred and recruited applicants were supposedly judged by objective criteria.

Upon approval, each political appointee's performance was continually monitored by the political personnel office, which also sponsored a system of awards, incentives, seminars, and institutes designed to maintain employee morale and policy consciousness. In perhaps the most extreme situation, the ACTION agency conducted intensive week-long institutes in five geographic regions that were compulsory for all agency employees.[95] ACTION politicization institutes included an explanation of the Nixon Administration's new political priorities with pre- and postinstitute attitudinal surveys administered to determine attitudinal changes in employee political orientations. ACTION's institutes were subsequently attacked in a petition filed before the Civil Service Commission by one-hundred-fifty past and present ACTION employees.[96]

How pervasive was the Malek manual's influence? Although only the tip of the iceberg was publicized by the national media, much more was documented in Civil Service Commission (CSC) investigations and House post office and civil service committee hearings.[97] Unfortunately much of this evidence was ignored because of more intriguing media interest in the CIA and the plethora of Watergate post-mortems. Regrettably, committee hearings into systematic exploitation of civil service "flexibilities" were finally discontinued after a frequent lack of committee quorums. However, the Civil Service Commission did appoint an "independent" merit staffing review team, which subsequently issued a report further documenting merit system abuses.[98] Despite committee apathy, accumulated evidence revealed a intricate network of referrals and political patronage in the following agencies:

The General Services Administration (GSA) GSA's problems were first publicized in 1974 when CSC investigators formally charged eight top GSA administrators with having operated a political referral system since 1971. Arthur Palman, GSA Region III personnel director, countercharged CSC commissioners with having approved of GSA's referral system from its inception but now being fearful of launching a comprehensive investigation.

Only in 1973, after a formal request from Palman and Congressman David Henderson (D-NC) did CSC conduct its GSA investigation and later request disciplinary proceedings against those operating the GSA referral unit. However, the CSC investigation into abuses dragged on over a year, causing the House committee to express concern regarding "the inordinate delays in implementing proposed disciplinary action" in GSA.[99] All disciplinary actions against GSA offenders were subsequently dismissed because CSC officials were doing the same things, and they were not apparently illegal at the time.

Housing and Urban Development (HUD) In a report released by Congressman David Henderson of the House Post Office and Civil Service Committee, investigation disclosed that HUD administrators kept political personnel files on more than 4,000 employees and applicant referrals up to the GS 15/16 level during the Nixon Administration. The CSC investigation indicated that virtually all job referrals came from the White House, Republican Congressmen, and national, state, and local political committees.[100]

Office of Economic Opportunity (OEO; now the Community Services Agency) A local union (AFGE) representing OEO headquarters workers requested the termination of political clearance procedures for exempted employees of OEO. The union, in a grievance filed in 1974, particularly opposed OEO's political clearance unit located under OEO Director Gallegos's office. The union claimed that Schedule A appointments and promotions were screened by White House advisors during the Nixon and Ford Administrations.[101]

Health, Education, and Welfare (HEW) Early in its development the Department of Health, Education, and Welfare created a referral unit, "Operation Talent Search," which relayed job applications from the White House and Congress. Ironically, the HEW political unit was administered by John Cole, a deputy assistant secretary, who later became the Civil Service Commission's director of personnel management evaluation. Also deeply involved in HEW's referral activities was the assistant to Secretary Robert Finch, Alan May, who later implemented much of the infamous Malek manual and pretested its applicability in the ACTION agency.[102]

ACTION (The Federal Volunteer Agency) Early in 1975, ACTION employees filed a complaint with the Civil Service Commission accusing the Nixon and Ford Administrations of systematically recruiting loyal Republicans while harassing Democratic employees.[103] The ACTION complaint charged that May's Office of Staff Placement applied all the political techniques outlined in Malek's manual to remove political undersirables—job reclassification, reassignment to meaningless jobs with superfluous titles, and restructuring of regional offices to remove political "agitators." Region IX (San Francisco) ACTION employees in 1972 filed a complaint with the CSC protesting attempts from the committee to reelect the president to utilize that office as a resource in the president's reelection campaign.[104]

The Civil Service Commission: Prosecutor and Defendant

The CSC was severely criticized on two counts: (1) for failing to investigate and prosecute those engaging in political patronage rings within federal agencies, and (2) for allowing some CSC commissioners and staff personnel to practice informal or *personal* referrals of their own. In the first instance, critics charged that CSC commissioners could not possibly have been ignorant of the Malek manual and the extensive personnel units within federal agencies during six years of the Nixon Administration. The second issue, although not actually a *political* patronage system, concerns personal referrals practiced by civil service commissioners in employee recruitment and selection.

The U.S. Civil Service Commission Personal job referrals are a common informal occurrence within public organizations at all levels. Even Congressmen have traditionally inundated the Civil Service Commission with thousands of requests from constituents for assistance in securing a government job. Most such requests are routinely sent to the Civil Liaison Office, which forwards the applicant standard employment forms and information. This office averages 3,800 phone calls and 1,300 letters per month from Congressionally referred applicants.

These personal referrals by Congressmen to the civil service commissioner are unlike the systematic political patronage units of the Watergate era. Nonetheless, these, too, represent a threat to the merit system concept and the 91-year-old Civil Service Act, which theoretically eliminated subjectivity in public employee personnel systems.

The primary threat to merit system principles results from personal referrals originating with civil service commissioners, which, though not illegal, are highly depreciatory for merit system credibility. Significantly, it is what occurs when a referral is received, not the referral itself that constitutes legal guilt or wrongdoing. Personal referrals, particularly verbal recommendations, are, therefore, common throughout the civil service. As long as referral requests from civil service administrators are not written as "must" requests but rather "for your consideration" they are perfectly legitimate.

Investigations reveal that three commissioners made thirty-five employment referrals.[105] Former CSC Chairman Hampton's records reveal only seventeen referral letters during his six years in office; these official letters, while hardly constituting a flood of requests and none written in imperative tones ("must"), represent the Achilles' heel of the "objective" merit system. Personally endorsed recommendations by civil service commissioners who are responsibile for administering the merit system, automatically interject the influence of the commissioner making the recommendation. The merit system is compromised and vulnerable to the familiar "old boy's club" of cronyism.

Political patronage does occasionally intervene in the civil service system, unless this is brought to light by countervailing partisan forces, the Civil Service Commission, the media, or even public employee unions. There is the expectation that the merit system would emerge stronger after the exposure of political patronage networks. However, the personal channels of influence allowed at the top levels of the CSC were not strenuously resisted by the majority of public employees; nor did this lead to a reaffirmation of the merit principle. Why should a public employee (or anyone else) be expected to understand that a friendly call from a civil service commissioner requesting "equal consideration" for a friend is morally different from that urging consideration of political criteria?

On a theoretical level, the merit principle is based on equalitarian and objective concepts that lie at the heart of a democratic public personnel system. Unfortunately, for the merit principle, the civil service has not always insisted on the rigid professional and procedural codes of the British civil service system. If civil service commissioners easily make personal referrals, it becomes acceptable for subordinates to select by political or personal preferences. Too often, public employees have been forced to accept the adage, "It's not what you know, but

Part I: Nature of Collective Bargaining

who you know" within civil service systems. It is significant that until 1975 the U.S. Civil Service Commission "had never established specific procedures for bringing action against agency officials held to be responsible for merit system violations."[106] Subsequent to the Malek manual investigations, the commission implemented a self-imposed ban on personal referrals by civil service administrators.

The credibility of the merit principle among public employees has also been eroded by the prevalent practice of selecting out civil servants and military officers if they are not promoted in regular increments. The subjective criteria and closed nature of this weeding out process obviously undermines morale. It also creates an embittered cadre of former public employees and presents a compelling argument for collectivization. In effect, the threatened public employee cannot easily turn to the civil service system for protection or grievance.

American Foreign Service Association (AFSA) elections in 1975 underscore the poor reputation of the merit system (Foreign Service classification) among State Department officers.[107] The association, which represents approximately 7,400 foreign service officers, is the exclusive bargaining representative for active and retired employees in the State Department, AID, and USIA. Significantly, the association presidency was won by a candidate who had been selected out of the State Department in 1969 because he had not been promoted over a long period. Not surprisingly, his "absolute top priority" as a campaign issue was the implementation of a foreign service grievance system. Although he was perhaps the most critical and outspoken of the AFSA candidates, all candidates expressed the position that the promotion process was not merit-based:

> *Everyone knowledgeable agrees that assignments, promotions and training opportunities often are given to buddies—and are not based on merits objectively applied to all.*[108]

Again, it is the fallacy of allowing the merit system to be subverted for personal patronage that persuades public employees that a civil service system is simply a management tool.

There are many labor-management experts who feel differently. Some believe that the U.S. Civil Service Commission and civil service system have emerged unscathed from political and personal patronage scandals and that they are entering an era of "renewed public interest." One past CSC executive director euphorically observed that "the merit system is temporarily closer to the high promise of the Civil Service Act than at any time in our history."[109] The former CSC chairman believed that CSC's "corrective actions . . . against possible furture abuses had rendered the merit system stronger today than at any time in its ninety-three-year history."[110]

The Performance of Civil Service Systems as Advocates of Minority Rights

The civil service system has also been attacked for its failure to anticipate the demands for justice by minority and ethnic groups. It is not necessary to recount the long and continuing struggle for individual rights and civil liberties as a philosophical ideal and a reality in the United States. Since its founding, the Republic has sought to preserve the tension between majority rule and minority rights. Certain institutions and principles, e.g., the Supreme Court and judicial review, have attempted to define the rights of the few. The political climate of the times now calls for civil service to exemplify this philosophical and institutional tradition through "affirmative action" selection and promotion.* However, the merit system is frequently viewed by minorities as a defender of the status quo and entrenched elites. On the other hand, majority individuals have viewed the implementation of "affirmative action" as a case of reverse discrimination and a violation of the merit principle. In fact, in a recent public opinion survey, preferential hiring and advancement of minorities and women was rejected by about eight to one nationally. (see chapter 7 for a full discussion of affirmative action.)

Those who argue that civil service has not done enough for minorities would have employee job classification and testing procedures dedicated to "social justice" and "cultural objectivity." Civil service commissions are not generally indicted for conspiracy or even covert discriminatory practices; their failure is perceived as one of omission rather than of commission. Too often, its critics charged, the Civil Service Commission did not question existing personnel practices and procedures.

As former CSC Chairman Hampton observed, the commission had "come a long way in providing equal opportunity for minorities and women ... and many discriminatory practices have been eliminated."[111] Yet, Hampton added, merely complying with equal employment laws is insufficient. The judicial branch defines minority rights by precedent not by statute. The result has been harsh criticism by a variety of racial, ethnic, and physically handicapped minorities with charges of alleged

---

* An affirmative action plan refers to "a set of specific and result-oriented procedures required of government contractors to achieve equal employment opportunity. An acceptable affirmative action plan must include: (1) an analysis of the areas in which the contractor is deficient in the utilization of minority groups and women; and (2) goals and time tables to which the contractor must direct his good faith efforts in correcting the deficiencies and increasing the utilization of minorities and women at all levels of the work force" Felicitas Hinman, ed. *Equal Employment Opportunity and Affirmative Action in Labor-Management Relations: A Primer* (Los Angeles: University of California, 1976), p. 1-2).

prejudice and discrimination. An example of how civil service objectivity may be viewed as discriminatory is exemplified by the Board of Examiners of New York City in its merit-testing procedures.

Specifically, because civil service commissions frequently complied with statute law but did not *advocate* change, they were viewed critically. They failed the test of advocating justice by assuming cultural objectivity. As Chairman Hampton noted:

> *The day of cutting and pasteing is over and we must look more realistically at our employment system to assure that the system is responding to human needs rather than its own requirements.*[112]

Even in the supposedly objective task of preparing tests and measurements, the civil service system is vulnerable to the pressures of interest group politics.

In 1971, a black and a Puerto Rican, Boston Chance and Louis Mercado, acting elementary school principals, brought a class action suit against the Board of Examiners of New York City.[113] Ironically, the board's originating purpose was to design and administer a competitive examination system "to place the appointment and promotion of teachers purely on a *competitive basis of merit* (italics added)." The plaintiffs claimed that competitive examinations given by the board to those seeking permanent supervisory positions, i.e., principals and assistant principals, were discriminatory against blacks and Puerto Ricans and, therefore, unconstitutional.

The cast of characters attacking or supporting the Board of Examiners' position illuminates the extent of interest in the case. Obviously, the board served as the principal defender of the existing examination system. Surprisingly, both the New York City Board of Education and its chancellor, Harvey Scribner, refused to support the Board of Examiners. In fact, Chancellor Scribner believed that to support the board "would require that I violate my own professional beliefs and defend a system of personnel selection and promotion which I no longer believe to be workable.[114]

Supporting the class action suit by *amicus* briefs were three unaffiliated groups: Public Education Association; Aspira of America, Inc.; and the New York Association of Black Educators.

Significantly, the board's position was supported with *amici* briefs filed by a number of public employee unions and associations: United Federation of Teachers (Local 2); American Federation of Teachers, AFL-CIO; Council of Supervisors and Administrators, (Local 1); School Administrators and Supervisors' Organizing Committee, AFL-CIO; and the Council of Jewish Organizations in Civil Service, Inc. These *amici* were joined by B'nai Brith and the Catholic Teachers' Association.

It is here tempting to approach *Chance* v. *Board of Examiners* from a policy rather than a personnel perspective. The emotional intensity of of the issue is obvious yet paradoxical. Why should major educational groups (both classroom and supervisory) align themselves with Catholic and Jewish organizations against a class action suit brought by Puerto Ricans and blacks? Why, particularly since the issue dealt with supervisory personnel rather than with classrom teachers? The implications of the court's decision for the merit system must be clarified before analyzing the policy's redistributive consequences. In sum, the court agreed with the plaintiffs that the board's examinations constituted "unintentional racial discrimination." Discrimination was determined by comparing New York to other major cities (see table 1-4) that did not use competitive examinations and by analyzing attrition rates of the same examination for other ethnic groups in New York City.

However, the court's decision continued, "the existence of such discrimination, standing alone, would not necessarily entitle plaintiffs to relief." *De facto* discrimination was not sufficient if examinations could be proven to be "job related" by either "content validation" or "predictive validation." In effect, the court felt that the board had not *proven* that its examinations were anything than "measuring a candidate's ability to memorize" or that its results were "better than drawing names out of a hat."

The district court, following appeal, shifted to the board the burden of proving that the examinations which it assigned were job related. In effect, the court now requires that public employers (including state and local employers), as was previously required of private employers, demonstrate test validity, i.e., that predictable job performance standards be established.

Several important trends are exemplified in the *Chance* case and should not be overlooked as anomalies:

1. Public employee unions and associations may support the merit system and merit principles only insofar as it protects and enhances the professional and personal career aims of employee members. In *Chance*, the traditional career mobility pattern for teachers was into supervisory positions. The existing examination system discriminated against certain groups and provided more supervisory positions for other groups.

2. The merit principle of objective and competitive examinations is not enhanced whenever judicial decisions redefine merit system policies and procedures. Merit objectivity should be a process not dependent on statute law or judicial decision.

3. Both the Malek manual and the *Chance* case demonstrate the lack of consensus concerning the merit system and the role of civil service systems. There is no safe, agreed-upon role for civil service systems. All of the functions of commissions are problematical

TABLE 1-4: Supervisory Personnel in Comparative Urban School Systems

City	Total No. of Principals	Percentage Black	Percentage Puerto Rican	Percentage Black and Puerto Rican
Detroit	281	16.7	——	16.7
Philadelphia	267	16.7	——	16.7
Los Angeles	1,012	8.0	1.7	9.7
Chicago	479	6.9	——	6.9
New York	862	1.3	0.1	1.4

City	Total No. of Asst. Principals	Percentage Black	Percentage Puerto Rican	Percentage Black and Puerto Rican
Detroit	360	24.7	0.2	24.9
Philadelphia	225	37.0	——	37.0
Los Angeles	——	——	——	——
Chicago	714	32.5	——	32.5
New York	1,610	7.0	0.2	7.2

and controversial. Even testing or employee referrals are no longer exclusively the civil service's jurisdiction.

The Civil Service System as a Liability to Public Management in Collective Bargaining

As Felix Nigro points out, even the role of the civil service commission in recommending pay plans and revisions is rendered virtually meaningless because pay and fringes are negotiated by management and union representatives.[115] In effect, the commissions do not represent management at the bargaining table nor do they significantly influence management positions. Public management (legislator/executive) often does not even consult the commission for its opinion. Obviously, neither will public employee unions consult with a commission that is viewed as "an avowed arm of management."[116]

The traditional function of the civil service commission as the principal arbiter of employee grievances is also eroded whenever collective bargaining contracts provide for final-step binding grievance arbitration.

As Professor Nigro observes, "Increasingly, important provisions of civil service rules and regulations are negotiated along with economic benefits, which reduces the commission's policymaking role.[117] The civil service's claim to objectivity or to a role as an impartial mediator is simply not feasible, given prevailing mistrust by public employees.

Not surprisingly, public management has discovered that public employee organizations often benefit from the dual existence of collective bargaining and the merit system by selectively bargaining on those issues that represented possible leverage while simultaneously attacking those civil service rules that are disadvantageous. For example, public employee unions might wish to bargain on issues of upwardly reclassifying jobs while refusing to bargain on stricter disciplinary procedures or on prevailing wage clauses designed to maintain civil service parity with the private sector.

In a startling but apocalyptic move, the Los Angeles County Board of Supervisors began preparing legislation that would eliminate civil service protection for all public employees represented by bargaining units "in all matters except hiring and promotions."[118] Civil service jurisdiction would be replaced with a process of compulsory arbitration by a third party to break bargaining impasses, it would be added to the county's existing system of collective bargaining. The board chairman believed that the action was necessary for county managers because:

> it is extremely difficult to discipline employees who are incompetent or insubordinate. This is demoralizing to the many conscientious employees who must work extra hard beside incompetent or idle employees.[119]

The effective or actual removal of civil service commissions from public personnel management systems is increasingly viewed by many labor relations experts as a means of aiding public management in collective bargaining. Public management's role in collective bargaining strategy can no longer be diluted by attempting to include the neutral civil service function.

With the weakening of the civil service commission's management role in collective bargaining, the role of personnel directors or the administrative officer is frequently enhanced. In fact, many labor relations experts are advocating that the personnel organization be designated and trained to "coordinate and unify the management position on issues that arise.[120]

The Impact of Collective Bargaining on the Merit System: A Summary

We have presented two trends that have weakened the power and role of civil service commissions. First, political and personal patronage by civil service commissions, e.g., the Malek manual, have somewhat tarnished their reputation for integrity and objectivity. Second, the accusation of not being effective as an advocate of juridical democracy in anticipating minority or individual rights has some critics regarding the commissions and personnel boards as conservative defenders of the status quo. Others see the civil service system as violating the merit principle through "affirmative action."

Yet, the commissions could probably survive by introducing more stringent codes of ethics and by aggressively pursuing a "justice as fairness" philosophy.[121] Again, it is the civil service system's liability to public management that demands its inexorable decline. Despite the existence of expert opinion concerning the civil service system's optimistic future, it appears that current trends support a view expressed in committee hearings by a former dirctor of the Civil Service League:

> *The merit principles and civil service systems* as we know them *are going to be non-existent . . . civil service commissions cannot effectively serve three masters [a neutral role, the employer, and the employee]. More and more commissions must decide where they stand. And generally they are choosing the "spokesman for management" role. Collective bargaining will push this farther because employees are turning more to their unions for help.*[122]

Impact of Public Employee Organizations upon Public Policymaking

Public employee organizations are an increasingly important variable in two spheres of public policymaking: (1) the external arena of political action, and (2) the internal environment of decision making within public bureaucracies. This study includes a subsequent chapter (4) analyzing the role of public employee unions as a political movement with avowed political objectives. Particular emphasis is given to the activities of public employee unions as pressure groups within the pluralistic group process and to an analysis of the strike as a political strategy. A later chapter (6) analyzes the role of public employee unions as a bilateral participant within bureaucratic policymaking. Particular emphasis is placed on the process of collective bargaining as a catalyst of bureaucratic change and reform.

Before examining the public policymaking arenas of political action and bureaucratic decision making, our analysis will survey the issues and concerns of policy analysts and researchers. Finally, we shall pinpoint the major areas of impact for public employee organizations on public policymaking.

The scholarly and practical literature in the field of policy analysis and research is diverse and fragmented. The normative issues, theoretical frameworks, and analytical models utilized by policy studies reflect the rapidly developing and burgeoning nature of the field.[123] Unlike the more applied and professional expertise of public personnel administration, public policy studies are a developmental hybrid of social science theory and applied professional methodologies. Nonetheless, as with its impact on public personnel administration, public employee collective bargaining is exerting and will continue to exercise a profound effect upon the traditional process of public policymaking within all levels of government and the larger political environment.

Process of Public Policymaking: An Overview

Although policy analysts are concerned with policy process, it must first be emphasized that there is no single process by which policies are formed. For example, variations in the policy issue will produce variations in participant behavior and the framework of public policymaking.[124] Criminal justice, education, taxation, and poverty are among the myriad issues that may each be characterized by distinguishable policy processes.

Second, the nature of policymaking is significantly affected by the primary locus of the institutional framework. Policymaking and, therefore, collective bargaining scope and issues will vary with the institutional framework of policymaking—legislative, executive, judiciary, administrative, or regulatory agencies; or federal, state, local, or district government.

Third, given the complexity and diversity in the public policy process, it is not now possible for policy analysts to present a "grand theory" of policy formation. Consequently, it is not possible to place public collective bargaining within a precise analytical model. But a useful approach toward including public employee unions within theoretical models of public policymaking would be to generalize on such collective bargaining concerns as how do policy problems develop; who is involved in policy formation, on what kinds of issues, under what conditions, in what ways, and to what effects?

Conceptually, any policy process must be viewed as a sequential pattern of decisions, each involving strategies and activities, that can be analytically (if not empirically) distinguished in the following longitudinal stages:

1. **Problem Formation** How does a perceived social problem get on the political agenda for policymaking? Somewhat simplistically, public policymakers were overtly compelled to recognize submerged issues of poverty, pollution, and equal employment opportunities at particular junctures longitudinally. Analagously, why did particular public employee problems become *political* action or strategy issues? Analysis must be especially attentive to linkages between varying perceptions of the problem held by policymakers, clientele groups (property owners, union members, etc.), and other political groups.

2. **Policy Formulation** How are the alternatives or options for dealing with the problem developed? Who participates in policy formulation and the generally closed decision-making process? Public employee organizations, obviously, through the demands for a bilateral decision-making process will increasingly present and advocate policy options to public policymakers.

3. **Policy Adoption** How is a particular policy option chosen and legitimized? What symbolic and material requirements must be met in policy adoption?[125] Public employee organizations work toward attaining their collective bargaining objectives within specific decision-making environments. The central strategy requirement is to persuade "the right people" to accept proposed policy options.

The following four decision-making models would seem particularly appropriate to organizational or community policy analysts in understanding the decision-making process peculiar to public collective bargaining:

a. **Elitist** model assumes that policy reflects elite rather than mass values.[126] Change and policy strategies are only symbolically affected by mass participation in voting and political participation.[127] Whether a single power elite or pluralistic elites, each community or political environment exhibits some degree of elitist decision making. Community power studies indicate a wide variety of elitist decision-making styles ranging from the hierarchy of former Mayor Daley in Chicago; the racial bifurcation of power in Atlanta, the fragmented elitism of Los Angeles, and the pluralism of New Haven.[128] Collective bargaining by public employees will obviously shape and be shaped by elite preferences and values.

b. **Group Theory** The pluralistic group model views public policymaking as a *compromise* process reached by competitive groups in society.[129] The collective public interest is achieved by the interaction among groups. Significantly for public employee organizations, group theory assumes that a group's influence in policymaking is determined by its numbers, wealth, organization, leadership, and access to policymakers. To this group model of influence must also be added the nature of public employee services. One can hypothesize that the critical nature of protective services provides police and firemen with political influence. The group approach sees the public interest protected by a "theory of countervailing forces." For every interest group (faction) e.g., labor, there is a countervailing interest group, i.e., management.

c. **Incrementalism: Policy as Incremental Change** As Charles Lindblom suggests, public policymaking is often "the science of muddling through,"[130] and public budgeting only a slight variation on last year's budget. Rather than rationally evaluating existing program objectives and activities, public administrators are compelled to advocate only slight changes in order to avoid conflict. Rather than proposing broad policy initiatives, incremental policymakers include programs that placate as many clientele support groups as possible. Comprehensive or rational policy planning is neither desired nor rewarded as appropriate administrative behavior in public agencies.[131]

d. **Institutionalism: The Bureaucratic Environment** Clearly the political policymaking environment is more comprehensive than governmental or institutional decision making. Yet institutional organizations and legal framework (both constitutional and statute) define an authorized cadre of those who legitimately should make public policy. Governmental structures are designed to define and monitor legitimate collective bargaining behavior. Clearly, in the public sector some governmental structures are becoming dysfunctional, e.g., civil service commissions, and new structures are being proposed, e.g., a public sector regulatory body similar to the National Labor Relations Board (NLRB).

e. **Policy Implementation** What is done, if anything, to programmatically implement policy objectives? As Theodore Lowi and others have observed,[132] contemporary interest group liberalism fails to implement policy objectives because its ambivalent nature does not allow it to achieve either planning or justice. Collective bargaining can potentially achieve both through a sound contract arrived at in good faith.

f. **Policy Evaluation** How is the effectiveness or impact of a policy measured? As Drucker, Lowi, and others have observed, too often budgetary *efficiency* in public institutions is disguised as program *effectiveness*.[133] Generally, public programs do not have tangible objectives nor does legislation provide specific authoritative guidelines. The result is often a perception of public employees as bureaucratic, inefficient, and insensitive.[134] Public employees suffer the stigma of inefficiency, and employee organizations the lack of public opinion support.

In essence, our analysis of public employee organization activities (including collective bargaining) is a systems analysis[135] of environmental forces that produce public policy. Within the political system one might productively utilize elitist, institutional, group, and incremental models in understanding the public policymaking environment of collective bargaining. Yet one must also include a systemic overview of other relevant variables in society. Comprehensive policy analysis must also consider both inputs (demands, supports) and outputs (consequences, actions).

Specifically, policy analysis should include public opinion as one environmental variable or political input. For example, a 1975 poll indicates that public opinion is overwhelmingly opposed to federal or state legislation authorizing union, closed or agency shops for public employees[136] (see table 1-5).

As indicated, public attitudes toward specific labor-management issues and general social values regarding collective bargaining are but two environmental variables in public policymaking.

Finally, any analysis of public employee organizations must examine the nature of bureaucratic decision making. As will be discussed, the public policymaking process is increasingly dominated by public bureaucracies. Public bureaucracies play a pivotal role in a public policymaking system that occurs in "closed decision-making loops," "arenas for power," or "whirlpools of power."[137] Generally, elected representatives function as policy watchdogs and only rarely as policy initiators.[138] It is the bureaucratic elites who function as the linchpin in the policymaking subsystem.

The bureaucratization of the policymaking process stems from two sources of bureaucratic power: (1) political support gained by mobilizing clientele groups, and (2) administrative expertise utilized as a means of controlling decisions and maintaining isolation from outside pressures.[139] Clearly, the bureaucratic elites do not reign supreme. Rather, these bureaucratic elites generally *share* policymaking power in an autonomous subsystem. As indicated, the degree to which this subsystem of power functions, the participants involved, and the policy process will vary with the type of issue, the level of policymaking, and the environmental variables.

Finally, the effect of public employee organizations in public policymaking will be evidenced in various budgetary management systems employed within public bureaucracies. Such budgetary management techniques as Management by Objectives (MBO); Planning-Programming Budgeting (PPB); Systems Budgeting; and President Carter's Zero-Base Budgeting (ZBB) are techniques to regain bureaucratic control and

TABLE 1-5: Public Opinion of Compulsory Unionism in the Public Sector

Question: Which of these arrangements do you favor for federal, state and local government employees: (1) A person can work for government whether or not he belongs to a union; (2) a person can go to work for the government if he doesn't already belong to a union, but has to join after he is hired to hold his job; (3) a person can get a job with the government only if he already belongs to a union; (4) no opinion.

(in percentage)

	Total U.S. Public	Union Members	Republican	Democrat	Independent
1	83	77	85	81	87
2	10	17	7	11	9
3	1	2	2	2	. . .
4	6	4	6	6	4

Question: Should the U.S. Congress pass a law that would allow agreements requiring employees to join or to pay dues to a union in order to work for the federal government?

(in percentage)

	Total U.S. Public	Union Members	Republican	Democrat	Independent
Yes	11	19	11	13	9
No	79	71	78	77	84
No opinion	10	10	11	10	7

Question: Should the U.S. Congress pass a law that would allow agreements requiring employees to join or pay dues to a union in order to work for state, county, and municipal governments?

(in percentage)

	Total U.S. Public	Union Members	Republican	Democrat	Independent
Yes	10	19	10	10	9
No	79	73	78	79	84
No opinion	11	8	12	11	7

Question: Should your state legislature pass a law that would allow agreements requiring employees to join or pay dues to a union in order to work for the state, county, and municipal governments?

(in percentage)

	Total U.S. Public	Union Members	Republican	Democrat	Independent
Yes	10	18	10	11	9
No	78	74	78	78	83
No opinion	12	8	12	11	8

Source: Opinion Research Corporation, Princeton, N.J.

Note: These findings are based on interviews with a scientifically constructed sampling of 2,038 citizens. The interviews were conducted in January, 1975.

accountability in policymaking.[140] An analysis of public employee collective bargaining must include an appraisal of the planning and reorganizational implications of various budgetary systems.

In essence, our analysis indicates that the introduction of public employee organizations into the public policymaking arena is causing a major change in both the heuristic models and the pragmatic realities of public policymaking. Public employee organizations are not just another pressure group casting its bid into the policymaking arena and demanding a share of the pluralistic prize.

Although public employee organizations frequently compete with interest groups on distributive policies (see chapter 4), they are also fundamentally different by virtue of their location *within* the bureaucracy. As will be examined, public employee groups exert political action strategies on legislatures and public opinion in order to obtain economic benefits. However, such strategies are properly understood as being incremental and group oriented. It is the public employee organization's demand through collective bargaining to participate in larger regulatory and redistributive policymaking that requires restructured analytic focus.

Conclusion

This chapter has explored in detail the organization of the public labor market. We have noted that despite the diversity of jobs in the public sector, the overwhelming majority of positions are classified as white-collar occupations. This has significant implications for labor organizations because traditionally white-collar workers have been reluctant to affiliate with unions. In addition, the relative job security of the white-collar worker, the opposition of government employers, and the jurisdictional rivalries between unions have all combined to make organizational attempts in the public sector a very difficult task. However, growth is being achieved at a rapid pace in spite of these difficulties. The most important reason results from what has been called "the proletarianization of the white-collar worker," who finds himself increasingly losing pay, status, and fulfillment due to technology, on the one hand, and the collectively bargained financial advances of the blue-collar work force, on the other. In conjunction with broader-based union appeals, effective competition from other associations, and a lessening of employer hostility in some quarters, the movement toward unionism in the public sector has showed a capacity and a capability to overcome obstacles and make increasing advances.

The important fact to note is that white-collar workers, the predominant group in the public sector, are joining unions because they apparently are convinced that unions are effective in securing better salaries, benefits, and working conditions for their members.

We have explored the rationale for the growing attractiveness of unionization even among professional groups. In this connection, a recent survey of college faculty attitudes toward unionization by Everett Carll Ladd, Jr. and Seymour Martin Lipset offers the most systematic examination of this phenomenon among these professionals. The 1977 Ladd-Lipset survey found that a leveling-off of general faculty support for the unionization of professors has occurred. At the same time, nearly three-fourths of all professors, including a majority at every type of institution, responded that they would vote for a collective bargaining agent if an election were held at their institutions. The respondents were clear about the perceived advantages and disadvantages of collective bargaining. About three-quarters attributed higher salaries and improved benefits to collective bargaining. Conversely, roughly the same number felt that unionization resulted in an "over-emphasis on rules and regulations" and a reduction in "collegiality between administrators and faculty" (see table 1-6).

Although a majority of the professoriate, even at elite research universities, indicated that they would vote for collective bargaining rather than for "no agent," a clear distinction regarding unionism emerges: (1) in terms of "professional status and interests, . . . the most secure, established, rewarded, and attaining academics are the least supportive of unionism," and (2) in terms of "sociopolitical ideology, . . . the most liberal professors [are] the most prounion and, conversely, the most conservative faculty members [are] the least inclined to support collective bargaining."

Despite the high percentage of declared support for collective bargaining, the actual occurrence of unionization among faculty does not support the data. About a quarter of the professoriate, or about five hundred campuses, is currently unionized. Ladd and Lipset explain this disparity by pointing to several factors: (1) Most unionization has taken place in institutions where the argument that collective bargaining can secure better econmic advantages from reticent legislatures has taken hold. (2) Experience has shown that unionization has been critically dependent upon state legislation providing collective bargaining for academics. Only twenty-four states have passed this kind of legislation. (3) Supporters of faculty unionism are spread across several organizations that are often bitter rivals. (The responses to their question, "If an election for a collective-bargaining agent were to be held at your institution, how would you vote?" were: for the A.A.U.P.: 35 percent; for the A.F.T.: 14 percent; for the N.E.A.: 13 percent; for another agent: 11 percent; for "no agent": 27 percent.) The issue over who will be the bargaining agent has, thus, hampered unionism. (4) The kind of leadership—its effectiveness and its placement on the question— is a key determinant in the success of unionism. Fundamentally, inertia must be overcome in order to propel a faculty toward unionism.

TABLE 1-6: Perceptions of Costs and Benefits of Collective Bargaining by Professors

	Percentage Agree	Percentage Disagree
Collective bargaining is likely to bring higher salaries and improved benefits		
1975	76	74
1977	76	24
Union grievance procedures serve to protect faculty members against arbitrary action by administrative officials		
1975	83	17
1977	74	26
Collective bargaining reduces collegiality between administrators and faculty members		
1975	69	31
1977	68	32
Collective bargaining results in overemphasis on rules and regulations		
1975	62	38
1977	66	34
Faculty unions have made it more difficult for institutions to deny tenure		
1975	64	36
1977	60	40

How Faculty Members Would Vote

	Percentage That Would Vote for Agent	Percentage That Would Vote 'No Agent'
Type of institution		
Ph.D.-granting universities	65	36
Liberal-arts colleges, comprehensive four-year institutions	74	26
Two-year colleges	91	9
Teaching load		
Four hours or less.	61	39
Five to eight hours	66	34
Nine to 16 hours	78	22
17 or more hours	84	16
Articles published in last two years		
Five or more.	58	42
One to four	69	31
None	78	22
Teaching v. research		
Heavily in research	59	42
Leaning to research	68	32
Leaning to teaching.	72	28
Heavily in teaching	80	20
Rank		
Professor.	60	40
Associate professor	77	23
Assistant professor	81	19
Instructor	82	18
Political point of view		
Conservative.	64	36
Moderate.	69	31
Liberal	83	17
Discipline		
Engineering	51	49
Agriculture.	55	45

Table 1-6 (continued)

Medicine.	59	41
Business administration	63	37
Physical sciences	73	27
Biological sciences	75	25
Education	75	25
Humanities.	79	21
Social Sciences	79	21

Source: 1977 Survey of 4,400 faculty members at 161 colleges and universities, by Everett Carll Ladd, Jr. and Seymour Martin Lipset in "Faculty Support for Unionization: Leveling off at About 75 Percent," *The Chronicle of Higher Education,* 13 February 1978, p. 8.

The authors conclude:

> *The future of unionism in academe is likely to depend much more on the strategic thrusts of the unions, on their leadership, on state enabling legislation, and on the financial future of higher education than upon professors' attitudes toward bargaining. The transformation of those attitudes—from a negative view of unionism to a rather positive one—has been completed.*[141]

This chapter has also noted the variety of public employee unions who participate in the public policymaking process. We have observed the variation in union objectives, leadership, and political objectives at each governmental level. The trend away from fragmentation, toward increasing interunion solidarity is increasingly important.

We have also observed the significant impact of collective bargaining on public personnel administration. We have concluded that existing civil service systems have not successfully met the employee needs which often precipitate unionization. This chapter presented three examples of the civil service system's vulnerability to the impact of collective bargaining. The first case study traced the U.S. Civil Service Commission's susceptibility to both systematic political patronage and private personnel referrals, thereby subverting the merit principle. The second case study analyzed the attack upon the civil service as defenders of the status quo by advocates of minority rights. Specifically, we examined the experience of the New York Board of Examiners in administering allegedly discriminatory examinations. Finally, the function of the civil service system has been discussed in terms of its being a liability to public sector management during collective bargaining. Viewed as management-oriented by employees, the civil service system has hindered management unity during collective bargaining by fragmenting its bargaining position.

Fundamental changes in the civil service system are possibly forthcoming. The Carter Administration has made civil service reorganization a major priority. The plan calls for the abolition of the Civil Service Commission and having its functions performed by two new agencies: Office of Personnel Management (OPM) and Senior Executive Service (SES). The OPM would handle administration, training, examination, and a new Merit System Protection Board that would operate an adjudicatory system which, among its other capabilities, would facilitate and expedite the dismissal of federal employees. The SES, responsible for 9000 of the senior executives in the federal bureaucracy, would provide the executives with greater managerial authority and flexibility and the opportunity to earn incentive bonuses, but it would remove their present job security. The virtually automatic annual pay raises for about 72,000 mid-level management employees would be replaced with a system of earned raises. Additionally, the plan calls for modifying the present policy of preferential hiring of military veterans in order to open more jobs for women and minorities.

Battle lines are being drawn around Carter's plan for civil service reorganization. The AFL-CIO and the largest of the federal employee unions, the American Federation of Government Employees, are supporting the plan, in return for Carter concessions on a yet-unspecified "greater union" role in federal labor-management relations. Veterans organizations and other civil service employee groups are opposing the plan. Kenneth T. Lyons, president of the National Association of Government Employees, told the House committee considering the plan that it amounts to "nothing less than the ruination of the merit system" and its replacement with a system of "personal favoritism and patronage."[142] In response to the employee groups' intense focus on the issue of job security, one of President Carter's principal reorganization operatives stated: "When the unions say we're trying to make it easier to fire people, they're right . . . . We are trying to make it easier to fire people—but for the right reasons. We're also trying to make it impossible to fire people for the wrong reasons—discrimination and politics." Administration officials are counting on "taxpayer unhappiness about the federal service" making it "something of a political imperative" for Congress to act on the reorganization plan.

Finally we must conclude that the impact of collective bargaining is significantly changing the nature of public policymaking. The traditional role of the civil service in maintaining a politically free, professional bureaucracy has been challenged. As we shall see, public employee unions, through the collective bargaining process, have come of age as participants in the political arena. Both as a decision-making force within public bureaucracies, and as pressure groups within the political process, public employee unions are now redefining the traditional power relationships of public policymaking.

Notes to Chapter 1

1. U.S., Civil Service Commission, *Occupations of Federal White-Collar Workers* (Washington, D.C.: U.S. Government Printing Office, 31 October 1969 and 1970), p. 1.

2. For a listing of government occupations see U.S. Civil Service Commission, *Handbook of Occupational Groups and Series of Classes* (Washington, D.C.: U.S. Government Printing Office, October 1969).

3. U.S., Civil Service Commission, *Occupations of Federal White-Collar Workers* (Washington D.C.: U.S. Government Printing Office, 31 October 1974 and 1975).

4. Ibid.

5. Leo Troy, "White-Collar Organization in the Federal Service," *White-Collar Workers*, ed. Albert A. Blum, et al. (New York: Random House, 1971), pp. 186-87. Cited hereafter as Blum, et al.

6. U.S., Civil Service Commission, *Occupations of Federal Blue-Collar Workers* Washington, D.C.: U.S. Government Printing Office, 31 October 1970), p. i.

7. Ibid., p. ii.

8. U.S. Bureau of Labor Statistics, *Handbook of Labor Statistics 1976*, tab. 142, p. 295. Cited hereafter as Bureau of Labor Statistics, *Handbook 1976*, and U.S. Bureau of Labor Statistics, *Handbook of Labor Statistics 1972* Bulletin 1735 (1970), tab. 153, p. 333. Cited hereafter as Bureau of Labor Statistics, *Handbook 1972*.

9. Bureau of Labor Statistics, *Handbook 1972*.

10. Bureau of Labor Statistics, *Handbook 1976*, tab. 142, p. 295.

11. Neil W. Chamberlain and Donald E. Cullen, *The Labor Sector* (New York: McGraw-Hill Book Co., 1971), p. 82.

12. Willem B. Vosloo, *Collective Bargaining in the United States Federal Civil Service* (Chicago: Public Personnel Administration, 1966), pp. 127-31.

13. Harry A. Donoian, "The AFGE and the AFSCME," *Collective Bargaining for Public Employees*, ed. Herbert L. Marx, Jr. (New York: H. W. Wilson, 1969), pp. 24-25. Cited hereafter as Marx.

14. Troy, op. cit., p. 195.

15. Wesley A. Wildman, "Teachers and Collective Negotiations," Blum, op. cit., p. 134-36.

16. Hervey A. Juris and Peter Feuille, *Police Unionism: Power and Impact in Public-Sector Bargaining* (Lexington, Mass.: D. C. Heath and Co., 1973), p. 11.

17. Ibid.

18. Allan M. Cartter and F. Ray Marshall, *Labor Economics: Wages, Employment and Trade Unionism* (Homewood, Ill.: Richard D. Irwin, Inc., 1967), p. 130.

19. Wilson R. Hart, "The Impasse in Labor Relations in the Federal Civil Service," *Collective Bargaining in the Public Service*, ed. Daniel H. Kruger and Charles T. Schmidt, Jr. (New York: Random House, 1969), pp. 142-43.

20. Juris and Feuille, op. cit., p. 11.

21. Troy, op. cit., pp. 197-98.

22. Ibid.

23. Ibid., p. 199.

24. Ibid., p. 197.

25. Blum, et al., op. cit., p. 24.

26. Ibid.

27. Ibid.

28. Ibid.

29. Ibid.

30. Troy, op. cit., pp. 196-97.
31. Ibid.
32. Ibid., pp. 201-202.
33. Ibid.
34. Bureau of Labor Statistics, *Handbook 1972*, tab. 150, pp. 327-30.
35. U.S., Civil Service Commission, *Union Recognition in the Federal Government* (Washington, D.C.: U.S. Government Printing Office, November 1974), p. 26.
36. Ibid.
37. Everett M. Kassalow, "A New Kind of Unionist," Marx, op. cit., p. 17.
38. Twentieth Century Fund Task Force on Labor Disputes in Public Employment, *Pickets at City Hall* (New York: Twentieth Century Fund, 1970), p. 5.
39. Morton R. Godine, *The Labor Problem in the Public Service* (New York: Russell & Russell, 1967), pp. 6-7.
40. Blum, et al., op. cit., p. 12.
41. Derived from Bureau of Labor Statistics, *Handbook 1972*, tab. 101, p. 226.
42. Ibid.
43. Ibid. and derivations from Bureau of Labor Statistics, *Handbook 1972*, tab. 104, p. 232.
44. Bureau of Labor Statistics, *Handbook 1972*, tab. 97, p. 220.
45. Bureau of Labor Statistics, *Handbook 1976*, tab. 102, p. 237.
46. Blum, et al., op. cit., p. 12.
47. Ibid.
48. Ibid.
49. Ibid.
50. Blum, et al., op. cit., p. 17.
51. Ibid., p. 16.
52. Stanley Aronowitz, *False Promises: The Shaping of American Working Class Consciousness* (New York: McGraw-Hill Book Co., 1973), chap. 6.
53. Joseph W. Garbarino, "Emergence of Collective Bargaining," *Faculty Unions and Collective Bargaining*, Edwin D. Duryea, et al. (San Francisco: Jossey-Bass Pub., 1973), pp. 7-9. Cited hereafter as Duryea, et al.
54. Ibid.
55. George W. Angell, "Two-Year College Experience," Duryea, et al., op. cit., pp. 89-90.
56. Edwin D. Duryea and Robert S. Fisk, "Epilogue," Duryea, et al., op. cit., pp. 203-204.
57. Derek C. Bok and John T. Dunlop, *Labor and the American Community* (New York: Simon and Schuster, 1970), p. 318.
58. Helen J. Christrup, "Why Do Government Employees Join Unions?" *Personnel Administration* 29 (September/October, 1966): 49-54.
59. Blum, op. cit., p. 15, quoting *Interviews on the American Character* (Santa Barbara, Ca.: Center for the Study of Democratic Institutions, 1962), pp. 22-23.
60. Troy, op. cit., pp. 193-94.
61. Joseph Krislov, "The Independent Public Employee Association: Characteristics and Functions," in *Collective Bargaining in the Public Service*, ed. Daniel H. Kruger and Charles T. Schmidt, Jr. (New York: Random House, 1969), p. 35.
62. Troy, op. cit., p. 205.
63. Garbarino, op. cit., p. 4.
64. Membership figures are taken from the following publications: U.S. Civil Service Commission, *Union Recognition in the Federal Government* (Washington, D.C.: U.S. Government Printing Office, 1972); U.S. Department of Labor, *A Directory of Public Employee Organization: A Guide to Major Organization Repre-*

senting State and Local Employees (Washington, D.C.: Division of Public Employee Labor Relations, 1974).

65. Vincent L. Connery, *Federal Legislation for Public Sector Collective Bargaining*, ed. Thomas B. Colosi and Steven B. Rynecki (Chicago: International Personnel Management Association, 1975), p. 47. Cited hereafter as Colosi and Rynecki. Also see "NTEU Picketers Ordered to Stop," *Federal Times* 9 July 1975, p. 3.

66. Connery, op. cit., p. 47.

67. *Statistical Abstract of the United States:* Washington, D.C.: U.S. Government Printing Office, 1976, p. 386.

68. *A Directory of Public Employee Organizations*, op. cit., p. 18.

69. Joseph R. Grodin et al., "A Symposium of the Supreme Court's Vallejo Decision," *California Public Employee Relations* 24 (March 1975).

70. Grodin et al., op. cit.

71. Edward L. Faunce, "L.A. SEIU 660 Claims Law Requires CSC to Meet and Confer," *California Public Employee Relations* 23 (December 1974).

72. City of Hayward, et al., United Public Employees, Local 390, of the Service Employees International Union, AFL-CIO; California Court of Appeal, First Appellate District (Sup. Ct. No. H 24764).

73. Eugene Eidenberg and Roy D. Morey, *An Act of Congress* (New York: W.W. Norton & Co., 1969), p. 63.

74. O. Glenn Stahl, *Public Personnel Administration*, 7th ed., (New York: Harper & Row, 1976), p. 327.

75. U.S., Congress, House, Committee on Education and Labor, Subcommittee on Labor-Management Relations, "Public Employee Labor-Management Relations," 94th Cong., 1st sess., 1975, p. 104.

76. Ibid.

77. Colosi and Rynecki, op. cit., p. 5.

78. Stahl, op. cit., p. 327.

79. Frederick C. Mosher, *Democracy and the Public Service* (New York: Oxford Univ. Press, 1968), p. 176.

80. Aronowitz, op. cit.

81. Jerry Lelchook and Herbert J. Lahne, *Collective Bargaining in Public Employment and the Merit System*, (Washington, D.C.: U.S., Department of Labor, Labor Management Services Administration, 1972), p. 45.

82. Fred Hustad, "The Legal Conflict Between Civil Service and Collective Bargaining in Michigan," *Public Personnel Review* 31 (October 1970), pp. 269-272; Charles Feigenbaum, "Civil Service and Collective Bargaining," *Public Personnel Management* 3 (May/June 1974), pp. 244-252.

83. David Lewin, "Collective Bargaining Impacts on Personnel Administration in the American Public Sector," *Labor Law Journal* 27 no. 7 (July 1976), pp. 426-436; David Lewin and Raymond D. Horton, "The Impact of Collective Bargaining on the Merit System in Government," *Arbitration Journal* (September 1975), p. 203.

84. U.S., Civil Service Commission, "Management Approaches to Insuring Compatibility of Collective Bargaining and Merit Principles," Collective Bargaining for Public Managers (State and Local); *Reference Material,* Bureau of Training, Labor Relations Training Center, 1975. See also Davil T. Stanley, "What Are the Unions Doing to the Merit Systems?" *Public Personnel Review* 31 (1970), p. 110; and *Managing Local Government Under Union Pressure* (Washington, D.C., Brookings Institution, 1972), pp. 32-45.

85. Stahl, op. cit., pp. 362-363.

86. See Stahl's quote from Felix A. Nigro and Lloyd G. Nigro, *Modern Public Administration*, 3rd ed. (New York: Harper & Row, 1973), p. 273; compare with Felix A. Nigro, "The Implications for Public Administration," *Public Administration Review* 32 (March 1972), pp. 123-124.

87. John F. Burton Jr., "Local Government Bargaining and Management Sturcture," *Industrial Relations* 11 (May 1972), pp. 123-139.

88. Fredrick V. Malek, "The Development of Public Executives: Neglect and Reform," *Public Administration Review* 34, no. 3 (May/June 1974).

89. *Federal Times* reprinted the Malek manual in ten weekly installments, 16 October-18 December 1974.

90. *Federal Times*, 16 October 1974, p. 12.

91. Ibid., p. 13.

92. Ibid.

93. *Federal Times*, 18 December 1974, p. 13.

94. R.W. Apple, Jr., *New York Times*, 13 January 1975.

95. Center for ACTION Research, *ACTION Institutes: Summary of the Report July 1973-January 1974* (Boulder, Colo: Univ. of Colorado).

96. Apple, op. cit.

97. U.S., Congress, House, Committee on Post Office and Civil Service, *Documents Relating to Political Influence in Personnel Actions at the General Service Administration*, hearings before the Subcommittee on Manpower and Civil Service, 93rd Cong. 2nd sess. 7 October 1974; *Documents Relating to Political Influence in Personnel Actions at the Department of Housing and Urban Development*, Subcommittee on Manpower and Civil Service, 93rd Cong., 2nd sess. 12 December 1974.

98. U.S., Civil Service Commission, "A Self-Inquiry into Merit Staffing: Report of the Merit Staffing Review Team," (Washington, D.C.: U.S. Government Printing Office, May 1976).

99. David N. Henderson, "Statement Regarding Alleged Political Influence in Personnel Actions at the General Services Administration," 10 October 1974), p. 2.

100. David N. Henderson, "Statement by Chairman of the Subcommittee on Manpower and Civil Service," House Committee on Post Office and Civil Service, handout, (16 December 1974), pp. 2-3.

101. Inderjit Badhwar, *Federal Times*, 19 January 1976, p. 9.

102. George C. Koch, testimony submitted to *Nomination: Joseph H. Blatchford*, Senate Hearings before Committee on Labor and Public Welfare, 1971, p. 35.

103. Badhwar, *Federal Times*, 9 January 1976, p. 9.

104. Rosetta Gainey, "Letter to A.T. Briley," testimony submitted to ACTION Act of 1972, p.t., pp. 106-111.

105. U.S., Civil Service Commission, "A Self-Inquiry into Merit Staffing," (Washington, D.C.: Government Printing Office), p. 3.

106. U.S., Civil Service Commission, "A Self-Inquiry into Merit Staffing," op. cit., p. 1.

107. *Federal Times*, 30 July 1975, p. 1.

108. Ibid.

109. Bernard Rosen, "The Merit System in the United States Civil Service," a monograph prepared for the Committee on Post Office and Civil Service, U.S., Congress, 94th Cong., 1st sess., 23 December 1975, p. 35.

110. Robert E. Hampton, "Civil Service: Past and Future," delivered at Annual Civil Service Commission Awards Ceremony, Washington, D.C., 16 January 1976, U.S. Civil Service Commission, Office of Public Affairs, S. Rept. 5, p. 5.

111. Hampton, op. cit., p. 10.

112. Ibid.

113. Chance v. Board of Examiners, 458 *Federal Reporter*, 2nd ser., (1972), p. 1167-1179.

114. Chance v. Board of Examiners, op. cit., p. 1167.

115. Nigro, op. cit., p. 124.

116. Connery, op. cit., p. 48.

117. Nigro, op. cit., 124.

118. Bruce Keppel, "End to Some Civil Service Rights Studied," *Los Angeles Times*, 13 April 1977, pt. II, p. 1.

119. Ibid.

120. Stahl, op. cit., p. 348; see also Kenneth O. Warner and Mary L. Hennessey, *Public Management at the Bargaining Table* (Chicago: International Personnel Management Assn., 1967) pp. 291-305.

121. See Nicholas Henry's effort to apply political philosopher John Rawls' "justice as fairness" philosophy to public administration in *Public Administration and Public Affairs*, (Englewood Cliffs, N.J.: Prentice-Hall, 1975), p. 40-42.

122. Jean J. Couturier, testimony "Labor-Management Relations in the Public Sector" Hearings, U.S. Congress, House Committee on Education and Labor, Special Subcommittee on Labor, 92nd Cong., 2nd sess. 8 March, 3 May 1972), p. 335.

123. Duncan McRae, Jr., "Policy Analysis as an Applied Social Science Discipline," *Administration and Society* 6, no. 4. (February 1975), pp. 363-388.

124. Theodore J. Lowi, *The End of Liberalism*, (Chicago: W. W. Norton & Co., 1969).

125. Murray Edelman, *The Symbolic Uses of Politics* (Urbana: Univ. of Illinois Press, 1964).

126. Charles Wright Mills, *The Power Elite* (New York: Oxford Univ. Press, 1956); Thomas Dye, *Who's Running America?: Institutional Leadership in the United States.* (Englewood Cliffs, N.J.: Prentice-Hall, 1976).

127. Thomas Dye and Harmon Ziegler, *The Irony of Democracy* (Belmont, Calif.: Wordsworth, 1975).

128. Robert A. Dahl, *Who Governs?* (New Haven: Yale Univ. Press, 1967).

129. Arthur F. Bentley, *The Process of Government* (Bloomington, Ind.: Principia Press, 1949).

130. Charles E. Lindblom, "The Science of Muddling Through," *Public Administration Review* 19 (Spring 1959), pp. 79-88.

131. Ralph K. Huitt, "Political Feasibility," *Political Science and Public Policy*, ed. Austin Ranney (Chicago: Markham Publishing Co. 1968), pp. 263-275.

132. Lowi, op. cit.

133. Theodore Drucker, "The Management of Public Service Organizations," *The Public Interest*, (Fall 1973).

134. Ibid.

135. David Easton, "An Approach to the Analysis of Political Systems," *World Politics* 9 (1957), pp. 383-400.

136. Opinion Research Corporation, Princeton, N.J., reprinted in "Public Employee Labor-Management Relations," op. cit., p. 104.

137. Randall B. Ripley and Grace Franklin, *Congress, The Bureaucracy, and Public Policy* (Homewood, Ill.: Dorsey Press, 1976).

138. Theodore Lowi and Randall Ripley, eds., *Legislative Politics USA* (Boston: Little, Brown & Co. 1972).

139. Francis E. Rourke, ed., *Bureaucratic Power in National Politics* (Boston: Little, Brown & Co. 1972).

140. For an overview of these budgetary techniques see Harley M. Hinrichs and Graeme M. Taylor, *Program Budgeting and Benefit-Cost Analysis* (Pacific Palisades, Calif.: Goodyear Publishing Co. 1969).

141. The discussion about the unionization of faculty was drawn from Everett Carll Ladd, Jr. and Seymour Martin Lipset, "The Ladd-Lipset Survey: Faculty Support for Unionization: 'Leveling-Off at about 75 Percent.' " *The Chronicle of Higher Education,* 13 February 1978, p. 8.

142. The discussion about Carter's civil service reorganization plan was drawn from, "Civil Service is Carter Priority," *Cincinnati Enquirer,* May 30, 1978, p. A-6.

Collective Bargaining in Public Employment: Scope, Issues and Conduct

For many years, personnel administration in the public sector operated in a bureaucratic setting under a complex system of laws and regulations that served a dual purpose. The first, brought about by the civil service reform movement, sought to free the public service of partisan politics and the "spoils" system, whereby appointments were given as rewards for loyal party service. Civil service reformers succeeded in having legislation enacted that substituted partisan service with a system of appointments and promotions based on "merit and fitness," determined by such objective standards as competitive examinations.

The second purpose of the laws and rules was to impose the principles of reform onto the internal administration of the public service. This was to be achieved by a system of position classification that clearly defined duties and responsibilities. In time, such functions as recruitment, position classification, performance ratings, promotions, training, and fringe benefits were to be standardly administered by personnel departments representing the chief executive. These functions were designed to promote the career concept and to make the public service attractive.[1]

The authority executives and civil service commissions exercised over working terms and conditions had gone largely unchallenged by public workers until recent times. Workers were accepting of "merit hiring, broad fringe benefits, almost absolute job security, and an assured income (not dependent on vagaries of weather, availability of risk capital, or the ebb and flow of fads and fashion). In truth, these were the trade-offs for the private sector unionism."[2] This has now changed. Public workers are unionizing, and are not only making the conventional demands for "more," but are also moving into areas traditionally controlled by civil service commissions or personnel offices. Public unions are seeking to participate in the setting of working conditions and work loads, job assignments, transfers, and promotions and to have a role in the reorganization of institutional structures. Thus, public workers are gradually making inroads into the governmental policy-planning and policy-making machinery. Some are boldly asserting that their real goal is the sharing of power.[3]

These union activities and objectives have given the merit system an unclear meaning. Unions, thus far, have not sought to question nor to weaken the merit principle, under which employees are recruited, selected, and promoted in a politically neutral environment. This is the portion of the merit system that sets the idealistic framework for public employment. But, the merit system also includes a broad program of personnel management activities and civil service commission controls. Activities such as position classification, pay administration, employee benefits and training, rule making, and the administration of appeals from employees fall under the latter category. It is the broader understanding of the merit system that has aroused the interest of public worker unions. The era of unilateralism—when management had sole authority over personnel functions—has thus ended. With the advent of unionism, "management-by-itself" has given way to a bilateral relationship where consultation, negotiation, and bargaining now take place. This has happened not because public employees "are clearly dissatisfied with existing merit systems but because they feel that unions will get more for them—more pay, more benefits, more aggressive protection against possible arbitrary management actions."[4]

How public employee unions evolved with respect to collective bargaining can be illustrated by a brief history of the fastest growing and most influential union representing municipal workers—the American Federation of State, County, and Municipal Employees (AFSCME), an AFL affiliate. In 1936 there were genuine merit systems in only eleven states and AFSCME perceived itself as part of the reform movement working for the enactment of civil service laws. At a time when the spoils system was commonplace, the union supported civil service as the best way to protect its membership from arbitrariness and political favoritism. According to the standards of the period, the emphasis on civil service rather than on collective bargaining made sense, and AFSCME relied on civil service and lobbying as the means to improve wages and working conditions. Yet, even then, the union was involved not only in conventional trade union objectives but in public policy questions as well. For example, it was active in such issues as the poll tax, consumer products, prices, rents, public power, and navigation projects. Finally, while not renouncing the right to strike, the union saw this as a counterproductive tactic in pursuit of union objectives.[5]

Since 1964, when Jerry Wurf captured the union's presidency in a bitterly fought election, the direction of AFSCME has changed. It now challenges the adequacy of the merit system, emphasizes its right to strike, has stepped up organizing efforts, and appreciably enlarged both its political and its collective bargaining roles. AFSCME and other public employee unions now clearly favor bilateral negotiations over what is regarded as the unilateralism of a management-dominated civil service personnel system.

In addition to proclaiming its right to bargain collectively and to strike, AFSCME has taken other significant policy steps. The executive board of the union urges the establishment of collective bargaining legislation where none exists, the expansion of coverage and scope of bargaining in existing laws, and the creation of impartial tripartite boards for the resolution of impasses and for administering collective bargaining laws. The board is opposed to compulsory arbitration as a means of settling bargaining disputes. The board favors the adoption of federal standards for collective bargaining (as represented in the federal Executive Orders dealing with collective bargaining) by states and municipalities and urges this as a stipulation for grants-in-aid programs to the lower governments.

As unions of public employees grow in strength and bargaining proficiency, public management faces institutional and legal barriers to effective labor relations. Collective bargaining in the public sector has been called "underdeveloped" by Harold Davey, noted labor relations expert, who believes this is a condition that will be difficult to overcome because of the nature of the American regime and of public employment.[6] The problem with the regime concerns the principle of separation of power and the limitations this places on the organization for labor relations. Who speaks for management in the public sector is unclear and varies from jurisdiction to jurisdiction. With some, negotiations are conducted by personnel offices; others employ a separate labor relations office or a specific administrator. Compounding this difficulty is the role played by "independent" civil service commissions in negotiations. Moreover, a personnel officer or civil service commission is faced with a dual and contradictory posture—to be both an impartial defender of employee rights and an adversary of employee unions as a management negotiator.[7]

Management's difficulties in negotiations are further exacerbated by the bifurcation of responsibility and authority in labor relations. Although a representative agency of the executive branch is responsible for negotiating with a union, it is an elected representative body—the legislative branch—that has ultimate charge of the purse strings and thus has the final authority to legitimize a settlement. This diffusion of authority complicates negotiations when an agreed contract is costed out to a sum exceeding an agency's existing ability to pay.

The nature of public employment also provides a complication in collective bargaining. At least 70 percent of the operating budgets of state and local governments are committed to personnel services. However, generally the public sector cannot rely on productivity gains enjoyed by the private sector as a way to hold down unit labor costs and actually enlarge real wages. In public employment negotiated salary increases invariably add to the cost of government by the amount of the increases. The only way to defray the mounting costs is through increased taxation or bond issues. Voter reaction to these measures has a direct influence on negotiations as well as introducing a third party—the public—to bilateral collective bargaining.[8]

Last, but not the least of the impediments to mature labor relations in the public sector has been the question of state sovereignty. In the early 1960s the claim of sovereignty served as one of the major arguments against recognizing representative organizations of public employees. The sovereignty argument has been used in defense of management unilateralism, management rights, and as a way of philosophically opposing collective bargaining. Sovereignty is defined as the "supreme, absolute, and uncontrollable power by which any independent state is governed. The sovereign is the person, body, or state in which supreme authority is vested." The orthodox claim of sovereignty further asserts that "government has sole authority which cannot be given to, taken by, or shared with anyone."[9] The argument against bilateral negotiations is founded on the premise that the state is sovereign in relation to its employees, and that it cannot—must not—delegate or share any of its authority because the supremacy of its authority in mass society provides the society with its sole rationality.

The claim of state sovereignty borrows from the concept of "divine right of kings." English common law tradition has in it the concept that the king can do no wrong. In "The Leviathan" Thomas Hobbes reasoned that an authoritarian state which compels every man to follow the rules is the basis for the common good. Otherwise, man left to his own designs would naturally promote his selfish desires with the end being a "war of all against all." The idea that man only excels in a collective state explains why individual or group desires, contrary to the common interest, should be ignored or crushed.

Bertrand de Jouvenal provided a modern version of the concept of sovereignty.[10] He justified sovereignty by claiming that the state exists to protect and refine the common interest. Further, the state must influence individual behavior if the behavior conflicts with the common interest. Most importantly, he defined man at his rational best when cooperating through the state and according the state recognition and respect. But, there are checks on the state as well. The law serves as the cornerstone of the state because it limits the discretion of the sovereign. Fundamentally, the common good must have priority over private will. A "good" sovereign, according to de Jouvenal, is the executant of the public will, not its creator. Since, ideally, the sovereign is restricted by the consent of the governed and the law, he becomes responsive to the collective will and not his own. "Thus the sovereign is no longer the crown of a complex social edifice, but rather the root of an edifice which has undergone arbitrary simplification."[11]

The American rendition of the sovereign nature of the state has sovereignty resting with the people. However, sovereign power in this country is exercised for the people by the national and the state governments. Morever, these governments, in turn, delegate some of their power to counties, municipalities, and special districts. Additionally, in democratic governments, there is a tendency to limit sovereign immunity and to restrict the absolute power of the sovereign in order to preclude a government's authority from becoming oppressive. Thus, sovereign immunity has been occasionally waived through legislation and court decisions in this country.

With respect to labor-management relations in the public sector, the orthodox position on sovereignty has been advanced by those who are wary of the effects of collective bargaining on government. The sovereignty concept is thus employed to ensure that only government be permitted to set the terms and conditions of employment. This posture is clearly incompatible with collective bargaining. It has taken state laws and executive orders in some cases, and voluntary action in others, for government agencies to come to terms with collective bargaining. They have done so despite a history of wishing for the unilateral determination of conditions of employment. They have done so despite the fear that collective bargaining would infringe on management prerogatives, diminish authority, and have an adverse impact on the efficiency of government operations. Not the least of some fears, too, has been the expectation that collective bargaining in government paves the way for crippling strikes against government. But, the growing political strength of public employee organizations and the law have either compelled collective bargaining or have made it necessary for government to agree to it.

Scope of Bargaining

The tension between management prerogatives and union rights leads to a conflict over the proper range of matters that should be negotiated. Realistically, in the absence of specific legislation that spells out management rights, the scope of bargaining is itself negotiable even when this involves matters that management feels is within its sole jurisdiction.

In the public sector, the locus of managerial authority is often difficult to pinpoint. The chief executive may delegate bargaining responsibility to a subordinate—a personnel officer, for instance—while retaining the authority to overrule a negotiated agreement. If the chief executive is an appointed official, he may be overruled by the legislative body; if he is elected, he may be opposed by the public if they disapprove of the agreement. Hence, management's authority in public sector labor relations is dictated by the political climate, the structure of government, and the executive chain of command. In local government, a weak mayoral structure and county governments generally end up having the final authority vested in the legislative body; strong mayoral and council-manager forms usually vest final authority in the chief executive.

Unions want to expand the scope of bargaining as much as they can. They want to negotiate over the traditional objectives of wages, fringe benefits, and working conditions as well as over policy issues that have a bearing on their objectives. For instance, organizations representing school teachers want bargaining to include such matters as class size, classroom discipline, and curriculum.

Union officials in the public sector feel that bargaining only over wages, fringe benefits, and working conditions does not fully consider the total welfare of the employees. Moreover, they argue that because of the vagueness of institutional arrangements for management decision-making in collective bargaining, they must pursue other means available to them in addition to collective bargaining. This means that the application of political power in the course of negotiations is an acceptable strategy and one that has become widely employed in public sector labor relations. For all practical purposes, it has become clear that the relative power of the negotiating parties will determine the scope of bargaining.

The power context of collective bargaining notwithstanding, many jurisdictions restrict the scope of bargaining by statutes, civil service regulations, and the legal restraints of sovereignty. Many public managers, too, feel that the scope of bargaining should be limited because they believe that an encroachment on policymaking by employee organizations is detrimental to their authority and to the public interest. Additionally, some managers feel that issues beyond their control should not be negotiable, for this invariably leads to a proliferation of actors involving themselves in labor relations. Accordingly, collective bargaining between labor and management becomes a mere facade and the real confrontation over issues takes place at other levels and institutions of government. Put another way, collective bargaining becomes a sideshow, while the main event is played in the political environment.

Some states, such as New York and Nevada, have statutes that define the scope of bargaining. Generally, where there is legislation dealing with scope of bargaining, these laws call for management to determine the nature and delivery of services; and give management the unilateral right to hire, fire, promote, discipline, assign, determine work loads, classify jobs, and exempt civil service regulations from negotiations. These laws do allow for unions to have consultation rights in many of these matters, however. Generally included within the scope of bargaining are wages, salaries, fringe benefits, retirement, union security, union stewards, working conditions, layoffs, rehiring, and grievance procedures. On the other hand, Connecticut, for one, has a progressive attitude and only excludes the recruitment and promotion functions of the civil service commissions from bargaining.[12]

Ultimately, managers believe that there should be residual rights of management if they are to perform as managers, and that these rights should not be negotiable. They maintain that they ought to have the right to set personnel policy, determine the work situation, and determine the nature and delivery of services. The scope of bargaining, it follows, should only include those issues that have a direct, practical impact on an employee. This attitude is reflected in New York City's statement on management rights in its Executive Order 52:

> It is the right of the city, acting through its agencies, to determine the standards of services to be offered by its agencies; determine the standards of selection for employment; direct its employees; take disciplinary action; relieve employees from duty because of lack of work or for other legitimate reasons; maintain the efficiency of governmental operations; determine methods, means, and personnel by which governmental operations are to be conducted; determine the content of job classifications; take all necessary actions to carry out its missions in emergencies; and exercise control and discretion over its organization and the technology of performing its work. The city's decisions on these matters are not within the scope of collective bargaining, but not withstanding the above, questions concerning the practical impact that the above matters have on employees, such as questions on workload or manning, are within the scope of collective bargaining.[13]

Labor unions hold to residual rights as well. Specifically, they feel that the right to strike is essential to real collective bargaining. Public employee unions contend that antistrike rules and legislation are an attempt to give management the upper hand in negotiations. While proclaiming that they dislike the strike as much as anyone, the unions believe that unless this ultimate weapon is available to them, they are reduced to begging rather than bargaining.

Another residual right claimed by unions is the right to bring in third parties for mediation and fact-finding in the event of an impasse in negotiations. They would like to see this procedure outlined in legislation. Finally, they would like to have legislation universally specifying that both management and labor in the public sector bargain in good faith. Unions would perceive this as a declaration that management must accept the bargaining process as a constructive method for rational and stable labor relations rather than an indication of personal failure or a rebellion against authority.

The present state of development in public sector labor relations has management more concerned with depth (the extent of influence on particular issues obtained by the union) rather than with breadth (the number of issues negotiated). Put another way, management is agreed to a comprehensive number of "negotiable issues" so long as the actual encroachment by the union upon the issues is limited. Thus, management negotiators show a willingness to "discuss" any issue with union representatives but are unwilling to admit that any issues are "jointly determined," for "joint determination" is an admission of a delegation of their authority. In the few instances where collective bargaining in the public sector is well developed there is a recognition of joint determination and thus, a likelihood of a trade-off by the parties between breadth and depth, or an outright attempt by management to limit breadth. Predictably, the latter condition of limiting breadth should prevail as time passes. This prediction relies on these factors: (1) Unions are gaining in strength vis à vis management, thereby increasing their capability for depth of penetration. (2) More formal written agreements are occurring. Written agreements reduce management's flexibility by committing them to the terms of the agreement. (3) Joint decision making on certain issues has already been mandated in some jurisdictions by public policy and this could suggest a growing trend.[14]

Ultimately, what is negotiable depends directly upon the power relationship of the negotiating parties. The power capability, actual or implied, of the employee group relative to the power held by management determines the scope of bargaining. Power, in public sector labor relations, is the ability of one side to apply the most telling pressure influencing the outcome of the negotiation in its favor. This may be done by mobilizing effective political support through lobbying of key institutions or key officials, or somehow gaining the support of the public. Another manifestation of power is the capability to, at least, inconvenience the public, and, at most, potentially or actually endanger their health, safety, and welfare, by the deprivation of public services. The latter manifestation clearly advantages public employees, whose occupations afford them this capability. Finally, the power capability of a union is also the product of the will of the membership, i.e., how strongly the members feel on an issue.

Public policy, insofar as it pertains to collective bargaining in the public sector, has an impact on the real scope of bargaining. Generally, legislation concerning unionization that deals with specific issues removes these issues from the scope of bargaining. Cases in point are the automatic granting of exclusive recognition to unions that enjoy the support of a majority of employees, prohibition of mandatory union membership requirements, and legalization of dues checkoff. Public policy also has a way of affecting the real scope of bargaining through an indirect influence on union strength. When a policy shift occurs that is favorable to union aims with respect to specific issues, especially when it concerns union security, it enables the unions to focus their resources on areas untouched by legislation. In any event, the real scope of bargaining is, in the main, determined by the relative strength of the involved parties.[15]

Issues in Collective Bargaining

The union agenda for bargaining is often determined during the recruitment and organization stage. In order to attract and retain members, the union must perceive their needs and frustrations and articulate these as issues in negotiation. This is necessary for self-perpetuation. Also tied to survival are issues directly related to the union's institutional needs. Management, on the other hand, is placed on the defensive. It is generally trying to hold the line on existing costs and to retain its authority on personnel and policy matters where practicable.

There are six general areas of concern to unions, and hence to management, in collective bargaining: bargaining unit determination, union security, individual security, wages and fringe benefits, employment and unemployment, and working conditions. These issues will each be examined.

Bargaining Unit Determination

Even before negotiations begin, the question of who will represent the employees in collective bargaining must be resolved. One issue of unit determination is closely related to the workers' quest for craft autonomy.

Within a work environment employees prefer a bargaining unit that consists of members having common work-related interests. Workers in certain crafts feel that they, as an exclusive unit, should have the autonomy to determine their own rules of the workplace because of their closeness to their work. The conflict between workers in different crafts can be illustrated by the internal split in the Transit Workers' Union in 1956. The machinists and motormen within the union formed a splinter union, the Motormens' Benevolent Association, because they believed that their narrow craft interests were not being protected by the leaders of the larger union.

Professional employees, too, feel that they deserve a separate unit because they have nothing in common with clerical or unskilled workers. State legislation varies as to its outlook on the establishment of separate units for professional and craft employees. Generally, professional employees must be separated from other workers unless the other workers vote to allow them to be included. New York State's Taylor Act declares that a separate unit for professionals is the "most appropriate unit."

The setting up of a bargaining unit is tied to the criterion of majority representation. Yet, the key question here is, "majority of what?" There are many interests to be considered prior to determining a bargaining unit: the integrity of a craft or occupation, the union, the public, and the experience and effectiveness of a public employer in labor relations. However, the critical determining factor generally concerns the range of occupation within a workplace and their common interests. The rational definition of a constituency to be represented concerns locating a power structure that can bring about effective collective bargaining without gerrymandering worker groups.

There is a great deal of difficulty in locating common interests within a bargaining unit. Legislation dealing with this matter provides management with a great deal of latitude in determining appropriate bargaining units. Some of the criteria employed by management for unit determination are "community of interest," the labor relations history of a bargaining unit, the traditional alignments of a group of employees with particular unions, and the locus of management authority. "Community of interest," the most prevalent criterion, is defined by New York State's Taylor Law as having common work rules, wage structures, personnel practices, and occupational concerns. Further, the Taylor Act is also helpful because of its precision in stipulating the "most appropriate unit" rather than resorting to "an appropriate unit" formula. Under the act, the state's Public Employee Relations' Board (PERB) has three standards for the most appropriate unit:

1. *The definition of the unit shall correspond to a community of interest among the employees to be included in the unit.*

2. *The officials of government at the level of the unit shall have the power to agree to, or make effective recommendations to, administrative authority or the legislative body with respect to the terms and conditions of employment upon which the employees desire to negotiate.*

3. *The unit shall be compatible with the joint responsibilities of the public employer and employee to serve the public.*[16]

Under the Taylor law, and similar legislation in other states, an individual or a group of employees have the right to appeal a bargaining unit decision to the state public employee board.

Another issue is whether or not supervisors should be included in a bargaining unit. The Taft-Hartley Act excludes supervisors in the private sector. In the public sector, the feeling is that supervisors should be excluded because they are representatives of management in their day-to-day dealings with the rank and file. Their inclusion in a bargaining unit would lead to divided loyalties and lessen their effectiveness as representatives of management.

However, the problem in the public sector is that a supervisor is often just a title which carries with it no real supervisory responsibilities. Accordingly, those who are charged with the responsibility of determining a bargaining unit must also determine who is truly a supervisor and who is not. The Wisconsin Employee Relations Board provides the clearest definition of a supervisor and delineates degrees of supervisory responsibility:

1. *Authority to effectively recommend the hiring, firing, promotion, transfer, discipline, or discharge of employees.*

2. *Authority to direct or assign the work force.*

3. *Number of employees supervised, and the number of other persons receiving greater, lesser, or similar authority over the same employees.*

4. *Level of pay, including an evaluation of whether the supervisor is paid for his skill or for his supervision.*

5. *Whether the supervisor is primarily supervising an activity or is primarily supervising employees.*

6. *Whether the supervisor is a working supervisor or spends a substantial majority of his time supervising employees.*

7. *The amount of independent judgement and discretion exercised in the supervision of employees.*[17]

In Wisconsin, employees whose responsibilities correspond with this definition of a supervisor are excluded from bargaining units.

Most other states exclude supervisory employees from bargaining units. Where supervisors are allowed to join bargaining units of employees, they are not permitted to participate in collective bargaining decisions. There are exceptions however. The Public Employee

Relations Board in New York has not made a definitive ruling on the exclusion or inclusion of supervisors. For example, state troopers in New York include supervisors in their bargaining unit because these supervisors merely assign work. Generally, most states also exclude top managers, confidential employees such as accountants, personnel officers, and others who have an impact on personnel policy—probationary, seasonal, part-time, and temporary employees—from bargaining units.

In some states supervisors have formed their own units. New York's Taylor Act does not prohibit supervisors from forming their own units. Even though some states allow supervisors to form unaffiliated units and to enjoy bargaining rights, the trend is toward allowing representative units with consultative rights, not bargaining rights. In general, personnel officers feel that when supervisors form their own unit for purposes of collective bargaining, it is a sign of management's failure.

Management prefers to have bargaining units as large as possible. Fragmentation of units and union competition for representation makes constructive bargaining difficult at best. Excessive units cause administrative breakdowns, employee jealousy, interunion rivalry, and irrational multiple negotiations. Bargaining unit fragmentation leads to a crazy quilt of wage and benefit packages that diverts negotiators from other problems. The advantages of having large bargaining units are that unions can afford to hire skilled labor relations practitioners facilitating constructive bargaining, the opinions of a large unit are more accurate reflections of general employee feelings, and a large unit minimizes jealousy over wage differentials that occur among fragmented units negotiating separate packages. A union also prefers a large unit, provided it is the sole bargaining agent for the unit.

Fragmentation of units has occurred where management has recognized any group that applied for representation without setting up specific criteria for bargaining units. The city of Philadelphia avoided this problem by recognizing only one bargaining unit, to be represented by AFSCME, for all its nonuniformed employees.[18] Proliferation of units occurs when governmental jurisdictions have recognized minority units within a larger unit as a way of solving representation disputes. Ultimately, recognition must balance between administrative discretion on behalf of rational collective bargaining and the freedom of employees to choose their representatives.

Union Security

Union security is a nonmonetary issue that is important to both unions and management. Unions need security clauses in order to provide institutional stability, optimize their membership, and establish

66   Part I: Nature of Collective Bargaining

their position as a power bloc. Union security provisions such as dues checkoff, exclusive recognition, the union shop, agency shop, and maintenance-of-membership clauses, while widely accepted in the private sector, are controversial points within public sector collective bargaining because some of them conflict with the merit system and invade management prerogatives. However, union security measures are seen as necessary for a stable bargaining relationship and for the establishment of good communication procedures for both parties.

Union security provisions are sought by unions in order to present a strong, united front to management and to prevent the encroachment of rival unions. Without the availability of statutory guidelines, unions must work out their own security arrangements. The concern with security is tied to the self-preservation of unions. It is also tied to the strike issue becasue a strong, financially secure union is less likely to strike. Finally, security provisions attempt to eliminate those who benefit from labor-management negotiations yet do not join the union.

The dues checkoff, a common practice in the private sector, is one union security device. The standard procedure has the employer deducting union dues and fees from the employees' paychecks and turning the collected funds over to the union, usually keeping a small amount to cover accounting and clerical costs. In 1962, AFSCME reported that thirty-eight states permitted a dues checkoff for state and local employees and that eighty percent of the union's members paid their dues through this method.[19] These numbers have since increased, and now most major municipalities permit the dues checkoff. Some of the advantages of this practice to a union are that it provides a steady, year-round income to the union, it permits the union to collect dues without pressuring employees, it cuts the union's cost of dues collection, and it makes withdrawal from the union more difficult. The checkoff also has the advantage of providing for management a reasonably accurate list of union members.

The question of recognition of employee representatives relates to management's attitude about union security and the union's organizational abilities. The issue for management to determine is which union should represent the bargaining unit; and then, whether or not the majority of employees in the unit want this union to represent them. The two basic forms of recognition are voluntary and certified. When voluntary recognition occurs, management relies on dues deduction cards, payroll lists, or union authorization cards to satisfy itself that a majority of the employees want a union to represent them in bargaining. Voluntary recognition, however, has two problems: the evidence presented may not be valid, and coercion may have been employed by the union. When there is doubt about the validity of the evidence or there is competition among unions for representation status, management usually resorts to a secret employee election, governed by legislation or by an appropriate state or local agency. The election must be conducted under consistent rules and management must be careful not to show favoritism toward one union. The bargaining agent is then "certified" according to the results of the election.

The most important kind of recognition is exclusive recognition. Here, one union has the right and responsibility to speak on behalf of all employees in the bargaining unit if the union can prove that it represents a majority of all employees. The institution and recognition of one bargaining agent discourages union competition, minimizes inter-organizational factionalism, simplifies negotiations for both sides, makes the administration of an agreement easier, provides the union with a strong and stable membership, and reduces the possibility of a strike.

The general trend is toward exclusive recognition. Executive Order 11491 mandated that only organizations granted exclusive recognition would be authorized to participate in collective negotiations in the federal service. Table 2-1 shows the extent of exclusive recognition in the federal service. Most recent state public employee legislation favors this posture. The New York Taylor Act called for a continuing study of exclusivity in light of experience. State study commissions, while concerned with the rights of the individual and the minority of employees, favor exclusive recognition. Most jurisdictions feel that the advantages of stability and clarity in collective bargaining with organizations enjoying exclusive recognition outweigh any disadvantages.

After recognition, negotiation rights are usually granted to the majority union in a bargaining unit. Bargaining rights are mandated in most state legislation; the rules of bargaining and impasse procedures, such as mediation and fact-finding, are administered by a state agency or board. The strike is used as a leverage if bargaining rights are not granted or if the negotiation process breaks down. The increasing legitimacy of exclusive recognition suggest that most states and municipalities recognize that exclusive bargaining rights are essential to union security.

In the private sector, the union shop is recognized as being perhaps the most important component of union security. With the restricted use of the closed shop, the union shop has been the industrial unions' chief way to ensure membership. The union shop requires that all employees hired must join the union after a specified period of time, usually thirty days. In the public sector, the union shop has met with opposition. Even though it is unlike the closed shop, where an employee has to be a union member to be hired, the union shop is nonetheless seen as being in violation of merit selection. Executive Order 10988

TABLE 2-1: Organization of Federal Blue- and White-Collar Workers by Major Unions (1974)

Union	Total Employees in Exclusive Units	Blue-Collar a			White-Collar b		
		Membership	Rank	Percentage	Membership	Rank	Percentage
American Federation of Government Employees, AFL-CIO (AFGE)	650,038	208,394	1	32.0	441,644	1	68.0
National Federation of Federal Employees (NFFE)	125,234	31,605	4	25.2	93,629	2	74.8
National Association of Government Employees (NAGE)	74,127	32,882	3	44.3	41,425	4	55.7
Metal Trades Councils, AFL-CIO (MTC)	58,366	55,661	2	95.3	2,705	6	4.7
National Treasury Employees Union (NTEU)	65,417	24	6	0	65,393	3	100.0
International Association of Machinists and Aerospace Workers, AFL-CIO (IAM)	30,166	26,903	5	89.2	3,263	5	10.8

Source: U.S., Civil Service Commission, *Union Recognition in the Federal Government* (1974), tab. F, and calculations.

a Wage-earners.

b Paid through General Schedule.

Note: Percentages are based on total nonpostal employment (2,014,704).

and 11491 do not authorize union shop agreements for federal workers. Court rulings and state public employee boards have also been unfavorable to the union shop. Despite negotiated modified union shop agreements in Philadelphia and Baltimore and transit unions having union shop agreements in several cities, the provision still appears to be of doubtful legality in the public sector. Spero and Capozzola reported, however, that labor relations have greatly stabilized in jurisdictions where the union shop has been implemented, because the unions become less concerned with organizational maintenance as a primary goal.[20]

As a compromise, a widely used modification of the union shop in the public sector is the agency shop. Here, the employee must pay a fee equivalent to union dues or have it deducted from his paychecks, but need not actually join the union. Unions contend that the agency shop does not violate the employee's right of association while providing the union with a guaranteed, steady income. The agency shop tends to eliminate "free riders," those who share in the benefits gained by union members in collective bargaining yet do not share in the costs of membership.

Unions contend that it is only equitable to have those who benefit from a collective enterprise to also contribute to the costs. Objectors to the agency shop believe that it conflicts with the merit system, is a case of "taxation without representation," and is a way of having compulsory unionism. It is also argued that the rights of an individual are violated by an agency shop because there is no choice but to contribute to the union treasury. A key issue is whether or not fees can be assessed against a nonunion member's will. Another objection is that the fees may be used for purposes other than securing bargaining agreements, e.g., political activity or union administrative expenses.

The issue of whether the agency shop violates the First Amendment right of free association has been resolved by the Supreme Court in *Abood* v. *Detroit Board of Education*. The 1977 decision upheld "agency shop" agreements for public employees just as earlier cases upheld similar agreements for private employees. The court held that the dues requirement, as used to finance collective bargaining, contract administration, and other nonpolitical purposes, is valid. But, the court added that employees may not be forced to contribute to the union's "ideological" causes, for this would be in violation of the First Amendment. However, the justices acknowledged that there would be "difficult problems" in drawing the line between "collective bargaining" activities and "ideological" activities.

The emergence of the agency shop as a union security provision is yet another attempt of public sector labor relations to emulate the experiences of the private sector. The rationale for the agency shop is that while individual rights must be accommodated, the most important consideration is for stable labor relations; this potential is best realized through an accommodation to union security provisions.

Another substitute for the union shop, permitted in some jurisdictions, is the maintenance-of-membership provision. Here, employees who are union members at the time of contract approval, or those who join the union subsequently, must remain union members for the duration of the contract.

Individual Security

Collectivity bargained agreements provide the rules for due process for employees. These rules establish for the workers their absolute claim to fair treatment in the employment relationship in exchange for an obligation to perform their duties as specified in the agreement or as called for by management. Moreover, the rules also establish for the workers their relative claim to available work. Interestingly, unionized employees have opted to secure due process through collective bargaining instead of relying on the due process procedures formed in most civil service rules. The reason for this is that workers prefer to have a voice in the process and not to rely on civil service, perceived as an arm of management, for adjudication.

The question of fair treatment in the employment relationship concerns the establishment of both the rules of employee conduct and the judicial system by which a violator is tried. The agreement, thus, would, on one hand, provide management with certain rights to define "reasonable" rules of employee conduct and to discipline workers for "just cause." On the other hand, the agreement would create a judicial system concerned with the grievance procedure and the arbitration provisions of the agreement.[21]

Employees also obtain job rights through collectively bargained agreements. This is done through specified hiring and promotion criteria in the negotiated agreements, usually tied to union security provisions. Hence, union security arrangements are more than an institutional concern; they bring with them clauses that establish the individual worker's job rights.

Union and agency shop provisions generally require that seniority and union membership be at least considerations in hiring, layoffs, firing, and promotion. Unions prefer to have seniority and union membership as the determinants in these personnel matters, thereby restricting management's freedom of selection.[22]* Further, unions

---

* Many civil service laws and procedures restrict the role managers may play in personnel matters. The union influence, in effect, reinforces this posture. The difference is that the union through collective bargaining, has replaced civil service as a controlling force.

would like to have a single salary rate for each employee classification level instead of the step schedule within a classification common in civil service.

Unions pose a challenge to the merit concept and to the policy-making authority of civil service commissions in personnel concerns. The challenge to the merit system is not so much because the system has failed in public personnel administration but because the system is being made superfluous by collective bargaining, despite the unions' professed support of the merit principle. And the public sector is clearly accommodating to the realities of power politics and the aspirations and demands of its employees for collective bargaining. The public sector is finding it difficult to have the merit system coexist with collective bargaining; the utility of the merit system is now, at best, unclear.

Wages and Fringe Benefits

To many public workers, wages or salaries and fringe benefits are often their most important concerns. Yet, ironically, in a number of jurisdictions and especially in the federal government, this issue is not often negotiable. Most unions representing federal employees are restricted to lobbying before Congress on the crucial concern of salaries or wages and fringe benefits, and must limit their collective bargaining with agency heads to other issues. The reason for this is that the wages and salaries of most classes of employees must be ultimately determined by congressional action. White-collar workers fall into the salary specifications and ranges as determined by the Civil Service Commission and approved by Congress.[23] Postal workers, however, are now governed by the NLRB and are able to bargain on wages. The wage of the federal blue-collar worker is usually determined by a formal calculation of the prevailing wage rate in the particular area of employment.[24] These conditions generally hold for the state and local levels of government as well, in that the authority for final decision making on financial matters rests with the state legislature or the city council.

Unions generally find it in their best interest to seek bargained wages and salaries (unless they consistently achieve success in their lobbying efforts); and they have made some achievements in this endeavor. (See chapter 3 for an expanded treatment of this issue.) The International Association of Fire Fighters is a case in point:

> *In recent years, the Fire Fighters have been changing the form of their relationships, in localities where the statutes and regulations permit, to incorporate their wages and conditions of work into collective bargaining agreements rather than into city ordinances and regulations.*[25]

Douglas Weiford and Wayne Burggraaff predict that this will be the trend of the future because the merity system of salary determination is based on "hard-to-defend subjective standards."[26] If this evaluation is correct, it means that union can come to rely increasingly on their negotiating skills at the bargaining table rather than on their political muscle alone to achieve gains in this vital area.

Since fringe benefits must be considered as a part of the total wage and salary package, they are inextricably tied to the bargaining practice used to negotiate wages and salaries. Fringe benefits comprised about twenty percent of the average worker's conpensation in 1972, as shown in table 2-2.[27] Fringe benefits are becoming increasingly important at the bargaining table because of the interest union members have shown in them; they are often considered to be a hidden cost to the employer, and they offer tax advantages over straight salary to the employee.[28]

Employment and Unemployment

Control of employment and unemployment is another issue of concern to union members and particularly to some white-collar workers who feel that automation is reducing both their number of jobs and the value of their work. Consequently, unions may bargain for shorter workweeks and shorter workdays in an effort to control employment. Management may also be more cautious in introducing technological changes and in the accompanying reduction of personnel due to the presence of a union.[29]

Automation is currently the main threat to employment in the public service and will undoubtedly have a great impact on collective bargaining in the public sector. With automation, old skills became obsolete, the emphasis is on labor saving and efficiency, and little or no regard is paid to job satisfaction. The application of automation techniques has already occurred to some extent in the following areas of the public service: the postal service, police communications, sanitation services, and data processing systems replacing the traditional government clerk. Workers who have been affected by technological innovation have thus far been the unskilled or semiskilled; however, as technology continues to expand, displacement may occur to the skilled and professional workers as well. At any rate, workers currently being displaced are usually union members. Thus, the threat of automation is already real to unions in the public sector, as they must extract concessions through bargaining in order to protect their members.

For comparison, the question of automation and technological displacement has had a longer history in the private sector. Unions in the private sector have met the challenge with varying responses. Among the powerful trade unions the results range from the building trades

TABLE 2-2: Average Employee Compensation, Private Nonagricultural Economy (1972)

Total Compensation	100.0
Item of Compensation	**Percentage of Compensation**
Pay for working time a	80.5
Pay for leave time b	5.6
Employer expenditures for retirement programs	7.0
Employer expenditures for health benefit programs	4.7
Employer expenditures for unemployment benefit programs	1.0
Nonproduction bonuses	1.0
Savings and thrift plans	.2

Source: U.S., Bureau of Labor Statistics, *Handbook of Labor Statistics 1976*, tab. 112, p. 235.

a Includes pay for overtime

b Does not include sick leave.

unions' successful shutting-out of laborsaving devices to the gradualist approach of the longshoremens' unions.* Generally, management has been able to implement laborsaving techniques at a quicker rate in industries where their power relationship vis 'a vis the union has been one of dominance, and at a slower rate or not at all as the power relationship evens or shifts. This is an instructive pattern for the public sector, as unions there engage in the battle to safeguard their members' job security.

The stakes surrounding job security are high. If the unions fail to provide for this, then their own survival is threatened as well. A hard-line management posture on the issue of laborsaving devices would be to hold firm on automation claiming it not a negotiable issue but a

---

* The longshoremen's unions allowed management to introduce automation to replace a gradually diminishing work force—diminishing through normal attrition (i.e., death, retirement, or resignations).

management prerogative. A management victory here would undoubtedly weaken or even destroy the union. However, for the sake of long-run labor-management relations, some government jurisdictions have done otherwise. In the federal service, management saw a unilateral introduction of automation as a way of increasing union militancy and thus, entered into negotiations over automation voluntarily. For instance, the postal service began negotiations over this issue in 1968 even though it was not required to do so. The negotiations took the form of consultation with the postal unions about how the service planned to move toward automation; the subsequent agreement called for a gradual implementation of automation and a retraining provision for displaced employees. Ultimately, while management agreed to negotiate over automation, the relative legal and political strength of the parties did not provide the unions with the leverage to alter the basic management decision to automate. The only recourses that unions may have to counteract management's strength on this issue are through public relations efforts or through political channels. Otherwise, it would appear that the advent of automation in the public service implies a general decline in union effectiveness in determining policy. How unions came to grips with this issue has a bearing on their long-run institutional stability. It should be recalled, however, that weak or unstable unions, seeking to gain parity in negotiations are the ones most likely to act in a militant way.[30] The choice for management is in favor of labor-saving efficiency, or rather, the right of management to manage human and other resources in the most efficient way; or in favor of stable and harmonious labor relations. In the real world, sometimes these two choices are mutually incompatible.

Working Conditions

Workers, in some cases and in some jurisdictions, are more concerned about working conditions than they are about significant pay increases. For example Juris and Feuille enumerate a number of bargaining issues for police unions: hours of work, shift changes, shorter workweek, standby duty, use of civilians in the department, one-man versus two-man squad cars, promotions, seniority, arbitrary transfers, moonlighting, name tags, uniform changes, and discipline and grievance procedures.[31] Agreements with teachers' unions also contain a number of clauses on conditions of work, which include such items as grievance procedure, teacher hours and loads, class size, nonteaching duties, transfers, assignments, promotions, teacher evaluations, discipline, teacher facilities, student control and discipline, programs for professional development, and textbook selection.[32] Other employee groups, principally professional and semi-professional employees such as physicians, nurses, and social workers, also accord a great deal of importance to matters related to working conditions in the course of collective bargaining. However, this is not to dilute the importance accorded economic concerns by *most* workers —especially in nonprofessional occupations (see table 7-4, chapter 7).

The importance of working conditions to professional employees and the militancy with which they pursue this interest may be demonstrated by the example of the Los Angeles County hospitals strike in April 1976. On 21 April 1976, intern and resident doctors went on strike at the three main Los Angeles County hospitals, "substantially disrupting services at all three."[33] The strike forced the cancellation of scheduled clinic visits and elective surgeries at County-USC Medical Center, Martin Luther King General Hospital, and Harbor General Hospital. However, emergency care continued at all three hospitals, as teachers and full-time doctors, as well as nonstriking interns and residents, continued to treat patients.

The Joint Council of Interns and Residents, representing the strikers, called the strike an effort to pressure Los Angeles County into improving patient care at the hospitals, as well as to increase the doctors' salaries. A key issue in the dispute that led to a breakdown in negotiations was the proposal by the doctors of a four-million-dollar patient care fund, to be used for added staff and new equipment. The doctors also wanted more nurses to be hired to help reduce the number of hours the doctors work. One of the strike leaders said that for four years the doctors had been "politely begging the county to do something to help get decent medical care," and now they "hope and believe that the message is getting through at last." He continued that the doctors would "seek help from county supervisors who have the final authority to decide whether county negotiators should increase their offer."[34]

The three-day strike ended when the young doctors voted to return to work while negotiations for a new contract continued. However, management granted the doctors a key concession in order to end the strike: more money would be put in a special patient care fund and the doctors would be given a share in the authority over spending of money from the fund. A raise in doctors' salaries was also assured. Still left unresolved was the strikers' demand for an administrative reorganization as the means to improve care. The doctors wanted a more centralized authority structure with a physician at the head, as well as an improvement in the system of medical records.

The federation representing all the doctors, while not ruling out subsequent strikes, but calling them "inappropriate" for doctors, stated that it preferred to employ job actions that "could create chaos in the entire county health care system." For example, doctors could refuse to fill out Medi-Care and Medi-Cal forms, thereby shutting off a chief source of income for county facilities. Another example would be to treat all patients "by the book," causing patients to accumulate in such numbers that county facilities would overflow. Interestingly, it is the magnitude of the federation's potential power that prompts some of its members to urge restraint. "We could make the system so unpalatable or so costly to the voters that they would prefer the county to get out of the health care delivery field," a spokesman said. "But," he added, "there comes a point in time where action is the only way workers can gain their goals."[35]

The issue of working conditions is so critical among professional employees that the impetus for collective bargaining for these employees may have been more of a concern over aspects of professionalism than over economic ones.[36] For public school teachers, while there is a focus on economic matters in their bargaining, there is also a sense of their inability to have a voice on such matters as curriculum, choice of teaching materials, and size of classes. And these are becoming issues in bargaining with increasing frequency in the school districts. Among faculties in higher education these matters are considered professional prerogatives. However, as austerity budgets have necessarily had an impact on what is taught, on sizes of classes, teaching loads, and so on, the control over teaching and research has shifted from the faculty to college administrators. Thus, collective bargaining has taken hold among college faculties, especially where the shift in control is more readily apparent, i.e., in the two-year and four-year teaching institutions, although not restricted to these institutions. Nurses have been moved to collective bargaining because of frustration in the absence of a voice on standards and procedures for patient care and other related issues. Social workers are unhappy with their case loads and the general administrative indifference to a professional servicing of their clientele. This is not to imply, however, that the sole reason for unionization among professional employees has been the degree of professional prerogatives, i.e., working conditions. Dissatisfaction with working conditions has often provided the impetus; but, dissatisfaction over economic matters is generally evident too.

Working conditions, which are specified for public employees, are frequently derived from the process of public policy formulation. The way management authority is actually exercised in government makes its actions strongly influenced by the need to weigh and balance the interests of divergent citizen groups. In many instances a union dispute may have a direct consequence on the nature of an essential service. For instance, the teachers' strike in New York City in 1968 had not only a labor-management confrontation; it included other groups representing educational, civic, political, racial, and religious interests. The real issue is, thus, one of public policy. In the case of the New

York teachers' strike, it was one of public educational policy; "a policy so fundamental to the welfare of the community that it was surrounded by a mixture of pressures, politics, and prejudice of such complexity as to obstruct any resolution through traditional dealings between the union and management."[37]

Fundamentally, public employee unions participate in the formulation of public policy through collective bargaining and political activities to secure bargaining advantages. For when unions act on their behalf they become concerned with issues that, in the main, are determined by legislation, the courts, civil service commissions, or other interests among the public. Because of the political nature of decision making and management authority in the public sector, collective bargaining provides a new dimension to public policy formulation. It is the way for public employees to be represented in the political arena where decisions affecting their working lives, as well as the nature and extent of their services, are determined. The crucial question is not whether public employee unions are now institutionalized interests, but whether their power capabilities are so unmatched as to allow no check or control over them. The critical question becomes whether they are, or could become, the major determinants of public policy in areas of concern to them.

The Government Standpoint

The government employer is also concerned with wages and salaries, fringe benefits, employment levels, and working conditions, but usually from quite a different perspective than the unions. The government goes to the bargaining table with issues of its own that are its chief concern; these issues form the nucleus of the negotiating stance of the public employer.

The first of these issues may be expressed by the question, "What is the cost of the economic package proposed by the unions?" A corollarial question is, "What is the maximum amount that the government can afford to spend on personnel costs?" To answer these questions requires knowledge of anticipated revenues for the life of the proposed union contract, a clear concept of priorities in governmental expenditures, and an accurate analysis of the explicit and implicit costs of union proposals. For example, the employer must always keep in mind that a dollar paid for fringe benefits such as a health care plan for employees "is a cost of production, just the same as a dollar of wage payments."[38]

A second issue of great importance to the government is the matter of legal and practical constraints on the source of funds to meet union demands as well as limitations on the bargaining authority of the employer. Some programs may have to be cut back, others may never get started. The relative gains and losses must be weighed by the government in consideration of the union proposals. The question of decision making on these matters is often quite complicated due to the number of officials involved and their respective powers and duties. For example, the agency directly involved in bargaining with a union may have one idea about how much it is prepared to accept in increased personnel costs, but the legislature may have an entirely different idea, and it is the legislature that has the final authority in fiscal matters.[39] The circumstances may vary from agency to agency, however; for example, there are some public authorities, such as public utility companies, that have "greater freedom in affecting revenues and costs than the executive departments of government.[40] At any rate, the appropriate legislative body must decide how much of its authority on fiscal matters it is willing to delegate to the executive branch for purposes of collective bargaining.

A third issue from the government standpoint is the timing of negotiations with the budgetary process. It is obviously advantageous to determine as early as possible in the budget cycle what the personnel costs will be in order to better assess the implications for fiscal planning. Furthermore, an early start at the negotiating table gives more time for bargaining, and more time to settle a dispute should an impasse develop.

The fourth perspective from which government views the bargaining issues is that of how union proposals relate to their prerogatives as managers. Some employers become very sensitive about their rights and their authority after hearing union proposals for employee participation in policymaking, for example. Indeed, it is over this issue that much of the hostility of government employers centers, for they may view as inappropriate any attempt by employees to bargain over their rate of compensation and work conditions. Consequently, employers are usually concerned over the question of policy determination and may be quite wary of bargaining proposals in this area.

It is interesting to consider the question of the government as a model employer in regard to the public manager's viewpoint of bargaining. The government feels that it should be a pacesetter in the area of equal opportunity employment; does the same attitude hold true for compensation and benefits? The answer is an emphatic No. The Employee Relations Officer of the Tennessee Valley Authority indicated that this would not be politically feasible; if government salaries were very much above the norm for comparable work in the private sector, a great deal of pressure would be brought on the offending agency from the affected business community through charges of unfair government competition and unfair interference in the market place.[41] As a result, TVA, at least, determines wages and salaries for both its white-collar and blue-collar workers by means of an annual survey of wage and salary rates prevailing in the TVA area among a large list of selected employers.[42]* The TVA spokesperson indicated that while the agency's rates of compensation would certainly be above some employers in the area, it was politically and economically practicable and defensible to set the rates as close to the area average as possible.[43]† Economist Morton Godine confirms the wisdom of this policy in the following statement:

> Government in an economic system based primarily upon private enterprise should not reward its own employees in such a manner as to place private employers at a severe competitive disadvantage. It would seem inequitable to require taxpayers to support model personnel policies at their expense. For it is true that government can support such wage scales by taxation and borrowing as it is that private enterprise is unable to do so because of resulting unprofitable operations and potential bankruptcy. Moreover, the very tax burden which would necessarily be imposed as a consequence of uneconomic public wage payments would tend to prevent private employers from paying the higher wages prevailing in the government service.[44]**

Since it is safe to assume that the market forces described are applicable to all levels of government, we can conclude that the government sector deliberately avoids any attempt at being a model employer in terms of determining a "fair" rate of compensation for each occupation in order to develop guidelines for private industry. Instead, government wages and salaries seem, for the most part, to be reactions to the trends generated in the private sector.

---

* The fact that TVA unions acquiesce to this position leads one to question the authenticity of collective bargaining there, at least in regard to compensation and benefits.

† It is interesting to speculate that the Salary Reform Act of 1962, which introduced the concept of the prevailing wage to federal employees and was hailed as progressive legislation, may have kept federal wages at levels lower than what they would have been in a collectively bargained situation. Indeed, this bill may have been anticipatory legislation that foresaw the potential impact of bargaining on personnel costs and was designed to undercut meaningful negotiation on compensatory matters should it develop.

**It should also be noted that low wage rates in the public service that are noncompetitive are also a disservice to the taxpayer in that low wages may entail the hiring of lower quality workers to manage the public business (Paul A. Samuelson, *Economics*, 9th ed. [New York: McGraw-Hill, 1973], p. 583).

Unique Features of Public Sector
Collective Bargaining

The monetary and nonmonetary issues in public sector collective bargaining are confronted not only at the negotiation table but in the broader arena of public policymaking, where competing groups make demands on government resources. Public sector decision makers are faced with having to weigh the private interests of unions with the private interests of other groups, while, at the same time, trying to protect the concept of the "public interest." Added to this problem, is the unclear source of decision making in the public sector. The separation of powers among the executive, legislative, and judicial branches with each branch often having different functional responsibilities and often serving different clienteles make it difficult, if not impossible, to identify who speaks for management in collective bargaining. The incomplete resolution of the question of delegation of authority has institutionalized bargaining in bad faith in the public sector. The vagueness about where the final authority in collective bargaining lies in government has fostered the practice by unions of circumventing management bargaining representatives and appealing to other branches and/or levels of government to obtain bargaining advantages. These are dilemmas that are uniquely associated with collective bargaining in the public sector. In the public sector, internal and external pressures on management negotiators limit their ability to rationally commit public resources.*

The political atmosphere of public sector negotiations is not the only difference between public and private sector bargaining. The public sector provides essential services for which there are generally no alternatives. In the private sector, there are usually alternatives to products or services priced too high for the consumer. Even though there is a "blurred line" between the public and private sector, the basic economic distinction prevails. The demand for public services is immune to price, and negotiators are aware of this when developing their economic packages. The necessity to provide essential services on a continuing basis is not a consideration in private sector negotiations. Stated another way, government must remain in business, no matter what.

Government services are such that increased labor cost in most cases will not be offset by productivity gains commonly relied upon in the private sector as a way of holding down unit labor costs.† Negotiated

* The political environment of public-sector negotiations will be further explored in a later chapter.
† Government efforts at reducing labor costs through productivity gains usually take the form of increasing employee workloads, e.g., enlarging the caseload of

increases in wages and salaries, in the public sector, inevitably add to the cost of government. In the private sector, too, where product costs are affected by a negotiated wage settlement, these costs may be passed on to the consumer, provided there is a constant consumer demand for the product, or demand is unaffected by the price increase (inelastic demand). Private sector bargaining decisions are determined by product market considerations; thus, private sector bargaining may be characterized as one that operates in an economic context. The public sector, on the other hand, must make bargaining decisions on political considerations. A major way to pay for the added cost of a negotiated labor agreement is to have the general public absorb it through increased taxes, because user charges are not generally feasible for most public services. The issue of raising taxes is a politically volatile one and, in addition, makes the general public an added party to the collective bargaining process. Another method for coping with added labor costs created by a negotiated agreement is for government to reallocate earmarked fiscal resources, shifting some resources already committed to other areas to pay for the increased labor costs. This would not be difficult to accomplish if employee unions were the only groups to be served by policymakers. However, this is not the case. Other groups are also in competition for government resources and for public funding. The task of policymakers is to try to allocate resources in an equitable fashion. Realistically, however, resources will not go to those who can demonstrate the most need; they will generally be allocated on the basis of political strength. Finally, government may react to rising labor costs by cutting back or eliminating services. This option, however, has a political price as well; affected clients are potentially able to mobilize against this tactic.

The issue of sovereignty separates public and private sector bargaining as well. Public policy has made collective bargaining mandatory in the private sector. There is no longer legitimate claim to universal rights of management in the private sector. However, in the public service, the claim of unilateral management authority and the restriction of the scope of bargaining is justified by legal arguments, specific legislation, and civil service regulations. Therefore, in public sector bargaining, there is a *de jure* inequality of the negotiating parties unless management voluntarily waives, or is pressured to waive, some of its rights.

---

social workers, increasing student-faculty ratios, and so on. These efforts are precisely the ones that are so vehemently opposed by employee groups, who see them as providing for onerous working conditions and as tactics that lead to a reduction in employee professionalism. Moreover, it is argued that these efforts at cost reduction do not result in productivity gains but in a deterioration in the delivery of public services.

The strike is generally recognized in the private sector as the final, ultimate weapon to be used when all mediation and other negotiation impasse procedures have been exhausted. The strike, walkout, and boycott are seen as legitimate actions by unions when all else has failed. Not so in the public sector. The essentiality and inelasticity of government services provide the rationale that strikes in the public sector should be prevented at all cost. Injunctions against strikes and legislation outlawing strikes and punishing strikers clearly demonstrate that strikes are not regarded as a residual right of public sector unions.

Having examined the issues of collective bargaining from the vantage points of both labor and government, we now turn our attention to the tactics used by both sides in pursuit of their negotiation objectives.

Tactics of Bargaining

In preparation for actual bargaining, both sides determine their goals and objectives, establish priorities, assess the strengths and weaknesses of their opponents and themselves, and anticipate their adversary's counterproposals. For example, a union may have the goals of improving salary and fringe benefits as well as maintaining employment at current levels. However, as personnel costs per employee begin to rise, the employer may begin thinking more seriously about cutting costs; one obvious way to do this is to reduce the number of employees. Cartter and Marshall state the economic philosophy with which unions must approach bargaining: "Rational economic behavior for a union can be seen as seeking some intricate balance of increased wages, increased total employment (and union membership), and increased leisure (decreased hours) for its members."[45] Unions must thus approach the bargaining process with a clear idea of their objectives, realize the short-term and long-term effects of the realization of these objectives, and be prepared to make appropriate trade-offs, if necessary, to achieve their priorities.

Juris and Feuille enumerate four economic conditions that greatly influence the bargaining process and that will determine the relative strength of the union vis à vis public management. They are local labor-market conditions; ability of comparable groups to raise their wages and benefits; cost of living; and the government's ability to pay.[46] Another consideration is that the union's stance in bargaining must be determined in part by the expectations of its members; union rivalry tends to make unions more aggressive in their bargaining than might be otherwise be the case.[47]

Once the two sides have ascertained their respective minimum and maximum parameters of settlement, the actual process of negotiation is ready to begin. Chamberlain and Cullen describe succinctly the objective of the process when they observe, "the art of bargaining is to probe for (and possibly alter) the true position of your opponent while concealing your own [position] for as long as possible."[48] There are numerous tactics and strategies in the arsenal of bargaining weapons that may be used to influence the outcome of bargaining. Four major tactics used in the public sector will be considered here as we examine the way in which the process of bargaining affects economic and political decision making.

The first of these tactics is the use of comparisons to other occupations, to other areas of the country, to the same occupations in other jurisdictions, and to ideal standards. Comparisons are also made to the current cost of living.[49] Such comparisons are made in great detail and length during the course of bargaining; they are also made extensively after bargaining in order to buttress membership support by demonstrating that the union was able to gain some favorable advances (hopefully). Arthur Ross clearly explains the importance of these comparisons to the union:

> Comparisons are crucially important within the union world, where there is always the closest scrutiny of wage agreements in the process of negotiation as well as of those already negotiated. They show whether the negotiating committee has done a sufficiently skilled job of bargaining. They demonstrate to the union member whether he is getting his money's worth for his dues. A favorable comparison becomes an argument for reelection of officers, a basis for solidification and extension of membership, and an occasion for advancement within the official hierarchy. An unfavorable comparison makes it likely that the rank-and-file will become disgruntled, rival leaders will become popular, and rival unions will become active.[50]

On the other hand, such comparisons are also important from the standpoint of the public manager for the same reasons. One can see that the comparisons introduced into the bargaining process are crucially important, since they become the evaluative standard. In the TVA, this issue itself is a subject of negotiation, because comparison of compensation in area industries is necessary in determining prevailing wage rates. Therefore, which area industries are compared is crucial.[51] In the cities of San Francisco, Oakland, and Cleveland provisions in the city charters statutorily require changes in police compensation to changes in the pay of other groups.[52] In 1971, the San Francisco police union attempted to compare itself with the higher paid construction craftsmen. In 1967-68 the Boston police union compared its salaries to the much higher ones of the New York police force.[54] The parity of fire and police salaries is a perennial issue; police feel that their job is more hazardous than that of firemen and it must be a better paid one in order to recruit properly, while the firemen argue that their job is just as hazardous in its own right and their salary should be the same as policemen's as a matter of equity.[55] These examples are only a sampling of the ways in which comparisons are made in the bargaining process in order to enhance one's negotiating stance.

A second important tactic of bargaining is utilization of those techniques used by political pressure groups, which include mobilization of public opinion, legislative lobbying, and political campaigning. For federal employee unions, this is a virtual necessity since, as previously noted, even those unions and associations with exclusive bargaining rights are usually unable to discuss matters of compensation at the negotiation table. Harry Donoian makes it clear:

> *Virtually all federal employees have their pay determined by congressional action. Similarly, Congress has jurisdiction over basic employee benefits such as annual and sick leave, compensation for injury, insurance, and employer contributions to health and welfare plans. Until Congress relinquishes authority over these areas, the only way that unions which represent Federal Government employees can secure increased pay and improved benefits is to use legislative tactics.*[56]

The postal unions have developed a great amount of expertise over time in this activity. They make an active effort to elect to Congress members who agree with their viewpoints and to influence appointments to the various post office committees and subcommittees; their success is measured by the fact that they are often able to get their proposals passed by Congress even over the objections of the president.[57]

In their study of police bargaining techniques in twenty-one cities, Juris and Feuille describe a number of political pressure tactics used by the police to influence bargaining.[58] In the absence of formal collective bargaining in San Francisco, Baltimore, Cleveland, and Los Angeles, police unions had developed such strategies as "private lobbying with various managerial officials; public lobbying via appearances at city council, civil service commission, or state legislative hearings; involvement in the election campaigns of various candidates; and putting police measures on the ballot."[59] Police measures placed on the ballot included such items as police pay amendments to the city charter and referendum approval of increases in the pension plan.[60] Juris and Feuille found four unions that were willing to campaign for increased city revenues if they would be assured of getting a portion of the increase in improved benefits; the techniques included:

campaigning for the passage of a referendum to establish a city payroll tax; lobbying in the state legislature for a bill enabling the city to levy a sales tax; campaigning for the incumbent governor's slate during an election in return for favorable consideration over the amount of state financial aid their city would receive; and lobbying in the state legislature for approval of the mayor's budget (the solvency of which depends upon the level of state financial aid).[61]

It can thus be seen that the unions' perception by and relationship to the public is very important to the success of its publicity campaign, in that public opinion may have a greater impact on influencing negotiations in this arena than in the private sector.[62] Some unions have learned to turn this sentiment to their advantage. For example, the community desire to have an efficient and honest police force in metropolitan Toronto has led the police association to maintain that this can be accomplished only through increasing pay and benefits.[63] "At negotiation time, reports of resignations appear in the press as 'proof' of the need to increase wages and improve working conditions."[64]

The third tactic used in influencing negotiations is the disguising of one's true position in order to strike the best possible deal for oneself. Governments, for example, may "hide" extra funds throughout their proposed budget by "padding" programs with more dollars than they would actually receive. These funds may be held in contingency in the event that the government is forced to settle at a higher cost than anticipated. Wesley Wildman notes this trend in the school system:

A few boards ... are proving quite adept at hiding even relatively large sums of money, which are released for salary purposes only at the eleventh hour. The additional amount can then be claimed by the teacher organization as a victory for the exercises of teacher power and the efficacy of the negotiating process.[65]

Unions generally assume that such a contingency fund exists; their strategy must be to explore through probing, estimate the size of the fund, and try to secure as much of it as possible for their membership.

The fourth tactic of bargaining is the threat or actuality of a strike or slowdown, or the threat by the government employer to discharge or penalize participants in a job action of this sort. Some argue it is only when this threat is truly present that meaningful bargaining can take place. Juris and Feuille contend that "agreement occurs not voluntarily because of altruism but rather because of the threatened or actual use of power."[66] Joseph Domitrz concurs when he argues that the degree of employee militancy, which may be reflected by their willingness to strike, plays an important role in the final settlement.[67] Eli Rock argues that the essence of bargaining is in both parties participating as equals

Part I: Nature of Collective Bargaining

in negotiations; without the threat of a work stoppage, employee negotiation is little more than a presentation of requests.[68]

A number of so-called job actions may take place without the membership actually going out on strike. Such tactics accomplish the same results as a strike, yet avoid the legal penalties that may be associated with a strike by public employees. Such strategems as mass resignations and mass utilization of sick leave time are two examples.[69] "Transport workers have run subways and buses 'by the rule book,' a strategem designed to slow operations to a crawl by meticulously observing procedures routinely ignored in the interest of effective transportation."[70] Similar tactics are available to every occupation and may be resorted to if necessary to display strength at the bargaining table. The effect of such tactics varies with the circumstances. However, A. H. Raskin encapsulates the strategy: "The more essential the service, the greater the chance that the government will have to capitulate."[71] This, of course, is applicable to both a work slowdown as well as a strike. A classic example of such pressure tactics at work occurred in Canada in 1969, when the Montreal police and fire departments walked off the job.[72]

The Case of the Montreal Police Strike

There were two key issues to be negotiated by the Montreal police union in 1969; salary parity with the Toronto police department and two-man patrol cars. The police had initially requested an increase of $1,900 per man for 1969-70, which would have placed them at the level of their Toronto counterparts. Because the sentiment among the Montreal police was that their job was more hazardous because of their city's higher crime rate, they felt that parity was the least for which they could settle. Negotiations reached an impasse and the case was sent to arbitration. The arbitrator's decision was to award a $730 increase for 1969 and a $400 increase for 1970. This left the Montreal policemen $1,100 behind Toronto in 1969 alone, and there was the possibility of a wider gap in 1970 because the contract of the Toronto police expired on 1 December 1969.

The arbitrator also ruled that the city was not required to staff each patrol car with two men. Then, 5 October 1969, a Montreal policeman was murdered while on solitary patrol. This added further emotional fuel to the situation and affirmed the convictions of the police that two-man patrols should be employed. In short, these decisions of the arbitrator, although compulsory and binding, were absolutely and unequivocally not acceptable to the Montreal police. Consequently, at eight o'clock on the morning of 7 October 1969, the police force walked off the job in defiance of the arbitrator's position.

The strike only lasted until midnight of the same day, but the effect was chilling, and the public was immediate in demanding a return to work. Consider the sixteen-hour toll: sixty-one armed robberies, including six bank robberies; two men shot dead in civil disturbances, one of them a provincial policeman; more than one hundred shops looted; twelve fires; two million dollars worth of windows smashed and an additional one million dollars worth of property damage by rioters in the downtown area (over forty carloads of glass were needed to replace shattered storefronts).*

The strike as a bargaining tactic is obviously the most extreme and the most controversial, although it has been resorted to with mounting frequency in the public sector.

In discussing the strike and its threatened use as a strategy of negotiations, mention should also be made of the financial capacity of public workers to sustain a long strike. Ironically, their capability is heightened as well as their credibility, by the fact that under certain circumstances strikers are eligible for public welfare benefits.[73] During the first month of the strike, the striker will probably become eligible for food stamps; during the second month he may become eligible for Aid to Families with Dependent Children.† Analysis by Armand Thieblot, Jr. indicates that, assuming the maximum eligibility for each worker and an eighty dollar per month strike payment from the union, "for the average worker, being on strike is monetarily equivalent to working forty hours per week for at least the minimum wage."[74] It is clear that the threat of strike looms over the bargaining table despite the question of its legality; it is the ultimate and perhaps the most potent weapon in the public union arsenal.

To review, we have analyzed in this section four major tactics employed in public sector bargaining: comparisons to other occupations and standards, political pressure and lobbying, disguise of true financial parameters within which bargaining can occur, and the threat or actuality of a strike or work slowdown. Given the issues discussed in the previous sections and these tactics of bargaining, let us examine how the mechanism of bargaining actually occurs in three major cities.

The three cities chosen as examples of bargaining approaches are appropriate models of the development of the state-of-the-art of public labor-management relations in American municipalities. Each was selected as representative of a typology. Philadelphia may be termed

* It should be noted, however, that no comparisons were made to the average number of crimes committed during a typical 1969 day in Montreal.
† In May 1977, the Supreme Court unanimously upheld an Ohio law which allowed the state to deny unemployment benefits whenever workers were idled because of strikes, even though the affected workers were not on strike.

the Developed Model, for its cohesiveness and sophistication in labor relations. The city government is not only functionally adroit in coping with collective bargaining with public employee groups, it has also structurally adjusted itself to confront this imperative. The Memphis example demonstrates the more typical Underdeveloped Model, all too prevalent in the public sector. Here, officials react (and even overreact) —rather than take the lead (proact)—to the exigencies of unionization. The building of a bilateral labor-management relationship has been a slow and enervating process. The third example, Cincinnati, was selected to show that even in a Developed Model labor peace may, from time to time, be broken. Nonetheless, the case study affirms the existence of Developed bargaining, by virtue of the way the impasse was ultimately resolved.

Developed Bargaining in Philadelphia

The City of Philadelphia devised an approach to negotiating with its unionized public employees that has operated very successfully since 1952.[75] The city's objective was to develop an approach to bargaining that would reconcile the features of collective bargaining with the traditional principles of the merit system. In addition, the city wished to develop a bargaining team that could deal authoritatively with the unions and that would undercut the union tactic of playing the council off against the mayor's office in order to achieve more gains. Consequently, the negotiating team of the city is composed of the managing director, the personnel director, the finance director, the labor relations advisor, and a key member of the city council. The union bargaining unit is composed of top officers and representatives of AFSCME.

Prior to the beginning of negotiations and at frequent intervals during negotiations there is communication with the Mayor and other important members of the council on the basic economic items that are at issue. A consensus is achieved as to what is acceptable, within a basic framework. On nonmonetary matters, a consensus is achieved between the city council service commission, the personnel director, and the labor relations advisor on matters that might fall within the confines of the merit system. Not only does this procedure have the advantage of unifying the city decision makers on the issues, it also means to the union that the agreement it reaches with the bargaining team is very likely to be accepted. Should a stalemate occur, the mayor himself may participate directly in the negotiations.

When an agreement has been reached between the negotiating teams, it will be drafted in the form of an informal document. At this point the mayor will incorporate the economic agreements into his budget document and the personnel director will draft the other appropriate agreements in the form of proposals for new regulations by the civil service commission. Negotiations are now at the most crucial stage.

Both the city and the unions appear before hearings on the proposals held by the council and the civil service commission respectively. Both the city and the unions must ask for implementation of only what was agreed in the informal document; to do otherwise would be to act in bad faith and would undermine the groundwork laid previously. Once the council passes the budget and the commission enacts the regulations, the city and the union write their informal agreements into a formal contract, which is then signed by both sides.

This case study of public sector bargaining in Philadelphia describes a sophisticated and effective manner of conducting collective bargaining with public employees. It is a model that has worked effectively with few variations for two decades, and it deserves serious scrutiny by those governmental entities that are unsatisfied with their current procedures.

Underdeveloped Bargaining: Memphis Light, Gas, and Water Division and the IBEW

The Memphis Light, Gas, and Water Division (MLGW) is a publicly owned utility in Memphis, Tennessee. The city bought the utility from the Memphis Power and Light Company in 1939. The city administration appoints the board of commissioners, the utility's governing board, and exercises budgetary review control.

There is no state legislation regarding public labor relations in Tennessee, although a comprehensive proposal was introduced and discussed in 1974. Restrictions on public jurisdictions in entering into contracts with labor unions are based on the famous Weakley County case in 1938. This decision stated that elected officials could not delegate their authority through collective bargaining because of legal restrictions on public spending and on the state tax rate. Moreover, legal opinion has interpreted the case as making collective bargaining agreements legally unenforceable. The only type of labor agreement that is acceptable in Tennessee is a memorandum of understanding; agreement to bargain and recognition of agreements are completely voluntary on the part of management. There is no no-strike statute for public employees in the state, however, cities and their agents insist on a non-strike clause in their memoranda of understanding.

The first substantial union contact with MLGW was made in 1969 when a representative of the International Brotherhood of Electrical Workers told MLGW officials that IBEW Local 1288 had signed up 200-250 MLGW employees as members. MLGW had no restrictions on its employees' right to join a union. IBEW wanted the right to organize utility employees within one broad unit. This request and a request to process grievances through union channels was refused because the union had no claim for recognition and because a discussion of grievances would have constituted a tacit recognition of the union.

The next year, the IBEW claimed that more and more MLGW employees were joining the union and were signing representation agreements. However, the union was forced to observe a Department of Labor regulation that a union cannot seek recognition for a year if it falls short of a majority of employees the first time it seeks recognition. At this time, it was estimated that IBEW had signed 700-750 of the division's 3,000 employees. In the atmosphere of the Memphis sanitation strike of 1968, the IBEW tried again for recognition by the utility. Taylor Blair, international representave for the union, issued a strike threat to Memphis City Hall unless the union was granted recognition. Because of the political and social tensions in Memphis after the assassination of Dr. Martin Luther King, Jr., in April of 1968, Mayor Henry Loeb wanted to avoid another labor confrontation at all costs. Loeb called MLGW President, Ray Morton, and asked for a meeting of the board of commissioners to consider negotiations.

IBEW did not claim a majority of employees in the utility and only desired recognition in those departments where it did have a majority. The MLGW Board of Commissioners met with IBEW representatives in late 1968. The utility officials conceded that the meeting with the union constituted *de facto* recognition. A meeting in early 1969 resulted in an agreement by the utility board to negotiate with the union. There had been no election among MLGW employees to determine majority status, and, in normal circumstances, Memphis citizens would not have tolerated recognition without an election among the employees of the utility. The social disorder of Memphis in 1968-69 did not allow for normal circumstances, however. MLGW administrative officials Jack Dodd and Al Grady were selected as the management negotiators for the impending bargaining sessions.

Negotiations for the first memorandum of understanding began on 3 March 1969. Dodd and Grady bargained with international representatives and six union members for ten months. The *de facto* recognition by the utility provided a great impetus for union organization and the union had enrolled 1,000-1,100 employees by the time negotiations ended. The noneconomic issues were negotiated first and comparative analysis was done of other utility agreements because of the inexperience of the management negotiators. There were eighty-five discussion items and thirty-seven articles in the final agreement. Many items about which there was no disagreement were formalized in the memorandum of understanding. Management's generosity prior to union organization was acknowledged and recognition of such existing items as time off with pay were formalized. Both sides allowed that the limits on management discretion would probably hurt the employees more than it would the company.

There was very little external pressure from politicians on the MLGW negotiators; their basic limitation was their lack of experience in collective bargaining. The union bargainers were under pressure from the employees and the international union to come up with a favorable contract. Political maneuvering was minimized by the refusal of the city council to deal with IBEW representatives. Strike threats were ignored by the management negotiators because of the minority status of the union and the knowledge that the rank-and-file were opposed to a strike. The demands and power positions of the parties were factors, but the long negotiations were largely the result of the attempt to draw a comprehensive agreement for a minority union and the absence of a legal framework for bargaining.

The agreement's union security provisions were more *de facto* than *de jure*. IBEW has no sole agent, union shop, or agency shop with MLGW. The utility does grant *de facto* exclusive recognition to IBEW by wording the recognition clause, "it is the policy of LGW to recognize only majority representation," by giving no stewards to minority unions, by giving IBEW and no one else the dues checkoff, and by refusing to deal with the representatives of minority unions. The bargaining unit excludes supervisors, professionals, confidential personnel, security personnel, and temporary and part-time employees. Supervisors are not permitted to form their own unit.

Management rights are a point of contention in MLGW labor relations. Officials have accused the union of trying to comanage the utility. MLGW has tried to retain its rights in the determination of personnel policy. For example, while the union contended that employees can refuse overtime, under the memorandum of understanding, employees can only trade-off overtime, with the utility retaining the right to direct overtime. The union has tried to reduce or eliminate educational requirements for hiring and promotion but the agreement states that the union cannot represent an applicant or set job requirements. The basic union effort to influence the level of utility services has been on size of crews and other items not covered in the agreement.

The prevailing wage for the memorandum was calculated by a compromise between the utility desire to compare wages with other

TVA-supplied utilities and the union goal of a nationwide comparison. The agreement prohibited strikes, sit-downs, slowdowns, secondary boycotts, and lockouts. Even though there was no negotiation over automation in the first agreement, MLGW officials said that if the company should profit from automation, so should the employees. The utility informally agreed to plans for consultation and retraining for automation.

A clause in the 1970 memorandum of understanding stated that ninety-days notice had to be given for the termination of an agreement. In June of 1971, the union gave such notice to MLGW. The negotiations to change the agreement began in October 1971 and ended on 4 January 1972. The forty-one articles included many changes and clarifications, but five articles remained the same—vacations, holidays, wages, shift differentials, and job evaluations. These negotiations were marked by more experience on both sides and by a common desire to improve the original memorandum.

Charges and countercharges have characterized the history of labor relations at MLGW. The minority status of the union and the inexperience of both parties have contributed to difficulties for the management of the utility. Harold Gillespie, business manager for Local 1288, says Jack Dodd has been one of the main causes of labor problems because of his "hard-nosed" stand during the negotiations. Dodd replies, "I am no more immune to criticism than anyone else. There are always people in any organization who have to say No."[76] Other problems are the structural problems in the managerial levels of the division, especially as it pertains to labor relations; the affirmative action programs, which push minority employees and threaten the union; and the job evaluation programs. Public utilities are in a unique situation because they provide and price services much like a private corporation, yet they are responsible to public legal and political authority.

Dodd, the present administrative manager at MLGW, feels that labor relations in the public sector is a new phenomenon that has minimal recognition. He believes that labor is not a dirty word and that unions are legitimate institutions if they are responsible. The major problems between MLGW and IBEW Local 1288 were (1) the political pressures to negotiate with a minority union were substantial because of the fear of another strike in Memphis and (2) a union that had never proved its majority status had been given exclusive recognition. Dodd feels that state legislation on collective bargaining is needed in Tennessee along with a powerful state public employee board to oversee labor relations; however, prolabor legislation in the public sector will have to coexist with the antilabor attitudes of most Tennesseans. Wage demands by unions will also be balanced and counteracted by the regressive Tennessee tax structures.[77] The experience of MLGW with collective bargaining shows how management must act in a decisive manner in the absence of enabling legislation.

Developed Bargaining and the Strike: Cincinnati

Cincinnati is noted as one of the nation's best-governed municipalities. The reform efforts of its charter committee and the Cincinnatus Club have led to a stable council-manager government, widely recognized for its ability to efficiently deliver services. The industrial environment of the city provided a constructive framework for public labor relations. As a model of professional municipal government, Cincinnati also became a model for public collective bargaining, due in no small measure to the influence of the Taft family and the power of the business community in Cincinnati politics.

AFSCME began organizing municipal employees in the city in 1938. It had a small influence compared to the power of the United Mine Workers in the area, whose garbage workers struck in 1943. The city refused to recognize or bargain with the small but growing AFSCME unions, which retained a business agent as a lawyer and spokesman before the city. After World War II, rising prices and the desire to keep pace with private industry spurred organization among municipal employees. AFSCME grew quickly. Other public sector unions grew as well; the Fraternal Order of Police and the International Association of Fire Fighters actively organized police and firemen respectively. Although union contracts for public workers were not legally enforceable under Ohio law, in 1948 the city council gave municipal employees the right to join unions and required the city manager to deal with the unions. Negotiations over wages and fringe benefits, according to the prevailing wage concept, were instituted, even though the relationship was voluntary and informal. The fact that the city manager had experience in private sector bargaining greatly facilitated the relationship.

In 1951, the city formalized its labor-management relations. The city manager was directed by the council "to bargain collectively with city employees, their unions, or other authorized representatives on all matters pertaining to wages and working conditions before determination by the city council."[78] There was no statement on the right to organize and the exclusion of supervisors, no mention of impasse procedures, a negotiation schedule, discussion of exclusive recognition, or elections. AFSCME grew in membership during this period, hired a business staff, and by 1958 had 2,200 dues-paying members, a majority of the nonuniformed employees of the city. In 1957, the city manager granted exclusive recognition to majority unions; and in 1958, dues deduction and fact-finding as an impasse procedure were instituted. Professional union leadership and the city's willingness to bargain created a harmonious relationship.

In 1960, after negotiations between the city and AFSCME, an agreement formalized the bargaining relationship. AFSCME obtained exclusive recognition for all nonuniformed employees in Cincinnati. A union was granted exclusive recognition if it could prove that it represented a majority of employees of an appropriate unit, as determined by the city manager. AFSCME did not want a competitor and the city wanted to avoid union jurisdiction battles. Supervisors and confidential employees were to be excluded from the bargaining unit. Management prerogatives were clearly spelled out in the agreement and the boundaries of bargaining clearly defined. Supervisors were given training in the city's labor policy and they conveyed these policies to the rank-and-file. The city manager, while retaining final authority in negotiations, delegated the negotiation responsibility to his personnel officer. The personnel officer bargains annually on city-wide issues with AFSCME, especially wage policies. Negotiations over specific working conditions are conducted with the relevant department heads. Central clearance with the personnel office is required in negotiations over these operating matters.

The success of labor relations until 1969 can be largely attributed to the acceptance of unionization and collective bargaining by the city council and the administration. The reputed dominance of the business community in civic affairs—a community in favor of harmonious labor relations—is partly responsible for this acceptance. Conflict had arisen with the civil service commission of the state, but the broad personnel authority of the city manager usually prevailed over the limited authority of the commission. Management has wide discretion in labor relations because of the Cincinnati open-shop policy and the absence of public employee labor legislation in Ohio. Another contributing factor is that the city manager has budgetary authority and negotiating responsibility at the same time.

But in 1969, Cincinnati experienced a strike by its public workers. The city faced a tight financial situation in 1968. There was a referendum to increase the municipal income tax and the city negotiators, fearing a taxpayer's revolt, put off economic negotiations until after the election. There was a feeling within AFSCME that uniformed employees were receiving preferential treatment over their own nonuniformed members. In an environment of public support for "law and order," the police were able to obtain a substantial wage raise. Thus, AFSCME demanded a twelve million dollar package consisting of a dollar-an-hour raise plus fringe benefits for its members. There was a public outcry because the demand exceeded private labor market trends. The city proposed a five percent wage increase for AFSCME members, but there was a report that the police and fire workers had secured a nine percent increase from the city manager. Donald Heisel, the City Personnel Director, and the unions went to the city manager when an impasse was reached. On 27 December 1968, the city's offer to the union was raised to six percent. This satisfied the union negotiators and they brought the offer back to the rank-and-file for ratification. However, a blue-collar union negotiator, who was absent when the offer was made, convinced the rank-and-file to reject the proposal. The negotiators were sent back to secure the same increases as were obtained by the police and fire workers. This was accompanied by charges of racial discrimination, since most policemen and firemen in the city were white while AFSCME membership was largely black. While the city manager agreed to wage modifications, albeit below the police and fire level, and the union leaders accepted the offer, the rank-and-file voted to strike on 12 January 1969.

The union leaders tried to continue meeting with the city negotiators and moved the strike deadline back three days to keep communications open. When the city obtained an injunction, however, the union worked out emergency procedures and went out on strike. The union showed restraint by only picketing municipal buildings and by preventing violence. Desiring a quick settlement, the city did not force the injunction. Federal mediators were called in and meetings lasted for twenty-one days during which time the city agreed to revise the grievance structure but refused to compromise on wages. The mediators kept the parties talking and the city agreed to some small concessions on wages if the strike ended. Services were finally resumed and a wage settlement was reached.[79]

Donald Heisel points out some of the reasons why the strike was peaceful and why mediation was successful. The city did not try to force the injunction because it realized that a settlement could not be reached in jail. The restraint displayed by both sides allowed the mediators to keep the parties talking. The city wanted fair wages but also wanted a consideration of its ability to pay. Hostility did not result because both parties understood the constructive nature of collective bargaining. Finally, the city administration presented a united front to preserve stability and to prevent the union from playing one governmental entity off against another.[50]

Conclusion

This chapter has described how public employee unions have moved from relying on the merit system to a self-reliance and especially to a

Part I: Nature of Collective Bargaining

reliance on bilateral negotiations about decisions that affect the work-place life of their members. We saw how collective bargaining grew out of the expanding political strength of public employee groups; this has led to public policy legitimizing this growing phenomenon. Described, too, were the needs and desires of the union membership and the insti-tutional union to have such issues as scope, bargaining unit determina-tion, union security, individual security, wages and fringe benefits, some control over employment, and working conditions placed on the bargaining agenda. On their part, the public managers have an agenda as well that contain such items as keeping the costs of union proposals to a minimum, keeping costs within certain legal and fiscal constraints, coordinating bargaining with the budgetary process, and preserving satisfactory managerial options. Additionally, the unique features of public sector labor relations were examined. Both sides have a store of strategies to use during the course of negotiations. We have suggested that the techniques of compensatory comparison, lobbying and other forms of political pressure, disguising of one's true bargaining position, and the threat or utilization of some sort of job action are among the more important strategies used in bargaining. Finally, case studies of collective bargaining in three jurisdictions were presented as illustrative of "developed" and "underdeveloped" labor-relations experiences.

The most important deduction from this analysis is that collective bargaining, in quest of both economic and noneconomic gains, operates in a political environment. Crucially, unions are now able to exert a decisive influence on public policy. By representing and articulating the interest of a sizeable group of constituents, unions are capable of and, in fact, play a major role in the determination of public resource allocations and public service provisions. But, has this capability re-sulted in comparative gains for union members? The next chapter will seek to answer this question insofar as economic gains are concerned.

Notes to Chapter 2

1. Sterling D. Spero and John M. Capozzola, *The Urban Community and Its Unionized Bureaucracies: Pressure Politics in Local Government Labor Relations* (New York: Dunellen Publishing Co., 1973), pp. 200-205.
2. Sam Zagoria, ed. *Public Workers and Public Unions* (Englewood Cliffs, N.J.: Prentice-Hall, Spectrum Books, 1972), p. 1.
3. Ibid., p. 2.
4. David T. Stanley, "What Are Unions Doing to Merit Systems?" *Collective Bargaining in Government: Readings and Cases*, ed. J. Joseph Loewenberg and Michael H. Moskow (Englewood Cliffs, N.J.: Prentice-Hall, 1972), p. 82.
5. Much of the discussion about the evolution of AFSCME relies on Spero and Capozzola, op. cit., pp. 18-19; and Jerry Wurf and Mary L. Hennessey, "American Federation of State, County and Municipal Employees," in Loewenberg and Moskow, op. cit., pp. 61-64.

6. Harold W. Davey, *Contemporary Collective Bargaining*, 3rd ed. (Englewood Cliffs, N.J.: Prentice-Hall, 1972), pp. 345-347.

7. Stanley, op. cit., p. 83.

8. Davey, op. cit., p. 347.

9. Michael H. Moskow, J. Joseph Loewenberg, and Edward Clifford Koziara, *Collective Bargaining in Public Employment* (New York: Random House, 1970), pp. 16-17.

10. Bertrand de Jouvenal, *Sovereignty: An Inquiry into the Political Good* (Chicago: Univ. of Chicago Press, 1957).

11. Ibid., p. 198.

12. W. D. Heisel and J. D. Hallihan, *Questions and Answers on Public Employment Negotiation* (Chicago: Public Personnel Association, 1967), p. 29.

13. New York City, "The Conduct of Labor Relations Between the City of New York and Its Employees," Executive Order Number 52, D5C (29 September 1967).

14. Paul F. Gerhart, "The Scope of Bargaining in Local Government Labor Negotiations," Loewenberg and Moskow, op. cit., pp. 128-129.

15. Ibid., pp. 131-132.

16. Joseph R. Crowley, "The Resolution of Representation Status under the Taylor Law," *Fordham Law Review*, May 1969, p. 521.

17. Harry H. Wellington and Ralph K. Winter, *The Unions and the Cities* (Washington, D.C.,: Brookings Institution, 1971), p. 116.

18. Heisel and Hallihan, op. cit., p. 58.

19. Arnold Zander, "Collective Bargaining in the Public Sector: The Union View," *Public Administration Review* Winter 1962, p. 7.

20. Spero and Capozzola, op. cit., p. 156.

21. Edwin F. Beal, Edward D. Wickersham, and Philip Kienast, *The Practice of Collective Bargaining* 4th ed. (Homewood Ill.: Richard D. Irwin 1972), pp. 428, 442-443.

22. Stanley, op. cit., p. 84.

23. Robert Repas, "Collective Bargaining Problems in Federal Employment," *Collective Bargaining in the Public Service*, ed. Daniel H. Kruger and Charles T. Schmidt, Jr. (New York: Random House, 1969), p. 25. Cited hereafter as Kruger and Schmidt.

24. Ibid.

25. Derek C. Bok and John T. Dunlop, *Labor and the American Community* (New York: Simon and Schuster, 1970), p. 317.

26. Douglas Weiford and Wayne Burggraaff, "The Future for Public Employee Unions," in Kruger and Schmidt, op. cit., p. 71.

27. U.S., Bureau of Labor Statistics, *Handbook of Labor Statistics 1976*, tab. 112, p. 235.

28. Davis Farrel, "The American Economy in 1974 and Beyond: Problems and Prospects," Proceedings of the Conference *Collective Bargaining in the Mid-1970's: Pressures, Problems, Issues* (Memphis, Tenn. 4 April 1974).

29. Albert A. Blum, et al., *White-Collar Workers* (New York: Random House, 1971), p. 22.

30. Harold L. Sheppard, "Approaches to Conflict In American Industrial Sociology," *British Journal of Sociology*, 5 (1959), pp. 324-340.

31. Hervey A. Juris and Peter Feuille, *Police Unionism: Power and Impact in Public-Sector Bargaining* (Lexington, Mass.: D. C. Heath and Co., 1973), pp. 119-146.

32. Charles T. Schmidt, Jr., "Collective Negotiations in Michigan Education: An Overview," Kruger and Schmidt, op. cit., pp. 181-182.

33. *Los Angeles Times*, 22 April 1976, pp. 1, 22.

34. Ibid., pp. 1, 22.

35. *Los Angeles Times*, 2 May 1976, p. 3.

36. Davey, op. cit., p. 374.

37. John W. Macy, Jr., "The Role of Bargaining in the Public Service," in Zagoria, op. cit., p. 11.

38. Belton M. Fleisher, *Labor Economics: Theory and Evidence* (Englewood Cliffs, N.J.: Prentice-Hall, 1970), p. 20.

39. Bok and Dunlop, op. cit., p. 322.

40. Ibid., p. 318.

41. Conversation with Ms. Anna M. Martinez, Employee Relations Officer, Tennessee Valley Authority, Knoxville, Tennessee 28 March, 1974.

42. Ibid.

43. Ibid.

44. Morton R. Godine, *The Labor Problem in the Public Service* (New York: Russell & Russell, 1967), pp. 33-34.

45. Allan M. Cartter and F. Ray Marshall, *Labor Economics: Wages, Employment and Trade Unionism* (Homewood, Ill.: Richard D. Irwin, 1967), p. 278.

46. Juris and Feuille, op. cit., p. 53.

47. Ibid., p. 37.

48. Neil W. Chamberlain and Donald E. Cullen, *The Labor Sector*, 2nd ed. (New York: McGraw-Hill Book Co., 1971), p. 208.

49. Samuelson, op. cit., pp. 587-88.

50. Arthur M. Ross, *Trade Union Wage Policy* (Berkeley, Cal.: Univ. of California, Institute of Industrial Relations, 1953), p. 51.

51. Martinez, op. cit.

52. Ibid.

53. Juris and Feuille, op. cit., p. 54.

54. Ibid.

55. Chamberlain and Cullen, op. cit., p. 297.

56. Harry A. Donoian, "The AFGE and the AFSCME," *Collective Bargaining for Public Employees*, ed. Herbert L. Marx, Jr. (New York: H. W. Wilson, 1969), p. 28. Cited hereafter as Marx.

57. Bok and Dunlop, op. cit., p. 316.

58. Juris and Feuille, op. cit., pp. 49-55.

59. Ibid., p. 50.

60. Ibid., p. 49.

61. Ibid., p. 55.

62. Twentieth Century Fund Task Force on Labor Disputes in Public Employment, *Pickets at City Hall* (New York: Twentieth Century Fund, 1970), p. 36.

63. Harry W. Arthurs, *Collective Bargaining by Public Employees in Canada: Five Models* (Ann Arbor: Institute of Labor and Industrial Relations, 1971), p. 93.

64. Ibid.

65. Wesley A. Wildman, "Teacher and Collective Negotiations," Blum, et al., op. cit., pp. 158-59.

66. Juris and Feuille, op. cit., p. 43.

67. Joseph Domitrz, "Collective Bargaining and Public Administration: The Role of Long-Term Contracts," *Collective Bargaining and Public Admistration* (Chicago: Public Personnel Association, 1971), p. 19.

68. Eli Rock, "A Local Government Experience—Philadelphia," Kruger and Schmidt, op. cit., p. 169.

69. Twentieth Century Fund Task Force, op. cit., p. 35.

70. Ibid.

71. A. H. Raskin, "A Strike Ban Is Essential," in Marx, op. cit., p. 100.

72. The following account is based on Arthurs, op. cit., pp. 96-97 and "The

Canadian System Breaks Down," *Time Magazine*, in Marx, op. cit., p. 168.

73. Armand J. Thieblot, Jr., "Public Support for Strikers," *Collective Bargaining: Survival in the '70's?*, ed. Richard L. Rowan (Philadelphia: Univ. of Pennsylvania Press, 1972), pp. 348-349.

74. Ibid. For a more detailed analysis, see Armand J. Thieblot, Jr. and Ronald M. Cowin, *Welfare and Strikes: The Use of Public Funds to Support Strikers* (Philadelphia: Univ. of Pennsylvania Press, 1972).

75. The following account is based on Eli Rock, "A Local Government Experience—Philadelphia," in Kruger and Schmidt, op. cit., 164-65. Mr. Rock is an arbitrator in the Philadelphia area.

76. *Commercial Appeal*, Memphis, Tennessee, 29 August 1973, p. 19.

77. Interview with Jack G. Dodd, Administrative Services Manager of the MLGW, 21 February 1974.

78. Arnold Zander, "Collective Bargaining in the Public Sector; The Union View," *Public Administration Review*, Winter 1962, p. 11.

79. W. D. Heisel, "Anatomy of a Strike," *Public Personnel Review*, October 1969, pp. 230-232.

80. Ibid., p. 232.

Part I: Nature of Collective Bargaining

Economics of Public Sector Unionism 3

In order to assess the impact of unionism in the public sector we must attempt an analysis of its economic achievements, since the economic issues are among the most important in bargaining. Significant and fruitful gains can be an invaluable organizing tool for unions in the public sector and can serve to break the resistance of those public employees who have some interest in joining a union but are uncertain of the benefits to be derived. On the other hand, if the gains achieved are more modest, discontent may develop in the ranks, other unions may compete for representation rights, and organizing efforts elsewhere in the public sector may be slowed. As a result, it is essential that union leadership interpret the results of bargaining favorably and attribute these results solely to union bargaining power. The union has the same desire to perpetuate itself as any other bureaucracy, and this is survival behavior.

In looking at the dynamics of the situation more objectively, however, we intuitively realize that every advance in compensation and benefits, every improvement in working conditions cannot be credited solely to union bargaining. We have already noted that in some cases, particularly in the federal sector, the union has only an indirect opportunity to influence rates of compensation. It is also reasonable to assume that most employers have enough concern about retaining and attracting a competent work force that they would be willing to raise salaries to accomplish this purpose whether or not there was a union to act as watchdog. Indeed, it is a well-known political strategy for a president, governor, mayor, or department head to upgrade salaries as soon as possible after taking office in an effort to secure the loyalty and cooperation of the bureaucracy. While government may not serve as a model employer in terms of compensation, efforts are maintained to pay at prevailing wage rates (which would have to be done anyway to attract a sufficient supply of workers). It is also in the employer's self-interest to appear to his workers as enlightened and concerned about their welfare, to discourage the union movement in the public sector for whatever reason, and to attempt to minimize its power and achievements.

It can thus be seen from the outset that the results of collective bargaining are subject to wide interpretation that often depends on the bias and vantage point of the commentator. This situation considerably complicates the task of the objective observer, however, because the research of some authors is weighted toward a particular viewpoint. As such, their findings are subject to cautious acceptance at best. Even under the best of circumstances, it is difficult to isolate the unionism factor and test its single impact on the structure of wages and working conditions because of inadequate statistical data and the absence of any generally acceptable formula to do this.

As a result, the announced purpose of this chapter, to make some assessment of the economic impact of unionism, is a bold one indeed. Some of the problems and research efforts in this area can be explored, however, and some effort made to come to terms with the issue.

Labor Economics

The first matter germane to this study is the argument of whether or not unions actually accelerate real wages. Before beginning the discussion certain aspects of labor economics in the public and private sectors must be clarified.

Wages over Time

In the long run, money wages and real wages have increased in this country. Compensation per man hour in manufacturing has increased about twentyfold since 1900. This amounts to a cumulative rate of 4.5 percent a year from 1900 to 1971. At the same time consumer prices have almost tripled. This represents a cumulative rate of increase of 2 percent a year. Thus, by 1971 real wages had increased at a cumulative rate of about 2.5 percent a year.[1]

The Demand Curve for Labor

The relationship between the level of wages and the quantity of labor demanded is called the *demand curve for labor*. The demand curve has

Part I: Nature of Collective Bargaining

a negative slope, i.e., increases in wages reduce the numbers of workers employed—everything else remaining constant (see figure 3-1).[2]

The significance of any change in wages depends on the elasticity of the demand curve. In a market where the demand curve is highly elastic, a small change in wages could produce an enormous change in employment (see figure 3-2).

Where the demand curve for labor is not very elastic or inelastic, the effect of a change in wages is relatively small on the amount of employment (see figure 3-3).[3]

In a perfect market the demand curve for labor would have unitary elasticity. A one-unit change in wages would produce a one-unit change in employment.

Several factors are important in determining the elasticity of demand for labor:

A. Possibility of Substitution[4]

The smaller the substitution possibilities for a group of workers, the less elastic the demand for their services. When substitution is difficult or impossible, there are few alternatives to employing the workers beyond going out of business or, as in the case of the public sector, discontinuing the services. With such essential services as police and fire fighters, this is out of the question. Thus, we can say that for policemen and fire fighters the demand curve is very inelastic.

B. Elasticity of Demand for Goods or Service[5]

In the public sector the derived demand for labor is less elastic. If wages are increased, say, in the Sanitation Department, citizens will not react by producing less garbage thereby reducing the demand for employment of sanitation workers. In this case, the demand curve tends to be inelastic.

C. Proportion of Total Costs Contributed by Labor Costs

The demand for labor tends to be more elastic as the rate of labor costs to total costs increases. In the public sector labor costs compose a large percentage of the budget, especially at the municipal level. Thus the demand curve for labor is highly elastic in this respect.

From these theories we can conclude that the demand curve for labor generally tends to be inelastic in the public sector. There is little chance of substitution for many essential services, and demand for these services will remain the same, regardless of relatively large wage increases. The demand curve will be more elastic at the local level however, since personnel costs tend to account for such a large percentage of the budget. In Memphis, for example, the figure for personnel is approximately 80 percent of the budget. Statutory limits on municipal

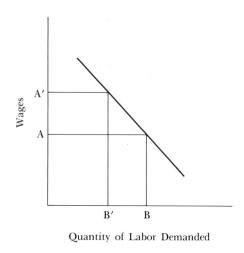

FIGURE 3-1: When wages are increased from A to A', the quantity demanded is reduced from B to B'.

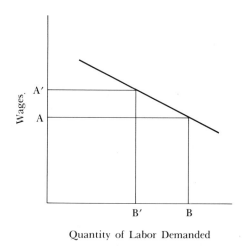

Quantity of Labor Demanded

FIGURE 3-2: A one-unit increase in wages from A to A' would reduce the demand for labor by almost two units from B to B'.

Part I: Nature of Collective Bargaining

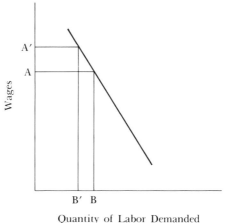

FIGURE 3-3: A one-unit increase in wages from A to A' would decrease the demand for labor by less than one unit from B to B'.

taxes and voter resistance to high taxes will dictate a point beyond which wages could not be raised without reductions in service due to lack of funds.

Now that the economic foundation has been laid, we can begin the assessment of union acceleration of actual wage increases.

Economic Environment of Public Sector Collective Bargaining

The wage rate for public employees, like that of private sector workers, is determined by the interplay of a host of labor market variables.* It is these variables which more of less dictate the extent to which public sector unionism can influence the wage rate. The number, nature, and importance of these market factors vary depending upon the

---

* The term "wage" is used here to denote the entire wage package which includes wages, hours, fringe benefits, and working conditions. The wage represents the total cost of employee compensation to the employer as used in Allan M. Carter and F. Ray Marshall, *Labor Economics: Wages, Employment, and Trade Unionism* (Homewood, Ill.: Richard D. Irwin, 1967), p. 226.

location of the particular market and the job classification being studied. For example, local governments generally do not have to contend with the prospect of their fire fighters opting for employment in privately owned fire fighting companies. They must, however, recognize the possibility of their teachers accepting employment in private school systems. But most importantly, they must be aware that a higher wage rate in private industry may induce members of both groups to leave the public sector and accept jobs that demand skills not directly related to those required by their present jobs. Thus, each market situation is influenced by variables unique to it, such as lack of competition from the private sector for a specific skill (fire fighting); and more common factors such as competition from the private sector for general skills (clerical work). Other common factors include the presence or absence of monopsony, spillover effects, wage-employment trade-off, ability of a governmental unit to substitute labor for capital, willingness of a governmental unit to pay, ability of a governmental unit to pay, and private sector labor market conditions. The impact of collective bargaining on the public labor wage rate is a function of one or more of these variables.

Before examining each of these more common variables it is important to note one noneconomic factor that affects all public employee wages. Wage rates are the products of governmental policymaking and are therefore political in nature.[6] Thus, in addition to the above economic factors, the public sector wage rate is partly determined by the values and interests of policy decision makers and by pressures exerted by various interest groups. If a particular local government decides to markedly increase the size of its police force, the wage and employment levels of policemen will rise, while those for other city workers will remain the same or show only slight increases.

The degree to which employers compete for labor is a basic determinant of the wage rate in any market. An employer is considered to possess monopsony power when, because of the large amount of labor he employs relative to other firms in the local labor market, his decisions on employment have a substantial effect on the local wage rate.[7] Put simply, a monopsonist is a labor buyer who can control the market just as a monopolist is a seller who controls the market.

Since governments must compete with private industry for labor they cannot be classified as monopsonists in the strict sense of the term.[8] However, public employers do enjoy a quasi-monopsonistic advantage in that they employ a large number of workers whose duties and skills have few direct counterparts in the private sector. Examples are policemen and fire fighters. Other occupations such as teaching have private sector members, but their numbers are very small relative to those in public employment. The extent to which a quasi-monopsony affects the market is dependent upon the size, population density, and the location of the government jurisdiction being examined.

Public employees working in large jurisdictions are limited in their work alternatives by the distances to adjacent jurisdictions. It follows, then, that public workers in small jurisdictions have more work alternatives in surrounding districts that would not require a change of residence.[9] The resultant increase in the number of prospective buyers increases their bargaining power and results in a higher wage rate.[10] To counter the effects of governmental jurisdictions competing against each other for labor it has been suggested that governments negotiate on a regional or statewide basis. The statewide approach is currently practiced in Hawaii.[11]

The population density of a jurisdiction has a similar effect on the market. Since it is likely that there will be more competition from other jurisdictions and from private sector employers for public workers in densely populated areas the governmental units in such areas will have to be more competitive in their wage offers. Conversely, governments in areas where the population is dispersed are faced with little competition for labor—a quasi-monopsonistic advantage.[12] Likewise, the location of a jurisdiction will affect the amount of competition for labor. A jurisdiction tucked away in a rural corner of a state surrounded by districts where the wage rate is low will be able to compensate its employees less than if it were located near a large metropolitan area.

The implications of quasi-monopsonistic markets are most evident in the field of education. Decentralization of school districts increases the number of units bidding for teacher services, thus forcing up the wage rate. On the other hand, consolidation of independent school districts reduces the competition for teachers, weakens their bargaining position, and results in a lower wage rate. Such a situation is likely to induce teachers to organize for collective bargaining.[13] This situation might be mitigated by noncompensatory advantages, where one school system with a low pupil-teacher ratio and better physical facilities enjoys a competitive advantage over another system lacking in these aspects even though both systems are paying the same wage. Another less likely influence in the event of decentralization is a conspiracy on the part of the local districts to fix the wage rate. This results in the revival of the quasi-monopsonistic market. However, the solidarity and effectiveness of this "buying cartel" would decrease as the demand for teachers increases.[14]

A similar result of the interdependence of jurisdictional labor markets occurs when the wage rates of employees in an ununionized jurisdiction rise because of the presence of strong labor organizations in surrounding jurisdictions. Such a "spillover" increase results from government efforts to remain competitive with the wage increases obtained by collective bargaining or to convince employees that they have no need to organize. Here again, geographically isolated jurisdictions tend not to be affected by the market situation in other jurisdictions.[15]

In the private sector, unions operate under the realization that high wage settlements are usually accompanied by reductions in employment levels. This threat of market imposed unemployment tends to moderate private sector union demands.[16] Because unions are concerned with employment as well as wages, their bargaining behavior will reflect their desire to obtain a compatible combination of wage and employment levels.[17]

The extent to which the threat of unemployment constrains union demands is determined by the elasticity of consumer demand for the product or service sold by the firm in question. *Elasticity* denotes the degree of response to a change in price. An elastic demand (supply) reflects a high sensitivity to a change in price, whereas an inelastic demand (supply) reflects a minimal impact of price changes on the quantity demanded (supplied). A highly elastic product demand severely limits union wage demands. High elasticities usually exist in markets where product competition is high. It follows that union wage demands are restrained in markets where product demand is inelastic, that is, where monopolies or near monopolies supply the product.[18] Since this is generally the case in the public sector, union wage demands usually are not limited by employment levels because of the inelastic demand for government services.[19]

Obviously, some government services are less essential to the community than others, and some services lend themselves to substitution more than others. In addition, some government services can be "contracted out" to private sector firms. These differences among services reflect differences in demand elasticities and thus differences in the bargaining power of unions that represent employees providing these services.[20]

When governments must limit employment levels because of high wage settlements they may choose to replace labor with capital rather than reduce services.[21] Replacing teachers with closed-circuit television instruction in schools and replacing clerical workers with data processing equipment are possible examples of such a policy. This approach is limited in its usefulness by the cost of the new capital and the extent to which it will successfully perform the functions of the labor it replaces. "Diminishing returns" from the added increments of capital dictate that at some level the new capital will cease to increase the amount and/or quantity of services.[22]

A public employee union's demands are also dependent on the willingness of the community to pay for the services rendered by the employees it represents.[23] Aside from the essential services of fire and police protection, the willingness of the community to fund other services is determined by the values of the community and those persons and institutions that influence and control them. As previously mentioned, politics is an important factor in determining what services will receive priority treatment. Willingness to pay for public services can be measured by the ratio of taxes to income.[24]

The willingness of the community to pay for public services and its ability to pay for them work together to determine the demand for public services. The ability of the community to pay can be determined by its tax base and by the amount of revenue in the form of intergovernmental grants it is eligible to receive from state and federal government.[25] This subject will be discussed in more detail in the section on budgeting.

The condition of the economy as a whole has a different effect on the wages of public sector workers than on private sector workers. The dependence of public workers on the usually slow-moving political process and the inflationary character of the postwar economy has often caused wage increases of public workers to lag behind those obtained by private sector workers. This effect is most notable in the case of federal employees and other workers that rely on legislation for wage increases.[26] Recent legislation, however, has sought to reduce this disadvantage of federal employees. Public employers must be able to adjust to the conditions of the economy in order to remain competitive with the private sector. The higher the wage for comparable skills in the private sector and the higher the cost of living, the higher will be the wage demands of public employees.[27]

Impact of Collective Bargaining on Public Employee Wages

Apparent Gains Achieved

Numerous examples may be cited of situations in which compensatory benefits were increased after the introduction of collective bargaining as a means of decision making for a particular public entity. To get a flavor for the kinds of settlements and gains achieved, we will review agreements in a number of cases. It should be noted at the outset that gains in the bargaining process can be achieved in basically two ways: the give-and-take of the negotiation process, and the use of force, as in a strike. Important gains are achieved with both methods, as we shall see.

An examination of the bargaining process shows that gains have been achieved both in remuneration and in conditions of work and that such advances are normally attributed to the introduction of the negotiation process. Walter Goodman attributes the improvement in starting salaries of Chicago's teachers from $5,500 in 1967 to $6,560 in 1968 directly to AFT bargaining.[28] In New York City, negotiators over time have successfully bargained for retirement benefits at half-pay after twenty and twenty-five years for sanitation workers, policemen, firemen, and subway operators; firemen have achieved full-pay pension after thirty-five years' service.[29]

Education is a field in which specific contractual changes are often attributed to collective negotiation. Wildman lists the granting of rights to teachers to challenge administrative judgments on teaching methods, provisions for election of department heads, provisions for peer evaluation to supplement a principal's evaluation, length of the school year, class load requirements, and establishment of committees for a number of administrative and decision making purposes as areas that have been successfully negotiated by teachers' unions.[30] George Angell notes that significant gains have been made by faculty unions of public institutions when compared to nonunionized public and private institutions; these gains are usually matched by approximately equivalent gains by faculty unions in private institutions. He observes:

> *Some community colleges now have higher salary scales than the majority of four-year colleges. [These are the unionized community colleges.] This may have a serious impact on the ability of private four-year colleges to compete successfully for quality in new faculty. . . . An analysis of the rise in community college salaries in comparison to increases in civil service salaries, four-year college salaries, and cost-of-living indices from 1968 to 1971 indicates almost spectacular relative gains for community college faculties, and these have been caused at least in part by bargaining. . . . In addition to salary increases, faculty unions have made unusual progress in obtaining fringe benefits formerly exclusive to faculties of older, more liberally oriented colleges.*[31]

Frederick Hueppe cites the experience with bargaining at a private institution, St. John's College, where the negotiated financial package constituted an increase in salary of over 25 percent in contrast to the previous year.[32] This contract was, in fact, as good as any gains achieved by public faculty unions in 1970.

Significant gains were also made by the police after they had achieved the right to negotiate collectively. Juris and Feuille observed that collective bargaining led to definite increases in police participation in policymaking decisions in most of the unionized departments that they surveyed; this participation did not occur before the advent of unionization.[33]

The strike has also been an effective economic weapon and has often produced dramatic gains for those employees willing to use it. Goodman states that a two-week strike by eleven thousand Detroit teachers in 1967 resulted in a raise of $850 a year.[34] A 1968 teacher's strike in East St. Louis, Illinois, resulted in an increase in starting salary from $6,250 to $8,000.[35] Striking teachers in Huntington, New York, raised their salary range from $6,300-$14,500 to $7,500-$17,700 in 1968.[36] Philip Grant describes a successful strike at Chicago City College in 1966 where faculty members were represented by the militant American Federation of Teachers:

> The AFT . . . gained a substantial reduction in class contact hours, a three-year tenure policy, a $500 salary increase for each professor as well as $300 in additional fringe benefits, and an enlarged role for the faculty in hiring of new professors, renewal of individual contracts, and selection of departmental chairmen.[37]

AFT also scored significant gains when it struck Michigan College in November 1967. "The terms of the settlement included a minimum salary increase of $1,000 for each professor, a two-week reduction in the length of the academic year, a limitation of both lecture hours and extracurricular duties, [and] guaranteed sick leave."[38]

It is evident that some definite gains in both compensation and working environment have been achieved in a number of different situations after the introduction of collective bargaining. Unions have been successful in convincing their membership that these gains are directly attributable to unionization. For example, in a survey conducted by Duryea and Angell there was an almost unanimous feeling among the more than one hundred faculty members from twenty-three New York campuses surveyed that collective bargaining negotiations had been successful in securing many benefits, and that this success would be helpful in recruiting new members as well as assuring the continued maintenance of bargaining.[39]

However, despite these apparent gains and the willingness of some members to attribute them directly and solely to unionism, this evidence is not conclusive. In order to make the generalization with confidence that unionism results in improved compensation over what could have been otherwise obtained, one must examine in more detail aspects of market structure, long-term trends in compensation, and other hypothetical influences on compensation. Such an analysis is the subject of the next section.

Gains Attributable to Unionism

The methodological challenge of isolating the impact of unionism on wages has been of interest to economists since the advent of collective bargaining organizations. Unfortunately, due to the complexity of the issue, the paucity of data, and the general absence of an accepted methodology of procedure, the problem is still unresolved. There are some studies, however, that have become classics in the field and have made significant advances in the state of knowledge. One such study was conducted by economist John E. Maher and published in the *American Economic Review* in 1956.[40] Maher notes in his article that simply a before-and-after type of wage comparison is too imprecise, in that it fails to isolate unionism as a variable.[41] Tables 3-1 and 3-2 present a graphic illustration of Maher's point. Table 3-1 indicates that general wage changes occurred far more frequently among unionized employees than among nonunionized workers in manufacturing. However, table 3-2 shows that when wage increases were granted, the median wage increases of nonunion manufacturing employees outstripped their union counterparts almost every time.* Thus, at least in some cases, nonunion workers have secured greater rates of compensation than they would have in a union, although perhaps at less frequent intervals.†

One way of approaching the problem of isolating unionism as a variable is to attempt to estimate what wage rates would have been if unionism were not present. However, this too is a difficult concept to qualify, as Belton Fleisher describes:

> In order to conclude that unionism ... has changed the wage rates of union members, we have to be able to discover what such wage rates would have been in the absence of unions. However, the very presence of unions in the economy is likely to make this kind of comparison very difficult by changing the wage rates of many workers besides those who are union members.[42]

This, in fact, may very well be the situation illustrated in table 3-2.

The impact of a union in influencing wage rates depends on its power as well as the market structure within which it operates. Melvin Lurie notes: "The power of a union is largely dependent on the inelasticity of demand for unionized services. The more inelastic the demand is, the more successful a union will be in pushing wages above competitive levels," which could lead to unemployment and reductions in its membership.[43] This leads Allan Cartter and Ray Marshall to conclude that unions will definitely raise wage levels above the nonunion norms to the degree that they have monopsonistic conditions in their

---

* Unfortunately, no comparable data is available for the public sector at this time.
† Of course, this does not demonstrate that nonunion members always enjoy these benefits. Indeed, if one hypothesizes that greater benefits were given to nonunion members to discourage union membership, we see that unionization still had an indirect influence on the wage levels.

TABLE 3-1: Percentage of Production Workers in Manufacturing Establishments Where General Wage Changes Were Effective (1963-74)

	1963	1964	1965	1966	1967	1968	1969	1970	1971	1972	1973	1974
All Manufacturing	75.8	71.4	84.6	80.2	88.1	92.9	88.9	90.7	87.0	90.5	94.4	95.6
All Unions	77.8	76.1	87.3	80.9	90.6	93.7	93.2	94.8	92.0	92.0	95.9	97.8
Nonunion	69.6	56.2	75.4	77.8	81.1	87.6	75.5	77.6	70.2	83.2	90.1	89.1

Source: U.S., Bureau of Labor Statistics, *Handbook of Labor Statistics 1976*, tab. 86, p. 162.

TABLE 3-2: Percentage of Median Wage Increases for Production Workers in Manufacturing Establishments Where Changes Were Effective (1963-74)

	1963	1964	1965	1966	1967	1968	1969	1970	1071	1972	1973	1974
All Manufacturing	3.1	2.7	3.3	3.9	4.3	5.1	5.1	5.9	6.1	5.3	6.2	8.4
All Unions	3.0a	2.6a	3.2	3.8	3.9	5.1	5.0	5.9	6.6	5.4	7.4	11.3
Nonunion	3.7a	3.2a	4.0	4.5	4.8	5.0	6.0	5.9	4.8	5.2	6.0	8.7

Source: U.S., Bureau of Labor Statistics, *Handbook of Labor Statistics 1976*, tab. 86, p. 187.

a Estimated.

particular sector and occupation.[44] The fact that conditions will vary from place to place, level to level, and job to job means that union power will vary accordingly. Consequently each situation must be judged on its own merits when trying to make assessments of union power and impact.

This explanation is not completely sufficient either, because it fails to explain how wage levels could rise in nonunionized occupations that do not have monopsonistic structures. Paul Samuelson, for example, notes that since 1933 such traditionally low-paid, nonunionized occupations as farm work and domestic service have shown greater percentage increases in compensation than unionized trades.[45] He cites the case of the Dupont Chemical Company, whose many plants have national as well as company unions represented, in addition to a number of plants that are not unionized. Nevertheless, between 1945 and 1973 his analysis indicated no substantial variation in the pattern of steady increase in wages at each of the three different kinds of plants.[46] It is clear then that the generalization that market power has a direct effect on union ability to achieve gains should be amended to hypothesize that a competitive market situation is likely to improve the economic position of any employee, unionized or not.

Some economists argue that union impact on wages, when it does occur, is only a short-run phenomenon. Lurie, for example argues that "unions achieve their largest gains during the early stages of unionization and thereafter union power diminishes so that over time movements in union wages are not very different from movements in nonunion wages."[47] This observation seemed to be confirmed, at least in part, in the education profession. Research by Wildman indicated that between 1946 and 1968 collective bargaining had "at least a short-run impact on both the *level* and the *structure* of teacher compensation."[48] * Maher adopts a slightly different position, arguing that union and nonunion employers may await the results of union bargaining, and then match or exceed the gains with their own employees.[49] This may make the appearance of short-term gains by unions deceptive, since, according to Maher, these gains may be matched at a later time.†

Maher offers another explanation for the differentiation between union and nonunion salary rates—namely, the inflexibility of rates as determined by a union contract, particularly a long-term contract. He explains, "If an inflationary situation develops during the life of a

---

* While Wildman's work did confirm Lurie's thesis on short-run impact, he does not necessarily concur in the hypothesis that long-term rates tend to seek an equilibrium. His research was not conclusive on this point.
† This is not to say that nonunion employers may grant their workers anticipatory increases on the basis of what union workers may obtain.

negotiated agreement that provides for no wage reopening, rates of unionized employees may remain unaltered. By contrast, the nonunion firm may quickly respond to such inflationary forces by raising wages."[50] In this respect, an employee might actually find it disadvantageous to be a union member unless his contract includes an escalator clause. In short, Maher seems to feel that there are no inherent differences in union and nonunion rates of compensation based on the power of collective bargaining or union manipulation of the market structure; he simply argues that differences in rates appear due to normal leads and lags in the market, and that one's results will vary over time as the economic conditions change.

These complex and conflicting viewpoints are illustrative of the problems in trying to come to grips with the issue of union impact on wages. One of the most provocative analyses in recent years on this question was done by Orley Ashenfelter, a Princeton economist. Ashenfelter uses regression and correlation techniques to study the impact of a public sector union, the International Association of Fire Fighters, on relative wage rates.[51] He concludes that "in 1966 the unionization of firemen may have raised the average hourly wage of unionized firemen by somewhere between 6 and 16 percent above the average hourly wage of nonunion firemen."[52] Ashenfelter notes, however, that these figures may be a bit high for most unions in the public sector which do not have certain market and bargaining advantages of IAFF.[53] This would seem to indicate that in at least one case, unionism has had a direct influence on wage levels despite the earlier reservations mentioned. This sets the stage for a more detailed look at conditions in the transit industry, perhaps the public sector industry that has been more exhaustively studied than any other.

Case Study: Unionism and the Transit Industry

A comprehensive study of labor economics in the transit industry was recently conducted by Donald T. Barnum; his analysis may be of some interest in attempting to determine the reasons for the industry's high percentage of union membership and in comparing wage rates in the public sector with comparable work in the private sector.[54] Approximately 95 percent of the transit industry is unionized, with the Amalgamated Transit Union accounting for over 79 percent of the agreements. During the past two decades, there has been an increasing shift to public ownership as well as a tendency to discontinue many service lines. The shift to public ownership is illustrated by the following statistics: Between 1950 and 1960 twenty-five private companies became publicly owned; between 1960 and 1965, twenty-seven; and between 1965 and 1970, fifty-one.

The growth in unionism played no small part in this trend with personnel costs accounting for approximately 74 percent of total expenditures in 1970. The rising costs of employee compensation and the inability of private companies to raise rates to a level sufficient to maintain service and still make a profit made the option of government subsidy or operation the only feasible alternative. Fringe benefits account for about 20 percent of standard payroll costs, and provide the standard benefits such as paid vacation and holiday, pension and insurance plans.

Wages rose rapidly in the transit industry along with the increase in union memberships. Between 1949 and 1969 wages increased by 158 percent, which was about the same rate of increase experienced by building journeymen and local truck drivers. On the other hand, the transit unions have not been successful in equating their wage level to that of local truck drivers, who have a similar job, but with perhaps less responsibility in terms of human life. In 1971, the average union wage rate for local transit workers was $4.38; the union rate for a local truck driver was $4.95.[55] Even at the reported rate of wage increases, private companies found costs too high to be profitable, and the feeling among unions and managers seemed to be that only government could continue to pay the high wages demanded. The government operated under less stringent financial conditions than private enterprise in that wages could always be covered by tax increases.

Barnum conducted a study to compare the wages of bus drivers working for both public and private systems in order to test the hypothesis that public workers would earn more in a public system because they could exact greater concessions from their employer. However, in his own words, "There was no significant difference between the wage rates after accounting for the variation caused by differences in labor market conditions and by differences in company size."[56] This contrasts quite markedly to Lurie's analysis of the Boston transit industry in which he determined that "a conservative estimate of the Boston transit union's power to raise the wages of its membership in the 1950's has been on the order of 20 percent."[57] Perhaps this seeming contradiction can be explained by dismissing Boston as a unique case, or as evidence for the hypothesis that a union may have considerable power over wages initially, but this may decline over time. Barnum notes that another factor may lead to higher wages once a system becomes public: small peripheral systems on the outskirts of the city are often merged into a regional system, and the wages of their drivers are brought up to parity with the rest of the group. This may explain the ability of Boston's transit unions to seemingly extract such high wages in comparison to both private transit unions and public unions in other cities.[58]

It would thus seem that public unions have about the same power as a private union in securing wages, which may moderate over time. This finding supports the prevailing-wage theory of government compensation, as opposed to the model-employer concept discussed in chapter 2. Distressingly enough, however, even this generalization cannot be made without qualification. A recent study by David Lewin finds "a consistent pattern of higher pay for municipal employees in a variety of occupations than exists for comparable workers in either private industry or the federal government.[59] Lewin's explanation is that, since the occupations mentioned are all at the lower end of the scale, these employees represent the largest segment of the governmental work force and the largest governmental voting bloc; consequently their loyalty is secured through use of highly competitive salaries.[60] On the other hand, the municipal government may try to garner a reputation for fiscal responsibility by depressing the salaries of the top people below what they could expect to earn in the private sector.[61] It would appear that an astute union can use this inclination to its advantage in the public sector in securing gains; on the other hand, the tendency will be present whether or not there is collective bargaining and cannot be fairly attributed to unionism alone.

Finally, it should be noted that minimum wage legislation, which newly applies to government workers, also has a positive effect on the wages of those at the lower end of the scale, although it may result in some unemployment as well. This circumstance cannot be directly attributed to unionism, although unions may take some credit for lobbying in behalf of such legislation.

Let us review some of the findings of this section. The reader is aware by this point of some of the complexities that the economist must evaluate and resolve in order to make any definitive judgments about the impact of unionism on rates of compensation. We have discussed the necessity of trying to isolate unionism as a variable of wage level determination; we have noted the theoretical impact of market structure as a determinant of union power, and, consequently, the union's ability to have an impact. We have noted that despite assessments of these factors, nonunionized employees make unpredicted gains. Even the innovative analysis of Ashenfelter, which found a definite union impact on wages, must admit to being done in an exceptional industry and only dealing with the short run. The transit industry was exceptional in its high rate of unionization, but not so exceptional in its lack of clarity in indicating union impact.

Despite the lack of authoritative supportive evidence, however, we will offer three impressions of the economic consequences of collective bargaining to summarize the preceding information. One, unionism may have a positive impact on compensation in some occupations in the short run, an impact that may vary from 5 percent to 20 percent. Two, whether or not a union has an impact on compensation and the degree of this impact will be determined by conditions generally beyond its control, although these conditions are subject to manipulation. These conditions include the monopsonistic structure of the market, the competitive conditions existing in this occupational category, and the degree to which the government entity sees its employees as voters. These conditions will also work to the advantage of the nonunion employee. Three, gains in compensation in the long run tend to be about the same for both union member and nonunion public employees.

It is to be hoped that this important subject will be a continuing topic of academic research, and that, at some time, a conclusive body of information can be compiled to substantiate or discredit these arguments.

Real Gains Achieved

We have previously observed that some notable gains have apparently been achieved through collective bargaining, although not necessarily directly attributed to unionism. We term these gains "apparent" because a wage or salary rate only has meaning when interpreted in terms of its purchasing power. Therefore, real gains are those that are achieved after the effects of inflation have been discounted.

It is obvious, then, that it is not enough for the union member to achieve gains; he must receive compensatory advances at least at the level of inflation in order to maintain his present standard of living, and he must receive gains in excess of the rate of inflation in order to improve his standard of living. A. H. Raskin provides a case in point:

> *Just to take New York City . . . money wages for factory workers went up by $29 dollars a week in the last half of the 1960's, but the average family head ended up $1.80 behind in what his pay envelope could buy after taxes and inflation had taken their ravenous bite.*[62]

The gains must be hefty indeed to beat the recent rates of inflation that Raskin indicates. Incredibly, the purchasing power of the dollar declined by 18 percent in the four years between 1967 and 1971.[63] The average weekly earnings of a production worker in 1971 were $126.91 in current dollars, but only $104.62 in 1967 dollars due to inflation.[64]

It appears that some public unions have been successful in achieving gains for their members that are above the current rate of inflation. Kenneth Mortimer and Gregory Lozier, after study of selected contracts of four-year colleges, came to the conclusion that "with one or two exceptions, salaries provided for in the contracts analyzed are keeping the faculty even with or slightly ahead of the current rate of national inflation."[65] The inflationary situation has led unions to seek shorter contracts, more emphasis on fringe benefits, and mandatory cost-of-living increases each year as an adaptation to the current market situation.

Another unresolved economic question is the cause of inflation. Some argue that inflation is the result of improperly controlled growth in the money supply; others adhere to the wage-push theory of inflation, which argues that wage settlements in excess of productivity lead to higher prices, which begins a vicious circle of wage and price hikes. In the case of the first theory, the prime culprit is the Federal Reserve Board, while in the latter case, labor unions get much of the blame. Some see the advent of public sector unionism as a guarantor of a permanent inflation in the U.S. economy, based upon the fact that the government is notoriously a soft bargainer due to political pressure, and that government settlements are highly visible in the economy as a whole.*

The Nixon Administration apparently subscribed to the wage-push theory of inflation and introduced wage-price controls in August 1971 in an effort to bring U.S. inflation under control. However, wage-price controls were generally ineffective in the public sector, perhaps due to the lobbying and persuasive efforts of some union organizations. Raymond Lee notes that the initial focus of the Pay Board (instrument effecting wage-price controls) was in the private sector.[66] This may partially explain why, for example, TVA had approved for its blue-collar workers increases of 4.01 percent in 1971, 7.9 percent in 1972, and 5.6 percent in 1973 in contrast to the alleged maximum rate of increase allowed—5.5 percent.[67] It would appear then that, on the whole, wage-price controls had little effect in the public sector.

As public sector wages increase, it should be remembered that the cost to government is also increasing. Since these rising costs are ultimately paid by the taxpayer, one public union member's gain may be one taxpayer's loss. It is ironic that these people are, in fact, one and the same. The union member who speaks favorably of the advances his union has achieved may not realize that these advances are passed along to him in the long run in terms of higher taxes or lost opportunities to finance other programs that might have some social benefit.

We have seen that the union must be cognizant of the real gains in compensation during the course of bargaining if its members are to improve their standards of living. We will look next at the effect that collective bargaining has had on nonwage provisions.

---

* This seems to imply the idea of government as a model employer, however, which has been elsewhere rejected.

Impact on Other Contract Provisions

As previously mentioned, the nonsalary components of the wage package have played an increasingly important role as bargaining objectives. In addition to raising the costs to government, they create important implications for employee morale and discipline. These nonsalary items can be divided into two general classifications. The first, representation in management policymaking, is a relatively new bargaining objective. It is confined, for the most part, to those decisions that will have an indirect effect on working conditions. The second classification is the more traditional goal of increasing fringe benefits.

Those having the greatest interest in and desire for representation in policymaking are the professional employees of state and local governments. Since most unionized workers at the federal level are blue-collar level there is little demand there for policymaking representation.[68] The working conditions of blue-collar workers are generally not products of the basic policies and goals of the agency involved. These conditions are usually set by clearly defined work rules. The working conditions of the professional worker, however, have different origins. Victor Gotbaum, an American Federation of State, County and Municipal Employees (AFSCME) representative stated that "[to] the professional—the teacher or the case worker—class size and case load become as important as the number of hours in a shift for the blue-collar worker."[69]

In an article published in the fall of 1973 Jerry Wurf, AFSCME president, wrote,

> We believe that the thrust in the years to come will be toward a higher level of participation by public employees in the decision-making process—particularly where the decisions affect them directly as workers.[70]
>
> Workers are demanding—and they'll be getting—a greater degree of bilateralism on the job. Much nonsense has been written about the new breed of worker, but it is true that younger Americans, those who grew up with no depression experience and no memory of its devastating impact, are less likely to grind out their lives at jobs that are unrewarding. The work ethic still lives, but with an amendment: work must have worthiness.[71]

Examples of these demands by the worker include greater control over his own job and more flexible job assignments and work schedules.[72]

This move to demand a voice in policy decisions formerly reserved for elected officials is a result, in part, of the lack of state legislation clearly defining what is negotiable. Most state laws require only that governments negotiate "wages, hours, and conditions of employment." This vagueness, especially the term "conditions of employment," leaves the policymaking area vulnerable to union demands.[73] In Spokane, Washington, however, the city took the offensive and used the vagueness of the law to its advantage. Police there attempted to persuade the city to hire more patrolmen in order to improve working conditions. The city refused to negotiate, arguing that such decisions were matters of policy that were not negotiable.[74]

Federal employees bargain directly for improvements in working conditions. A 1971 survey by the Bureau of Labor Statistics showed that more than eight out of every ten federal collective bargaining agreements contained procedures for handling employee grievances. The study also showed that federal employees were increasingly obtaining contract stipulations concerning hours and overtime (as shown in table 3-3).[75]

Collective bargaining by public employees has resulted in an increase in fringe benefits.[76] Since fringe benefits traditionally have been used by governments to supplement relatively low salaries in order to compete with private sector firms, the advent of public employee unionism has made the fringe package extremely costly to government.[77] A 1972 study conducted by the Labor-Management Relations Service of the National League of Cities, the United States Conference of Mayors, and the National Association of Counties, found that in 1970 public employee benefits amounted to 28.2 percent of their salaries. Workers in the private sector received benefits valued at 30.8 percent of their wages.[78] This figure breaks down to an average cost of $2,274 for each municipal employee.[79] To make matters worse for budget makers, the cost of fringe benefits are expected to continue to rise dramatically. One prediction estimates that by the middle of the 1980s fringe benefit costs will equal salary costs.[80]

The term "fringe" is applied to a variety of nonsalary benefits, the most common of which include hospital, medical, and life insurance; sick, vacation, and holiday leave; pension and retirement allowances; severance, longevity, and education incentive pay; overtime; and medical care.[81] Other less conventional fringe benefits now being demanded by most public employee unions include leaves for conventions, funerals, jury duty, and union meetings, among some others.[82] For example, in 1972 a bargaining council of the American Federation of Government Employees, representing 2,000 employees of the Office of Economic Opportunity, bargained with the agency for free abortions and birth control devices.[83]

In addition to the surface advantages of fringe benefits to employees there is a hidden value. Unlike salaries, fringe benefits are generally not

TABLE 3-3: Provisions on hours, overtime, weekends, holidays, and shifts in federal collective bargaining agreements, by occupational group (late 1971)

Provision	Agreements	Workers
Total	671	532,745
Provision for regularly scheduled hours.	463	429,783
Daily and/or weekly overtime provisions	490	456,056
Premium pay for early start.	45	60,676
Equal distribution of overtime	429	399,582
Right to refuse overtime	253	269,339
Premium pay for weekend work	98	103,534
Premium pay for holiday work	202	227,402
Shift differential	168	153,942
Notice of work schedule changes	365	358,551

Source: U.S., Bureau of Labor Statistics, as shown in Richard R. Nelson, "Collective Bargaining Agreements in the Public Sector," *Monthly Labor Review* 96 (September 1973): p. 77.

taxable.[84] Therefore, when salary increases are traded-off for fringe benefits the employee achieves a real gain.

The next section turns to some of the costs of bargaining in terms of real losses from the standpoint of the public employer.

Costs of Bargaining

Collective bargaining can result in four kinds of costs or potential costs for the public employer. The first of these is in the area of inefficient work practices. If the public manager feels restrained by collective bargaining in terms of his hiring or firing practices, then the staff may not be at the optimum size and of the optimum abilities to work at peak efficiency. Derek Bok and John Dunlop argue that because public managers are not restrained by market forces, they "are probably less alert, on the whole, in detecting and avoiding inefficient work practices."[85] Wildman notes that in the educational sphere the single, uniform salary schedule has long been regarded as inefficient because it takes no account of supply and demand factors within the various teaching specialties.[86] Any changes in this area, along with any plan to introduce pay differentiation based on classroom performance, and any introduction of automatic teaching devices are likely to face tough going in bargaining sessions.[87] Collective bargaining may result in a loss of innovation and a preservation of inefficient work practices, all of which represent an immeasurable yet important cost of bargaining.

The second cost is in terms of lost or underfunded projects and proposals that may have been a casualty of increased personnel costs attributable to bargaining. Ziedler notes that "[The] challenge of organized public employees can mean considerable loss of control over the budget, and hence over tax rates and over governmental programs and projects."[88] The cost of the loss in this case is again indeterminate; it can only be measured in terms of lost opportunity.

The third cost to government is in higher tax rates. Obviously, after every settlement the government is faced with the choice of either cutting back programs, as suggested earlier, or raising tax rates to finance the increased costs of operating government. David Selden advocates the latter course for government decision makers, particularly in terms of higher income and sales taxes.[89] However, the costs of even modest gains in compensation can add an enormous burden to government expenditures. Bok and Dunlop point out:

> Wages and salaries make up almost half of state and local government expenditures, and fifteen percent of federal expenditures. A five percent wage and salary increase to all government employees would cost taxpayers $4 to $5 billion exclusive of related fringe benefits.[90]

A miscalculation of the costs involved can have disastrous consequences for the government treasury. For example, New York mediator Ted Kheel observes that the early retirement plans of the city of New York, whereby transit and sanitation workers, policemen, and firemen can retire at half pay after twenty years of service "is causing a critical exodus of skilled workers sorely needed to maintain city services."[91] In addition, an increasing number of early retirements has bankrupted one system, with pension costs more than doubling in the city as a whole, going from $342 million in 1966 to an estimated $750 million in 1975.[92]

Cleveland was trapped in the fiscal dilemma of spiraling personnel costs and spiraling tax rates during the 1960s. The situation was so desperate that in 1971 the city declared a freeze on compensatory increases for all its employees.[93] However, this could not be done with the police and fire departments because they were protected by provisions in the charter against just such an eventuality. The result was that 193 police officers were laid off because the city did not have the funds to pay them.[94] It can be seen, then, that it is not in the long-term interest of the unions to take advantage of the lack of bargaining expertise in the public sector; otherwise they may find the economic situation worsening. Raskin cites a disturbing example of what can happen unless costs are controlled:

> *Earlier this year (1972) all our principal industry groups—the State Chamber of Commerce, the Commerce and Industry Association, the Economic Development Council and the Citizens Budget Commission—joined in a warning to Mayor Lindsay that one of the elements prompting business to move out of New York was the extent to which the City's profligacy at the bargaining table not only was driving up taxes but also was acting as a spur to inflated demands by unions in the private sector.... Whatever one union wrings out of a not too resistant municipal administration becomes the jumping off point for an even bigger exaction by the union next in line.[95]*

It can be seen how the situation can easily get out of hand unless all parties are aware of the economic parameters within which bargaining must occur; any union success in taking advantage of public management's relatively weak position may be detrimental in the long run.

The fourth cost to government is in the area of administration; it concerns the costs of negotiation, impasse resolution, and strikes. The cost of administering a personnel system that employs collective bargaining is likely to be higher. In order to negotiate with employee groups, the administration must hire personnel skilled in collective bargaining or train existing personnel to handle the job. More often than not, personnel charged with negotiations will require staff assistance as well. From time to time attorneys must also be consulted. All add to the cost of administration.

Strikes in the public sector are almost universally illegal and generally undesirable for the government, the workers, and the public. A logical solution to impasses in collective bargaining, which, if unresolved, cause strikes, is in the form of third-party intervention, such as arbitration. As collective bargaining in the public sector has increased, so has the need for arbitration. Yet, the supply of qualified arbitrators has failed to keep up with the demand. As a result, the arbitration process has become very costly. Costs of arbitration hearings commonly include the arbitrator's daily fee; the arbitrator's travel and study time, normally paid at the daily rate; fees for the parties' attorneys; wage payment to personnel taking part in the proceedings; rental of a hearing room; and, if the services of the American Arbitrators Association are used, payment to the association for furnishing the parties a panel of arbitrators. Added to these costs is the time involved between requesting an arbitration panel and the receipt of an arbitration award.

The cost of a strike in the public sector cannot be measured in economic terms as it would be in the private sector. The difference between the sectors is that in the public service the employer does not normally lose money during a strike. In fact, there is a savings as revenues continue to come in while wages are not being paid out. However, there is a cost to the public employer; the cost is the political and social pressure put on the employer because a strike holds back essential services from the public.

We have examined four aspects of the costs of union gains in terms of in-bred inefficiency, loss of programs, increased tax rates, and increased administrative costs. Let us next examine the prospects for future gains by public sector unions in the governmental arena.

Prospects for the Future

There are some indications that taxpayer resistance is developing to the higher and higher taxes needed to support the proposals of public sector unions. Goodman notes that in spite of a concern for quality teachers and facilities, many towns are beginning to vote down their proposed school budgets.[96] The implication is that teacher demands for more salary increases are also being voted down, since a school budget increase is usually the only way to finance them. Wildman predicts that the rate of gain in teachers' salaries may level off in the future, in part because of taxpayer attitudes, and in part because of more sophisticated bargaining by the public employer.[97]

Another trend that is likely to continue into the immediate future is this increased bargaining sophistication of the public employer. This is reflected structurally in increased centralization of decision making on as many issues as the legislative body will permit. In addition to improving the government negotiating stance, such centralization may be helpful in achieving parity among other employees doing equivalent work and in maintaining an appropriate salary differential between workers performing different functions.[98]

A final prospect to look for in the future is the increasing tendency of government agencies to "contract out" some of their work. In other words, instead of maintaining an in-house capability to perform a certain job or hiring someone to do it, the job is given to a consultant.

Should this trend accelerate, it could reduce direct public employment in both blue-collar and white-collar positions over time and become an issue of controversy between public unions and the government.

Collective Bargaining and the Budgetary Process

The advent of unionism in the public sector brings an immediate and direct problem to the process of budget preparation and approval. Another party has been added to the decision making process; a party that has the potential (or actual) power to change priorities, reallocate designated funding amounts, and even force increased tax rates by threat or the exercise of collective force.

Collective bargaining has been the cause of a variety of headaches for municipal budget makers. Legal restrictions on their taxing authority, inadequate tax bases, and inflexible tax structures have made it difficult to fund wage increases won by public employee unions. In addition to the problems of funding, public administrators must cope with nonmonetary difficulties posed by budget schedules and deadlines and union efforts to use these deadlines to obtain a bargaining advantage. It is estimated that employee compensation accounts for 50 to 74 percent of local government expenditures.[99] As we have seen, these costs will continue to skyrocket.

Since cities and municipalities are "creatures of the state" and, therefore, dependent on the state for their taxing authority, their ability to adapt to these rapidly increasing costs is limited.[100] Cities rely on the property tax and federal and state grants-in-aid for most of their revenue. Of these revenue sources the property tax is the most productive. In 1966, 44.8 percent of local revenue was supplied by the property tax, while state and federal grants contributed 33.4 percent. The remainder of the revenue was supplied by miscellaneous charges and taxes.[101]

Spero and Cappozzola found that the yield of the property tax is inelastic, i.e., it does not respond adequately to the rising costs of city government.[102]* If this is the case, local governments, initially anyway, must look to other revenue sources to finance large wage settlements. State and federal grants make up most of the remaining revenue. State aid takes the form of the traditional grants-in-aid and shared taxes,

* However, another expert found the property tax to be "quite elastic." See Maxwell, p. 128. James A Maxwell, *Financing State and Local Governments* (Washington, D.C.: The Brookings Institution, 1969), p. 128.

Part I: Nature of Collective Bargaining

which are the products of state efforts to use their larger tax base to make tax collections more efficient and productive.[103] However, because of allocation procedures and restrictions on use, shared taxes provide little relief for cities attempting to finance increased wages. Since grants-in-aid also tend to be earmarked, state revenues offer little help to a cost-ridden city.[104] Likewise, federal grants are usually accompanied by restrictions on their use.[105] Federal revenue sharing ostensibly was an effort to endow local governments with "no strings attached" funds. However, it is expected that most cities cannot use these funds for wage increases, because they must use the revenue sharing to finance earmarked projects funded by categorical grants.[106]

The budget-making rules and procedures used by public administrators before the advent of large scale collective bargaining have proved to be inadequate in dealing with the problems presented by unionization.[107] Budget schedules and deadlines often have lacked the flexibility necessary to accommodate settlements for increased wages reached during the approval process. To strengthen their bargaining power unions may plan for bargaining to reach a climax while the legislative body is considering the budget.[108] Such action further complicates the matter.

Another impediment to predicting labor costs is escalator clauses, which have become a part of many contracts. Their purpose is to protect the worker from losses of real income due to inflation. These wage additions are based on the cost of living and are, therefore, subject to quick changes (almost always upward).[109] Such clauses put the budget maker in the position of having to predict the behavior of the economy in order to determine the total cost of labor. In order to absorb cost of living increases and/or higher than predicted wage increases reached after budget approval, some cities have built "cushions" or "hidden money" into their budgets.[110] To facilitate budget making, many states have enacted legislation requiring cooperation between bargainers and negotiators.

The following sections explore the issue of collective bargaining and the budgetary process, focusing on the issues of timing and fiscal planning as elements of the budgetary process, and examine how collective bargaining may influence them.

Timing of Negotiations

From the standpoint of the government employer, it is important that collective bargaining be conducted so that the agencies can submit their funding requests for the next fiscal year at the appropriate time of the budget cycle. Generally speaking, agencies submit their budget requests to the executive or his designee about six to eight months before the beginning of the next fiscal year. The tentative budgets of each department and agency are discussed and debated within the executive branch from thirty to sixty days. Then the chief executive prepares and submits to the legislative body his administration's budget proposals. Agency heads may be called upon to testify before legislative committees as the legislative branch reviews each budgetary item. Finally the legislative body adopts a budget for the ensuing fiscal year. It is normally built around the framework that the executive submitted, but with certain changes that the legislature felt were desirable and in accordance with its own priorities. It can be seen then that any delays in this process could disrupt the entire cycle.

When an agency deals with a union in setting compensation rates, it cannot make any immediate or unilateral decisions on this issue; as a result, it does not know until this issue is resolved just how much anticipated money it can request to finance its proposed activities.[111] Obviously, it is to the agency's advantage to reach a settlement with the union as soon as possible, preferably in time to submit a definite budget request to the chief executive. It would be advantageous, then, to begin collective negotiations about nine months before the start of the next fiscal year. (See chapter 2, the Philadelphia model.)

When bargaining begins late in the budgetary cycle or when an impasse occurs and delays the negotiation of an agreement until after a budget has been submitted or adopted, a nightmarish situation may develop for the legislature and the affected agency because funding allocations may have to be completely reordered. Bok and Dunlop explain:

> *If bargaining takes place after a budget has been adopted, negotiation becomes much more difficult. An increase in compensation under a pre-established budget involves either a deficit or a drastic reordering of public priorities. In the latter event, public officials are forced to take funds from capital budgets, from agencies less able to resist cuts, from services whose recipients have least political muscle, or—for some purposes—from federal agencies.*[112]

As public agencies have gained experience with the bargaining process, they have come to realize that, despite the best efforts of all parties, bargaining will not always flow smoothly. Occasional stalemates and even strikes are bound to occur. Consequently, it is imperative for the public agency to devise some means of coping with this inevitability in a way that will make it as least disruptive as possible for the process of budgeting. In general, four mechanisms or combinations of these mechanisms are used in varying degrees by public agencies.

Part I: Nature of Collective Bargaining

One, recent legislation establishes specified time limits on collective bargaining. For example, legislation in Connecticut and New York requires negotiation and bargaining be completed before the date that the governor or mayor must submit a budget to the legislature.[113]

Two, in the absence of such legislation or in the event that it fails to work properly, agencies may estimate liberally the amount of compensatory increases they think may be negotiated and plan their remaining expenditures around this figure. This estimate will be "hidden" within the total budget estimate, however, since the government obviously does not want to reveal to the union from the outset exactly how much of an increase it is willing to grant; if it can bargain for less than the maximum estimate, the employer will have bargained successfully. Since the union is aware of this contingency on the part of the public employer, the initial stage of public sector negotiation is often referred to as the budget search process.[114] James Craft explains that "[in] the budget search process, either one or both of the parties concentrate on finding 'misallocations' or 'overallocations' of money on specific items in the proposed budget and then work to reallocate the 'discovered' funds."[115] The implication is that public sector bargaining is becoming a test of the skill of public fiscal officers in disguising the entity's true financial condition and the maximum amount it is prepared to pay for increased compensation and benefits; thus, it is also a test of the ingenuity of the union accountant in exposing and estimating these hidden amounts.[116]

Three, bargaining is prevented from upsetting the timing of the budgetary process in some localities by the granting of retroactive wage and salary benefits at such time as an agreement is reached. Juris and Feuille cite this mechanism in the area of police bargaining:

> *Perhaps the most important factor in understanding the lack of time pressure in police bargaining is the easy granting of retroactivity by most jurisdictions: the union loses nothing by not reaching agreement when the previous contract expires. Retroactivity also allows the union to take full advantage of municipal election campaigns.*[117]

Juris and Feuille cite the case of the New York City patrolmen's contract scheduled to expire in December 1972 as an illustration of retroactivity. The police union and the city did not reach agreement for almost eighteen months; the contract that was finally signed in July 1972 was retroactive in payment of the newly bargained salaries and benefits through the date of expiration of the old contract.[118] Similar events have also taken place in Milwaukee, Hartford, New Haven, and Rochester.[119] It would appear that in some areas, "when the budgetary and bargaining processes conflict, the bargaining process will not necessarily be subordinated to the time constraints of the annual budgetary process."[120]

Four, public jurisdictions are experimenting with a variety of methods to work out their own best solutions to the problem of timing negotiations and budgeting. One such method of experimentation is the long-term contract. If an agreement can be negotiated for a two- or three-year period, this considerably reduces the opportunities for disagreements and stalled negotiations, which can be so disruptive to effective budgeting. In addition, long-term contracts save the government considerable time in having to prepare for bargaining and in having to negotiate.[121] There are other forms of experimentation as well. For example:

> *The New York Board of Education has experimented in this area in three ways; the first year, they bargained before knowing how much money would be appropriated to them. The second year, they bargained after submitting a budget and after the extent of their appropriation became known. This year [1968] they bargained in advance of submitting a budget request, with a view to arriving at a mutually satisfactory estimate of the cost of improved salaries and working conditions.*[122]

It is likely that such experimentation will continue during the embryonic stages of public sector collective bargaining, as government bargainers search for an approach to bargaining that best suits their needs and constraints.

We have examined the importance of timing in order to efficiently incorporate the process of collective bargaining into the budget cycle, and we have reviewed four methods that have been utilized as strategies to facilitate this merger. We will now examine how collective negotiations can influence fiscal planning.

Fiscal Planning and Collective Bargaining

As the previous section suggested, collective bargaining has often been detrimental to fiscal planning from the standpoint of the government manager. The public employer is less free to assign priorities to spending based on his own judgment and values once unionization enters the decision-making process. As Wildman says, "Teacher power exercised in negotiations on salary and other cost items has resulted in significant reassessment of budget priorities and forced boards to make reallocations with definite policy consequences."[123] Higher teacher salaries may force cutbacks in textbook purchases, building maintenance, capital construction, or hiring, to cite only a few examples.[124] Thus, program cutbacks, changes in priorities, increased deficits, or higher taxes may have quite disruptive effects on a rational planning process.

Although such disruption will be inevitable to a certain extent in this transitional stage of public sector bargaining, disruption in this sphere can be minimized by introduction of long-term contracts and the designation of a specific and authoritative bargaining unit for the government.*

Both of these ideas have already been discussed; suffice it to say that the long-term contract can facilitate fiscal planning by adding an element of predictability to contract administration. Joseph Domitrz states it quite simply when he observes, "[The] long-term contract provides the administrator with greater certainty over economic costs than annual negotiations."[125] The designation of a special bargaining team for the government with authority to speak for both the executive and the legislative branches facilitates planning in that all parties can seriously negotiate from authority, and the union is prevented from circumventing this tentative agreement and lobbying for more from the legislature. Consequently, the atmosphere of negotiations is more serious and likely to be more definitive. This means that fiscal planning can be conducted with more certainty after initial compromises are reached.

As a final note on the relationship of collective bargaining and budgeting, the reader should remember that the government employer is more isolated from market pressures than is his private industry counterpart.[126] As a result, government bargainers are often tempted to pass the costs or potential costs of their agreements on to a group not represented in bargaining, i.e., the taxpayer.[127] We should keep in mind, therefore, that when we discuss the importance of collective bargaining on fiscal planning we are discussing its effect on the wise and efficient expenditure of public funds.

Case Study: Collective Bargaining in Memphis

Budgetary Effects of the Sanitation Strike of 1968

Memphis entered into collective bargaining because of the conflict and confrontation of an all out strike—the Sanitation Workers' Strike of 1968. The history of the strike and the facts surrounding the assassination of Dr. Martin Luther King, Jr. are well known and will not be elucidated here. Because of the strike, Local 1733 of the American Federation of State, County, and Municipal Employees became a powerful force in Memphis, Tennessee.

---

* Refer to chapter 2 for discussion of the governmental bargaining unit and the Philadelphia model.

The aspect of the strike most important to this chapter is its impact on the budgetary process of the city. There was difficulty in obtaining data on personnel costs in the Sanitation Department prior to the strike in 1968. Prior to 1968, Sanitation was part of the Public Works Department and no separate accounting of sanitation personnel costs was kept.[128] One effect of the strike on the budget, then, was that the city began keeping detailed records of sanitation costs. This was necessitated in large part by the need for accuracy in dealing with the union representing the sanitation workers. The city would have to know previous years' costs for negotiating purposes and estimating future costs and cost increases in order to plan the budget accurately. Sanitation was thus removed from the Public Works Department and made into a separate department.

The figures in table 3-4 dealing with the Sanitation Department were obtained through personal interviews at Memphis City Hall, as data for the years prior to 1968 had not been published nor presented in any other study. We were unable to obtain cost figures for years prior to 1967 due to the length of time it took for the city's budget personnel to gather and compute the data, coupled with the fact that they were busy working on the upcoming budget. It was indicated, however, that large dollar or percentage increases in wages had not immediately preceded 1967.

That the strike had an impact on the personnel costs of the Sanitation Department is obvious from figures presented in the table. Costs jumped by 17.8 percent from June 1968 to June 1969. Further increases followed but at a decreasing rate. The initial jump and the subsequent increases were products of two factors. First, wages were increased across the board; second, equalization increases were instituted to grant all workers equal pay for equal work. Before the strike, different wage rates were being paid for essentially the same work. Black workers received considerably less than white workers for the same jobs.

The Bargaining Process

In the city of Memphis, salaries, work practices, and fringe benefits for city employees are determined by administrative actions of the mayor, subject to the approval of the city council. The mayor has delegated a great deal of his administrative authority by designating the director of personnel as the chief negotiator for the city. In that capacity, he receives the initial proposals of the employee associations, responds to them, and develops counterproposals prior to the beginning of negotiations.

TABLE 3-4: Memphis Sanitation Personnel Costs

Fiscal Year	Sanitation	Percentage Increase
1967	$5,139,868	——
1968	5,256,082	2.2
1969	6,198,270	17.8
1970	7,119,477	14.8
1971	7,912,470	11.1
1972	8,113,222	5.5
1973	8,939,584	10.1
1974	9,633,753	7.7

In general, this is how the negotiating process is structured to operate in Memphis: The union initiates action by serving notice that it wishes to negotiate. This notice may be in the form of a reopener, as provided for in the existing agreement, or at the termination of an agreement, or it may come from an organization seeking initial recognition. Reopeners are provided for in case either party should desire to modify the existing agreement prior to termination. It must be submitted from sixty to ninety days prior to the anniversary date of the agreement. Reopeners at the termination of the agreement must be submitted ninety days prior to the expiration date of the contract.

The city responds to the initial notice and sets up a first negotiating meeting. At this meeting, union proposals are requested and discussed so that everyone understands them. Subsequent meeting are scheduled; at the second or third meeting, the city presents its proposals. These are not counterproposals but specific issues that the city wants to have changed or altered in the agreement. After this matter is settled, the city presents its counterproposals and the bargaining process actually begins.

In the case of initial recognition of a union the city requests evidence that the union represents a majority of the employees in a specific labor unit. If there is a question as to the appropriateness of a unit, then this matter is discussed in the first meeting. After the unit is established, the procedures follow the pattern set for existing unions: present proposals, city proposals, counterproposals, and bargaining.

The fiscal year for budgetary purposes runs from 1 July to 30 June. Normally, budget hearings are concluded and the tax rate set by mid-May—six weeks prior to 1 July. The negotiating cycle is about a sixty to ninety-day period prior to the negotiation date. The negotiation cycle, however, is not timed to coincide with the budgetary cycle. With police and fire fighters the contracts usually expire and negotiations are completed prior to the setting of the tax rate. But with AFSCME the contract does not expire until 30 June, well after the tax rate has been set.

Negotiating After the Tax Rate Is Set

Sometimes it may be necessary to negotiate an unexpected contract after the tax rate has been set. The decision must then be made of whether the negotiated increase is to be put off until the next fiscal year or whether adjustments are to be made within the present budget to accommodate the increase. The city generally tries to make adjustments within the budget that is already set. While the tax rate sets the level of revenue coming into the city's treasury, the city council and the administration can make changes within expenditures at times other than called for in the budget. Thus, if it were determined that the city needed an additional one million dollars, they would try to find it somewhere within the operating budget and shift money from capital projects to personnel salaries. Also it might be possible to postpone expenditures on a project until later in the year and pick up extra money in this manner.

Setting Fiscal Limits on Negotiated Wages and Benefits

The city is aided in determining fiscal limits in that it generally knows which unions it will be negotiating with and what their demands will be. The city administration presents it budget recommendations to the city council and then sits down with them to work out the fiscal limits on allowances for wage and benefit increases. This takes place during the budgetary process prior to setting the tax rate. The outside limit on the city's ability to pay is ultimately determined by the tax rate, as the bulk of the city's income is from property and sales taxes. There are legal restrictions limiting the amount by which the tax rate can be increased in any single year. That limit determines how much money can be raised in the fiscal year. In some years the mayor and the city council may decide not to increase the tax rate at all. In that case the city can still count on revenue increases due to inflationary pressures on spending, i.e., the sales tax. The city council has the final say on what percentage increases will be allowed for labor contract negotiations within the confines dictated by the tax rate.

Determining Costs

The city performs a detailed costing of all union requests. In the event of a wage increase in the Fire Department, for example, the city will look at total dollars presently being expended within the bargaining unit. That is, the total dollars being paid out in salaries. Then, if a five percent increase is desired, the negotiator could easily see what 5 percent on top of present expenditures would cost the city. The negotiator also knows that a percent increase in salary would be accompanied by an increase in the amount of fringe benefits. That is also costed out. Thus, the negotiator knows what every percentage increase will cost the city in total dollars when he begins negotiating. He knows at each step the cost liability of any increase he may make.

In dealing with AFSCME, increases are costed out on a cents-per-hour basis. So the negotiator knows how much total money each one-cent-per-hour increase will cost.

This detailed costing out of salary increases is extremely useful in preventing budget overruns. It is also useful in that it puts the negotiator in a position where he can present figures to the union representatives. Often union negotiators do not realize how much an increase will mean in total dollars to the city.

In drawing up the budget the city does not specifically earmark a certain sum of money for anticipated personnel cost increases and then designate it as such. To do so would be showing its hand to the union negotiators. As an example of this, in 1972 the Personnel Department submitted its budget proposals with no forecasted wage increases. But it had concealed money in the budget for the negotiating process, and the city council knew where it was. The amount was not, however, telegraphed to the unions on the front end.

Negotiation

Planning is essential in negotiations. The city must be able to deal from a strong, well-prepared and well-informed position. A consequence of improper preparation is the "leap-frog" effect. When this occurs, the first union that negotiates gets the lowest wage package. Subsequent unions, seeing what the previous union got, argue for larger wage increases and get them, with the last union negotiation getting the highest wage settlement.

The city takes precautions to avoid this effect. It generally knows across the board what kind of wage package it is confronting. As stated before, it also usually knows which unions it will be negotiating with and what the union demands will be. A percentage of available funds is set aside for each union. The formulas may differ as to how the unions get the money, e.g., flat dollar-per-month increase or cents-per-hour increase. But the percentage increase for each negotiating unit is about the same.

The Psychology of Negotiating

While cost economics play a considerable role in collective bargaining, of great importance is the psychology of negotiation. The city always has the union proposals first; from there it can deal. Also, the city never puts its final offer on the table in the early negotiating sessions; neither does the union. There is a psychology involved at the bargaining table whereby the union has to be able to show its members and its bargaining committee that it got the city to change from one offer to a higher offer. If the city presented its best offer at the beginning of negotiations and the union bought it, it would be extremely difficult for the union to communicate to its members that it was doing a good job. It would appear that the union came in with a request and then accepted the first offer it could get. So there is a bargaining process by which both parties start out at extreme positions and negotiate to a middle ground.

Conclusion

The economic impact of unionism is significant and the key to the success of the movement. Gains have undoubtedly been achieved in public employment after the introduction of collective bargaining, but the degree to which they can be attributed solely to unionism is unclear and a situational variable. Real gains are the most important, yet the skyrocketing rate of inflation in recent years has made even substantial monetary advances seem inconsequential. In addition, the mounting costs of running government and the higher tax rates implied are serving to toughen the bargaining stance of the public employer and the taxpayer and making the possibility of dramatic gains in compensation and benefits less likely in the immediate future.

This somewhat gloomy analysis should not obscure two very important points, however. One, while the influence of unionism on rates of compensation may be a matter of great debate, this debate is occurring in the academic world and not necessarily among those public employees who are members or potential members. An individual makes a decision to remain in or to join a union on the basis of *perceived* benefits, not on the basis of *actual* benefits. Thus, if unions can continue to get credit for what was termed "apparent" gains, then they are in an excellent position to increase their membership. Two, unions have been dramatically and unquestionably successful in bargaining over working conditions and employee participation in policy making when these factors have been at issue. There is little reason to believe that employees would have achieved a voice in these matters without unionization.

This chapter also reviewed the relationship between collective bargaining and the process of budget preparation. We have examined first the importance of timing negotiations to mesh with the budgetary cycle. We then noted how fiscal planning has been negatively affected by the introduction of public sector unionism. It was suggested, however, that through such devices as long-term contracts, retroactive negotiations, centralized negotiating teams, and legally specified periods of bargaining some of the potential disruptions and confusion could be minimized. The chapter concluded with a case study of bargaining in Memphis and its influence on the city's budgetary process.

Notes to Chapter 3

1. Richard B. Freeman, *Labor Economics* (Englewood Cliffs, N.J.: Prentice-Hall, 1972), p. 73.
2. Ibid., p. 54.
3. Ibid., p. 64.
4. Ibid.
5. Ibid.
6. Harry H. Wellington and Ralph K. Winter, Jr., *The Unions and the Cities* (Washington, D.C.: Brookings Institution, 1971), p. 14.
7. Allan M. Cartter and F. Ray Marshall, *Labor Economics: Wages, Employment and Trade Unionism*, Homewood, Ill: Richard D. Irwin, 1967, p. 256.
8. Ronald G. Ehrenberg, *The Demand for State and Local Employees* (Lexington, Mass.: D.C. Heath and Co., 1972), p. 17.
9. Robert Baird and John H. Landon, "Monopsony in the Market for Public School Teachers," *American Economic Review* 61 (December 1971), p. 967.
10. Roger W. Schmenner, "The Determination of Municipal Employee Wages," *Review of Economics and Statistics* 55 (February 1973), p. 84.
11. Arnold M. Zack, "Meeting the Rising Cost of Public Sector Settlements," *Monthly Labor Review* 96 (May 1973), p. 38.
12. John E. Drotning and David B. Lipsky, "The Influence of Collective Bargaining on Teachers' Salaries in New York State," *Industrial and Labor Relations Review* 27 (October 1973), p. 23.
13. Baird and Landon, op. cit. p. 970.
14. Ibid., p. 967.
15. Drotning and Lipsky, op. cit., p. 29.
16. Wellington and Winter, op. cit., p. 18.
17. Cartter and Marshall, op. cit., p. 282.
18. Wellington and Winter, op. cit., p. 30.
19. Ibid.
20. David Lewin, "Public Employment Relations: Confronting the Issues," *Industrial Relations* 12 (October 1973), p. 315.
21. Wellington and Winter, op. cit., p. 19.
22. Cartter and Marshall, op. cit., p. 231.

23. Baird and Landon, op. cit., p. 967.

24. Ibid.

25. Ibid.

26. Wellington and Winter, op. cit., p. 14.

27. Schmenner, op. cit., p. 84.

28. Walter Goodman, "Why Teachers Are Striking," *Collective Bargaining for Public Employees,* ed. Herbert L. Marx, Jr. (New York: H. W. Wilson, 1969), p. 66. Cited hereafter as Marx.

29. E. S. Willis, "Pension Opportunities and Problems," *Collective Bargaining: Survival in the '70's?* ed. Richard L. Rowan (Philadelphia: Univ. of Pennsylvania Press, 1972), p. 362. Cited hereafter as Rowan.

30. Wesley A. Wildman, "Teachers and Collective Negotiations," *White-Collar Workers,* ed. Albert A. Blum, et al. (New York: Random House, 1971), pp. 148-149, 156. Cited hereafter as Blum, et al.

31. George W. Angell, "Two-Year College Experience," *Faculty Unions and Collective Bargaining,* ed. C. D. Duryea, et al. (San Francisco: Jossey-Bass Inc., Pubs., 1973), pp. 95-96. Cited hereafter as Duryea, et al.

32. Frederick E. Hueppe, "Private University: St. John's," in Duryea, et al., op. cit., pp. 186-87.

33. Hervey A. Juris and Peter Feuille, *Police Unionism: Power and Impact in Public Sector Bargaining* (Lexington, Mass.: D. C. Heath and Co., 1973), p. 114.

34. Goodman in Marx, op. cit., p. 65.

35. Ibid., p. 66.

36. Christopher F. Vagts and Robert B. Stowe, *The Anatomy of a Teacher Strike* (West Nyack, N.Y.: Parker Publishing Co., 1969), pp. 13, 182.

37. Philip A. Grant, Jr., "Unionism in Higher Education," in Marx, op. cit., p. 77.

38. Ibid.

39. Angell in Duryea, et al., op. cit., p. 100.

40. John E. Maher, "Union, Non-union Wage Differentials," *American Economic Review* 46 (June 1956), pp. 336-352.

41. Ibid., p. 337.

42. Belton M. Fleisher, *Labor Economics: Theory and Evidence* (Englewood Cliffs, N.J.: Prentice-Hall, 1972), p. 182.

43. Melvin Lurie, "Government Regulation and Union Power: A Case Study of the Boston Transit Industry," *Journal of Law and Law and Economics* 3 (October 1960), p. 122.

44. Cartter and Marshall, op. cit., p. 357.

45. Paul A. Samuelson, *Economics*, 9th ed. (New York: McGraw-Hill Book Co., 1973), p. 589.

46. Ibid., p. 142.

47. Lurie, op. cit., p. 124.

48. Wildman in Blum, et al., op. cit., p. 145.

49. Maher, op. cit., p. 247.

50. Ibid., p. 347.

51. See Orley Ashenfelter, "The Effect of Unionization on Wages in the Public Sector: The Case of Fire Fighters," *Industrial and Labor Relations Review* 24 (January 1971), pp. 191-202 for a complete discussion of his methodolgy.

52. Ibid., p. 201.

53. Ibid., p. 202.

54. Darold T. Barnum, "Labor Relations in Urban Transit," Rowan, op. cit., p. 373, pp. 275-298. The following account is based on this article unless otherwise noted.

55. U.S., Bureau of Labor Statistics, *Handbook of Labor Statistics 1972* tab. 96, p. 208.

56. Barnum in Rowan, op. cit., p. 297.

57. Lurie, op. cit., p. 131.

58. Barnum in Rowan, op. cit., p. 298.

59. David Lewin, "Aspects of Wage Determination in Local Government," *Public Administration Review*, 34 (March/April 1974), p. 151.

60. Ibid., p. 153.

61. Ibid.

62. A. H. Raskin, "Reflections on Public Sector Bargaining and the Wage-Price Freeze," in Rowan, op. cit., p. 480.

63. Bureau of Labor Statistics, *Handbook 1972*, tab. 121, p. 276 and calculations.

64. Ibid., tab. 103, p. 229.

65. Kenneth P. Mortimer and G. Gregory Lozier, "Contracts of Four-Year Institutions," in Duryea, et al., op. cit., p. 115.

66. Raymond Lee, "Federal Regulations of Wages and Prices," *Municipal Year Book, 1973* (Washington, D.C.: International City Management Association, 1973), p. 107.

67. Correspondence with Ms. Anna Martinez, Employee Relations Officer, Tennessee Valley Authority. For an example of a proposed increase in the public sector that was disallowed, see Lee, op. cit., p. 109.

68. "Who's in Charge? Public Employee Unions Press for a Policy Role; States and Cities Balk," *Wall Street Journal*, 7 September 1972, p. 1.

69. Ibid.

70. Jerry Wurf, "The Future of Fringe Benefits: View from the Union," *Public Management* 55 (October 1973), p. 16.

71. Ibid., p. 17.

72. James L. Caplinger, "The Future of Fringe Benefits: View from the Municipality," *Public Management* 55 (October 1973), p. 20.

73. *Wall Street Journal*, 7 September 1972, p. 1.

74. Ibid., p. 21.

75. Richard R. Nelson, "Collective Bargaining Agreements in the Public Sector," *Monthly Labor Review* 96 (September 1973), p. 76.

76. Sterling D. Spero and John M. Capozzola, *The Urban Community and Its Unionized Bureaucracies* (New York: Dunellen Publishing Co., 1973), p. 223.

77. John A. Hanson, "Fringe Benefits in the Negotiation Process," *Public Management* 55 (October 1973), p. 7.

78. Wurf, op. cit., p. 15.

79. Dana R. Baggett, "Growing Pains in Fringe Benefits: Critical Issues," *Public Management* 55 (October 1973), p. 7.

80. Ibid.

81. Hanson, op. cit., p. 8.

82. Spero and Capozzola, op. cit., p. 223.

83. "Delicate Demands," *Wall Street Journal*, 4 January 1972, p. 1.

84. Hanson, op. cit., p. 8.

85. Derek C. Bok and John T. Dunlop, *Labor and the American Community* (New York: Simon and Schuster, 1970), p. 341.

86. Wildman in Blum, et al., op. cit., pp. 162-63.

87. Ibid.

88. Frank P. Zeidler, "Public Servants as Organized Labor," in Marx, op. cit., p. 12.

89. Goodman in Marx, op. cit., p. 68.

90. Bok and Dunlop, op. cit., pp. 314-15.

91. Willis in Rowan, op. cit., p. 363.

92. Ibid.

93. Juris and Feuille, op. cit., p. 120.

94. Ibid.

95. Raskin in Rowan, op. cit., pp. 477-78.

96. Goodman in Marx, op. cit., p. 66.

97. Wildman in Blum, et al., op. cit., p. 146.

98. Ibid., p. 147.

99. David T. Stanley, with the assistance of Carole L. Cooper, *Managing Local Government Under Union Pressure: Studies of Unionism in Government* (Washington, D.C.: Brookings Institution, 1972), p. 120.

100. Spero and Capozzola, op. cit., p. 216.

101. James A. Maxwell, *Financing State and Local Governments* (Washington, D.C.: Brookings Institution, 1969), p. 128.

102. Spero and Cappozzola, op. cit., p. 216.

103. Maxwell, op. cit., p. 73.

104. Ibid., p. 75.

105. Spero and Cappozzola, op. cit., 216.

106. "City Workers Can't Count on Revenue Sharing to Boost Paychecks," *Wall Street Journal*, 4 September 1973, p. 1.

107. Milton Derber, et al., "Bargaining and Budget Making in Illinois Public Institutions," *Industrial and Labor Relations Review* 27 (October 1973), p. 49.

108. Stanley, op. cit., p. 116.

109. Spero and Cappozzola, op. cit., p. 224.

110. Stanley, op. cit., p. 119.

111. Bok and Dunlop, op. cit., p. 330.

112. Bok and Dunlop, op. cit., p. 330.

113. Neil W. Chamberlain and Donald E. Cullen, *The Labor Sector*, 2nd ed. (New York: McGraw-Hill Book Co., 1971), p. 153.

114. Bok and Dunlop, op. cit., p. 330.

115. James A. Craft, "Public Employee Budget Negotiations: Budget Search and Bargaining Behavior," *Public Personnel Review* 31 (October 1970), p. 245.

116. Juris and Feuille, op. cit., p. 68.

117. Ibid., p. 67.

118. Ibid.

119. Ibid.

120. Juris and Feuille, op. cit., p. 68.

121. Joseph Domitrz, "Collective Bargaining and Public Administration: The Role of Long-Term Contracts," *Collective Bargaining and Public Administration* (Chicago: Public Personnel Association, 1971), pp. 16-17.

122. Daniel H. Kruger and Charles T. Schmidt, Jr., eds., *Collective Bargaining in the Public Service* (New York: Random House, 1969), p. 17.

123. Wildman in Blum et al., op. cit., p. 155.

124. Ibid. See also p. 145.

125. Domitrz, op. cit., p. 19.

126. Barnum in Rowan, op. cit., p. 297.

127. Lurie, op. cit., p. 122.

128. The information for this case study was attained through interviews with elected public officials and career administrative officials of the city of Memphis. These individuals were also helpful in allowing us access to their documents.

Politics of
Collective Bargaining

Part one provided a descriptive framework for collective bargaining in public employment. Part two deals with the political environment of public collective bargaining and how this environment shapes, and is shaped by, public employee unions. The political context of labor-management relations in the public sector governs the way it can and does operate; thus, it is crucial to the understanding of collective bargaining. This part opens with a historical description of labor in politics, looks at labor and collective bargaining as interest group phenomena, and treats the strike as a compelling weapon in interest group politics. The next chapter describes how public policy has shaped the formation and evolution of collective bargaining in this country, with a special emphasis on policy regarding and affecting the strike. The last chapter in this part describes the content and process of public policymaking from a theoretical standpoint and then integrates collective bargaining within the policymaking framework. Thus, collective bargaining is employed as a case study to illustrate the public policy process; and, policy analysis is used to assess the impact of public employee unions on the political arena.

Public Employee Unions and the Interest Group Process

4

Traditionally, the role of organized labor has been to pursue aims of economic self-interest. But, because labor unions operate both in a sociopolitical environment and within a bureaucratic framework, they have influenced public policymaking in both decision-making arenas. As discussed in a subsequent chapter (6), public employee organizations are demanding that bureaucratic elites practice bilateral policymaking through the collective bargaining process. Secondly, public sector unions pursue objectives in the political system by participation in the interest group process. This pursuit of policy objectives by political action strategies has produced mixed policy consequences.

Every demand and support articulated by public unions carries with it a political implication. The employment relationship of public employees is defined by the political and administrative structure; for this reason, events in the political environment have a direct effect on the working life of public employees. Thus, public unions proclaim that they are justified and prudent in attempting to influence these events. The political activities of organized labor serve as an appropriate model of interest group politics and provides for an assessment of the impact of an interest group on public decision making in the American regime.

Unions are faced with several impediments to their political activities. The public images of unions is sometimes an obstacle, especially when surveys indicate that 60 percent of the nonunion public is opposed to union efforts to elect preferred candidates.[1] Other restrictions to their political capabilities include internal union disputes and divisions, inability to present a united front, and disagreement over the political goals of labor. Public employee unions nonetheless pose a formidable political challenge. In the public sector, for example, the political leverage of New York City's 300,000 unionized employees has created intense pressures on city government over a period of time. The pressure has been all the more compelling as the intensity of union demands increase, urged by a growing power capability, and the concomitant management ability to confront these pressures has diminished. The proliferation of collective bargaining relationships in public employment is illustrative of the gains achievable in the political arena when political power is clearly apparent and manifested.

Public and private labor unions play a key role in the American political system. For instance, the voting strength and organizational ability of labor is decisive in Michigan, where the United Auto Workers exercises influence over the Democratic party throughout the state. AFL-CIO, through its political wing, the Committee on Political Education (COPE), urges union members to participate in such electoral activity as voter registration, door-to-door canvassing, and financial contributions. COPE also conducts lobbying activities and disseminates political information to union members and the general public. Even though the official position of AFL-CIO is to take a nonpartisan stance, organized labor has a major policymaking influence upon the hierarchy of the Democratic party on the national level. On the state and local levels, unions maintain an autonomous posture with respect to their granting or withholding of political support; this has given the local unions the flexibility to act as political power brokers. The voting power of the labor unions in large municipalities has provided them with a leverage in deciding elections. For example, labor's support of Mayor James Tate in Philadelphia in the 1967 mayoral election contributed to his victory and resulted in a number of subsequent bargaining gains for municipal unions of this city.

Public employee unions employ a variety of tactics in pursuit of their bargaining goals. Some of these tactics fall within the scope of traditional labor-management negotiations; many of the tactics are clearly political activities. The political alternatives to collective bargaining include advancing their collective interests before legislative bodies and a political executive while negotiating at the bargaining table, involvement in electoral politics at all levels, attempting to influence judicial decisions, and attempting to influence public opinion. Labor unions have also promoted and supported progressive social welfare and prolabor policies by government.

The political capability of public employees takes a variety of forms. Organized employee groups have acted as electoral "machines." For example, the AFSCME coalition in Philadelphia and the sanitation and transit workers' unions in New York City operate much like the traditional political machines associated with an earlier era. Unions, providing a bloc vote, campaign workers, and money are a very attractive resource for any aspiring candidate. In order to get the support of organized labor, a candidate must come before it as a supplicant, and offer something in exchange for its support.

The threat of a strike is a potent political weapon. For example, the late Michael Quill, long-time president of the Transit Workers' Union in New York City, often threatened a mass strike by TWU to "bring the city to a grinding halt" in order to gain his bargaining demands. The strike is the ultimate political weapon of public employee unions because of the political impact caused by the denial of essential, monopoly services. Public employee organizations also rely on their association with the larger labor movement to help gain their objectives; for instance, a Central Labor Council of AFL-CIO will support the demands of an AFSCME local in collective bargaining. Finally, bargaining advantages can be obtained by exploiting the cleavages between branches of government as a result of the separation of governmental powers, a characteristic of the American regime. The experience of lobbying for favorable legislation and rulings shows the unions' sensitivity to the locus of administrative and legislative power and their ability to substitute lobbying for the bargaining process.

Development of Labor's Political Consciousness

Public and private sector unions generally choose the alternative for political action that results in the largest anticipated benefits for the lowest anticipated costs. The labor movement has always had five basic alternatives: abstinence from political participation, participation in labor-oriented issues only, participation in all sociopolitical issues, the formation of a labor party, and radical syndicalism. All of these political alternatives have been pursued at one time or another by any number of labor groups. The general movement, however, has seen an evolvement from a pattern of political nonparticipation to participation in labor-related issues only, to an active participation in all issues. The other political alternatives have been confined to splinter groups in the movement; attempts to form a labor party were limited to relatively small socialist and working-class groups, and radical syndicalism was advocated by the International Workers of the World (IWW).

The early history of the American labor movement is associated with an advocacy of reform and socioeconomic panaceas, such as land reform, antimonopoly, bank reform, and producers' cooperatives, among others. During these years the labor movement was weak, unsure of its identity, and confused. Not until the 1880s, with the formation of the American Federation of Labor (AFL), when it was captured by pragmatic leaders of the order of Samuel Gompers and Adolph Strasser, was it to find itself.

The intellectual and social development of American society mirrored the political development of the early labor movement. J. David Greenstone sees the dominance of liberal democratic values, the diffusion of property ownership, and the lack of class solidarity as reasons for the pluralistic development of labor's political orientation in the late nineteenth century.[3] A popular belief in upward mobility and equality encouraged most workers to aspire to the middle class and to eschew the Marxian dogma of social stratification. The central aim of the dominant groups in the American labor movement has been to achieve for its members an "American standard of living." They have sought not the overturn of the bourgeoisie, but the restructuring of the proletariat into a new bourgeoisie. "Middle-class respectability" was what most labor leaders and most rank-and-file workers have desired. Hence, the organized labor movement in America, for the most part, has been directed toward "bourgeois" goals.

The Protestant ethic and assertions of rugged individualism of the capitalist entrepreneurs during the early period of the labor movement's development contributed to an atmosphere of hostility toward labor organizations. The violence surrounding early strikes are indicative of the lengths employers would pursue to prevent the organizing of workers. Thus, the early unions, motivated by economic goals, were preoccupied with the need to attain organizational stability and to survive in the face of employer hostility. Their desire to create a leverage on economic issues did not include the use of direct political activity nor of a mass assertion of class power. Consequently, this orientation conflicted with the broader concerns of socialist groups that called for the establishment of a working class political party.

The Knights of Labor attempted to unite the divided and self-interested American workers by an appeal to a "fraternity of workers" and by a vague endorsement of political action in pursuit of economic goals. The organization supported the populist Greenback party in its attempts at currency reform and actively supported Henry George and his "single tax" concepts in New York City's mayoral campaign of 1886. The Knights, however, suffered from a divided and weak leadership and from their reluctance to endorse the strike as a weapon. The failings of their leadership, the ineffectiveness of the organization's socialist appeals, and the willingness to embrace all workers within the rubric of class solidarity led to the demise of the Knights in the late 1880s.

Labor's real contribution to interest group politics began with the development of the American Federation of Labor. AFL began as an exclusively craft-union organization in pursuit of narrow economic and craft goals. Mindful of the hostility toward unions and labor's lack of political leverage at this time, AFL had organizational survival as its major goal. The organization's political posture, as advocated by its leader Samuel Gompers, was a modified noninterventionist alternative. There was the expressed desire for minimum governmental interference in labor affairs and a policy of nonpartisanship and nonendorsement in political campaigns. Union members were free to take political initiatives on their own. However, the organization's objective of survival necessitated some political activity. AFL openly opposed government programs with a potential for lessening the tie of an individual member to his union. The organization thus opposed such programs as medical insurance, minimum wage and maximum working hours laws, and unemployment compensation, because it saw them as having a deleterious effect. The organization avoided partisan commitment; instead, it pursued a policy of "reward your friends and punish your enemies." This practice was facilitated by publishing the voting records of legislators on bills of special interest to labor. The political attitude of AFL, at the time, reflected only the position of a small segment of the movement—the craft unions—and it was designed to work for the organization's self-perpetuation.

Samuel Gompers and AFL

It is unclear who first arrived at an explicit formulation of "pure and simple trade unionism."[4] But, it is a term and an orientation generally associated with Samuel Gompers, the most prominent personality of the early American labor movement. Labor historian Philip Taft had this to say about him:

> No man in his time or since has had his pervasive influence upon organized labor in North America. . . . The directions in which he led have not been reversed, even though the movement has grown in size and influence.[5]

Any study of the American labor movement must therefore be anchored around this man, who guided it from nineteenth century reformism into the twentieth century.

Gompers undoubtedly owed a great deal to his youthful encounters with socialists and intellectuals, and particularly to Karl Malcom Ferdinand Laurell. Gompers recognized the influence of Laurell and his labor philosophy in these remarks:

> His kindly talks and warnings did more to shape my mind upon the labor movement than any other single influence. The principles of trade unionism that I learned then remained the basis upon which my policies and methods were determined in the years

*to come. I have always felt that he watched over me with chasten-
ing criticism, for he wanted to save me from allowing my sentiment
and emotion to be perverted into the channel of "radicalism."*[6]

It was Laurell who instructed Gompers to attend, listen, and understand the meetings of the socialist movements, but not to join the
party. Gompers, looking for something on which to base a constructive
program, sought out Laurell, who promptly translated and interpreted
the *Communist Manifesto* paragraph by paragraph. After a crash self-
taught course in German, Gompers read the works of Marx, Engels,
and Lassalle, among others. The young Gompers imbued with pie-in-
the-sky notions from his readings would periodically be deflated with
Laurell's caveat, "Study your union card, Sam, and if the idea doesn't
square with that, it ain't true." He was soon to formulate the concept
of the primacy of the trade union as the immediate and practical
agency which would bring wage-earners a better life.

Gompers learned early about the counterproductivity of radical
tactics. The Panic of 1873 marked the beginning of his experiences
with financial crises. A mass meeting of workingmen was planned for
Tompkins Square in New York City on 13 January 1874; the mayor
even promised to address the meeting. However, a short time before the
event was to occur, a group of radicals, associated with the sponsor-
ship of the meeting, made revolutionary speeches and issued revolutionary circulars, which brought a great deal of press coverage. Fearing
an uprising, the city issued an order demanding the return of the permit
for the meeting. However, the organizers of the meeting failed to notify
the workers about the cancellation and they assembled the following
day in the square. Mounted policemen greeted the marchers with a
billy club charge; hundreds were injured. A wave of repression swept
the city. Gompers, who witnessed the "orgy of brutality," was convinced of the futility of political radicalism and the danger of entrust-
ing the direction of the labor movement to intellectuals:

*As the fundamentals came to me, they became guideposts for
my understanding of the labor movement for years to come. I
saw how professions of radicalism and sensationalism concentrated all the forces of organized society against a labor movement and nullified in advance normal, necessary activity. I saw
that leadership in the labor movement could be safely entrusted
only to those into whose hearts and minds had been woven the
experiences of earning their bread by daily labor. I saw that
betterment for workingmen must come primarily through workingmen. I saw the danger of entangling alliance with intellectuals
who did not understand that to experiment with the labor movement was to experiment with human life.*[7]

It was not that Gompers universally condemned radicalism, but he believed that conditions in the United States neither warranted nor necessitated it. He once said that in the United States he was a trade unionist, but in Germany he would be a socialist, while in Russia he would be a revolutionary.[8] Because of this country's safeguards for free association, free speech, free assemblage, and a free press, the American labor movement had the opportunity for evolution rather than revolution.

Although Gompers and AFL avoided political radicalism and had "no ultimate ends," they did fight for immediate goals. These were "realistic," they could be obtained in a few years, and they did not imperil the organization as a whole:

> *The primary essential in our mission has been the protection of the wage-workers, now; to increase his wages; to cut hours off the long workday, which was killing him; to improve the safety and the sanitary conditions of the work-shop; to free him from the tyrannies, petty or otherwise, which serve to make his existence a slavery. These, in the nature of things, I repeat, were and are the primary objects of trade unionism.*[9]

These objectives may have been "bread crumbs" from the tables of capitalists, but these crumbs were more than what the radical movements were able to realize in this country. Implicitly, the decision was the acceptance of the capitalist system and the desire to work within it in order to promote and protect the interests of the workers. This is what distinguished the philosophy of Gompers and AFL from the labor movements that preceded them. Gompers and AFL did not oppose the inevitable—industrialization and the concomitant changes in the relationships of production.

The immediate workplace goals sought by AFL were to be obtained by use of the trade union. But what of political action? In the early 1870s Gompers and the cigarmakers' union zeroed in on the evils of poor housing, specifically on the question of use of tenements as workplaces and the related public health problems. Attempts to bring about appropriate federal legislation were blocked by the large tenement lobby in Washington. After waging a public education campaign, which included detailed reports on the various tenements published serially in an ethnic newspaper, efforts were focused on the New York State Legislature and on supporting legislators favorable to their cause. The cigarmakers saw the importance of having men in sympathy with their tenement legislation elected to office and were successful to the extent of having three trade unionists elected to the assembly. Their efforts were rewarded with the enactment of the law they were seeking; however, the courts subsequently found the law unconstitutional. A revised bill was drafted, introduced, and enacted in May 1884. In October the State Supreme Court declared the second enactment null and void. These experiences caused Gompers to charter a new course of action:

> *After the Appeal Court declared against the principle of the law, we talked over the possibilities of further legislative action and decided to concentrate on organization work. Through our trade unions we harassed the manufacturers by strikes and agitation until they were convinced that we did not intend to stop until we gained our point and that it would be less costly for them to abandon the tenement manufacturing system and carry on the industry in factories under decent conditions. Thus, we accomplished through economic power what we had failed to achieve through legislation.*[10]

Gompers now believed that the workers must be taught to rely on safeguarding their interests nearly exclusively through their trade unions. Realizing that what government can give, it can also take away, he now simply wanted the labor movement to be left unhampered by government. In the heyday of laissez-faire this was not only a pragmatic attitude but a necessary one; economic problems could be best dealt with by an economic organization. Workers and employers could jointly determine and enforce their own standards through collective bargaining. The success of these methods were guaranteed because they represented fundamental American values—individualism and distrust of government. Gomper's concept of voluntarism—the idea that it is better to do things for yourself than have the government do them for you—was an embodiment of these values.

Only legislation of a negative type was desired, since the objectives of labor were to be achieved by strong and efficiently managed trade unions bargaining with employers in a businesslike manner. Negative legislation would be legislation to restrain the courts in their indiscriminate suppression of the boycott and strike, and in other interference with the legitimate activities of unions.

The limited political goals meant that it would be unnecessary to develop an independent political labor party to represent workers in the political process. The trade union was to be the organization of the workingmen. But there were other concerns too:

> *An independent political labor party becomes either radical, so-called, or else reactionary, but it is primarily devoted to one thing and that is vote-getting. Every sail is trimmed to the getting of votes. The question of the conditions of labor, the question of the standards of labor, the question of the struggles and the sacrifices of labor, to bring light into the lives and the work of the toilers—all that is subordinated to the one consideration of*

votes for the party. . . . The organization of a political labor party would simply mean the dividing of the activities and allegiance of the men and women of labor between two bodies, such as would often come in conflict.[11]

A political party or government concerned with the protection of the workers by labor and social reform legislation would only introduce factors that would entice the workers from the union. A separate political party would constitute a rival organization striving for the loyalty of the workers; this could prove destructive to the interests of labor. Nor would an independent political labor party be representative of the interests of labor, since its primary goal would be vote-getting. The interests of workingmen would be compromised in the exchange.

The negative approach to politics did not mean an absolute ban on politics. Recognizing that some interest in politics was inevitable because of the power of government over the life of the people, an aloof, but polite, strategy of "rewarding friends and punishing enemies," was adopted. Significant efforts were made to affect public policy, elect representatives who embraced the negative political philosophy, and unseat those who did not. In 1906, Congressman Charles E. Littlefield of Maine, a labor opponent and a member of the Judiciary Committee, experienced the punishment of labor. Gompers collected a small campaign fund and spearheaded an effort to unseat him. Littlefield was returned to the House with a greatly reduced majority only after national leaders such as Secretary of War Taft, Senator Beveridge, Senator Lodge, Speaker Cannon, and President Roosevelt came to his aid.[12] The nonpartisan approach of "rewarding friends and punishing enemies" has been maintained up to recent years. When Woodrow Wilson became president in 1912 with the support of AFL, its position was slightly modified; organized labor has since then been closely linked to the Democratic party.

Various unions brought together in a loose federation formed AFL. Organization along craft lines (organization of workers according to their occupational functions, e.g., carpenters, brick masons, etc.) was the natural outgrowth of nineteenth-century experience. Craft unionism seemed the most logical approach to the problem of organizing workers since skilled craftsmen predominated over general factory workers in this period (in terms of numbers and prestige). Also, by fusing the skills and abilities of a single craft into a union, a measure of job monopoly and market strength could be maintained.

The pragmatism of AFL allowed for the autonomy of craft union locals. The member unions were left free to pursue their particular interests. Problems with the earlier centralized Knights of Labor caused the unions to be jealous of their sovereignty.[13] Strikes, boycotts, and picketing were the proper concerns of member unions, while AFL devoted its time and money to organizational campaigns, issued appeals for financial support of strikes, provided experienced negotiators to assist locals, and served as a clearinghouse of information. Gompers explained that previous efforts at unifying labor had failed because of:

> *the non-recognition on the part of all who have hitherto attempted it of the principle of autonomy, or the right of the several bodies composing the organization to self-government. The American Federation of Labor avoids the fatal rock upon which all previous attempts to affect the unity of the working class have split, by leaving to each body or affiliated organizations the complete management of its own affairs, especially its own particular trade affairs.* [14]

The words of Samuel Gompers define what has come to be the majority position of the American trade union movement. It has been a movement that, for the most part, has restricted its parameters to advancing the day-to-day interests of its members, that has recognized the trade union as the legitimate workingman's organization, that has eschewed any rigid ideological position, that has denied any interest in overthrowing the existing economic order, that has decided against political action as its primary method, and that has asked the government only to be left alone. These characteristics are not wholly absent from the European labor movements, but the dominance and combination of these characteristics in the United States represent a uniquely American brand of trade unionism.

Many students of the American labor movement have attempted to provide explanations of this uniqueness. Inevitably, these explanations are responses to the question: Why have the European-type politically grounded left-wing trade unions failed in the United States? *Prima facie* the answer is simply that the European-type trade unions have failed because this is not Europe, but the United States. Although simplistic, it is a good starting point. Seymour Martin Lipset addresses himself to the question: How has the American social order shaped the American labor movement? Lipset identifies two fundamental American values—equality and achievement—that exclude a class-consciousness, emphasize immediate material goals, and encourage militant tactics. He points out the social basis of American pragmatism in this remark:

> *The stress on equality and achievement in American society has meant that Americans are much more likely to be concerned with the achievement of approved ends, particularly pecuniary success —than with the use of appropriate means—the behavior considered appropriate to a given position or status. In a country which stresses success above all, men are led to feel that the most*

*important thing is to win the game, regardless of the methods
employed in doing so. American culture applies the norms of
a completely competitive society to everyone.*[15]

There are many other explanations of the American labor movement, such as the flexibility of the two-party system or the generally
high wages in the American economy. John M. Laslett, a well-known
labor historian, however, believes that the reasons are more complex.
He suggests that the more conservative unions pursued policies within
the trade union itself that proved more successful than the socialist
unions. The internal policies that contributed to the success of the more
conservative unions (such as AFL unions) were high dues, a large
financial reserve, an extensive benefit system, a strong central union
control, and the use of the strike weapon. The absence of these internal policies in the socialist unions contributed to their demise. The
socialist unions, based on the European union model, kept dues low,
did not maintain a large financial reserve, thought strong union control
was undemocratic, and participated in partisan politics. Laslett believes
that as a result the interests of the workingmen were better served by
the more conservative unions.[16]

Another labor historian, Selig Perlman, in his book, *A Theory of the
Labor Movement*, argues that the failure of the socialists was due to the
inability of the intelligentsia to secure control of the movement. On the
continent of Europe, Perlman argues, the intellectuals succeeded in
establishing an alliance between themselves and the proletarian leaders
of the labor movement. Perlman believes that without such an alliance
there can be no successful socialist movement.[17] Richard Hofstader, in
his book, *Anti-Intellectualism in American Life*, concurs that there has
been an absence of intellectual leadership, if not outright hostility toward intellectuals, in the American labor movement. He also points
out that the feeling was mutual, for intellectuals were "estranged from
labor leaders like Gompers because their expectations . . . were altogether different. The intellectuals tended to look upon the labor movement as a means to a larger end—to socialism or some other kind of
social reconstruction."[18]

Radical Unions

The literature attempting to explain the uniqueness of the American
labor movement does not provide a proper perspective. A broadly
based movement in opposition to the philosophy of "pure and simple
trade unionism" did exist before, during, and shortly after the First
World War. For purposes of expediency the opposition unions will be
termed *radical*. They espoused a wide range of ideologies ranging from
evolutionary socialism to anarcho-syndicalism. The socialists controlled

many important unions and held approximately one third of the vote at AFL conventions. They were quite a vocal and active group and commanded a greater influence than their numbers would indicate. The multiplicity of factions, perpetual schisms, and the ephemeral existence of many of these groups make classification difficult and a continuous tracing of their evolutionary development almost impossible. For the purpose of classification, the socialists can be broken into two groups:

> One group favored boring from within; the other sponsored dual unionism. One faction believed in opportunistic and evolutionary methods; the other was equally firm in its opinion that drastic and revolutionary procedure was the more essential. One element favored purely economic action as a means of furthering the radical cause; the other taught that economic and political action must be correlated.[19]

However different they were in their means, they both agreed that "pure and simple trade unionism" had to go.

Probably the two men most representative of the "dual unionists" were Daniel De Leon and William Haywood. De Leon, a graduate of Columbia Law School, first became involved with the labor movement in the George campaign in 1886. After failing to bring socialism to the Knights of Labor and AFL he formed the Socialist Trade and Labor Alliance in 1895. Although the alliance proved to be a failure, it was here that his labor philosophy began to crystallize. He opposed the policy of "boring from within," thinking coordinated economic and political fronts were the proper course. Later, as a member of the International Workers of the World (IWW), it was this emphasis on political action that got him expelled from the union he helped establish. His most identifying feature was his invective attacks against "stop-gap reforms and non-revolutionary leaders."[20]

For a number of years De Leon's failure discouraged other dual unionists. However, in 1905, another attempt at "smashing from without" AFL came in the form of the International Workers of the World. William D. Haywood can be considered as a representative theorist of IWW-ism as well as dual unionism in general. He advocated control of society by a large industrial union that would have several subdivisions. Each subdivision would control a major sector of the economy. The road to this syndicalist society was not by way of nationalization, as some thought, but by way of the general strike and direct action. This demonstrates the antipolitical bias of Haywood's class-conscious, revolutionary industrial unionism.[21]

The International Workers of the World (called Wobblies), a textbook example of a dual union, sought to organize workers into industrial unions as opposed to craft unions. Craft unions, it was thought,

Part II: Politics of Collective Bargaining

made solidarity impossible because related crafts that continue to work when men of an allied trade were on strike often facilitated the breaking of that strike. The craft idea was also thought wrong because it created a kind of "union snobbery" by separating the skilled from the unskilled. At the opening IWW convention, it was stated that:

> a movement to fulfill these conditions must consist of one great industrial union embracing all industries, providing for craft autonomy locally, industrial autonomy internationally, and working-class unity generally.[22]

Only by breaking through the craft lines and organizing a great industrial union could the workers present an effective united front in the class struggle.

Rejecting the AFL belief that the worker must improve his lot within the system of capitalism, the Wobblies committed themselves instead to revolutionary socialism. The preamble to their constitution asserted that "the working and employing class have nothing in common. Between these two classes, a struggle must go on until all the toilers come together . . . and take hold of that which they produce by their labor through an economic organization of the working class." It went on to say, "Instead of the conservative motto, 'A fair day's wage for a fair day's work,' we must inscribe on our banner the revolutionary watchword, 'Abolition of the wage system.' It is the historic mission of the working class to do away with capitalism."[23]

This overthrow of capitalism was to be sought solely through direct action tactics, which would increase the class-consciousness of the workers, their sense of power, and their solidarity. The general strike was viewed as the most effective final weapon against capitalism. IWW disapproved of trade agreements with employers because this would mean abandoning the right to strike at any time or on any occasion. Other tactics emphasized by IWW were more revolutionary in nature. They included sabotage, complete disregard for the law, and violence—all of which were accepted as a necessary phase of the labor struggle.[24]

These methods of action were in complete accordance with the Wobblies' syndicalist philosophy, since they considered the capitalist system to be a heartless exploitation of the worker, and thought that all laws and institutions were the creation of the capitalist class to preserve its status. IWW ideology was in agreement with the revolutionary movement of syndicalism, which attempted to use labor unions to overthrow the state and capitalism by violence. Syndicalists, adopting many Marxist principles, also viewed the labor unions as the backbone of the future society. They were opposed to participation in democratic elections and to attaining power through the democratic process. Syndicalists were also influenced by anarchists in believing that the future society should dispense with the state and with every political institution (hence, anarcho-syndicalism). They envisaged a society in which each industry would be managed by its workers, forming so-called syndicates; these syndicates would work together harmoniously without any external compulsion. However, it should be pointed out that the philosophy of IWW, especially during its formative years, was an indigenous product of this country. The French influence came only later in the movement and was confined to the adoption of a few French words such as *sabotage* and *la grève perlée* for tactics already existing in practice.[25]

Max Hayes and Victor Berger were two socialists who opted for the method of "boring from within." Along with many other socialists they advocated a moderate evolutionary pace in the economic and political fields rather than revolutionary bursts. Since the Socialist Labor party was committed to dual unions such as De Leon's Social Trade and Labor Alliance, they founded the Socialist party in 1901. All sorts of methods were utilized to "bore from within." They attempted to elect socialists to offices in AFL and its affiliated unions. There they tried to secure resolutions and endorsements consistent with their socialist principles. Among these were endorsement of social-ism, commitment to political action, socialization of industry, advocacy of government ownership, social insurance, short-hour legislation, and other reform legislation.[26]

Twentieth-Century Unionism: AFL and CIO

Pragmatism is a method of testing for truth. An idea works and is useful if the idea has consequences for human behavior, and if the consequences for human behavior are successful in meeting the problems of living. Consequently, pragmatism implies a good deal of adaptability and flexibility. It shuns ideology. By the 1930s the pragmatic nineteenth-century "pure and simple trade unionism" of Gompers required modifications if it was to remain a pragmatic philosophy for labor. Changes in the environment necessitated that philosophical and institutional changes be made in the labor movement. AFL began to change early. At the turn of the century, AFL began to expand its influence and move slowly toward the second political alternative—participation only on labor issues. Gompers became a member of and expressed the labor view in the National Civic Federation. AFL presented a labor "bill of grievances" to the President and Congress in 1906. Gompers chose to associate himself with the progressive move-ment and, as AFL sought to enlarge its political role, the federation supported the progressive legislation of the Woodrow Wilson Administration. Gompers personally endorsed Wilson in his 1916 reelection campaign. One of the highlights of labor's political efforts before the New Deal was the full support given the third party effort of Robert La Follette in 1924. When management hostility increased and membership contracted during the twenties, AFL retreated to the voluntarist banner again, opposing unemployment compensation in 1929 because it threatened member loyalty to AFL.

The development of mass industries had created new labor conditions that required new methods of organization. The member unions of AFL were for the most part organized on a craft basis. However, the number of skilled workers in industry was declining relative to unskilled workers. With the introduction of the assembly line, an ever-increasing number of the workers were unskilled. Also, unity was of the essence because these mass industries were dominated by very powerful capitalists who were determined to be free of any troublesome labor unions.

The New Deal Administration of Franklin Delano Roosevelt marked a revolution in the American labor movement as well as a revolution in American government. The relationship of labor vis-à-vis government was fundamentally reordered. The Great Depression took a heavy toll on labor unions. Union membership declined precipitously and most unions were reduced to penury because of the loss of union dues. The Roosevelt Administration, cognizant of the plight of labor, enacted legislation which it hoped would make labor a viable partner in a balanced economy of business, government, and labor. The New Deal labor legislation included five general areas: relief of unemployment, better wages and reduction of working hours, abolition of child labor, social security, and government recognition of collective bargaining.[27] An unofficial alliance between the labor movement and the Democratic party came about because the unions had no where else to go. The Democrats were accepted because they were the least hostile to union demands. The influx of industrial workers, the beginning of the Great Depression, and the passage of prolabor legislation under the Roosevelt Administration in the thirties solidified labor's partnership with the Democrats. The receptiveness of Franklin Roosevelt to labor demands and the New Deal programs made organized labor the cornerstone of the Roosevelt electoral coalitions.

Two environmental changes—the development of mass industries and the New Deal coalition—brought about corresponding changes in the philosophy and constitution of the American labor movement. These changes were manifested in the great labor schism of 1936 and the rise of the Congress of Industrial Organizations (CIO). The schism occurred because of disagreement between the old line labor leaders, who advocated organization on a craft basis, and the industrial labor leaders, who advocated organization on an industry-wide basis. Moreover, the heterogeneity of the labor movement and the resulting awakening of a class consciousness among industrial workers also contributed to the schism.

Once organized, CIO took a somewhat different attitude toward political action. Recognizing favorable changes in the political environment, it took the more active role of direct political action. CIO, a pragmatic organization, accepted the traditional American political strategy of nonpartisan political action, but went further than the "reward your friends and punish your enemies" philosophy of Gompers. Undeterred by the long tradition of negative politics in AFL, these younger labor leaders had fewer qualms about mass action and politics. CIO was active in the Non-Partisan League, which supported the election of candidates sympathetic to the cause of labor irrespective of party.[28]

CIO became the dominant force in the Roosevelt coalition between 1940 and 1944. It established the Political Action Committee in 1943 as a continuing political action and education organization for industrial unions. PAC and CIO began to support social welfare and civil rights legislation after World War II. For example, the CIO influence was largely responsible for the passage of the famous civil rights plank at the 1948 Democratic convention. This was an indication of the evolution of labor to its third alternative—participation on all issues. The Communist influence within CIO was largely purged by the 1948 presidential campaign, when AFL and CIO jointly endorsed the Democratic candidate, Harry Truman, and by the anti-Communist atmosphere of the Alger Hiss case and McCarthyism. AFL set up a counterpart to PAC, the Labor League for Political Education, to motivate political action and organize opposition to the Taft-Hartley Act. The increasing labor activism was illustrated by the joint AFL-CIO unsuccessful effort to defeat conservative Ohio Senator Robert Taft in 1950. The passage of the Taft-Hartley Act and the proliferation of right-to-work laws showed organized labor that it had a large stake in the political process.

In 1955 the two houses of labor consummated a merger with the formation of the American Federation of Labor and the Congress of Industrial Organizations (AFL-CIO). Also, the Committee on Political Education (COPE) was formed. Its mission was to ensure sound political education for its members. This was to be accomplished by encouraging workers to register and vote for the candidate most favorable to the labor cause. It plays an active role in federal, state, and local elections. With the formation of a consolidated federation, both groups had to compromise on their views on political activism. In practice, the federation joins with liberal Democrats to gain electoral majorities.[29]

Politicization of Public Employee Unions

Historically, public employees have been legally limited in their political activities by "gag" orders, the Hatch Act, and civil service regulations and rulings. But, over the years, public sector unions have steadily increased their political activism. Postal unions have long practiced supporting and withholding support from political candidates as well as making intense lobbying efforts before Congress. Municipal employee unions use their electoral power as a leverage over elected officials and as a political alternative to the collective bargaining process. AFSCME has long realized its members' stake in the political process and has encouraged their participation in elections and lobbying. In many cities, coalitions of municipal unions contend for political dominance in the community.

Transit Workers' Union of New York City

The experience of the Transit Workers' Union in New York City highlights the extent of participation by labor movement in the political process. The founder and leader of TWU, Michael Quill, immigrated to the United States from Ireland, where he had been involved in several radical movements in the twenties, including the Irish Republican Army. Quill began to work in the New York subways, which were privately owned and where management provided the employees with company unions. The young immigrant, shortly thereafter, opportunistically joined with communist organizer John Santo in organizing the transit workers. The leadership of the newly formed TWU then urged the city to purchase the entire transit system, and affiliated with CIO in 1936. Using his TWU organizational skill and union manpower, Quill was elected to the New York City Council in 1938. He managed to use the strike threat to pressure the city to buy the transit system and gave political support to Mayors LaGuardia, O'Dwyer, and Impellitteri, according to their degrees of responsiveness to TWU demands.

Quill, possessing a keen ability to recognize political realities, purged the union of its communist association in 1948. TWU gave its support to the prolabor candidate, Robert Wagner, in the election for mayor in 1953, in exchange for exclusive bargaining rights for the union with the Transit Authority. Quill was also influential in the New York Democratic party and in the government of CIO where he met some of his greatest challenges, through occasional and unsuccessful internal union disputes over his authority.

Mike Quill's greatest political skill, however, lay in his ability to exploit the collective bargaining process. The public and its officials became familiar with the routine of TWU demands for large pay raises and expanded fringe benefits and its threats to strike and destroy the city's transit system if the requests were not granted. To retain the backing of TWU and other municipal unions, Mayor Wagner established a "private" bargaining relationship with Quill, thereby continuing to enjoy his support and preventing a major transit strike. Public negotiators knew that behind Quill's charm and flair for publicity was the power of a superbly organized union.

The 1966 New York transit strike illustrates the degree of power of TWU in municipal politics. John Lindsay, who was to become mayor on 1 January 1966, would not agree to a forty million dollar wage package privately negotiated by Quill and Mayor Wagner because he was determined not to appease the union nor to allow it to dictate bargaining terms. Quill, angry over Lindsay's attempt to establish open bargaining procedures and determined to test the will of the new mayor, called a strike for the first of the year, thus, employing the tactic he had avoided for years. The personality clash between Quill and Lindsay (Quill said, "My men understand Yale locks, not Yale men.") resulted in the public's suffering a prolonged and bitter strike of the city's transit workers. During the strike, Quill alternated between the role of a martyr and a militant. His response to an injunction issued against the strike was, "Let the judge drop dead in his robes."[31] The melodrama ended with a highly successful settlement for TWU despite the jailing and death of Mike Quill.

The forty-year experience of TWU shows that public employee unions have a significant impact on the political process. A. H. Raskin feels that in New York City the political experiences of TWU parallels those of Tammany Hall. In both cases, immigrants were brought into the political system and given a sense of participation in the system in exchange for cooperating with leaders who "had their best interests at heart." In both cases, their political leverage has been decisive. Winning candidates now have to receive the support of a coalition of municipal unions, instead of relying on a traditional partronage-based machine.[32]

Pros and Cons of Political Involvement by Public Employees

Restrictions on the political activity of civil servants came in response to the abuses of the patronage system, whose main criterion for government employment was service to the party or the political machine. The job security of public employees was directly tied to the fortunes of the party or the political machine of which they were an intregal part. The reform movement in public personnel administration promoted merit and political neutrality in the civil service system. The

1883 Pendleton Act established the federal merit system, in which civil servants were to be hired because of their competence for the job and not because of their political affiliation. Thus, the first civil service regulations were sensitive to the relationship of public workers and politics.

There are several arguments for the political neutrality of civil servants. Political neutrality seeks to insure that public workers will render governmental services fairly and impartially to all citizens, regardless of the political affiliation of those citizens. "Shakedowns" of public employees by political parties for political contributions are to be prevented, and these employees should serve all public officials with loyalty and in the public interest. Restrictions on running for office, campaign activity, party activity and membership, and political contributions are designed to prevent potential conflicts of interest and the compromising of the impartiality and integrity of the public job.

Glenn Stahl poses the question, "Where does protection of the employee's freedom of speech reach the point where the supposed agents of government are undercutting the responsibilities they swore to uphold?"[33] The role of policy development, it is asserted, should be a function that is free from internal political conflict. Other cited advantages of restricted political activity include the prevention of political coercion, the prevention of civil servants acting as agents for political leaders, and the insurance of impartiality in government contracts and employee compensation.

Arguments on the disadvantages of political restrictions center on the political rights of public employees. The denial of the right to full political participation to a group of citizens necessarily relegates them to a second-class citizenship by undercutting their ability to assert their constitutional rights. Even though public employees can vote, privately state their convictions on public issues, petition the government for grievances, and communicate with government officials, they cannot fully participate in a process that will have as some of its consequences the nature and performance of their jobs. It is argued that the civil service has become so professionalized and specialized that direct political action will not necessarily compromise the integrity and impartiality of civil servants. Restrictions have been more stringently applied to the lower levels of the civil service while upper-level career people and political appointees are allowed more freedom in political action. The argument has also been advanced that if a strong interest group of public employees is to be restricted from the political process, then other strong interest groups should be restricted as well. Moreover, restrictions reinforce the notion that politics is dirty, by holding that public employees would be corrupted by joining the process.

The legal framework for political restrictions on public employees is based on a philosophic principle and on an idealistic conception of an administrative class. Governmental sovereignty has been the rationale used for the interpretation that government alone can set the terms of employment. The gag orders of President Theodore Roosevelt, which prohibited federal employees from participating in political activity, were followed by Civil Service Rule 1, which said, "persons in the competitive classified service, while retaining the right to vote as they please and to express privately their opinions on all political subjects, shall take no active part in political management or campaigns." The gag orders were partially lifted by the Lloyd-LaFollette Act of 1912, which gave employees the right to petition Congress for grievances. The Civil Service Commission made 3,000 rulings between 1906 and 1939 regarding political activity until the definitive standards of the Hatch Act were established in 1939.

The 1939 provisions covering federal employees were expanded in 1940 to affect state and local employees who were totally or partially compensated by federal funds, and again in 1966 to comply with the Equal Opportunity Act. Furthermore, many state and local governments enacted their own "little Hatch Acts." These laws, while varying on some specific restrictions, were largely based on the federal law. The laws forbid civil servants running for public office unless they first resign their career position. This provision was included to preserve the mantle of impartiality and to prevent conflicts of interest in the public service. Federal employees are allowed to run for nonpartisan elected posts so long as all other candidates are nonpartisan and the position sought does not interfere with the performance of the federal job. Career employees are also forbidden from participating in the management of political parties or campaigns, including the making of speeches. Exceptions again include nonpartisan elections insofar as the activity does not interfere with job performance. Employees are protected from making or soliciting political contributions, even though the federal government and many other jurisdictions permit voluntary contributions provided no pressure or coercion is involved.

The Hatch Act originally gave the Civil Service Commission a great deal of discretion in enforcing the law. However, the lack of true specificity in the statute, the patchwork pattern of restrictions in varying jurisdictions, and the pressure of public employee unions have led to a gradual lessening of the restrictions by administrative rulings and the courts. The amount of discretion granted has varied with the employee's governmental function, his contact with the public, his job security, and the impact that the activity would have on the merit principle. The case of *United Public Workers of America* v. *Mitchell*

(1947) upheld the Hatch Act in a four to three Supreme Court decision. In that decision, the Court held to the privilege theory of government employment, where an employee gives up certain constitutional rights, such as the freedom of speech, when he accepts government employment. The Mitchell decision was challenged in 1971 by a federal district court in Georgia in *Hobbs* v. *Thompson*, and in Rhode Island, in *Mancuso* v. *Tafts*, in which municipal ordinances restricting political activity were struck down. A federal appeals court in 1972 set aside the Mitchell decision for federal employees in *National Association of Letter Carriers* v. *United States*. This decision held that the Hatch Act was unconstitutional for federal employees because Congress did not make specific provisions. In 1973, the Supreme Court upheld the Hatch Act and overturned the *Letter Carriers'* decision as well as upholding the Oklahoma Hatch Act. The Court stated that there was no violation of rights involved because the act was necessary for the protection of the merit system and that legislative and administrative power to determine personnel policy should not be challenged by the courts. The Court did urge, however, that the doctrine of reasonableness be used in the application of political restrictions.[34]

Even though some jurisdictions prohibit political activity by public employee unions on the theory that employees should not be permitted to do collectively what they cannot do individually, the very existence of unions is a political act and their restriction has not been effectively enforced. Unions continue to support or oppose candidates, make endorsements, contribute funds, and lobby, so that union demands to eliminate or reduce political restrictions are only reflections of reality. "It could be said that the plight of the civil servant in political expression has been offset to some degree by the reality of power in his organizing for the welfare of his group and by the resulting lobby of such organizations directly with legislative bodies."[35] AFSCME has sponsored several test cases to challenge the constitutional validity of political restrictions. Even though some union members oppose the lifting of the protections tied to political restrictions, public unions continue to lobby for the removal of Hatch Act provisions since they already ignore them in their other political activity.

Political restrictions have recently attempted to strike a balance between the desire to insulate the merit system from undue political influence and the need to protect the political rights of the individual employee. The size and complexity of modern government make the relationship between politics and administration clear as policymakers become further involved in the political implications of their decisions. Moreover, there is now an acceptance of the subtle, as well as overt, implications of politics in the administrative process. The federal Commission on Political Activity of Government Personnel in 1966 recommended an expansion of the permissible areas of political activity for government employees provided those activities did not interfere with job impartiality and performance. The commission also recommended that Congress make specific the prohibited areas of activity. The reality of noncompliance alone should indicate the need for reform of these restrictions. The move toward liberalization in Oregon, California, and Wisconsin is not only a recognition that civil servants are being constantly bombarded by political pressure, but also a recognition that public employees have a significant stake in the outcome of the political process and that the denial of their rights in the process carries with it a denial of their right of self-determination.

Collective Bargaining and Interest Group Politics

Collective bargaining in the public sector, a bilateral decision-making process, carries with it political overtones in every step of the procedure. The allocation of public resources and the determination of the work situation directly affects the nature and quality of services because of the limited resources available to public officials. The roles assumed by labor and management in the negotiations take the form of psychological warfare between the adversaries, within the organizations themselves, and with the public. Negotiations and their outcome reflect the nature of political conflict.

Municipal unions are able to resort to political power devices to secure bargaining goals that are inappropriate to the private sector. Unions have several political alternatives in forcing a favorable agreement—use of an electoral bloc, pressure tactics, propaganda, the strike threat, and the strike. The political environment of collective bargaining is also seen in the public pressure on elected officials to provide continuous services at a minimum cost, compounded by fiscal shortages and budgetary pressures. The voters' anticipation of increased taxes, the low visibility of a tax because of the complexity of municipal budgets, and the pressures not to appease union demands are other conditions that the public management negotiator must face. The union leader is under pressure from the rank-and-file to not be overly cooperative with management and to obtain the best settlement possible. He must mount a façade of toughness with the ability to make effective arguments and yet remain flexible during negotiations. The balancing act of the union leadership also holds during a negotiated settlement's ratification process among the membership where the rising expectations of the rank-and-file can lead to the overriding of a settlement. Internal splits in the union organization, such as the revolt of the Motormen's Benevolent Association during the 1956 TWU negotiations with the New York Transit Authority, can greatly reduce the union position of leverage at the bargaining table.

Spero and Capozzola point out that all municipal labor-management negotiations invariably follow a "script." The union's initial demands, presented against a background of proposed budget deficits, are exorbitant beyond any range of the city's ability to pay. The unreasonable demands draw a dazed reaction from city officials who claim that the union is attempting to bankrupt the city. Both the union and management know that the actual settlement will fall somewhere in between the initial union demands and management's first offer. Each side employs rhetoric and innuendo to try to make the other side look unreasonable; the script calls for psychological and public relations warfare. As negotiations begin, the public utterances of the parties bear little relationship to the actual compromises occurring at the bargaining table. The parties generally negotiate on mutually agreeable items first, then move on to the points of contention. As the negotiation deadline approaches and breakdowns occur, each side blames the other for the need for third party intervention. The final portion of the script involves constant negotiations and a race to the contract deadline. The negotiations end in either a settlement or a strike.[36]

Mike Quill was the acknowledged master at manipulating the script. Every two years, the TWU leader threatened a transit strike that would cripple New York City during the Christmas rush season unless the union demands were granted. Quill, skilled at playing a dual role of militant union leader and compromising negotiator, would promise the workers a pie-in-the-sky settlement while privately working out an acceptable agreement with city officials, notably with Mayor Wagner. The bombast and professed differences in the negotiations were for public consumption only. It was the way for Quill to convince TWU members that he had triumphed over hostile city negotiators. City officials cooperated with Quill because they realized political advantages by circumventing normal bargaining procedures. Quill's script served the dual purpose of building a strong TWU union in New York as well as preventing a major transit strike for thirty years. Quill was always militant enough to placate TWU rank-and-file and frighten the public, and was flexible enough to negotiate an agreement with which the union and the city could live. The successful union leader, necessarily concerned with producing "gains for the boys," must be a skilled negotiator, a media and public relations manipulator, a politician with an extensive network of contacts, and must be able to keep internal union strife at a minimum.

The establishment of an official bargaining relationship does not preclude a union's attempts to circumvent normal bargaining procedures in trying to better achieve its goals. Unions have access to several pressure tactics to force politicians and the public to appease their demands. Mass rallies and demonstrations are staged by one or many unions to pressure officials and to show a united front. One of the largest union rallies was staged at Madison Square Garden in New York City in 1967 to display the political power of a coalition of public employee unions and to protest the antistrike provisions of the New York Taylor Act. Another mass display of support is the national union convention, where the national organization shows sympathy and support for local union positions. Rallies are flamboyant demonstrations of the power of public relations as defiant speeches are made to convince the union member that his goals are laudable and that in unity there is strength.

Union meetings are designed to promote internal unity, disseminate information, and crush internal dissension. Regular union meetings are used to formulate bargaining demands, air grievances, and plan political strategy. The gatherings are usually low-key and worker attitudes are largely shaped at these meetings. Quill used the regular TWU meetings to crush internal opposition and to maintain his own position. His ability to retain power for thirty years was directly related to his ability to convince TWU members of their own worth, of the value of TWU, and of his value to them.

Strike meetings are designed for public and institutional purposes in order to mobilize and convey a direct threat to management negotiators. Union leaders try to secure a unanimous mandate for a strike, but the rank-and-file cannot always be controlled in the emotionalism of these meetings. The 1969 strike of AFSCME employees in Cincinnati illustrates how a worked-up rank-and-file can overrule their leaders on a strike vote. With the media looking on, AFSCME employees voted to strike, even though the leaders moved the strike deadline back twelve days to give the city time to propose alternative bargaining solutions. Even though the emotionalism of strike meetings can be exaggerated, the threat to essential services or the political power displayed cannot be ignored.

Political pressure on elected and administrative officials is one of the most effective tactics employed by unions during the bargaining process. The union will demonstrate, picket, exploit the media, use innuendo and out-and-out falsehoods agaۇnst elected officials in order to force an acceptable settlement. The official can respond that he is defending the public interest of the sovereign state, that he is a champion of the taxpayer, and that he will allow the union to push the city only so far. The appointed official, who is usually responsible for negotiating an agreement and must bear the brunt of the union attack, may be charged with incompetence and inflexibility even though he is carrying out the orders of his elected superior. During the 1968 sanitation strike in New York City, John Delury, the head of the sanitation union, who claimed that he could deliver 99 percent of the votes of his union, went over the heads of both the city negotiator and Mayor Lindsay to appeal to Governor Nelson Rockefeller to mediate a settlement. When the Governor's representative negotiated a pay increase with the sanitation workers, Mayor Lindsay dissented, claiming that he was not going to appease the unions further and that he was protecting the taxpayers of the city. Even though the agreement was ratified by the union, the final outcome was that the union effort to go over the head of the mayor to appeal to the governor caused a negative public opinion of Rockefeller and the union, while the mayor emerged as a public hero for not acquiescing to union demands. This experience demonstrates that a union must not only consider the weak points of the officials it chooses to pressure, but the public reaction to that pressure as well.

The legislative "end run" is a tactic that has the union negotiators rejecting management's offer and then trying to negotiate with the responsible legislative body or get the legislators to pressure the management negotiators for a better settlement. This process gives the union the opportunity to use its political power directly, subverting the normal bargaining process. The process whereby a union negotiates an agreement and then tries to improve that agreement through lobbying a higher legislative body, is called "double-deck" bargaining. The end run also applies when the union circumvents the management negotiator to appeal to his elected superior. End runs do give the union options within the bargaining process, but they tend to destroy trust and adversely affect future bargaining relationships. End runs can divide the ranks of management by further muddling the locus of management authority. When a politician intervenes in order to settle an impasse by himself, he usually ends up harming the bargaining process. Leapfrogging or interunion competition to obtain higher benefits than other unions, can be prevented by established bargaining procedures and by a refusal of legislative bodies to listen to union demands until all possible impasse procedures have been exhausted.

The fragmentation of bargaining units in most cities promotes leap frogging. A union notes the benefits that a rival union settles for and claims that it has the right to the same or higher benefits. The 1969 AFSCME strike in Cincinnati was caused by the denial of a wage package to AFSCME that had been granted to the police union. AFS CME set the police package as its goal and would accept nothing less.

The power plays inherent in the interunion competition for benefits often reflect the political relationships in the city. The "me too" effect created by a large settlement by one union could be minimized by bringing all unions to the bargaining table at one time or by appreciably reducing the number of bargaining units.

The script that guides the public bargaining process, based on public relations and a psychological adversary relationship, shows that there is a thin line between bargaining and politics. The public conflicts between interest groups and the private bargaining between individuals suggest that collective bargaining is a microcosm of the nature of political conflict in the community as a whole. Racial conflict, the urban fiscal crisis, interunion rivalries, the municipal political and administrative structure, and internal union dissension are factors in the success or failure of a negotiating session. Real world experiences posit that established bargaining procedures in the private sector are not always applicable in the public sector because of legal restrictions and political alternatives to negotiation.

Public Employee Unions in the Broader Political Arena

Public employee unions use several tactics to supplement and circumvent the bargaining process. Political power is employed as a countervailing force to adverse administrative decisions and as a curb on administrative discretion. The tactics employed and the goals desired by the union must be selected within the bounds of feasibility. Organizational unity, the political environment, the nature of public services, and the degree of leverage that a union possesses over elected officials are other variables in determining the success of a political tactic.

Lobbying

Lobbying, the direct representation of union interests to the legislative branch, is one method employed by unions to augment the bargaining process as well as the most direct method for securing favorable legislation. In the face of administrative hostility to union recognition and collective bargaining, organized public employees have had to resort to political pressure to convince legislators to give governmental management the legal framework to establish stable labor relations. The greatest lobbying goal for all unions has been to eliminate right-to-work clauses, but public unions also lobby against antistrike legislation, which they claim relegates public employees to a second-class citizenship. Lobbying concerns of AFSCME include revenue sharing, extension of the Civil Rights Act to state and local government, national health care, emergency public service employment and halting comprehensive welfare reform because it would destroy many jobs. The communication process and subtle political pressure involved in lobbying provides organized labor with access to legislators to effectively present their case.

Lobbying can serve as a substitute for the collective bargaining process when legislatively mandated personnel policies are not included within the scope of bargaining on the local level. For example, police unions in New York were successful in pressuring the New York State Assembly in 1969 to repeal the provision prohibiting moonlighting by New York law enforcement officers.[37] Public worker organizations also lobby legislators to secure favorable changes in civil service codes. The lobbyist is adept at finding out the real source of power to exert pressure in the right place. The consultation and grievance process between labor and management may be considered a form of executive lobbying on an informal basis. Union lobbyists must be aware that they are involved in a group process in which there may be a countervailing administration lobbyist; but management negotiators should not depend on legislators to relieve them of the pressure of a negotiation deadline. The familiar lobbying technique of the legislative end run in which the union puts pressure on the legislator to exert pressure on the management negotiator is one illustration of how lobbying can circumvent and replace the bargaining process.

The most active concerns of public employee unions have been with obtaining and strengthening collective bargaining laws on the state level. Public unions have also had an impact on the national level, lobbying in concert through the public employees' division with the national legislative program of AFL-CIO. Postal unions have been active lobbyists before Congress since the turn of the century. The labor lobbyist is more than an advisor to legislators or administrators; he speaks for the entire union membership. *Communication* and *access* are the watchwords for the lobbyist. The limitations on the success of the labor lobby are organizational cohesiveness, the public attitude toward unions, and the degree of the identification of labor's goals with the general welfare. AFL-CIO's well-financed and highly influential lobbyists and their advocacy of welfare state issues makes labor the most important organized interest group before Congress. Generally, labor has been more successful in promoting progressive social and economic legislation (Minimum Wage, Civil Rights Act, etc.) than in preventing adverse labor legislation (Landrum-Griffin, Taft-Hartley, etc.).[38]

Coalition of Unions

Public employee unions, in a coalition with the private labor lobby, are pressuring Congress for the enactment of a federal collective bargaining law for public employees. The claim for the legislation is based on the rapid increase in public employee strikes and on the patchwork pattern of state legislation regarding public labor relations. NEA and AFSCME lobbyists state that the law is needed because of state inaction. Jerry Wurf, president of AFSCME says, "We seek federal legislation because most states won't do the job.... Only twelve of the fifty states have comprehensive bargaining laws covering all state and local government employees."[39]

The legislation, designed to create minimum standards for public labor relations, could take one of two forms. One form would extend coverage of the National Labor Relations Act to all state and local employees, including the right to strike. The second form would create a national public employee commission that would determine bargaining units, hold representation elections, and prevent unfair labor practices. The board would encourage binding arbitration to settle impasses, provide mediation services, and permit strikes if the public safety is not threatened.[40] The lobbying efforts for this federal legislation by public employee unions demonstrate how employee organizations will take affirmative action to rationalize labor relations in the absence of governmental initiative.

Interunion rivalries can greatly diminish the political impact of employee organizations. However as discussed earlier (chapter 1), public unions on all governmental levels, are beginning to band together for maximum political impact and to achieve common goals. In Michigan, a coalition was formed between AFSCME, teachers' unions, and law enforcement unions for joint lobbying efforts at the state level. The AFSCME-NEA-NTEU coalition (CAPE) at the national level and the public employee division of AFL-CIO's efforts in pressing for a national collective bargaining law have been previously described (chapter 1). Compromising and the sacrificing of goals will usually occur for the sake of building an effective coalition. Many old hatchets must be buried, for example between AFT and NEA, before unions can again effectively coordinate their political activities.

New York provides a graphic example of the political power of union coalitions. The 1967 mass rally of AFSCME, AFT, and TWU in Madison Square Garden demonstrated the power of a municipal union coalition. The city's 1969 election for mayor was a display of the predominance of the electoral power of a municipal union coalition even over that of the private sector unions. The Lindsay coalition of the sanitation union, TWU, and AFSCME defeated Mario Procaccino, the Democratic candidate supported by the Central Labor Council.

A labor coalition can provide an overpowering electoral bloc because of a commonality of goals and organizational ability. The support by the Central Labor Council of the bargaining position of public unions is another political asset. The internal conflicts within the coalition, however, can be damaging. In the 1968 teachers' strike in New York, the growing black membership in AFT and AFSCME along with their concern for community control of schools greatly dissipated the solid front of labor in support of the teacher demands.

Electoral Politics

Organized labor can have its greatest political impact in electoral activity for political candidates. Private AFL-CIO unions have long been active in electoral politics. Now, public employee unions, realizing their stake in the electoral process, are beginning to assert themselves, especially on the municipal level. Unions are able to provide manpower, a voting bloc, money, information, endorsements, and other supports for candidates on all levels. The labor alignment with the Democratic party that solidified during the New Deal era has been mutually beneficial. The impact of public unions as an electoral bloc will become more important in large cities because of the growing number of members, their ability to define issues that concern them, and their organizational ability.

The capability of AFL-CIO and its political wing, COPE, to maintain control over local union electoral activities has diminished; however, as the union membership grows more heterogeneous, labor is thwarted in its ability to "deliver the votes" of the working class. However, COPE had been extremely successful in its mission in the past. For instance, the 1960 Tennessee Democratic primary for U.S. Senator demonstrates the political effectiveness that COPE can provide. In that election, COPE made 60,000 telephone calls, distributed 300,000 pieces of literature, set up extensive ward and precinct organizations, and maintained a central labor file for the reelection of Senator Estes Kefauver.[41] This effort for an incumbent in an antilabor state is magnified many times in industrial states. The UAW in Detroit is able to develop an electoral machine for state and municipal elections. The union meeting provides a candidate with a captive audience and these meetings are used to facilitate political organization and disseminate information. A basic manpower concern for labor is the mass registration of voters, with a recognition that labor can hold the balance of power in elections in industrial areas. Many observers attribute the 1960 election of John F. Kennedy to the mass registration efforts of COPE before the balloting. For example, in 1960, COPE and UAW registered 200,000 voters in Detroit and its suburbs, and they cast two-thirds of the state's total vote.[43] COPE utilizes television, radio, literature distribution, and doorknocking in its registration efforts. Other union electoral activities include canvassing, mailings, recruiting workers, holding parties and rallies, distributing literature, transporting workers, baby sitting while working parents vote, and generally getting out the vote on election day.

Public unions can provide a substantial electoral bloc and campaign unit. The nonpartisan nature of elections in many cities gives municipal unions a great deal of leverage because they are not automatically identified with one of the political parties. One of the first mass efforts was the work of the postal unions against an antilabor congressman in Kansas City in 1918. Their effort almost succeeded in unseating him. Nonpartisan elections in the Washington D.C. metropolitan area are usually determined by the large numbers of organized federal employees living in the area. Organized municipal employees, thus, have the potential to become as effective as the traditional city machine in delivering votes, as the electoral power of the New York sanitation workers illustrates. In 1972, AFSCME announced a policy of taking an active part in registration campaigns and local elections.

The information provided through labor publications, advertisements, and propaganda is another important electoral tactic. COPE maintains an annual scoreboard on the voting records on labor issues of members of Congress. Labor speakers present the labor viewpoint, and the attitudes of candidates toward labor issues are carefully documented. COPE conducts national information campaigns and local unions attempt to influence the political attitudes of their members. The information function is usually more effective in rallying internal union support than in influencing public opinion.

Financial contributions provide a leverage over a candidate—rewarding a candidate for supporting prolabor legislation and guaranteeing access to a candidate after the election. Bok and Dunlop report that 80 percent of the nonunionized public oppose labor's financial contributions because they feel that legislators will then become beholden to labor.[43] To prevent this possibility, Congress has tried to limit the level of political contributions made by trade unions even though the Supreme Court has tended to say that such laws limit the freedom of expression of trade unions. In elections, the impact of labor contributions is felt more in the distribution of funds rather than in their volume; labor's campaign contributions average approximately 5 percent of the total.

An important consideration is the problem of reconciling union democracy with the use of union dues for political purposes. The question of the personal freedom of the worker who must indirectly contribute to a candidate whom he may or may not support is important, especially if the worker must belong to the union to continue working. A similar dilemma exists for nonunion workers in an agency shop in the public sector.

Union endorsements have a mixed impact on a campaign effort. The union can endorse a candidate, support a candidate but not endorse him, or remain neutral. An endorsement of a winning candidate will usually provide access to that candidate, but endorsement of a losing candidate can reduce the political leverage of the union. Union endorsements are a powerful boost for candidates running in industrial areas. For example, UAW-endorsed candidates in Detroit rarely lose a state or local election. The mere statement of a platform can lead to a tacit labor endorsement or rejection. Endorsements by public sector unions go to candidates who favor collective bargaining or who have provided them access in the past. Nicholas Masters's findings in Michigan were that unions will generally endorse the strongest and most sympathetic candidate; but, they will endorse a mediocre or weak candidate if his opponent is hostile to labor or is supported by business interests.[44]

Union endorsements often have adverse effects, however. Before the AFL-CIO merger, a CIO endorsement was considered a "kiss of death" for candidates in antilabor states. The impact of a labor endorsement is dependent on the past history of labor relations in the area, the degree of electoral support given by the union, and the socioeconomic character of the area. A labor endorsement in an industrial city such as Detroit, for example, where unions are well organized, will have a greater impact than in Los Angeles, where the unions are divided and the socioeconomic level of the general population is higher. Another negative factor surrounding union endorsements is the lack of member solidarity within the unions. Union leaders, despite the ability to make a strong suggestion, cannot force the membership to vote for the union candidate. Union members are not a monolithic voting bloc, and the growing heterogeneity of the movement could mean that a union endorsement will only mean organizational and leadership approval and not necessarily mass support. The union member, feeling that his union is losing its economic orientation, is increasingly rebelling against the dictates of his union leaders. Many members still adhere to the early voluntarist philosophy and the younger members of unions, especially those from minority groups, are increasingly independent.[45]

Unions and Political Parties

When the labor movement emerged from the voluntarist philosophy, it permanently aligned itself with the Democratic party because it had no where else to go. Even though AFL-CIO remains officially nonpartisan, it holds a great deal of power within the national hierarchy of the Democratic party. The close relationship between the party and the unions on the national level does not hold at the local level. David Greenstone studied the impact of unions on the structure and effectiveness of the Democratic party in Detroit, Chicago, and Los Angeles. His findings revealed that the power of UAW and the municipal employee unions in Detroit practically made the Democratic party in Michigan an arm of COPE. In Chicago, labor organizations competed with the nation's most powerful party organization. The COPE organization there accommodated the pluralistic nature of the patronage-based Daley machine because the party regulars went to great lengths to attempt to shut them out of the political process. The mixed effectiveness of COPE in Los Angeles results from the political disorganization of this metropolitan area; there labor had some influence on, but did not dominate the California Democratic party.[46] Greenstone summarized his findings by stating: "The American labor movement, in other words, functions as a major Democratic party electoral organization within limits imposed by its own economic structure and its political environment."[47]

The relationship of public unions to the party structure on the local level reflects the intense factionalism of municipal parties. Mike Quill was able to establish a strong position for TWU in the New York Democratic party by accommodating the reform group of Robert Wagner while maintaining his connections with the Tammany Hall Organization of Carmine de Sapio. Even though public employees have a special stake in participating in the party system, their activities are limited by the public suspicion of the partisan political activity of civil servants and the need to retain the flexibility to "reward our friends and punish our enemies."

Central Labor Councils

The political power of union coalitions is clearly seen in the influence of Central Labor Councils. While the council cannot speak for all unions, it can give policy direction and organizational ability to union political efforts within a city. It serves as a mediator for union rivalries and to achieve maximum political impact it combines and directs labor resources for electoral battles and bargaining disputes. The council assists in settling disputes between a public employee union and a city by bringing pressure to bear on both parties, as it did during the 1968 teachers' strike in New York City. The council can take a militant position, however, if a member union is threatened with an injunction or is being coerced, even to the point of threatening a general sympathy strike. The party structure can be strengthened by the actions of a Central Labor Council; the council in Los Angeles has been a strong influence in the California Democratic party in spite of the fragmentation of the labor movement in this city. Public employee unions benefit from the council's support because with it they do not stand alone when making bargaining demands and they have access to the general labor movement.

Legislative Impact

Now that most of organized labor's legislative goals have been achieved, the new objectives concern organizational maintenance conditions and the influencing of social and economic legislation. The impact of labor's influence is diminished, however, by the decreasing level of the private sector's unionized work force. The individual union member, having achieved the middle-class economic security that is his basic drive, now has something to protect; this has led to a basically conservative political orientation on the part of many working-class people. The political effectiveness of unions is also limited by their inability to effectively "deliver the labor vote." The assessment of the labor movement as a powerful interest group must be understood within the context of the nature of group pluralism in the American political system; organized labor is only one group among many providing decision makers with demands and supports.

The political power of group self-interest is emerging more graphically in the case of public employee unions. Public unions are not only interested in securing economic and working condition goals, but their political influence in collective bargaining, elections, and lobbying can dominate the development of public policy. Collective bargaining in the public service, a bilateral decision-making process concerning the allocation of scarce public resources, is inherently political because its outcome is affected by the challenge to governmental sovereignty, the public pressure for a settlement, and the inelastic demand for governmental services. Power considerations prevail in the determination of control over desired resources, or desired outcomes, and power considerations key management's response to a growing union militancy. The political assets of public employee unions include their voting strength, their ultimate ability to affect the nature and delivery of services, the impact of public opinion, their ability to circumvent bargaining procedures, and the strike. Their liabilities include their limitations on delivering votes, restrictions on the political activity of civil servants, and interunion rivalries. The structure of decision making, the legitimacy of union demands, the threat to management prerogatives, and the status and prestige of the municipal power structure are other factors. Ultimately, the public interest goals of economy, efficiency, and constancy of monopoly services will be threatened by the unchecked growth of union power and strikes. The development of established labor relations procedures can rationalize the growth of public unionization, but it cannot remove the inherent political conflict.

Political Efficacy of Police Organizations

Police employee organizations have existed in many cities since the turn of the century. Over the years, these organizations have provided welfare benefits for their members, lobbied for higher pay, and fulfilled certain social and fraternal needs. Police organizations in various jurisdictions affiliated with the organized labor movement after World War I, but the counterproductive 1919 Boston police strike quelled this development and chilled police union organization efforts by organized labor for several decades.

Despite this setback, police during the post-1919 period continued to form local associations, many of which affiliated with larger state or national groups. By the 1960s the two largest of these national organizations were the International Conference of Police Associations (ICPA) and the Fraternal Order of Police (FOP). By the time police militancy captured the public's attention in the late 1960s, most urban policemen were members of some kind of employee organization that served as an articulator of police demands.

There are a number of factors contributing to police employee dissatisfaction and their willingness to engage in militant tactics. One factor has been the manifestation of public hostility toward police beginning in the 1960s. The antipolice behavior took the form of black and student riots and unrest, court decisions seen as restricting police discretion, efforts on behalf of civilian complaint review boards, increased violence directed at police, the rising crime rate, and a perception among police officers that there was a lack of support for the police rank-and-file from police executives and city officials. Moreover, while the police were faced with a perceived mounting public hostility they were also faced with the problem of dealing with increased public demands to solve the urban crime problem. Another source of dissatisfaction was that the more hostile and demanding environment had increased the police workload and the perceived danger of the job without, it was felt by police, a commensurate increase in economic rewards. Finally, dissatisfaction was caused by a perception of unsatisfactory personnel practices within most police departments (e.g., lack of grievance procedures, no premium overtime pay or court time compensation).

There are factors that contributed to the overt expression of police militancy. The success of the confrontation tactics of blacks, students, and organized labor made an impression on policemen. Today's urban police forces have a high proportion of young officers who appear to be more than willing to engage in overt action in pursuit of their goals. Finally, the high degree of occupational cohesion among police officers contributes to a propensity for this occupation group to aggressively pursue group goals.

The phenomenon of police unionization has served to crystallize the self-perception of policemen as craftsmen demanding freedom from infringement on their autonomy in the discharge of their occupational responsibility.[48] Police fraternal organizations, through strength of numbers and demonstrated solidarity, have been able to neutralize controls over police officials by both internal and external means. These organizations have advanced the principle of worker initiative on the part of the police rank-and-file. In order for the police to preserve their worker initiative, they have had to fend off restraints imposed by institutional controls as well as the rule of law. Police organizations, through collective action, have been successful in many cases in challenging all actors, either within the police bureaucracy or in the political system, who are sympathetic to the needs for constraint and review of individual police practices.

Police organizations possessing a great deal of political power have the capability to negotiate autonomy with civil authorities in the political system and with the administrators of police departments. Police organizations wield power on several different levels. As labor organizations they employ standard weapons of economic warfare such as strikes, threat of strikes, and slowdowns, or rather, modified and imaginative versions of these practices. The police version of economic pressure consists of "job actions": the "blue flu" or threat of the "blue flu," slow down in ticket writing, overenforcement of the laws, or varying enforcement of the law. At another level, still as labor organizations, they act as vehicles for negotiating and presenting employee viewpoints to management. Finally, they operate as political organizations employing traditional political techniques for gaining their objectives. On this level they have been extremely active in lobbying, supporting political organizations friendly to their aims, overtly working for propolice candidates, as well as working against those whose policies and ideologies are rejected by the police rank-and-file.

In line with their activities to preserve the autonomy and authority of police officials, police organizations have devoted their efforts to combating external control over police operations. Their most notable victories came in the fight against the Philadelphia and New York civilian review boards. In Philadelphia their efforts were mainly confined to obtaining court injunctions against the operation of the board;

after eight years of litigation the Philadelphia chapter of the Fraternal Order of Police was rewarded by Mayor Tate, who disbanded the board by an executive order.

In New York City, the Patrolmen's Benevolent Association was the driving force behind the collection of signatures on a petition calling for a referendum on a civilian-controlled complaint review board. PBA was supported in its opposition against the review board by the conservative party, American Legion posts, parents' and taxpayers' groups, and the Brooklyn Bar Association. In support of the board were such groups as the New York City Civil Liberties Union and a number of civil rights, civic, religious, and labor organizations. The surface argument against the board was that it threatened police efficiency and morale, and would contribute to a breakdown in public order and safety by handcuffing the police in their dealings with criminal elements. The proboard coalition justified the civilian review agency for the sake of restoring public confidence in the police. But, at the heart of the matter, this was a racial issue. Civilian review grew to be linked with civil rights issues. The result of this identification was "to make the referendum a measure of the degree of 'white backlash,' that is, resentment by white voters against blacks and rights for blacks."[49]

The vote in the referendum was 1,313,161 against civilian review and 765,468 for the board, with whites voting against the board and blacks overwhelmingly favoring civilian review. The solidarity of labor's front was broken on this issue. The police organization was joined by conservative groups in the community; labor joined the liberal coalition. However, the issue was resolved on racial lines. The exploitation of an emotional issue resulting in a white-black racial dichotomy in the vote was useful to the police organization and its allies in their efforts to preserve police autonomy.

The Strike as a Weapon in Pressure Group Politics

Public employees, like their private employee counterparts, claim that the strike and work stoppages are essential strategies in achieving both short-term and long-range objectives. In the private sector, most labor relations observers agree that such tactics are essential in obtaining economic benefits for union members. However, the acceptability of public sector strikes or work stoppages is much more controversial. Whereas private sector job action is frequently economically motivated, all "public" organization pressure is political by definition. Therefore, to what extent, if any, can society sanction the public employee strike?

More importantly, how effective is the strike, threatened strike, or work stoppage as a political weapon for the union?

The strike case studies of Atlanta, San Francisco, Vallejo, and Albuquerque suggest that the strike is a much more complex and unpredictable strategy than its advocates have generally realized. It has not been the irresistible weapon that cripples cities and brings local officials to their knees. As a political tactic, the strike and work stoppage necessitate a much more careful analysis than they have received.

As Harry Wellington and Ralph Winter observe, generally those who oppose public employee strikes do so for four basic reasons: (1) market restraints are weak in the public sector, primarily because public services are essential; (2) the public puts pressure on public officials to arrive at a quick settlement; (3) other pressure groups have no weapons comparable to a strike; and (4) the strike distorts the normal political process. Concomitantly, many union representatives assume that the strike tactic would provide them with an almost inexorable means of obtaining quick, significant economic gains. Hence, the strike used by such groups as police or firemen would inevitably be effective. It would give public employees substantial leverage vis à vis other interest groups in attaining their objectives. However, public sector strikes have neither confirmed the fears of its critics nor the promises of its proponents.

First, the relative lack of market restraints in the public sector suggests that economic rewards are easily obtainable by public employee strikes. The public treasury becomes like a poorly guarded, small town bank—an open invitation to be robbed. Yet, such is not the case in reality, particularly at the local level. The property tax concerns of local property owners are no longer randomly or occasionally manifest. As in the Atlanta (1977) and San Francisco (1975) strikes, public concern over increased municipal spending was an important stimulus encouraging public managers to not compromise. Ad hoc property owner groups are now organized and careful to observe each proposed spending increase. The tendency to coordinate strike action with the local budgetary process has frequently embroiled strike issues with debate over budgetary spending levels. Given that most budgetary appropriations are fixed or irreducible, proposed increases by unions would automatically be resisted by both management and concerned interest groups.

Secondly, the thesis that strikes are usually effective in forcing local officials to make quick settlements is also unsubstantiated. Supposedly, because certain public services are essential, public officials are forced into quick and complete acquiescence. The essentiality of service depends on the extent to which disruption of the service by a strike would "immediately endanger public health and safety."[51] It is generally agreed that the protective services, i.e., police and firemen are most essential. Most observers assume that a strike by protective service employees cannot be tolerated because it would severely threaten public safety. Conversely, protective service unions have oftentimes viewed strikes and work stoppages as almost invincible weapons in achieving their objectives.

To the surprise of many, the prospect of a protective services strike has thus far been more awesome than its reality; even when police and firemen strike simultaneously. That strikes by protective services were always considered catastrophic by public managers and scholars was probably shaped by the 1969 Montreal police strike, which was accompanied by anarchy and a dramatic crime increase. The following examples, illustrative of the surprising lack of crime increase, generally reveal an unexpected impotence of the strike as a political weapon:

1. *In July, 1969, police in Vallejo, California, joined forces with local firemen in conducting a five-day strike. Only a chief, two subordinates, and a few reserves, together with a core of Solano sheriff's personnel and highway partolmen maintained the peace. Significantly, there was no appreciable increase in crime or looting, although there were confrontations between strikers and management.*[52]

2. *In January, 1971, approximately 25,000 patrolmen in New York City walked out over a back pay issue and remained out for six days. The strike did not result in an upsurge of crime as had occurred in Montreal two years earlier.*[53]

3. *In July, 1975, the 500-member Albuquerque Police Officers Association, staged a ten-day strike. The city's chief administrative officer remarked that every one feared the worst but instead, the city remained "very quiet." "In fact, crime actually went down.... All we had were 90 men working 12-hour shifts to handle only the direst emergencies. But our people cooperated beautifully and stayed cool."*[54]

4. *In our 1975 case study of the San Francisco firemen and police, the most serious incidents occurred between striking policemen and hecklers, and the bombing of the mayor's home. If anything, the strike served to mobilize community support for the Board of Supervisors against perceived police opportunism.*

5. *In the following instances, police/firemen (1969-1970) strikes occurred without accompanying increases of crime: Anderson, Antioch, Monterey, and Hollister (California), Ravenna and Toledo (Ohio), and Livonia (Michigan).*[55]

As clarification, strikes by protective services employees are always disruptive and occasionally a threat to public safety. However, they are hardly the dreaded apocalypse. They are frequently a double edged sword with the potential to either pressure public officials or mobilize community support against the strikers and their objectives.

The strike has not proven to be a consistently effective political weapon in achieving union objectives for two reasons. First, protective services are not monopolies or exclusive services held by local police or fire units. Specifically, even though police go on strike, law enforcement does not cease. In the examples cited, emergency services were successfully provided during the strike by a core police group composed of supervisory personnel and augmented by outside officers, usually sheriffs, reserves, and state police. Similarly, emergency fire protection is continued by nearby fire districts (which are quite accustomed to cooperating on major fires, anyway). Second, public opinion, far from reacting with fear and intimidation, has frequently responded with virulent indignation against the strikers. Examples of communities organizing neighborhood watch patrols or contracting with private security organizations are also not uncommon. Third, the strike supposedly provides public employee unions with an inordinate amount of political power in comparison to other interest groups who do not have a weapon comparable to the strike. Neither can the public sector management initiate a retaliatory lockout. Both criticisms assume that a group's political power is derived from the existence of a technique, the strike. However, the variables affecting a particular group's power and influence have proved to be much more complex.

Traditional interest group theorists assumed that rationally self-interested individuals voluntarily joined interest groups that reflected the collective interests of their members.[56] Interest groups supposedly serve to integrate the individual with the state and to act as a buffer between the individual and the state. This interest group model of politics includes a system of group interaction by which groups ultimately determine policy through conflict and compromise. Thus, a stabilizing social equilibrium is achieved and the interests of each group is represented.

Some group advocates claim that this pressure group process produces a form of indirect democracy: pluralism,[57] or "democratic elitism."[58] Theoretically the government functions as an arbiter of the group conflict process. Therefore, for government to be compromised by public employee unions' participation in the group process would simply lead to "a war of all against all."

Actually, modern group theory is very similar to the theory of factions, described by James Madison in *The Federalist*. According to it differences among individuals inevitably led to factions of like-minded persons. Each faction was opposed to each other faction. Controlling factional conflict became the principal task of modern legislation.[59]

Despite the importance of the group model as an analytic tool, more so with certain policy issues than with others, one must agree with Douglas Fox that the "thousands of interest groups at the city and state levels" make it "especially hazardous to generalize about their behavior."[60] Undaunted, Harry Eckstein identifies the following three variables which seemingly have the most impact on a pressure group's (1) form or structure, (2) scope and intensity, and (3) its policymaking effectiveness. Eckstein suggests that a pressure group's form, scope, and intensity are primarily affected by governmental structure, activities, and public attitudes toward groups. However, the group's effectiveness in achieving its objectives is dependent on both internal group characteristics (size of resources, cohesiveness, leadership), and external governmental structures (where power is concentrated, type of electoral system, and political party system).

The pressure group literature, from cross-national theory building to empirically oriented case studies at the local level, is vast and fertile.[62] Importantly, it suggests the improbability that the public employee organizations' use of the strike would provide them with any significant leverage in their struggle with other groups. In fact, the evidence indicates that the public employee union's acquisition of the strike would provide more of a psychological placebo effect than a panacea for union economic objectives.

Fourth, as its critics argue, the strike by public employees "introduces an alien force in the legislative process."[63] Theoretically, union strikes are antidemocratic and detrimental to representative government. Whereas, private sector unions seek legitimate economic objectives, public sector unions seek a role in the political policymaking process itself. From another perspective, strikes make public employee unions illegitimate participants in the political process. To union leaders, the strike offers a means for attaining policymaking influence on a competitive basis with private sector interest groups.

It is important here to distinguish the empirical reality of pressure group interaction from the theoretical assumptions of representative government. Normative theories of democracy, republicanism, and equality are vital in shaping American institutions and values. However, such constitutionally legitimized values affect but do not explain the behavior of political man, pressure groups, or political parties. We can heed Machiavelli's methodology of seeking reality without becoming advocates of "back room bossism." It should not be surprising that elected representatives seldom formulate major policies or represent the consensual will of the people. Policymaking at all levels of government is essentially a political rather than a representative process.

Several important characteristics of governmental policymaking must be emphasized in determining whether or not the public employee strike would alter that process. First, public policies are characteristically affected by multilateral group, bureaucratic, legislative, and executive interaction. The public employee union may thus be typically interacting with a number of political actors (see figure 4-1).

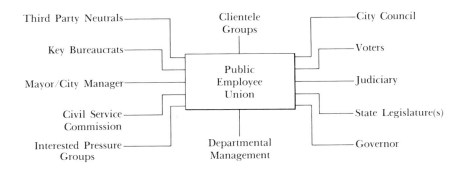

FIGURE 4-1: Actors in the Local Political Process

Not only is the policymaking process multilateral, the participants vary depending on the issue.[64] Most pressure groups and public agencies are only concerned with and possess expertise in areas of specific interest, e.g., agriculture, health, welfare, etc.[65] They are seldom interested in issues beyond a very narrow sphere of interest. Consequently, pressure groups attempt to influence decisions made in only those public agencies which develop and implement policy in relevant issue areas. For example, teachers' unions, the PTA, and taxpayer groups will consistently conflict and compromise on educational spending issues. The professional bureaucrat, pressure group leaders, and key legislative committeemen or individuals will form a subsystem[66] of governmental policymaking. Most issues will be decided within this private framework rather than by a legislative body acting as a whole.

In both policy formulation and subsequent implementation, pressure groups utilize various strategies in an effort to gain mutually advantageous objective, e.g., a joint police and firemen's strike; or a group, such as a union, will seek reciprocal cooperation in exchange for future support, e.g., labor solidarity.

It is instructive that one factor in the surprising ineffectuality of many police and firemen's strikes has been a general failure to formulate realistic strategies that reflect the union's role or status in the interest group process. For example, a key variable affecting the success of most interest groups is its ability to persuade other groups to coalesce, or join a common cause.[67] Consequently, when police go on strike, they generally do it unilaterally, or occasionally in conjunction with firemen. They go it alone; the true blue knight who is generally isolated in social and professional life from the community.

Despite the essentiality of protective services, the police and firemen generally lack clientele support groups. There are no interest groups that are concerned with the political objectives of protective agencies. The Department of Agriculture has powerful allies and lobbyists in the Grange, Farm Bureau, and other farm groups. The local health department has linkages with a reliable core of clientele interest groups that will lobby for agency objectives. However, the police and firemen are isolated.

Wallace Sayre, in a suggestive typology, categorizes "the political strength that agencies may derive from alliance with interest groups."[68] A category germane to this discussion is the *underprivileged* agency, which can only expect minimal support from its clientele. As an example, a metropolitan fire department is underprivileged because:

> Businesses subject to inspection and licensing do not like its activities; economy groups are cautious lest its budget be expanded too much; and the National Board of Fire Underwriters has endorsed recommendations for a reduction in the force."[69]

Similarly, police departments are without any natural allies or clientele groups whose primary concern is the well-being of the police department.

Police unions have even exacerbated their professional isolation by disdaining their once natural allies, firemen. In the period from 1927 to 1967, the salaries of police and firemen were usually maintained at parity.[70] Generally, they did not diverge more than two points. However, since 1967, municipalities have tended to pay police more than fire fighters on the justification that the recruiting, training, and professional standards for police are now higher.[71] The result is that police and firemen often engage in an internecine struggle over the parity issue rather than bargaining collectively for mutual objectives.

In conclusion, the interest group process and its function in the prevailing subsystem of government is an essential component of public policymaking on all levels. The achievement of political power and exercise of political influence is dependent on group and elite models of interaction. No political group, i.e., public employee unions, can achieve either by ignoring the interest group process and relying on the supposed omnipotent strike weapon to achieve its objectives. The strike as a political tactic has only proven effective when used by unions which are well organized, possess ample resources, have clearly defined objectives, and can win allies for the strike effort. Therefore,

Part II: Politics and Collective Bargaining

it should not be surprising that public employee strikes sometimes fail in achieving their immediate and long-term objectives.

Public Employee Strikes: Three Case Studies

The relatively brief but intense period of public employee strikes during the last ten years provides several suggestive case studies in which strikes were employed to gain political objectives. On the basis of these case studies and numerous other public employee job actions we have constructed three models for evaluating a strike's political effectiveness:

1. **Effectual Model** wherein both short-term objectives, those related to the immediate interest impasse, and long-range objectives, those strengthening the collective bargaining process and future impasse resolutions, are attained. The 1970 postal workers' strike is utilized as a case study.
2. **Ineffectual Model** wherein neither short-term nor long-term objectives are achieved. Consequently, both the union and future collective bargaining prospects are seriously undermined. The 1977 Atlanta city employees' strike is explored as a case study.
3. **Mixed Model** wherein short-term objectives are achieved but long-term prospects are seriously jeopardized. For example, a particularly hostile strike environment may result in increased pay in the short run, but arouses public hostility toward unionism and collective bargaining for the future. Consequently, strikes end up as pyrrhic victories. The 1975 San Francisco police and firemen's strike is analyzed as a case study of the mixed model.

Effectual Strike Model: The Postal Workers' Strike (1970)

The first major strike of federal workers against the United States government occurred with the postal workers' strike in 1970. The causal issue was the Nixon Administration's proposal for postal reform. The proposal was submitted to Congress in late 1969, and it contained no provisions for postal pay raises[72] (although congressional action would raise salaries somewhat). It did, however, propose to reduce the amount of time for an employee to move from the bottom of the pay scale to the top from twenty-one to eight years ($6,176 annually to $8,442 annually).[73] The walkout of the mail workers began in New York City on 18 March and quickly spread to other large cities. The employees voted to strike in defiance of a federal court injunction with employees on Long Island and in New York City the first to walk out.

By midnight, locals of the National Association of Letter Carriers (NALC) in parts of New Jersey had voted to strike. To avoid further confusion, the postal service ordered an embargo on all mail for the affected area. While many locals were reluctant to oppose the federal court injunction, others were not so timid; the first strike in the 195-year history of the postal service was initiated.

NALC picket lines were observed for the most part by an increasing number of other postal workers. The letter carriers' main complaint was that railway express workers, who held comparable jobs, were paid $3.81 an hour versus the postal service's $2.97 average hourly pay. If the workers' increase were granted, it would mean a forty percent pay hike. There was a great disparity between this figure and the 5.4 percent increase the House of Representatives was considering retroactively (to 1 January).

On a policymaking level, the Nixon Administration continued its power struggle to tie any pay raise to an overall postal reform. The main thrust of the reform was to set up an independent postal authority. However, postal workers insisted that they would not support reform of the service unless pay raises were instituted. Postal union leaders emphasized that the strike mood had been evident for some time with the rapid job turnover of employees. Furthermore, union leaders felt the time opportune for bringing problems to the public attention, even though they were forbidden by federal law from striking. Postmaster General Winton Blount hoped to minimize the strike's impact by asking for the continued support of loyal employees.

Simultaneously Congress began debating the issue of higher wages, despite Blount's comment that Congress was inept when dealing with emergencies. Perhaps the major obstacle was that many members of the Senate opposed the postal bill because they wanted to maintain congressional control of the post office.[74]

A *New York Times* editorial implied that "anarchy" would prevail if federal service employees began flouting court orders and civil law: "If the postal workers succeed [with the strike], the no-strike policy that has prevailed with almost perfect effectiveness in all branches of the Federal Civil Service will henceforth be at the mercy of every employee group with control over a strategic public operation."[75] Although perhaps somewhat harsh in its response to a public employee strike, New York City had recently suffered crippling strikes on the local level by police, teachers, and sanitation workers, and many New Yorkers labeled the postal strike as a clear abuse of economic power by the public sector.

The *Times* also linked the prevailing lawlessness in society with the action taken by the postal workers in breaking their oath; it urged government officials to invoke full penalties on the workers to restore

Part II: Politics of Collective Bargaining

"respect for the law." This is perhaps an overstatement, since it is doubtful that the postal workers' action had any significant effect on criminal attitudes in New York City or anywhere else.

While the *Times* could see the need for a pay hike, it could see no justification for a strike. Yet it believed that the federal government was duty bound not to equivocate on the subject of an illegal strike. No negotiations were to be held under an "outlaws' umbrella." It urged the Administration, congressional leaders, and union officials to meet and break the legislative deadlock.[76]

While the media and officials debated the issues, New York City's economy was being seriously affected by the strike. A major department store, Macy's, reported difficulties operating. Also affected adversely were brokerage houses, banks, law offices, and thousands of other firms.[77] Critics claimed that the populace was being held ransom in a conflict that was beginning to have costs of many different forms.

On 20 March, the walkout spread around the country, with almost 200,000 workers involved in the strike. Most major cities outside the South were without mail service, and sentiment among postal employees was still heavily strike-oriented—the vote at the Manhattan center was 8,322 for a walkout, 940 against.

The strike grew when the AFL-CIO Post Office Clerks local in New York City voted to strike. This was significant because it was a larger national organization than the Postal Union Employees, whose locals in Philadelphia and Detroit ignored injunctions and remained on strike.[78]

On 21 March President Nixon announced that he would ensure movement of the mail. When asked if he would use troops, he simply replied that the government would move the mail.[79] The commander of the National Guard also announced that he had conferred with Pentagon officials earlier in the day about the feasibility of troops moving the mail, indicating that this is what the president meant.

Meanwhile, negotiations between the National Association of Letter Carriers (NALC) and the Secretary of Labor proceeded. However, NALC warned that if negotiations were not fruitful within five days, a nationwide strike of all employees would be called. The inability of the Administration to take urgent steps to remedy the situation was heightened as Congress stalled on efforts to solve the problem.[80]

The next day, President Nixon declared a national emergency stating, "The strike violates prohibitions in the United States code against walkouts by government employees."[81] The president also announced and subsequently implemented "Operation Graphic Hand," by which 12,000 guardsmen and 15,000 reservists were called up in order to move the mails. He justified the use of troops because of the unions' obstinacy in continuing the strike, even though Labor Secretary Schultz and several union leaders had agreed to negotiation as soon as workers returned to work.[82]

George Meany, president of AFL-CIO, criticized the Administration's overreactive use of troops; nonetheless, he urged postal workers to return to work. Postmaster General Blount, late on the twenty-fourth, also appealed to workers for an end to the strike and promised renewed negotiations the next day if they did so. By this time over 150,000 workers were on strike across the country. At the same time, over 10,600 guardsmen and reservists were sorting and attempting to handle several million pieces of mail in the Manhattan, Brooklyn, Queens, and Bronx main post offices. Fortunately, there were no serious incidents between postal strikers and troops.[83] No troops were delivering mail, but large businesses and institutions were allowed to pick up what mail had been sorted.

The move by President Nixon in using troops to try to break a public employee strike successfully underscored the problem's severity to Congress.[84] Nor was it without effect upon the strikers, as thousands began a return to work. By 25 March, the strike was virtually over. This was due to several factors: the involvement of troops, promised congressional action on the pending postal bill, and Postmaster Blount's plea. Not an inconsequential element was that the pending postal package in Congress contained a 12 percent pay hike, over twice the original request.

Consequently, President Nixon ordered all troops withdrawn from the post offices on the night of 25 March, as postal workers continued to report for work. Postmaster Blount announced that further militancy was not anticipated and that he had been assured of this by the leader of the local which had initiated the initial walkout. The union leader provided this assurance explicitly because of pending congressional action that provided, in addition to the 12 percent pay increase, full health benefit payments, top pay after eight instead of twenty-one years, and a provision for collective bargaining with binding arbitration in an impasse.[85]

Negotiations began immediately, with the unions demanding a minimum salary of $6000 and amnesty for all workers who participated in the strike. As indicated, the unions were negotiating for a 12 percent pay increase retroactive to October 1969, plus other benefits included in the congressional proposals. The first Administration offer afforded the postal workers a 6 percent increase and promised an additional increase in return for union support of postal reorganization. This offer was rejected on 28 March. On 3 April, the Administration and the seven national postal unions agreed on a two-step 14 percent wage increase accompanied by an agreement on postal reform. Six percent of the increase was to be retroactive to 27 December 1969, with the remaining eight percent effective when Congress voted on postal re-organization. The agreement also gave the postal workers the right to negotiate on the same subjects of collective bargaining as workers in the private sector.[86] On 17 April, the postal reform plan was announced by President Nixon. It included giving postal workers the right to bargain with management concerning pay and working conditions and provided binding arbitration for the settlement of impasses in addition to the aforementioned pay provisions.[87] By any standards, the postal employee strike succeeded in accomplishing objectives even beyond those which precipitated the strike.

The postal workers strike accomplished several important and interrelated union objectives. First, the union succeeded in enlisting public and congressional support for its demands. Apparently for the first time, many congressmen and the general public became aware of the letter carriers' low pay scale. Public support pressured the Executive Office and post office management into granting a significant pay increase and improvement of working conditions.

Second, the strike initiated by the letter carriers forced management to abandon its coercive tactics against the union. For several years, the Nixon Administration had attempted to pressure postal unions into accepting a *quid pro quo*—increased pay in return for political support of post office reorganization. There were numerous critics to the inclusion of pay matters in the postal reform measure; this was the major issue preventing the workers from returning to their jobs. The *New York Times* chided both the Administration and Congress for allowing the pay issue to become the "pawn in the frustrating tug-of-war over postal reform."[88] Postmaster General Blount implied that "the Administration might accept Congressional action on a pay increase without insisting that the increase be tied to postal reform."[89]

Third, the postal workers' strike greatly strengthened the movement for federal legislation that would legalize collective bargaining and impasse resolution to avoid future disruptive strikes. Even though strikes were banned in the new law, the unions agreed because "a settlement involving collective bargaining and binding arbitration was viewed as the possible opening wedge in a drive to get similar rights for all Federal employees."[90] The major impact of the postal workers' strike was viewed direly by some: "In prospect are further crucial conflicts between the Federal government and its increasingly militant employees. . . . "[91] The *New York Times* noted that, "The postal strike . . . has caused concern . . . that other Federal unions will be forced to take more militant stands against the government."[92] Many union leaders, according to the *New York Times* viewed the postal strike "as the final test of the laws and principles barring strikes against the Government."[93]

Clearly, the postal service strike of 1970 must be viewed as a model to public employee organizations of the strike's effectiveness when properly timed and executed. As the first contemporary strike by federal employees, the significance of its success as a precedent can hardly be underestimated.

Ineffectual Strike Model: Atlanta City Employees' Strike (1977)

Labor Relations in Atlanta (1970-77)

In 1970 garbage workers in Atlanta went on strike for thirty-seven days. Since then, there had been numerous one-day demonstrations and several wildcat walkouts. The most recent had been a five-day sanitation walkout that had occurred only the preceding month (February). During the February walkout, AFSCME membership voted again to strike.[94] In summary, even though the 1977 strike was Atlanta's first in seven years, there had been little labor peace during that period.

This same seven-year period coincides with the rise to power of Maynard Jackson, largely with the support of civil rights, liberal, and labor groups. Before his election as vice mayor in 1969, Jackson was an attorney with the National Labor Relations Board. As vice mayor, Jackson marched with AFSCME picketers protesting the perceived antilabor policies of the then mayor Sam Massell. After assuming office in 1973, Mayor Jackson announced his support of state collective bargaining legislation (excluding police and firemen)—although prohibited by state law. The mayor also established a separate Labor Relations Bureau at City Hall with Sam Hider as director. As the city's chief negotiator and a black, Hider came from a prolabor background. He had been regional director of the International Union of Allied and Technical Workers and involved in organizing several large corporations.[95]

Yet it is a third action taken by Mayor Jackson that caused him to be labeled a prounion mayor—the resurrection of a dues checkoff system for public employees that had been rescinded by former Mayor Massell in 1970. The dues checkoff procedure compelled the city comptroller to deduct union dues from an employee's paycheck if so authorized by the employee. Mayor Jackson successfully persuaded the city council to pass a checkoff ordinance in January 1975, in return for a no-strike contingency provision. During the 1977 strike, the mayor expressed a deep sense of betrayal for his checkoff support: "AFSCME gave me a promise before they ever got (dues) checkoff that they would never strike the city—and that is a lie, clear and simple."[96]

The dues checkoff system, together with wage rates emerged as the two foremost issues of the strike.

The Precipitating Strike Issues: Checks and Checkoffs

Impasses existed over four issues, although only two were of major importance and even discussed during strike negotiations. The union had demanded that the city provide liability insurance protection for on-duty employees while driving city vehicles. In addition, AFSCME demanded hospitalization benefits for employees and their families.

Of more importance was AFSCME's demand that union dues be increased and that the city include this increase in each employee's assessment. Specifically, the union voted to raise dues from $5 to $7.50 per month but the city refused to immediately increase the amount deducted because "they'd have to get every employee to sign a new card."[97] In essence, the city wished to wait and implement the new deduction rate in July. Union members could drop themselves from the checkoff list only in January and July, although they could join at any time.

The checkoff system carried added significance as a public indicator of union strength. The city and the Atlanta media later attacked AFSCME for trying to provoke a confrontation in order to revive sagging union membership. Mayor Jackson asserted that "AFSCME is looking for a way to restore its membership. . . . They're looking for a fight, spoiling for a confrontation."[98] Yet analysis of the number of eligible employees utilizing the checkoff was down only slightly at strike time. Of the 2,736 eligible employees for AFSCME membership, the following members utilized the system:[99]

Jan. 1975	July 1975	Jan. 1976	July 1976	Jan. 1977
1395	1177	1126	1290	1290

However, the checkoff figures are significant for another reason: only 47 percent (1290) of the eligible members (2736) had dues deducted for AFSCME. The union was hardly dealing its hand from a position of numerical strength.

Despite the checkoff system's importance as a secondary issue, the key issue proved to be one of proposed wage increases. The union was unequivocal in its demand for an across the board increase of fifty cents per hour. The mayor adamantly refused to discuss this amount, claiming that it would cost the city at least five million dollars. He argued that borrowing to meet the strikers' demands could hurt the city's credit rating. Consequently, Mayor Jackson vowed:

> I'm not going to be the first mayor since 1937 to take us to the bank. . . . Before I take the city into a deficit financial situation, elephants will roost in trees.[100]

The city had indicated in the few prestrike negotiations that it might be willing to grant a 5 percent pay increase but never the 15 percent increase that the union sought. Certainly neither side argued that the prevailing wages were embarrassingly low at the $7,400 annual average ($6,000 minimum wage). The city simply claimed not to be able to financially raise wages.

The Atlanta Strike: Short and Sour

The strike was intended by AFSCME to be a surprise tactic that included both a national publicity campaign against Mayor Jackson and coercion to grant an immediate pay raise before the budgetary deadline in four days (31 March). Caught in this coordinated pincer movement by AFSCME, it was believed that the mayor would be pressured into yielding.

The National Anti-Jackson Campaign

On Sunday, 27 March, the day before AFSCME members voted to strike on Monday or Tuesday, the union launched a vituperative publicity campaign against Mayor Jackson. The first volley appeared with a one-quarter page advertisement (costing $4,008) in the Sunday *New York Times* with the title, "The Falcons Aren't the Only Losing Team in Atlanta. Try City Hall."[102]

The union announced that it had budgeted other ads in the *New Republic, New Times, Columbia Journalism Review, More,* and *Crisis* (NAACP). Such advertisements were phase I of a budgeted $60,000 campaign that also included spots on Atlanta radio stations.[103] One Atlanta editorial claimed that AFSCME was prepared to spend up to $120,000 in its anti-Jackson campaign, scheduled to continue until the October election.[104]

The Southeast regional director of AFSCME claimed that the purpose of the anti-Jackson advertising campaign was simply to:

> apprise the public of the kinds of duplicity and double crosses we have encountered so the nation will see that the image of Atlanta being the "next great city" is not reflected in its leadership."[105]

Clearly, AFSCME hoped to discredit Mayor Jackson's liberal image with liberal and civil rights groups, particularly in the Northeast.

Predictably, many Atlantans and civic groups such as the Chamber of Commerce were incensed at what they perceived as an anti-Atlanta rather than an anti-Jackson campaign: "It's anti-Atlanta. How many dollars from Forward Atlanta is it going to take to offset this?"[106]

"Forward Atlanta" was the Chamber of Commerce's project to lure more investment into the city. It had just opened a new office in New York City in an effort to create more jobs.

AFSCME Strikes the City of Atlanta

Approximately 150 members of AFSCME took a strike vote in the lobby of city hall Monday morning. The vote took place following a boisterous meeting with the mayor earlier that morning. The union head promised "a 100 per cent shut down and curtailment of all city services by Tuesday morning."[107] The union announced that it would stay out until its fifty-cent pay demand was met. The strike was timed as last minute pressure upon the city before it had to legally close its books on 31 March (Friday).[108] In other words, if the city was going to accede to a raise for the next year, it had to do so within the next four days.

The strike among city employees was initially quite effective, particularly among sanitation and water works employees. By the next morning (Tuesday) more than 1,300 of 8,000 city employees were off the job. By Wednesday, only 10 of 62 residential garbage crews and 7 of 40 street cleaning crews were working (apartment and commercial pickup was not affected). Field operations of water and sewage works were heavily affected with only emergency work being performed.[109]

Neither side seemed disposed to negotiate and the positions of both sides seemed to rigidify even further. Each party blamed the other for refusing to negotiate. Union organizer Leamon Hood claimed that the city negotiators had turned a deaf ear for months:

> We have been trying to negotiate a pay increase for the past several months. . . . At a meeting about a week ago, city representatives walked out on us and we have not heard from them since.[110]

City representatives denied that they had walked out or refused to negotiate. Although no negotiations were immediately scheduled, AFSCME sent the mayor a telegram on Tuesday announcing its availability to meet with city officials.[111] This followed an abortive Tuesday session in which city representatives left before talks even began, "claiming there were too many union representatives at the bargaining table."[112] Meanwhile incidences of violence between strikers and nonstrikers served to heighten the tension.

Rather than being pressured into negotiations, the mayor reacted decisively and forcefully. Mayor Jackson announced on Wednesday that any striker who did not report to work by Friday would be fired. The notification was sent to each striker by mail or hand-delivered and signed by the appropriate department head. The union defiantly responded, "We do not intend to give up our jobs under any circumstances; they belong to us."[113] Meanwhile, strike negotiations were nonexistent and garbage continued to pile up in the streets.

Unwaveringly, the city's media and business community supported the mayor's strike ultimatum. The somewhat liberal *Atlanta Constitution* carried a Thursday editorial, "Fire the Strikers," which reflected on the mayor's past sympathy with AFSCME:

> Perhaps the time for being sympathetic to the union is over. The mayor needs to show some sympathy for taxpayers and residents of the city and notify the strikers that unless they intend to work they will be fired immediately.[114]

The Atlanta business community's response to Jackson was typified by Richard Kattel, president of the Citizens & Southern Bank, "The guy's got guts and is willing to stand up for what's right."[115] Even more surprising was Jackson's support from local NAACP and Urban League chapters as well as an endorsement from the Rev. Martin Luther King, Sr., who stated, "If you do everything you can and don't get satisfaction, then fire the hell out of them."[116] Residents were urged to dump their own garbage in city landfills, to which they responded favorably.

Both sides finally met on Saturday, 9 April, for a four-hour discussion. They exchanged proposals but made no progress. Monday, 11 April, was set as the last day when strikers would be given priority status over new job applicants. After that, all applications would be reviewed equally. However, the city council urged the mayor to extend the deadline for priority reapplying until noon Tuesday (12 April) to which Mayor Jackson complied. By the Tuesday deadline, 331 of 832 fired employees had been rehired in addition to 101 new applicants. Thus approximately 400 job slots were still unfilled.[118] The city offered to discuss rehiring strikers with AFSCME in order to provide "a graceful way out." Yet the unions steadfastly refused all such discussions.

The union desperately tried to rally sagging striker morale. James Farmer, former civil rights leader and now a director of the Coalition of American Public Employees (CAPE), led a Monday rally in front of city hall to inspire strikers to continue the movement. Not surprisingly, Farmer expressed his dismay with former civil rights activist Maynard Jackson. Farmer also exhorted the approximately 100 picketers from AFSCME with the promise that the 3.5 million CAPE members were behind their efforts.[119] More significant than Farmer's exhortations was the fact that normal residential garbage collection began on Monday, 11 April.

By Thursday (14 April) the city had rehired 400 strikers who joined over 250 new workers on the job. This followed an extension of the priority reapplication deadline to a Thursday evening deadline. Consequently, only 250 remaining slots were still available to the strikers whose position had clearly become untenable. Meanwhile approximately 200 AFSCME members voted to continue the strike, picketing and advertising against the city indefinitely.[120]

The mayor's tactic of expressing concern and making conciliatory offers toward the strikers but showing open contempt for the union was clearly effective. To union members Mayor Jackson announced that the city had gone the extra mile. To AFSCME leaders the city was less sympathetic: "Our concern is not to talk to AFSCME. Our concern is to save and protect jobs of those who have been discharged. They were a victim of circumstance."[121]

The mayor still contended that he was "pro-labor, pro-union, but I'm no friend of AFSCME."[122] Clearly, in two short weeks the mayor had broken the back of the Atlanta AFSCME local.

The strike theoretically continued for another two weeks until Thursday, 28 April, when the union officially admitted that the strike had failed.[123] On that day the national AFSCME headquarters withdrew from the field and left the shattered Atlanta local on its own. Significantly, the city still held open 200 vacancies in addition to the 500 reclaimed positions. The once proud union had begun one month earlier by demanding a fifty-cent an hour raise. By Tuesday (26 April) it was willing to merely get jobs back for its fired workers.

The AFSCME national headquarters admitted that its Atlanta strike had been beaten by Mayor Jackson: "He has broken the strike but he hasn't broken the union."[124] A national spokesman pledged an intensified national campaign against Mayor Jackson and a renewed organizational drive among Atlanta city employees. The Atlanta local had no comment.

In retrospect, the 1977 Atlanta city employees' strike is a classic case study of ineffectiveness. Neither short-term economic goals nor long-term political objectives were attained. Rather, the prospects for securing either immediate pay raises or collective bargaining in Atlanta were greatly diminished. Instead of the strike being utilized as a union weapon, it came to be employed as a device against the union.

The reasons for the failure of the Atlanta city employees' strike bear closer examination, for they may be factors in other strikes, particularly in the urban South.

First, unlike the 1968 Memphis sanitation strike, the Atlanta strike was not provoked by the refusal of a white city government to recognize a union made up primarily of black workers. Rather, Atlanta's mayor and chief negotiator were both long term and respected civil rights supporters; both are black. Both had extensive labor relations backgrounds and prolabor track records.

Consequently, the question was appropriately phrased by an *Atlanta Constitution* editorial: "Why are Wurf and his union singling out a liberal black mayor of a southern city as a target for a bitter advertising blast?"[125]

Mayor Jackson believes the answer lies in a "domino theory," of which he was the first domino. According to this theory, AFSCME looked for "the soft underbellies of the municipal South" and identified cities that have or soon will have liberal black mayors "who have been friends of labor consistently and who never want to be painted as anti-AFSCME."[126] Yet Mayor Jackson feels that the strategy failed because he was too politically strong in Atlanta and was in no danger of losing his impending November election.

The mayor believes that the Atlanta strike ruptured cooperative relations between the labor and the civil rights movements that were forged together during the Memphis crusade:

> *Until now, major black political leadership has supported union organizing in the South. . . . But if organized labor makes a move on black political leadership in its efforts to get a stronger foothold in the South, I think that it's going to have severe consequences for labor Southwide, particularly AFSCME."*[126]

The mayor evidently feels that labor organization and strikes of sanitation workers will be more successful among white dominated cities in the South.

Second, the Atlanta city employees' strike failed tactically because of its timing and a counterproductive national advertising campaign. The strike's timing was off in several respects. It is doubtful that attempting to pressure the city into agreement within four days of its budgetary deadline lent credibility to the union's demands. Certainly the declaration of a strike following anti-Atlanta advertisements in Northern and national media did not lend believability that the union was acting in good faith. Finally, timing the strike to coincide with the mayor's own reelection campaign only charged the air with a ready made political issue for the mayor. One that won him many votes.

In conclusion, one must question AFSCME's wisdom in choosing Atlanta for muscle flexing, particularly since there were only 1,200 members in the local. As indicated, these union members represented only 40 percent of the employees in sanitation and water works departments. By comparison, there are 130,000 AFSCME members in New York City. Finally, the words of then Vice Mayor Jackson, when he marched with AFSCME against Mayor Massell in 1970, are most ironic in retrospect:

> *The city's attitude has been one of winning or losing, not one of finding creative solutions to the dispute. It is the obligation of the city to anticipate the needs rather than react to demands.*[128]

The Atlanta city employees could not agree more.

Mixed Model: San Francisco Police and Firemen Strike (1975)

The San Francisco police and firemen strike (1975) is an important case study of the strike's mixed effectiveness as a political weapon. Although short-term pay gains were achieved, the long-term consequences for both police and firemen were negative.

Labor Relations History in San Francisco and California

Approximately a year earlier (1974) public employees, led by the militant transit, sewage works, and sanitation workers, walked out and effectively curtailed most city services. Within a few days, public school teachers initiated a separate strike, leaving only firemen and police as nonparticipants. The strike inconvenienced millions of San Franciscans and created a severe health hazard as tons of raw sewage were dumped into the bay and garbage remained uncollected. Mayor Joseph Alioto proclaimed a local state of emergency after five days. The mayor also served as a mediator and was particularly effective in resolving the teachers' strike.

The 1974 strike by sanitation, sewage, transit and hospital workers and teachers accomplished its primary short-term objectives of increased pay raises and fringe benefits. Furthermore, San Franciscans had stayed relatively uninvolved except to pressure the Board of Supervisors into concluding the strike in order to avoid further inconvenience. The mayor had performed a mediating role, saving the city from further inconvenience and loss of tourism. The 1974 strike had accomplished its objectives by a well-coordinated effort among several public employee organizations.

By 1975, police strikes were hardly an unknown phenomena in the United States, including Northern California. Although not as common an impasse resolution tactic as the work stoppage, i.e., blue flu or red rash, it was not unusual. However, the police strike had yet to undergo its first implementation in a major American city since the New York City strike in 1967. Although a major ten-day strike occurred among Albuquerque police one month earlier, it did not result in disruption of major city services.[129] Neither was it accompanied by a coordinated firemen's walkout.

In Northern California, a number of police strikes had occurred in smaller communities.[130] The first strike occurred in Vallejo on 17 July 1969 when the police chief was dismissed; it lasted five days. Antioch police staged a three-day walkout on 11 July 1970 after rejecting the city pay offer of an 8.5 percent raise; the issue was settled by a 12¼ percent raise. Finally, Hollister police participated in a walkout on 13 November 1970 because of a delayed start of an agreed raise.

Clearly the San Francisco police and firemen were determined that 1975 would be their year to reap the financial rewards of pressure group politics. They would utilize the 1974 strike tactics of other municipal employees to gain salary parity. A *San Francisco Chronicle* editorial during the height of the strike summarized the police and firemen's predicament:

> *It is difficult to fault police and firemen for asking for special wage consideration when almost every other group of city employees has been granted special consideration, often after considerable pressure.*[131]

Much like the frequent military revolutions in developing societies have become the legitimized means of changing leaders in these countries, so public employee strikes, through common usage, have become legitimized as the acceptable means for accomplishing political objectives.

Specifically, the San Francisco police and firemen's strike objective was to achieve economic parity with two other public employee groups —other San Francisco public employees and the Los Angeles police. San Francisco police and firemen were generally paid less than their craft and blue-collar counterparts, as shown in table 4-1.[132] Consequently, the city/county civil service commission recommended that police and firemen salaries be raised to a parity with other municipal employees.

An even more important issue concerned the city's twenty-three-year practice of compensating firemen and police on a parity with other protective service pay scales in California. Specifically, the city charter allowed the San Francisco Board of Supervisors to grant a maximum pay raise equal to the top pay scale paid in any other California city.[133] In recent years, the civil service commission had selected Los Angeles for the comparison wage. In 1975, a Los Angeles police corporal received significantly more than a San Francisco patrolman. An order to raise police and firemen salaries to the Los Angeles level would have increased the city budget by 13 percent.[134] The issue of parity with Los Angeles police was also clouded by a more complex pay scale used in Los Angeles. San Francisco police and civil service commission believed that all San Francisco patrolmen should be paid at the top of the Los Angeles scale; supervisors felt they should be paid at the lowest rung. As a compromise, the supervisors proposed a 6.5 percent increase roughly comparable to the current Oakland police salaries. However, the San Francisco police and firemen would not discuss any sum less than a 13 percent increase. The Police Officers Association (POA) remained firm on parity with Los Angeles: "It's been a good formula, and it worked well for 23 years . . . the police took a .008% or $9 dollars per month in 1972 without complaint because that was the formula."[135]

Part II: Politics of Collective Bargaining

TABLE 4-1: Comparative Pay of Cops, Crafts

The civil service commission yesterday provided the following figures comparing representative salaries presently received by San Francisco police personnel and various city crafts employees:

Police Department (Annual Salaries)	
Patrolman	$16,644*
Lieutenant.	$19,344*

City Crafts Employees (Annual Salaries)	
Laborer	$17,312**
Painter.	$21,121**
Electrician.	$21,601**
Carpenter	$21,893**
Plumber.	$24,112**
Plumbers' foreman	$26,530**

Source: *San Francisco Chronicle*, 20 August 1975, pt. I, p. 2.

* Police personnel, in addition to salaries, receive an additional 55 percent of the annual salary figure that is paid into their pension plan by the city.

**Crafts employees, in addition to annual salaries, receive an additional 16 percent of the annual salary figure that is paid into their pension plan by the city.

The difference between the current salary, salary proposed by both sides, and adjustments to include pensions and fringe benefits annually for a typical patrolman is as follows:[136]

	Current Salary	Supervisor's Proposal	POA-IAF Demand
Base	16,644	17,724	18,816
Adjusted	26,131	27,797	29,540
Difference	9,487	10,073	10,724

The San Francisco Police Officers' Association (POA) timed its strike pressure to coincide with the city's budgetary decision-making process. In the weeks preceding the 19 August budgetary deadline, POA persistently reiterated its nonnegotiatory stance on the 13 percent pay increase. Association spokesmen announced that police would walk off the job immediately if their demands were not met. For emphasis, POA emphasized that it would not negotiate with the city's negotiating team, which it termed "just high paid messengers."[137] Nonetheless, the supervisors continued to urge POA to meet with the negotiating team in order to "work something out."[138]

Consequently, POA members voted overwhelmingly to strike if wages were not increased 13 percent across the board. Significantly, the association leadership rejected the work stoppage or blue flu approach. The actual timing of the strike was dependent on the supervisors' budgetary actions. In a not too subtle forecast, POA president, Crowley predicted that "if the supervisors turn down our offer at 2:02 p.m., we'll go out on strike at 2:03 p.m.," on Tuesday (19 August).[139]

It is important to outline the dilemma faced by the San Francisco Board of Supervisors. On one hand the voters had approved a 1974 proposition amending the city/county charter to increase the police-firemen retirement contributions: police were to receive fifty-seven cents per dollar earned, firemen, forty-five cents per dollar earned. This pension plan provided San Francisco police and firemen with the highest pension payments in the state.[140] This alone, without raises, would increase the municipal budget by fourteen million dollars in 1975. Yet the public applied increasing pressures on the supervisors to cut budgetary spending. Consequently, the supervisors had publically pledged to slice the tax rate from its current $2.75 per $1.00 assessed valuation.[141] Furthermore, they promised to curtail budgetary spending.

Specifically, each one percent raise for the police and firemen would require an additional one million dollars in property taxes or a five-cent increase in the tax rate. Similarly, each percentage increase for San Francisco Municipal Railway Drivers (MUNI) employees would require $300,000 more revenue or a two-cent property tax rate increase. Supervisor Robert Mendelsohn, chairman of the board's budget committee, predicted that even proposed budget cuts of nine to eleven million dollars, resulting from the dismissal of temporary employees, would still leave the city with an increase of approximately 5 percent. Supervisor Mendelsohn emphasized the board's position: "I think its fair to say that virtually the entire board is unified on the concept of giving an increase which is satisfactory to the taxpayer."[142] Even more conciliatory, Mayor Alioto admitted that San Francisco salaries were lower than Oakland or Los Angeles, but justified a lower wage on the basis that "this is the year that we take special regard for the taxpayer."[143]

By Monday, 18 August, the Board of Supervisors was confronted with the imminent probability of strikes within two days by police, firemen, and transit workers. MUNI authorized a strike in a near unanimous vote on Sunday. MUNI workers were demanding a 15½ cent-per-hour overall pay increase package.[144] The International Association of Firefighters local AFL-CIO was scheduled to appear before the San Francisco Labor Council on Wednesday, 20 August, to seek strike sanction. POA had already committed itself to strike Tuesday if its demands were not met.

Finally, one last participant in the San Francisco strike scenario deserves notice. Mayor Joseph Alioto had built an image as a prolabor, liberal executive. He attempted to play a self-defined mediating role between the seemingly intransigent unions and the Board of Supervisors. Reportedly, the mayor worked "feverishly" to avert a strike by meeting frequently with key supervisors and staff budget analysts to discuss budget cutting options. Alioto flatly refused to either support or oppose the 13 percent parity issue; instead he hoped for compromise while reiterating his threat that any striking policeman would be dismissed.[145]

The Police Strike

On Tuesday, 19 August 1975, the San Francisco Board of Supervisors offered its police and firemen a 6.5 percent pay raise. The vote was unanimous. Within the hour, off-duty policemen were picketing the Hall of Justice. The police chief announced that only emergency calls would be answered by the remaining on-duty policemen. During the strike's first eight hours, not a single arrest was made in the city (an average day would yield thirty to forty bookings).[146]

The solidarity of the striking Police Officers Association is impressive. Although only 1,800 of the 3,500 police were POA members, over 90 percent of the nonsupervisory personnel did not report for duty Tuesday. The department's 719 supervisory personnel included 334 captains, lieutenants, and sergeants, and 285 inspectors and assistant inspectors. Furthermore, 15 percent of the inspectors and assistants joined the strike in sympathy.[147] Even discounting the fact that perhaps two-thirds of those police not reporting were either sick or on vacation, the strike was clearly cohesive.

Mayor Alioto immediately responded by offering both the carrot and the stick. At a Tuesday morning press conference, the mayor produced an April 1974 agreement with POA forbidding strikes or slowdowns. He again refused to tolerate a strike against public safety while expressing his hope that many police would return to work.[148] Alioto scorned the idea of asking Governor Brown to call out the National Guard: "We can maintain law and order in this town and we're not talking about bringing in amateurs."[149]

Meanwhile the mayor shuttled back and forth as an emissary between the supervisors and POA; both refused direct negotiations but were sequestered in nearby rooms of the Jack Tar Hotel for "consultation."

By Wednesday, 19 August, little apparent negotiating success had been achieved, feelings became embittered, and the city was enmeshed in rising violence. Early Wednesday morning the mayor's residence was rocked by a loud bomb placed at his doorstep. A sign left on the lawn read, "Don't Threaten Us." The crime increase was somewhat isolated to Chinatown as patrons at several large restaurants were robbed en masse. On a less significant level, numerous incidents of individual violence were reported. Many normally law-abiding citizens used the opportunity to park in tow away zones and run red lights. In a symbolic gesture to allay mounting fear, Mayor Alioto walked through the high-crime Tenderloin district at night.[150] Despite these fears and incidents between strikers and angry citizens, the city did not experience a crime wave, looting, or massive violence.

The mayor again reemphasized his intent to dismiss all striking police who did not return to work by Thursday. The POA responded determinedly:

> We realize that our jobs are on the line. We knew it when we walked out. Now we're backed into a corner, and we're going to fight to a finish—win, lose or draw.[151]

In essence, the association did not really believe that the mayor would actually fire several thousand trained police officers and replace them with new recruits. So the strikers' cohesion continued; only about forty-five men and twenty cars patrolled the city (compared to a normal force of 300 men and 100 cars).[152]

"Me Too" : The Firemen Strike

On Thursday evening, San Francisco members of the International Association of Firefighters (IAF), which included 98 percent of the total 1,775 firemen, initiated a strike action.[153] The vote was overwhelming: 1,121 to 42. Within an hour only eleven of forty-nine pumper cars and three of eighteen truck companies were operative. Only eighteen officers and forty-six firemen remained on duty. In one instance the FAA was pressed to train forty volunteers to assist the one remaining fireman in operating the airport's two crash and rescue trucks for the runways.

The firemen were obviously piggybacking on the police effort and hoped to achieve the same 13 percent parity raise. Union spokesman John Sherry defended IAF's opportunism:

> We feel that if the city can run around with millions of dollars for a cultural center, it can do something for us. . . . A guy sweeping streets makes as much as a captain in the department. . . . A guy operating a lawn mower at golf courses makes $22,000 and those guys aren't thrown into any tight spots.[154]

Firemen had evidently not coordinated their strike with the police in advance. Both groups together with MUNI workers had made strike contingency plans based on the city's budgetary cycle. Nonetheless, firemen were quite prepared to seize the moment created by striking policemen.

The Board of Supervisors reacted swiftly, once again demanding that the mayor sign the board's declaration proclaiming a local state of emergency.[155] The supervisors also wired Governor Brown directly, requesting the immediate dispatch of 200 highway patrolmen. However, Mayor Alioto refused, stating that he still hoped for a negotiated settlement. The mayor believed that the highway patrol's presence would only precipitate a "police-to-police confrontation."[156] The only note of optimism for the city occurred when the supervisors averted a MUNI strike by approving a 6.5 percent pay raise.

The supervisors were angered by what they perceived as the mayor's preemption of their sovereignty. They accused the mayor of shifting his role from mediator to the board's negotiator: "We never asked him [the mayor] to negotiate."[157] The supervisors refused to negotiate directly with the strikers until the public safety had been adequately secured. The supervisors' stance was fortified by constituency calls which averaged forty or fifty to one against compromise. Supervisor Feinstein described the board's mood: "In all my five years on the Board I've never seen so much unanimity on a labor issue as there exists today on this board."[158]

The board was supported by organized interest groups as over thirty neighborhood organizations coalesced within the Coalition for San Francisco Neighborhoods attacked the continuing police strike.[159]

The Mayor's Finesse; The Supervisors' Game

On Friday morning, 22 August, Mayor Alioto swiftly signed the local emergency measure proposed by the supervisors. However, rather than notifying the governor, the mayor utilized his new emergency powers to sign a new labor agreement. In effect, the police and firemen's strike had accomplished most of their objectives.[160] The mayor agreed to a 13.5 percent raise, costing $9,634,206, which would begin 15 October 1975. POA had demanded this percent raise totalling $13,601,232 for the entire year. Thus, the mayor's offer was $2,651,646 more than the supervisors' 6.5 percent ceiling. Although the strikers were not to be paid for the period of strike, all were granted total amnesty.

To overstate the supervisors' anger with the mayor would be difficult. The supervisors had only wanted emergency power to obtain the highway patrol. They had emphatically rejected the mayor's settlement offer originally. Among other appellations and expletives deleted, the supervisors called the mayor a "dictator"[161] and accused him of acquiescing to brute force: "The mayor's position was that they [the police] have the guns and so we should give in."[162] The mayor dismissed such criticism: "The supervisors and I have a different approach. They believe in making threats and I believe in sitting down and talking to people."[163]

In retaliation, the supervisors threatened to drastically cut the police and firemen budget.

However, the supervisors did not exercise direct vengeance against the police and firemen. Rather, they played to the voice of the people. Even before the strike's resolution, the supervisors had extended the deadline for entering propostions on the November ballot. On Friday, immediately following the mayor's announcement, the supervisors submitted the following charter amendments as propositions on the November ballot:

1. Automatic dismissal for any police or fireman who participated in strikes.
2. Abolition of the parity clause which pegged police and firemen's salaries to the highest paid in California.
3. Repeal of twenty-four-hour shifts by firemen, to be replaced by eight-hour shifts.
4. Revocation of the generous retirement benefits which had been approved by voters in 1974.
5. Requirement that a majority of supervisors must approve any declaration of emergency by the mayor.

The resulting mandate of the voters in November was definitive and devastating to the mayor, police, and firemen.[164] Each of the propositions submitted by the supervisors passed by overwhelming majorities, several by more than two-to-one. In addition, all of the incumbent supervisors won reelection. Clearly, the police and firemen had won a classic pyrrhic victory. Short-term objectives had been achieved but previous gains, made primarily via the electoral process, were cancelled.

The Strike's Failure: Observations

The San Francisco police and firemen's strike, unlike the 1977 Atlanta sanitation strike, had every potential for long- and short-term success. The San Francisco strike was conducted by two well-organized unions, whose protective services were vital to the city. Furthermore, it was following the strike precedent so effectively utilized by the city's public employees only one year earlier. Public opinion was seemingly sympathetic, as evidenced by its recent approval of munificent pension benefits. Yet the strike weapon became a cudgel used by the citizenry to destroy police and firemen gains. Three factors are partially explanatory:

1. The Police Officers' Association failed to persuade, even ignored public opinion. Public opinion had recently been an ally of POA at the voting booth. Voters had earlier forced the supervisors to

increase police and firemen benefits. There is no indication that the public might not again be mobilized to grant modest pay raises. One could have envisioned a well-organized campaign to bring San Francisco police and firemen up to the level of Los Angeles. In essence, the police assumed that they did not need public support to attain their objectives. They were obviously wrong.

2. The police officers used an excessive amount of coercion. By obviously exerting pressure in tandem with the firemen and to a lesser extent with MUNI workers, POA acquired a bully image. Both police and firemen appeared to gang up on the city, to be insensitive to its plight. It seems probable that an epidemic of blue flu and red rash would have been a more effective means of securing economic objectives while allaying citizen fears.

3. POA and IAF allowed themselves to negotiate and settle with the mediator rather than with management itself. Only the supervisors could approve pay raises. The mayor never served as its representative. No true settlement exists if it has not been agreed to by management itself. A mayor who is not seeking reelection cannot force supervisors, all of whom are seeking election (two for mayor) to effectively conclude an agreement that both parties would view as binding.

Conclusion

Private sector unions have won legitimacy to participate in the broader political environment for political goals and objectives. Private labor unions have also become an integral part of the interest group process within the American political system. However, it was only after achieving their economic objectives that unions became participants in the political process. They have since become major components of the Democratic party's electoral coalition. Private sector unions have also achieved legitimacy in lobbying and campaigning for political objectives.

By contrast, public sector unions and the collective bargaining process are still in a developmental stage. Public employee union activities are still legally limited by a myriad set of state and local codes, federal legislation, judicial decisions, and public antipathy toward public sector collective bargaining. Public employee unions have not achieved political legitimacy, consequently, they have increasingly resorted to illegitimate means, i.e., strikes and work stoppages, in impasse resolution. The strike has been viewed by employees as the panacea to gain political and economic power now denied. By management, the public employee strike has frequently been viewed as an unfair tactic that would provide unequal leverage to unions vis-à-vis other interest groups.

The history of the American labor movement until the 1960s and 1970s was written in the private sector. Although labor growth is now focused in the public sector, the basic models and concepts of collective bargaining were formulated by private sector experience. Consequently, the impact of the labor movement on the American economy has been significant and unique in shaping economic policymaking.

The labor movement's uniqueness stemmed from its absence of ideology or lack of politicization. Unlike the revolutionary or ideological orientation of the trade union movement throughout Europe, the American labor movement focused primarily on economic objectives. In essence, the American labor movement never adopted the class ideology or political orientations of its European counterpart. This economic emphasis was due primarily to the character of Samuel Gompers, who sought to preserve capitalism while increasing the workers' share.

The labor movement went through several stages in its evolutionary relationship with government, from persecution to final legitimacy under Franklin Roosevelt in the New Deal. President Roosevelt's National Labor Relations Board (NLRB), despite postwar modification by the Taft-Hartley Act, shaped the current adjudicatory emphasis of contemporary labor relations. Consequently, collective bargaining in the private sector has become highly formalized and regulatory in nature.

The political efficacy of public employee strikes in obtaining long- and short-term objectives is developed in three models: effectual, ineffectual, and mixed. These three strike models are applied in the following three case studies: the postal workers' strike (1970), the San Francisco police and firemen's strike (1975), and the Atlanta city employees' strike (1977). These three case studies indicate that the public employee strike, although always disruptive, may only be partially effective or even ineffective in achieving union objectives. The union's potential for gaining its objectives is not necessarily enhanced by a strike action. Rather, the union's probable success is much more likely to be determined by variables that generally determine any interest group's success: group size, resources, political allies, leadership, and strategy.

Notes to Chapter 4

1. Derek C. Bok and John T. Dunlop, *Labor and the American Community* (New York: Simon and Schuster, 1970), p. 384.

2. For a complete account of the reform interests of the early labor movement see chapter 2 of Gerald N. Grob, *Workers and Utopia* (Evanston, Ill.: Northwestern Univ. Press, 1961).

3. J. David Greenstone, *Labor in American Politics* (New York: Alfred A. Knopf, 1969), p. 18.

4. H. M. Gitelman, "Adolph Strasser and the Origins of Pure and Simple Unionism," *Labor History* 6 (Winter 1965), pp. 71-83.

5. Philip Taft, *Organized Labor in American Life* (New York: Harper & Row, 1964), p. 116.

6. Samuel Gompers, *Seventy Years of Life and Labor*, vol. 1 (Fairchild, N.J.: Augustus M. Kelley, Pubs., 1967), pp. 70-72.

7. Ibid., pp. 97-98.

8. Fred Greenbaum, "Social Ideas of Samuel Gompers," *Labor History* 7 (Winter 1966), pp. 35-61.

9. Samuel Gompers, *Labor and the Common Welfare* (Freeport, N.Y.: Books for Libraries Press, 1969), p. 20.

10. Gompers, *Life and Labor*, op. cit., p. 197.

11. Gompers, *Common Welfare*, op. cit., p. 144.

12. Gompers, *Life and Labor*, op. cit., pp. 244-246.

13. Grob, op. cit., pp. 152-153.

14. Taft, op. cit., p. 117.

15. Seymour Martin Lipset, *The First New Nation* (New York: Basic Books, 1963), pp. 170-199.

16. John M. Laslett, "Socialism and the American Labor Movement," *Labor History* 8 (Spring 1966), pp. 136-155.

17. Selig Perlman, *A Theory of the Labor Movement* (Fairfield, N.J.: Augustus M. Kelley, Pubs., 1949), pp. 280-303.

18. Richard Hofstader, *Anti-Intellectualism in American Life* (New York: Alfred A. Knopf, 1962), p. 284.

19. David J. Saposs, *Left-Wing Unionism* (New York: Russell & Russell, 1967), p. 28.

20. Mark Perlman, *Labor Union Theories in America* (White Plains, N.Y.: Row, Peterson, 1958), pp. 76-81.

21. Ibid., pp. 83-87.

22. Paul F. Brissenden, *The IWW: A Study of American Syndicalism* (New York: Russell & Russell, 1957), p. 63.

23. Joyce L. Kornbluh, *Rebel Voices: An IWW Anthology* (Ann Arbor: Univ. of Michigan Press, 1964), p. 48.

24. Harold M. Faulkner, *Labor in America* (New York: Oxford Book Company, 1955), p. 114.

25. Brissenden, op. cit., pp. 53-54.

26. Saposs, op. cit., 34-35.

27. Joseph G. Rayback, *A History of American Labor* (New York: Macmillan Publishing Co. 1959), pp. 320-346.

28. Ibid., p. 356-373.

29. Charles M. Rehmus and Doris B. McLaughlin, eds., *Labor and American Politics* (Ann Arbor: Univ. of Michigan Press, 1967), p. 418.

30. Sterling Spero and John M. Capozzola, *The Urban Community and Its Unionized Bureaucracies* (New York: Dunellen Publishing Co., 1973), p. 251.

31. A. H. Raskin, "Politics Up-Ends the Bargaining Table," *Public Workers and Public Unions*, The American Assembly-Columbia University (Englewood Cliffs, N.J.: Prentice-Hall, 1972), p. 127.

32. Ibid., p. 145.

33. O. Glenn Stahl, *Public Personnel Administration* (New York: Harper & Row, 1971), p. 305.

34. Philip L. Martin, "The Hatch Act in Court: Some Recent Developments," *Public Administration Review*, Sept/Oct 1973, pp. 443-447.

35. Stahl, op. cit., p. 309.

36. Spero and Capozzola, op. cit., 109-110.

37. Michael H. Moscow, J. Joseph Loewenberg, and Edward C. Koziara, "Lobbying," *Collective Bargaining in Government: Readings and Cases*, eds. J. Joseph Loewenberg and Michael H. Moskow (Englewood Cliffs, N.J.: Prentice-Hall 1972), p. 218. Cited hereafter as Loewenberg and Moskow.

38. Rehmus and McLaughlin, op. cit., p. 230.

39. Dale McFeathers, "Pressure for Bargaining Law to Cover Public Employees," *Memphis Press Scimitar*, 27 March 1974, p. 8.

40. Ibid.

41. Mary Goddard Zon, "Labor and American Politics," *Law and Contemporary Problems* (Spring 1962), p. 247.

42. Rehmus and McLaughlin, op. cit., p. 218.

43. Bok and Dunlop, loc. cit.

44. Nicholas A. Masters, "The Politics of Union Endorsement of Candidates in the Detroit Area," *Midwest Journal of Political Science* (August 1957), pp. 37-46.

45. Ruth Alice Hudson and Hjalmar Rosen, "Union Political Activity: The Member Speaks," *Industrial and Labor Relations Review.* 7, no. 3 (April 1954), pp. 404-418.

46. Greenstone, op. cit., pp. 81-175.

47. Ibid., p. 175.

48. The balance of the material in this section originally appeared in Alan E. Bent and Ralph A. Rossum, *Police, Criminal Justice, and the Community* (New York: Harper & Row, 1976), pp. 227-229; and, in Alan E. Bent, *The Politics of Law Enforcement: Conflict and Power in Urban Communities* (Lexington, Mass.: D.C. Heath and Co. 1974), pp. 76-87. For a detailed account of police in politics see Bent, *The Politics of Law Enforcement*, op. cit.

49. Murray S. Stedman, Jr., *Urban Politics* (Cambridge, Mass.: Winthrop Publishing Co., 1972), p. 276.

50. Harry H. Wellington and Ralph K. Winter, Jr., "The Limits of Collective Bargaining in Public Employment," in Loewenberg and Moskow, pp. 264-273.

51. Wellington and Winter, "More on Strikes by Public Employees," in Loewenberg and Moskow, op. cit., p. 289.

52. Allen Z. Gammage and Stanley L. Sachs, *Police Unions* (Springfield, Ill.: Charles C. Thomas, 1977, p. 65; William J. Bopp, *The Police Rebellion* (Springfield, Ill.: Charles C. Thomas, 1971), pp. 209-210.

53. Gammage and Sachs, op. cit., pp. 81-82.

54. Frank Kleinhenz, quoted by Michael Grieg, *San Francisco Chronicle*, 20 August 1975, pt. I, p. 2.

55. Robert A. Liston, *The Limits of Defiance: Strikes, Rights, and Government* (New York: Franklin Watts, 1971), pp. 6-7.

56. David B. Truman, *The Governmental Process* (New York: Knopf, 1951); Earl Latham, "The Group Basis of Politics," *Political Behavior*, eds. Heinz Eulau, Samuel J. Eldersveld, and Morris Janowitz, (New York: Free Press, 1956).

57. Robert A. Dahl, "Further Reflections on 'The Elitist Theory of Democracy,'" *American Political Science Review* 60, no. 2 (1966), pp. 296-305.

58. Peter Bachrach, *Theory of Democratic Elitism: A Critique* (Boston: Little, Brown & Co., 1967).

59. The Federalist, Number 10, *Federalist Papers* (New York: Random House, 1976).

60. Douglas M. Fox, *The Politics of City and State Bureaucracy* (Pacific Palisades, Ca.: Goodyear Publishing Co., 1974), p. 58.

61. Harry Eckstein, *Pressure Group Politics: The Case of the British Medical Association* (London: Allen & Unwin, Inc., 1960).

62. For an excellent overview of the comparative analysis of groups, see Harry Eckstein and David Apter, eds., *Comparative Politics* (New York: Free Press of Glencoe, 1963), pp. 389-430.

63. John F. Burton, Jr. and Charles Krider, "The Role and Consequences of Strikes by Public Employees," in Loewenberg and Moskow, op. cit., p. 279.

64. Theodore Lowi, *The End of Liberalism* (New York: W. W. Norton & Co., 1969).

65. Robert H. Salisbury, "The Analysis of Public Policy: A Search for Theories and Roles," *Political Science and Public Policy*, ed. Austin Ranney (Chicago: Markham Publishing Co., 1968).

66. Randall B. Ripley and Grace B. Franklin, *Congress, The Bureaucracy, and Public Policy*, (Homewood, Ill.: Dorsey Press, 1976), pp. 5-7.

67. Fox, op. cit., p. 58.

68. Ibid., p. 57.

69. Wallace S. Sayre and Herbert Kaufman, *Governing New York City* (New York: Russel Sage Foundation, 1960), pp. 264-69.

70. *Midwest Monitor* (Bloomington, Ind.: Indiana Univ. Press, March/April 1977), p. 2.

71. Ibid.

72. *New York Times*, 24 March 1970), p. 1.

73. Ibid.

74. Loewenberg, "The Post Office Strike of 1970," in Loewenberg and Moskow op. cit., p. 196.

75. *New York Times* 19 March 1970, p. 46.

76. Ibid.

77. *New York Times*, 19 March 1970, p. 1.

78. *New York Times*, 21 March 1970, p. 1.

79. Ibid.

80. Ibid.

81. *New York Times*, 24 March 1974, p. 1.

82. Ibid.

83. *New York Times*, 25 March 1971, p. 1.

84. Ibid.

85. *New York Times*, 26 March 1971, p. 1.

86. *New York Times*, 3 April 1970, p. 1.

87. *New York Times*, 17 April 1970, p. 18.

88. *New York Times*, 24 March 1970, p. 46.

89. Ibid., p. 1.

90. *U.S. News and World Report*, 6 April 1970, p. 16.

91. Ibid.

92. *New York Times*, 25 March 1970, p. 16.

93. Ibid., p. 30.

94. Jay Lawrence, *Atlanta Constitution* 29 March 1977, p. 1.

95. "Key People in City Strike," *Atlanta Constitution*, 31 March 1977, p. 18-A.

96. Maynard Jackson, quoted by Lawrence, op. cit., 31 March 1977, p. 18-A.

97. Lawrence, op. cit., 31 March 1977, p. 18-A.

98. Maynard Jackson, quoted by Lawrence, op. cit., 31 March 1977, p. 18-A.

99. Lawrence, op. cit., 31 March 1977, p. 18-A.

100. Maynard Jackson, quoted by Tom Matthews in *Newsweek*, 25 April 1977, p. 29.

101. Lawrence, op. cit., 31 March 1977, p. 1.

102. *New York Times*, 27 March 1977.

103. Lawrence, op. cit., 29 March, 1977, p. 7-A.

104. Bill Shipp, editorial, *Atlanta Constitution*, 29 March 1977, p. 4-A.

105. Leamon Hood, quoted by Lawrence, op. cit., 29 March 1977, p. 7-A.

106. *New York Times*, 27 March 1977.

107. Lawrence, op. cit., 29 March 1977, p. 1.

108. Ibid.

109. Lawrence, op. cit., 31 March 1977, p. 18-A.

110. Lawrence, op. cit., 29 March 1977, p. 1.

111. Jay Lawrence and Ken Willis *Atlanta Constitution*, 30 March 1977, p. 1.

112. Lawrence, op. cit., 31 March 1977, p. 1.

113. Ibid.

114. Shipp, op. cit.

115. Tom Matthews, *Newsweek*, 25 April 1977, p. 29.

116. Ibid.

117. Lawrence, op. cit., 31 March 1977, p. 1.

118. Lyn Martin, *Atlanta Constitution* 12 April 1977.

119. Ibid.

120. Ibid., p. 1.

121. Ibid.

122. Ann Wodner, *Atlanta Constitution*, 10 April 1977, p. 1-A.

123. Lawrence, op. cit., 10 April 1977, p. 1.

124. Ibid.

125. Shipp, op. cit.

126. Woolner, op. cit.

127. Ibid.

128. Ibid.

129. Michael Geieg, *San Francisco Chronicle*, 20 August 1975, pt. I, p. 2.

130. Ibid.

131. Editorial, *San Francisco Chronicle*, 20 August 1975, p. 46.

132. *San Francisco Chronicle*, 20 August 1975, pt. I., p. 2.

133. Bill Bodenweck, *San Francisco Examiner*, 17 August 1975, pt. 1, p. 45.

134. Larry Liebert, *San Francisco Chronicle*, 20 August 1975, pt. I, p. 2.

135. Bodenweck, op. cit., p. 4.

136. Liebert, op. cit., p. 2.

137. Bodenweck, op. cit., p. 1.

138. Ibid.

139. Robert Bartlett, *San Francisco Chronicle*, 18 August 1975, p. 18.

140. Liebert, op. cit., p. 2.

141. Bartlett, op. cit., p. 18.

142. Bodenweck, op. cit., p. 4.

143. George Williamson, *San Francisco Chronicle*, 20 August 1975, p. 20.

144. Bodenweck, op. cit., p. 1.

145. Williamson, op. cit., p. 1.

146. Jerry Carroll, *San Francisco Chronicle* 19 August 1975, p. 1.

147. Ibid.

148. Ibid., p. 20.

149. Ibid.

150. Williamson, op. cit., p. 1.

151. Ibid.

152. Eugene Robinson, *San Francisco Chronicle*, 20 August 1975, p. 20.
153. Ralph Craib, *San Francisco Chronicle*, 21 August 1975, p. 1.
154. Ibid., p. 30.
155. Carroll, op. cit., 21 August 1975, p. 1.
156. Ibid., p. 30.
157. Ibid., p. 1.
158. Ibid., p. 30.
159. *San Francisco Chronicle*, 21 August 1975, p. 3.
160. Carroll, op. cit., 22 August 1975, p. 1.
161. Ibid.
162. Carroll, op. cit., 21 August 1975, p. 30.
163. Carroll, op. cit, 23 August 1975, p. 1.
164. *San Francisco Chronicle*, 5 November 1975, p. 1.

5 Collective Bargaining and the Law: Strikes and Impasse Resolution

This chapter will present and analyze the legal environment that shapes contemporary public sector labor relations, particularly the legal ramifications of public employee strikes. Our analysis is divided into three parts. First, we will present a three-stage overview of the legal development of labor relations in the United States. Next, we will examine the efficacy of legal prohibitions against public employee strikes, i.e., legislation, judicial decisions, and court injunctions, as well as the rational arguments for and against strike legislation. We will conclude with an evaluation of the role of legislation in shaping behavior and attitudes toward strikes in the public sector. Finally, impasse resolution techniques and experiences will be discussed.

The legitimization of basic principles and precepts in public sector collective bargaining is inherently linked to the private sector experience. Our analysis isolates those concepts and legislation in the private sector which are crucial to the public sector experience. We will analyze the overlapping application of private sector principles to public collective bargaining at two discrete levels—among the states and in the federal government.

Phase One (1932-1947): Formulation of the Basic Principles of Labor Relations

The American industrial relations system is undoubtedly one of the most legally complex among Western societies. No major aspect of the private sector management-employee relationship is free from detailed regulation by both federal and state legislation. All long-term indications suggest increased regulation at all governmental levels. Furthermore, there has been a continuing trend in labor relations for federal laws to take precedent over state laws. In fact, many observers criticize labor-management laws as being too regulatory and overly prescriptive. Supposedly, the collective bargaining activities of both private sector unions and management are so constricted that experimentation and creativity are seldom possible.

Yet formality and procedural rigidity were not always the *modus operandi* of the private sector. For approximately fifteen years, from 1932 until 1946, federal policymaking in private sector labor relations experienced mercurial extremes. As Harold Davey notes, from 1932 until 1947 the federal executive pursued a policy of encouraging unionism and collective bargaining.[1] In quick succession, the Roosevelt presidency built upon the existing Norris-LaGuardia Act to facilitate union growth by formulating the National Industrial Recovery Act (1933-1935) and its successor, the Wagner Act (1935), as the pinnacle of New Deal unionism. The Wagner Act together with its progeny, the National Labor Relations Board (NLRB),[2] provided the "psychological climate and legal support"[3] necessary for continued union growth and the legitimization of the collective bargaining process.

The development of federal policymaking in private sector labor relations has undergone several stages since the passage of the National Labor Relations Act (Wagner Act) in 1935. The various developmental stages of this policy are indicated by subsequent amendments to the NLRA: the 1947 Labor Management Relations Act (Taft-Hartley Act), and the 1959 Labor Management Reporting and Disclosure Act (Landrum-Griffin Act). In essence, the NLRA from 1935 until 1947 encouraged collective bargaining by guaranteeing employees the right to join the union of their choice. Conversely, since 1947, the NLRA has secured the right of employees to refrain from joining a union if they so desired.

Specifically, the Wagner Act's injunction against "unfair labor practices" by employers formalized more than an objective for the NLRB. The regulation of unfair labor practices by a neutral agency, imbued with permanent and final arbitrary powers, set an inviolate principle: the federal government, through its regulatory commission, should guarantee an equalized bargaining process between two equal parties. For example, the NLRB's consistency in recognizing appropriate units of bargaining as those complying with certain majoritarian procedures has become established precedent. Consequently, it has become unlikely that public management can continue to resist the cry for recognition from any public employee union that claims majority representation. It is this regulatory function, based on procedure and policies, which makes the role of an independent commission, i.e., the NLRB, seemingly essential to labor-management relations.

The National Labor Relations Board

The Wagner Act authorized a National Labor Relations Board (NLRB) as a regulatory body with authority over certain types of private sector employees. The NLRB's jurisdiction over collective bargaining evolves from the Constitution's commerce clause. Consequently the NLRB's jurisdiction is limited to those businesses which significantly impact either commerce or defense. Although expanded by later legislation, e.g., Taft-Hartley and Landrum-Griffin, NLRB jurisdiction was initially prohibited for the following employee categories:

- Agricultural workers
- Domestic servants
- Workers employed by parents or spouses
- Independent contractors
- Supervisors
- Government employees at all levels
- Hospital employees
- Employees covered by the Railway Labor Act

The NLRB's jurisdiction over employee groups remained relatively constant until a 1974 expansion to include employees of not-for-profit hospitals. A number of public employee organizations have pressured for further NLRB expansion to include regulation of public sector labor relations.

The Wagner Act intended the National Labor Relations Board (NLRB) to be an independent commission mandated to enforce its provisions. As such, the NLRB is authorized to investigate, conduct hearings, and issue decisions that are subject to judicial oversight for final review. Although somewhat modified through subsequent legislation, the NLRB is viewed by Harold Davey as performing two essential functions: (1) regulation of "unfair" labor practices, and (2) service, by administering representation elections. In actuality, both NLRB functions are regulatory of labor-management relations. Consequently, the NLRB workload consists primarily of either representation or unfair labor practices cases. In the first instance, representation cases deal with three questions of union recognition:

1. What is an appropriate unit?
2. What is the majority will of unit employees?
3. How can changes in majority will be indicated?

As several observers note, there are three important principles that govern NLRB decisions on union recognition and representation issues:

1. Employees are the sole judges of whether or not they should be represented by a union.
2. A majority of the employees can commit what may be a very unhappy minority to representation by a particular union.
3. It is the job of the NRLB to determine what the majority wants.[4]

The accepted method of determining these issues has been through NLRB encouraged "ballot box organizing."

The second area of NLRB responsibility includes regulation of unfair labor practices by either labor or management. Initially "unfair labor practices" were exclusively defined by the Wagner Act as employer actions. This definition was radically amended by the Taft-Hartley Act of 1947 to include a variety of employee or union practices. As a result, the NLRB's most difficult task has not been the adjudication of obvious legal infractions. Rather, it has been the application of either party's obligation to bargain together in good faith. Over the years, the NLRB has developed guiding principles, e.g., the "totality of conduct" during the bargaining process to assess good faith behavior. Throughout the war years, unions and management agreed informally to a hiatus in impasse and strike action as both parties agreed to a shotgun marriage of convenience. Both also accepted the imposed governmental domination by the War Labor Board (WLB) during these four years. As Harold Davey suggests, the WLB functioned as a final arbiter in all impasse disputes.[5] Consequently, both labor and management bargained in an unnatural no-strike environment in which both parties learned for the first time to appreciate:

> the desirability of providing for final and binding arbitration of contract interpretation or application disputes. They also learned to appreciate the uses of rate ranges in wage administration. Some unions lost much of their traditional fear of job evaluation and wage incentive systems. Such matters as paid vacations, paid holidays not worked, sick leave and night-shift differentials also received considerable impetus. . . .[6]

In effect, collective bargaining contract provisions were peculiarly shaped by the distinctive influence of the war environment and National War Labor Relations Board policies.

The Post-War Era of NLRA

In retaliation against the explosive increase in strikes following the war's end, Congress passed an amendment to the NLRA, the Taft-Hartley Act in 1947. It would be difficult to overstate the impact or importance of the Taft-Hartley amendment to the NLRA. In summary, Taft-Hartley employers are prohibited from engaging in the following activities:

1. Taking prejudicial action against their employees for participating in or supporting labor organizations.
2. In any way pressuring employees who exercise their right to organize or bargain collectively in choosing their own representatives.
3. Initiating prejudicial action against their employees for testifying in NLRB cases.
4. Refusing to bargain collectively with a union that was elected by majority vote, in compliance with NLRB guidelines.
5. Financially contributing to or attempting to set up a management controlled labor union.

Employee organizations are prohibited from engaging in the following activities:

1. Pressuring an employer to discriminate against any employee.
2. Coercing an employer to fire any employee at the union's behest unless the employee has refused to comply with agency or closed shop provisions in the agreement.
3. Attempting to influence employer selection of his representatives for collective bargaining or negotiation of impasse.
4. Refusing to bargain in good faith with employers.
5. Coercing employers into paying fees for services not performed.
6. Charging excessive initiation fees to prospective members.
7. Pressuring nonunion employees to join a union. Such employees are guaranteed the right to refrain from participating in or joining union activities.

Although Taft-Hartley contains both employer and employee restrictions, it is perceived by most observers as a successful effort to establish parity between management and labor. As such, it is clearly a management victory. Two crucial and controversial precedents were established by Taft-Hartley: (1) ban of the secondary boycott and (2) allowance of state right-to-work laws. Both precedents have withstood concerted attempts for over three decades by organized labor to either eradicate or revise their intent. Analyses of the public sector experience also indicate that both principles are already ensconced there as well.

Briefly, the most controversial, complex, and publicized area of union unfair practices is found in section 8 (b) (4) of Taft-Hartley. Among other unfair labor practices, this section bans strikes classified as "secondary boycotts." This means that unions are prohibited from applying economic pressure, i.e., strikes, boycotts, etc., against any organization other than the primary employer. Frequently, secondary boycotts are applied against the employer's business suppliers or customers in an effort to economically affect his profits.

In perhaps a more profound precedent for the public sector, Taft-Hartley's controversial section 14 (b) has provided the legal justification for a variety of right-to-work laws among the states. In essence, this section allows state laws regarding union security clauses to preempt federal legislation. In a rare reversal of the Constitution's Tenth Amendment, state regulation of union security clauses are to have precedence. Consequently, twenty states prohibit compulsory union membership, although in seven states an agency shop arrangement may be permissible.* Theoretically, any employee should have the right to work without being compelled to join or support a union. Both the right-to-work and the secondary boycott ban provisions of the Taft-Hartley Act have obviously profoundly shaped the nature of private sector labor-management relations for over thirty years. Despite continued intense debate, there is no evidence of the imminent demise of either precedent.[7] Both concepts have already been transposed to the public sector. As with the right-to-work precedent, state statutes have been allowed to prevail over federal legislation.

Perhaps the real significance of the Taft-Hartley Act is that it denotes the evolutionary zenith of major labor-management policymaking in the private sector. Although the Landrum-Griffin Act was subsequently passed in 1959, it served primarily to solidify the existent collective bargaining process rather than signify a new development in private sector labor relations. In fact, union membership in the private sector following Taft-Hartley barely maintained its overall percentage of the total labor force. Only rapid growth in public sector unionization beginning in the late '60s would again stimulate AFL-CIO growth. With Taft-Hartley, the process of labor-management relations was finalized. Only procedure and specific application remained to be somewhat refined by the NLRA's final amendment, the Landrum-Griffin Act in 1959.

The final shape of governmental policy formulation and regulation in private sector labor relations occurred with the last major amendment to the NLRA, the Landrum-Griffin Act of 1959. Although one observer notes, "the provisions of the Landrum-Griffin Act that strictly belong in the field of labor-management relations are relatively minor," the act has two important objectives:

> (a) to set minimum standards of democratic procedure, responsibility, and honesty in the conduct of the internal affairs of unions

---

* Arizona, Florida, Kansas, Nevada, North Dakota, South Dakota, and Texas.

and (b) to clarify congressional intent on basic labor relations policy as stated in the Taft-Hartley Act.[8]

The latter objective further clarifies the Taft-Hartley Act by defining the role of the NLRB, plugs up loopholes in the Taft-Hartley ban on secondary boycotts, and reauthorizes the closed shop in the construction industry.

The importance of Landrum-Griffin rests in its first objective, as a precedent for governmental regulation of internal union affairs that had heretofore been essentially self-governing. In a radical policy departure, Landrum-Griffin specifically regulates a variety of issues, designed to guarantee union democracy.

The crux of the act is a "bill of rights" for union rank-and-file that guarantees union membership participation in elections, holds union officers individually responsible for act violations, and provides safeguards for union funds.

Phase Two (1962-1969): Application of NLRA Concepts to Federal Employees

Accepting the conclusions of a presidential task force headed by Labor Secretary Arthur Goldberg, on 17 January 1962, President Kennedy issued Executive Order 10988, which established the first guidelines for federal employee-management cooperation. It is important to note that E.O. 10988 applied only to federal employees. Some observers feel that existent collective bargaining models in New York City had "served as a model for President Kennedy's Executive Order."[9] As Kenneth Warner and Robert Presthus note, the Kennedy order combined with legitimization of collective bargaining in New York and Philadelphia and increased teacher militancy during the '60s, were interrelated "steps toward the industrial pattern of collective bargaining... taken on all levels of government."[10] Despite its initial gratuity to federal employee organizations, neither the Kennedy nor a later Nixon Executive Order legally compromised Congress's right to determine wages and fringe benefits. However, the initial transposition of NLRA concepts and procedures to the public sector had begun.

Despite the fact that the Kennedy Order established an important precedent for federal employees, reactions were mixed. According to one observer, this Order was "an affirmative statement of the desirability of employee-management cooperation... well beyond the Lloyd-LaFollete Act's protection of the bare right of organization."[11] However, unions criticized the Order because "the determination of bargaining units and judgments regarding labor practices were left in the hands of the employing department."[12] The Kennedy Order was also criticized because it limited the scope of bargaining, offered no substitute for the right to strike, lacked a central administering agency, did not include a provision for a central bargaining representative, and failed to specify procedures for the resolution of grievances.[13]

Following the recommendations of a Civil Service Commission advisory committee, President Nixon issued Executive Order 11491 in 1969, which significantly expanded the earlier Kennedy Order. The Nixon Order mandated secret ballot elections and neutral party procedures in impasse resolution. Such techniques were intended to achieve exclusive representation for federal employee organizations.

In order to implement the Nixon Order's objectives, E.O. 11491 authorized a Federal Labor Relations Council (FLRC), which was commissioned to resolve major policy disputes by negotiation.[14] However in "Catch-22" logic, the commission neither possessed ultimate arbitration authority in cases where negotiation failed, nor could the council make decisions concerning bargaining units, representation, and unfair labor practices. Decisions in the former case were delegated to a newly created federal service impasse panel.[15] Decisions in the latter instance were referred to the assistant secretary of labor for labor-management relations. In effect, the FLRC followed the interest group liberalism model formulated by Theodore Lowi, in which public agencies are given ill-defined ambiguous policy objectives, while other agencies are provided responsibilities to accomplish overlapping objectives.[16]

Both the Kennedy and Nixon Executive Orders made federal employee-management relations more closely parallel to labor-management relations in the private sector and provided a limited form of collective bargaining for all federal employees. However, several public employee organizations remain critical of these attempts to encourage employee-management cooperation in the public sector, because they feel that collective bargaining without the right to strike is meaningless.[17]

In September 1971, President Nixon issued Executive Order 11616, which served to expand the scope of his 1969 Executive Order by requiring negotiated grievance procedures in all subsequent contracts and strengthened the role of bargaining by union representatives. For example, an employee in a grievance proceedings was guaranteed certain rights: (1) time off to prepare his own case, (2) hearings must be conducted by qualified examiners, (3) materials used by management as evidence must be made available to the employee in advance of the hearing, (4) such material not provided to the employee in advance was inadmissible as evidence, and (5) verbatim transcripts of the hearings must be made available to the employee.[18]

The scope of negotiations was further expanded in May 1975 by President Ford's Executive Order 11838.[19] Based on FLRC recommendations, the order essentially classified all agency regulations negotiable unless the agency could show a "compelling need" not to negotiate. Furthermore, any proposed changes in personnel policies were designated as mandatory bargaining subjects, even when a contract was already in force. The Ford Order also expanded the scope of grievance procedures to include the interpretation and application of agency regulations as well as negotiated agreements.

However it is important to realize both the symbolic and real consequences of the Kennedy and Nixon Executive Orders. Congress still has sole constitutional authority to determine wages and fringe benefits by *de jure* authority. However, federal employees exercise *de facto* power through joining a union and conducting strikes, to coercively determine wages and fringe benefits. Significantly, the two major nationwide federal employee work stoppages, i.e., the 1970 postal service strike and the air traffic controllers' job action, are both conceded to have been highly successful. Therefore, one perspective is that Executive Orders merely symbolize the status quo rather than ushering in a new era. Important precedents have already been established, as some observers note:

> There was no change from the historic exclusion from negotiated grievance/arbitration procedures of matters subject to statutory appeals such as discharge, demotion or discrimination based on race, sex, etc. Neither did the new amendments to E.O. 11491 repeal its ban on union or agency shops or the requirement that the management rights clause. . . be part of all negotiated agreements.[20]

The importance of the presidential Executive Orders lies not in their substantive reshaping of public sector labor-management relations. Rather, their significance is their symbolic encouragement of collective bargaining for all public employees.

Phase Three (1965-Present): State and Local Emulation of NLRA Principles and Procedures

State and local emulation of NLRA principles and procedures became apparent with the adoption of state collective bargaining legislation, beginning with Wisconsin and Michigan in 1965. Since many concepts in state legislation were transposed from the NLRA, it was also logical that NLRA precedents and procedures were utilized in collective bargaining implementation. That NLRA principles should reappear in state and local variations should therefore not be surprising.

> *Concepts in the field of labor relations which have prevailed over the years have been broad enough in nature and sound enough in logic to survive numerous "exceptions to the rule." Their durability offers pragmatic evidence of their merit.*[21]

Despite the uniqueness of public sector employment, collective bargaining policymaking and procedures will continue to be shaped by the private sector experience, specifically the NLRA and the regulatory role of the National Labor Relations Board (NLRB).

A recent survey comparison of various state statutes with NLRB concepts and concomitant NLRB interpretations corroborates their significant impact:

> *NLRB decisions are frequently cited in legal briefs and memoranda by employers and unions in public sector disputes involving unit determinations and unfair labor practices. . . .*
> *Perhaps more importantly, various state courts and public employee relations boards throughout the United States have specifically sanctioned the application of NLRB precedent in construing language under their state's public sector labor statute. For example, . . . the 1974 case—*Firefighters Union 1186 *vs.* City of Vallejo, *in which the California Supreme Court specifically held that the NLRA and cases interpreting the Act may properly be referred to in interpreting similar language in public labor statutes.*[22]

The NLRA statutes and NLRB decisions have been legitimized despite the fact that neither are legally applicable to public sector labor-management relations.

The comparative importance of the legal framework on which private and public labor-management relations is based is evident in various arguments concerning the public employee's right to strike. The Norris-LaGuardia Act and the National Labor Relations Act have given private sector employees the right to strike. As Spero and Capozzola observe, "In the private sector the law now sanctions an area of 'permissive economic warfare' in sharp contrast to the public case law, which held illegal the deliberate commission of harm to another without justification recognized by law."[23] All federal employees are without the legal right to strike and in fact federal employees are specifically forbidden to continue employment as civil servants if they participate in a strike. A number of collective bargaining experts and union leaders advocate that Congress pass legislation authorizing the right of public employees to strike.

Despite frequently introduced legislation, thus far only Alaska, Hawaii, Pennsylvania, and Oregon have passed legislation granting most state and local employees the right to strike. However, these states do not include police and firefighters or "essential" employees. In all four states, this right may be rescinded if a strike threatens public safety, health, or welfare. Vermont prohibits local employee strikes but states that employees may be prosecuted only if the public welfare is threatened. Montana allows nurses to strike only if no other health care strike is in progress within 150 miles and following thirty-days notification of intent to strike.

Most state legislatures outside the South have considered or are currently reviewing various forms of collective bargaining legislation. All such legislation stems from a common concern: the impact of a public employee strike upon the public welfare. As will be noted, such legislation focuses on the fear of strikes rather than on meaningful collective bargaining or negotiating impasse resolution. For example, the California Senate's Revenue and Taxation Committee in 1977 passed and sent to the floor a bill (S.B. 164) that prohibited strikes and included mandatory and compulsory arbitration in all police and fire fighting contracts.[24] Hence, negotiation or bargaining over an impasse is excluded a priori.

Consequently, these are the issues: Should public employees have the legalized right to strike? If so, what are the possible and appropriate methods of interest impasse resolution? Finally, what has been the experience of various public employee strikes (both legal and illegal)? To what degree, if any, were such strikes effective in accomplishing their objectives? And, to what extent were employed methods of impasse resolution effective? We shall analyze the major arguments offered affirmatively and negatively on the issue of legalizing public employee strikes.

Why Public Sector Strikes Should Be Legalized

Advocates generally present a number of interrelated reasons for legislatively legitimizing the public employees' right to strike. First and perhaps most compelling, public employee strikes already occur and there are no clear signs of their diminishing. Although frequently called "quasi-strikes," "job actions," or "work slowdowns," public employee strikes are contemporary phenomena that are not being legislated away.

Advocates argue that the prudent course for both labor and management would be to legalize the right to strike and establish procedures

Part II: Politics of Collective Bargaining

for resolving impasses similar to those established in the private sector. Strike legalization proponents believe the increasing number of "sickouts" and "study days" suggest that if government employees were allowed to strike, attention could be redirected toward substantive issues. Management time and energy would not be spent attempting to enforce untenable no-strike, or slowdown measures.[25]

A second argument supporting the public employees' right to strike is based in the supposed positive function of legitimate group conflict.[26] As Lewis Coser suggests, social conflict in legitimized ways may actually be constructive for group identity and member satisfaction. Clark Kerr, chancellor of the University of California during the strike-torn 1960s supported the strike's integrative function:

> *In modern industrial society the sources of unrest and hostility are enormous. The strike provides an outlet for them when they are so severe as to require forceful expression. . . reconciliation follows more easily if retribution has preceded. In a sense, thus, strikes are constructive when they result in the greater appreciation of the job by the worker and of the worker by management.*[27]

Kerr states that underlying hostility can be detrimental to production and efficiency, and that strikes clear the air and form the basis for a new beginning. He asserts that the lack of strikes in an industry is not necessarily indicative of good labor-management relations. Furthermore, even if strikes do not occur, the threat of strikes or lockouts facilitates the resolution of conflicts at the bargaining table.[28]

The third reason advanced for strike legalization is that it functions as the ultimate test of the union's strength as a bargaining representative. If the union cannot obtain its demand through collective bargaining, it can threaten to call a strike as further incentive for management to negotiate in good faith. Then, union leaders must amass the support of a large, individualistic group and mold it into a solid, powerful unit with high morale and enthusiasm for any eventual strike action. Strike legalization proponents reiterate that many strikes in the public sector are caused by interunion struggles for recognition; consequently, the union that encompasses the greater number of workers becomes the bargaining agent with which management must deal in the future. The union is forced to demonstrate its strength to management through the number of workers supporting a strike. In essence, supporters contend that the strike is "the natural concomitant of collective bargaining."[29]

Public sector unions feel that the strike threat is essential to back up their demands at the bargaining table:

> *Only such force will induce meaningful bargaining and subsequent agreement. Without the right to strike to back up their*

demands, public employees are merely able to make suggestions and recommendations, which the employer is free to reject without fear or reprisal. The strike or the threat of a strike thus resolves impasses in public employee negotiations in the same way it operates in private employment.[30]

Traditionally, unions in both the public and private sectors have felt that strikes are necessary for the survival of the union. The primary mission of a union is to improve working conditions and terms of employment for its members by bilateral negotiation with management. In order to bargain effectively, union leaders believe that they must have the ultimate threat of a strike behind their demands. If the union cannot bargain effectively and is unsuccessful at improving the individual lot of its members, the union serves no constructive purpose. Therefore, the strike is necessary for the effectiveness and very survival of the union.

In the public sector, strikes have frequently occurred to obtain recognition of a union as a bargaining unit. In fact, strikes for recognition have been the second major cause of work stoppages in the public sector.[31] Strikes for recognition are generally brought to demonstrate union power and solidarity and create a strong bargaining unit. Most labor leaders feel that strikes will continue to be necessary in reaching an agreement with management. In the public sector, union leaders are pressuring for the legal right to strike. However, some authorities feel that strikes are outmoded and that the alternative means for settling a dispute are more satisfactory and should be utilized more frequently. Nonetheless, the potential strike, like the potential executive veto, is a strategy in bargaining rather than necessarily a weapon to be utilized.

Those who wish to permit strikes in the public sector state that many government functions, including transit, health care, garbage collection, and teaching, are also performed by private institutions whose employees legally possess the right to strike. They believe that the same right should be granted to employees in the public sector. The executive director of CAPE gives an example:

When a U.S. city hires a private firm to pick up trash, the firm's truck driver is by federal law, guaranteed a minimum wage, time and a half for overtime, working conditions that insure his health and safety, the right to organize and bargain collectively with his employer, and a right to strike for better wages, hours, and other terms of employment. But when the city itself hires the truck driver, he has none of these same guarantees, unless the city or the state legislature has granted them. Moreover, what the city or state has by law and ordinance granted, it can by law or ordinance repeal.[32]

In essence, strike advocates object to the prohibitions of a strike by all categories of public workers, even grass cutters and leaf pickers, as a crime "when the government upholds the right of a private employee to diminish the free flow of food, fuel and other necessities of life until they actually imperil society."[33] Because the government performs so many of the same functions as private enterprises, it is contradictory for government to use the public interest as an argument against public sector strikes.

Finally, both proponents and opponents of strike legalization by the states base arguments on data from those states where collective bargaining has been already legalized. The issue is formulated thusly: Does collective bargaining legislation reduce the number of public employee strikes? At least three empirical studies indicate that collective bargaining legislation has *not* increased the number of public employee strikes.[34] Conversely, an analysis by the Bureau of National Affairs of public sector strikes before and after enactment of bargaining legislation from 1958 to 1974 suggests that "passage of a compulsory public sector bargaining law has resulted in increased strike activity."[35] The bureau's analysis indicates an overall, significant increase of public sector strikes the year immediately following bargaining legislation in comparison to the preceding year. In conflicting conclusions, two other surveys of legislative strike remedies indicated no correlation with such legislative measures.[36] Surveys or data which purport either a significant increase or decrease of strike activity due to collective bargaining legislation should be viewed carefully. Overall analyses or summaries of strike data tend to overly simplify or prove inadequate hypotheses. Whether or not legislation is effective in reducing the number of strikes will be dependent on two key legislative variables: (1) the type of impasse resolution technique prescribed, and (2) the extent to which the strike itself has been legalized.

Union Efforts to Obtain National Strike Legalization: The Dual Strategy in Washington

Public employee unions applied increasing pressure throughout the '70s in hopes of obtaining federal legislation that would regulate public sector collective bargaining, excluding federal employees. As with the War on Poverty earlier, the federal government seemed far more willing to support revolution in Washington State then in Washington, D.C. In each congressional session since 1972, sympathetic congressmen have fruitlessly introduced bills attempting to make state and local employees subject to the National Labor Relations Act (Taft-Hartley).[37]

Generally, public employee unions have pursued a twofold strategy of seeking to be included under NLRA jurisdiction and passing discrete legislation for public sector labor relations. Public employee organizations within the Coalition of Public Employees (CAPE) have actively lobbied for the inclusion of public employees under the National Labor Relations Act (NLRA).[38] However, such unions have not advocated an unqualified inclusion under NLRA and NRLB jurisdiction. Specifically, the National Education Association advocates particular amendments to the NRLA that would protect its interests:[39]

1. A well-defined impasse resolution technique involving mediation and fact-finding, and ultimately the right to strike.
2. Supervisors in public employment be given the right to bargain.

Furthermore, the NEA proposed that the states be encouraged to enact their own bargaining laws. This was to be accomplished by strengthening the NLRB's option of delegating its funtions to any state which passed enabling legislation for collective bargaining legislation.[40] However, the primary section in the NLRA that the unions sought to amend dealt with methods for resolving bargaining impasses. Supposedly by amending the NLRA, a balance of power similar to that existent in the private sector would be created.

In a second strategy, public employee unions have lobbied for discrete federal legislation that would include state and local public employees. Such hoped for legislation would include a regulatory commission similar to the NLRB, e.g., the National Public Employee Relations Commission (1972). The scope of particular bills is far-ranging. For example, a bill introduced by Congressman Ford (D-Mich.) in 1977 sanctioned negotiations on all matters

> concerning working conditions and environment, pay practices, fringe benefits, work hours and schedules, overtime, work procedures, automation, safety, transfers, job classifications, details, promotion procedures, seniority, assignment and reassignments, reductions in force, job security, contracting-out, disciplinary actions and appeals, training, method of adjudicating grievances, leave, union security, travel and per diem.[41]

Seemingly the most controversial provisions of the federal legislative proposals have been the agency shop and strike procedures. Given the slow progress in obtaining collective bargaining laws among the states and congressional opposition by right-to-work groups, union leaders may have to compromise by agreeing to a no-strike provision and loss of the agency shop proviso.[42]

The situation in 1972 wherein three separate bills were pending before the House Special Subcommittee on Labor was not unusual. The subcommittee was faced with three decision-making options: (1) coverage of public employees under the NLRA (H.R. 12532), (2) regulation of public labor relations through the formation of a separate National Public Employee Relations Commission (H.R. 7684), or (3) a more specialized commission, the Professional Education Employment Relations Commission.[43] By 1975, the renamed subcommittee on labor-management relations was confronted with five pending bills relating to both federal as well as state and local employees.[44]

Those who oppose federal legislation for public sector bargaining vary on a continuum from critics who oppose legalization of collective bargaining on any governmental level to bargaining advocates who believe activity by the federal government inappropriate. Those opposing bargaining legislation at all levels are considered elsewhere in this chapter. Those opposing federal legislation for collective bargaining generally do so for three reasons:[45]

1. Such legislation would destroy the "uniqueness of structure and operation of local government" by mandating undesirable uniformity among the states. Federal legislation proponents argue that such legislation would rather create uniformity of *process*, not substance.
2. Such legislation would transfer control of state and local budgets and ultimately power to the federal government. In essence, the purpose of federalism's decentralized power would be subverted.
3. Such legislation would preempt existing statutes in some states. Critics respond that federal legislation would not obviate state legislation. Rather, states would still be free to develop varying collective bargaining techniques, particularly of impasse resolution.

Finally one is confronted with a number of arguments generally offered to legalize public employee strikes. We shall briefly examine the various arguments offered against and in favor of legalizing public sector collective bargaining. We shall be particularly concerned with the issues concerning the legalization of public employee strikes.

Why Public Sector Strikes Should Be Prohibited

Arguments against the public sector strike are varied and frequently based on private sector analogies. One argument often advanced is that public sector management is at a distinct disadvantage because it lacks private sector market constraints. Specifically, a strike potentially threatens reduction of a private employer's efficiency, productivity, and profit. Even though a secondary boycott is expressly forbidden by Taft-Hartley, the private employer will usually lose business and consumers if a strike occurs. Concomitantly, private sector strikers will also suffer economically with loss of pay and possible loss of jobs. Though the actual strike causes economic harm, the realization of a strike's potential economic consequences is a significant positive stimulant in keeping the disputing parties at the bargaining table rather than experiencing a strike. One author notes that in some instances a company's financial troubles may even persuade unions to make economic concessions rather than lose jobs.[46]

Although perhaps inflationary, public sector strikes obviously do not result in direct profit loss to public sector managers. Scholars vary in their assessment of the degree, if any, that market constraints are operative in the public sector. Certainly, collective bargaining concessions might increase budgetary spending levels. Yet, a strike does not generally produce a resulting loss of revenue to the organization. Nor is there a loss of personal income to public managers. Public employees, except in rare instances where they are fired and not rehired, are equally impervious and indifferent to the economic consequences of a strike action. Wellington and Winter suggest that the absence of economic sanctions and the existence of political pressures cause public employers to settle quickly (not bargain hard). If, as Kenneth Clark suggests, the purpose of a private sector strike is "to bring economic pressure on the employer by depriving the employer of sales and profits,"[47] then, clearly the public sector strike has a totally different rationale. Hence, the antistrike critics reason, economic objectives should be settled at the bargaining table and political objectives in the political arena.

Antistrike proponents suggest that strikes are essentially political strategies designed to inconvenience citizens so that they will pressure politicians into acceding to union demands. This position holds that allowing strikes would hinder public administrators from preparing and implementing budget priorities.[48] The unions could then easily obtain excessive wages and benefits. Strike critics argue that budgeting is generally an incremental process in which clientele groups compete for a larger slice of the budgetary pie. Hence, strikes would simply allow public employee groups to compete unfavorably with other groups in the prevailing political process.

Finally, public recognition of the public sector's right to strike is believed by many to be a further erosion of governmental authority. Quite literally this view states that it is contradictory for the government to legitimize rebellion against authority. In part, this argument includes the previously discussed doctrine of sovereignty which "holds that as the sovereign employer, the government cannot be compelled to accept any obligation it shuns, or to continue to respect a commitment if it later decides it cannot or should not."[49] The government is ultimately responsible for determining the rules and conditions of employment. Consequently, those who use the sovereignty argument against the right to strike consider strikes *a challenge to the authority of government and thereby an invasion of the sovereign's prerogatives. To submit to such strikes, they contend, would be to submit to illegal coercion, would be an abdication of responsibility entrusted to public officials by the people, and would contravene the public welfare.*[50]

A related authority issue concerns "the nondelegation doctrine."[51] Legalized strikes force public officials to constrict their decision-making authority and share it with public employee groups. The public sector problem of divided authority is "concerning the extent to which the legislative branch of government, charged with the appropriation of funds, can delegate to others the determination of compensation and other rules governing the employment relationship."[52] Other labor observers do not accept this as a valid argument since court decisions have recently upheld delegations of authority that have been given with guidelines and standards. They contend that it is managerially sound to receive consultation from public employee groups when developing policies as a technique for strike prevention. An accompanying argument concerns "the theory of special responsibility"[53] by which government employees serve the public and should feel an obligation to carry out their duties as a sign of their patriotism and loyalty.[54] Even the trade unions feel "that every occupation has its special responsibility."[55] Although this ethical responsibility is supposedly shared by those employed in the private sector, it applies particularly to those employees sworn to uphold the public interest. As one local community leader asked of striking teachers, "if teachers have no respect for authority, then how can they teach the students respect for authority?"[56]

Those who oppose the legalization of public sector strikes contend that public employees already are employed by a "model employer" and thus have no valid job insecurity fears. Public employees work for an employer with no avarice or profit motives and within a protective civil service system. Many citizens believe that public employees receive high pay and excellent fringe benefits. Therefore, public employees should not need a right to strike because of their secure working conditions. For example, the Los Angeles County Charter has since 1913 contained a clause requiring that county employees be paid at least the same rate prevailing in the private sector for similar work. In some cases the county even pays more than the prevailing private rate.[57] It cannot legally pay less. Consequently, it is not surprising that perturbed taxpayer associations might question the county employees' contention that they also require civil service protection, collective bargaining, and the right to strike in order to feel secure.

A second argument is that legalization of public employee strikes would become a major cause of inflation and increased taxes. Some economists and many labor relations experts believe that "prices are often 'pushed up' by rising costs caused by wage increases forced upon the economy by powerful unions issuing strike threats and aided by government policies."[58] Unions disagree, stating that other economic variables, e.g., the push for profits by big business, are a major cause of inflation. Some observers believe that the ideal way to measure the impact of unions on inflation would be "to compare existing wage levels and differentials with those that would prevail in the absence of labor unions."[59] Although a difficult task because of the myriad factors including labor unions that collectively create the market economy, collective bargaining is viewed as an important influence in keeping wages up.

> In an economy with widespread and decentralized collective bargaining, where unions possess a measure of political influence, economic policies which seek adjustments through extensive reductions in wages and prices are likely to prove highly disruptive; other measures involving expanded demand have been substituted, and these tend to be somewhat more inflationary in the long run.[60]

There is no quantitative way to definitively measure the impact of union activities, including the strike, on the economy. There have been a great number of analyses on this issue (including our own), but no one has yet been able to precisely offer an absolute summation of the effect of public unionization on inflation.

The third argument against legalizing the strike in the public sector is that it harms third parties who have no influence on the outcome of negotiations. Disruption of services in the private and public sectors can adversely affect a third party. For example, merchants in a small town suffer when a plant employing much of the local population is shut down by a strike. A public employee strike may prove economically beneficial to competing private interests, i.e., "innocent bystanders may reap unexpected gains as larger profits and greater employment and overtime go to competitive enterprises not shut down by a disputes";[61] however, such rewards are only marginal to the greater public interest. Perhaps the most commonly used argument by those who oppose legalized public sector strikes is that such strikes are detrimental to public welfare and safety. When any public employee group strikes, i.e., transit workers, hospital workers, and teachers, the public is immediately inconvenienced. Strikes by protective service employees directly imperil the safety of citizens.

As a fourth argument, antistrike advocates claim that even if strikes were banned for only certain categories of employees, such as fire fighters and police, there would be continual debate as to which groups should be justly excluded from the right to strike and which groups

Part II: Politics of Collective Bargaining

most affect public welfare and safety. Certain categories of workers, such as park attendants and zoo keepers, would not have the power to inconvenience the public to the extent that public pressure would be brought against the government to meet their demands.[62] Therefore, proponents of the ban on public employee strikes believe it is only just and essential for all strikes to be banned. In actuality, the trend in those states which have legalized strikes has been to legalize strikes only for certain classifications, i.e., nonprotective services.

One measure of the degree to which legislation affects collective bargaining is the correlation between level of negotiation rights granted by the states and the proportion of employees organized. For instance, among state employees, New York's Taylor Act includes extensive bargaining rights, which is indicated by its relatively high rate of organization, 69 percent. California, with 58 percent organized, has more restrictive legislation. Michigan, with only 50 percent of its state employees organized, has not granted legal bargaining rights to its employees.

As Paul Staudohar and others have pointed out,[63] one finds a similar correlation with local public employees. Michigan's Public Employment Relations Act permits extensive bargaining rights to local employees. As noted, Michigan's police and firemen have had binding arbitration since 1973. Consequently, 75 percent of Michigan's local public employees were organized in 1974. New York, whose Taylor Act also provides extensive bargaining rights for local employees and compulsory arbitration for police and firemen, has 78 percent of its employees organized. Finally, California, with its somewhat weaker Meyers-Milias-Brown Act, has only 67 percent of its local employees organized.

Finally, the impact of legislation on strikes among the states may be viewed from yet another perspective. In one analysis of the six leading states in the number of public employee work stoppages (1971-1974), the number of strikes in more permissive Pennsylvania and New York would appear to have had a salubrious effect (table 5-1).

On the other hand, if one observes the total number of work stoppages in these same six states from 1973-75 an interesting pattern emerges (table 5-2).

The figures suggest a growing concentration of the national strike total in these six key industrial states.* Furthermore, these six states represent the spectrum of collective bargaining legislation. Ohio and Illinois are virtually without collective bargaining legislation; California, New York, and Michigan have legislation that allows limited collective bargaining; and Pennsylvania permits public employee strikes under most conditions.

---

* It must be noted that the percentages given and the trends discussed are our conclusions, not those of Ms. Cebulski.

TABLE 5-1: Summary of State and Local Government Work Stoppages (12-Month Periods Ended October 1972 and October 1974)

	Work Stoppages		Employees Involved			Days of Idleness		
	Oct. 1971 to Oct. 1972	Oct. 1973 to Oct. 1974	Oct. 1971 to Oct. 1972	Oct. 1973 to Oct. 1974	Percent Change	Oct. 1971 to Oct. 1972	Oct. 1973 to Oct. 1974	Percent
United States	382	471	130,935	162,115	23.8	1,127,911	1,404,768	24.5
California	18	49	10,891	40,433	271.3	128,021	434,554	239.4
Illinois	29	28	6,619	4,392	- 33.6	27,045	31,614	16.9
Michigan	29	66	8,173	15,365	88.0	65,138	162,293	149.2
New York	27	16	15,816	9,062	- 42.7	54,856	38,245	- 30.3
Ohio	34	51	6,972	21,836	213.2	32,554	94,923	191.6
Pennsylvania	77	80	34,240	17,781	48.1	486,363	130,415	- 73.2

Revised Source: Paul D. Staudohar, "Organization, Bargaining, and Work Stoppages in California Public Employment," *California Public Employee Relations* 29 (1974), pp. 19-24.

TABLE 5-2: Strikes in Six Leading States

	1973	1974	1975
† California	17	43	44
* Illinois	32	26	41
††Michigan	73	53	28
††New York	16	18	32
* Ohio	23	42	53
††Pennsylvania	65	78	110
	226	260	308
	58.3%	67.7%	64.4%
National total:	387	384	478

Source: Bonnie Cebulski, "A 1975-76 Tabulation of Strikes in California Public Sector" *California Public Employee Relations* 33 (June 1977), p. 2.

* No state level collective bargaining legislation.

† Limited state collective bargaining legislation.

††Comprehensive state collective bargaining legislation.

In summary, we can find no conclusive evidence that antistrike legislation or even the nature of collective bargaining laws have any effect on the number of strikes. The evidence on strikes is somewhat similar to Thomas Dye's emphasis on the importance of socioeconomic variables in public policymaking.[64] To paraphrase: those states with socioeconomic indicators of greater wealth, education, per capita spending, etc., will be those states which have more liberal spending policies for public education, social welfare, transportation programs. The accumulated evidence suggests that these same heterogeneous, industrialized states will also experience the greatest degree of public employee unrest, regardless of their work stoppage legislation.

Yet, our case study with the Rodda Act in California, as well as the evidence from other states, indicates that the type of legislation can affect the nature of public employee collective bargaining. Specifically, various types of negotiation impasse resolution techniques, when prescribed legislatively, may have a significant impact.

Case Study: Impact of the Rodda Act in California

Can collective bargaining legislation reduce the number and intensity of public employee strikes? In 1975, Governor Brown of California signed the Educational Employment Relations (Rodda) Act, which was to become partially effective 1 January and fully effective 1 July 1976.[65] The Rodda Act was California's first collective bargaining legislation, designed to include both certificated and classified school employees in more than 1,200 state public school districts. As such, it is important to note the legislation's impact or lack of impact on public school labor relations, specifically its impact on school employee strikes.

First, it is essential to understand previous educational labor relations in California and the legislation that had been in effect since 1965, the Winton Act.[66] Under the Winton Act's "professional" approach, both educational management and employees were prohibited from entering into legally binding contracts. In effect, the Winton Act encouraged an Alice in Wonderland world in which neither party could be held responsible for its agreement. Agreements were unenforceable by third parties. It was attacked by major teachers' unions and the California Teachers' Association (CTA) as a "meet and defer" process.[67] Consequently, neither educational employees, management, nor third parties had responsibility for bargaining in good faith or seeking a mutuality of interest.

In a major step the Rodda Act supposedly enforced responsibility to the agreement by requiring that a negotiated agreement shall "when accepted by the exclusive representative and the public school employer become *binding on both parties*" (italics added). However, in a key omission, the Rodda Act does not prescribe the type of impasse resolution to be utilized; this is to be agreed upon by both management and educational employees. The act simply promises to recognize whatever impasse resolution procedure is agreed upon by the two parties.

The failure to prescribe a specific technique for impasse resolution apparently did little to accomplish the act's objective "to promote the improvement of personnel management and employee-employer relations. . . . "[68] Statistics indicate several somewhat surprising trends. First, the number of work stoppages increased significantly during the first six months of 1977 to approximately the peak year (1974) immediately preceding the act's enactment (table 5-3).

Even more revealing than the increase in stoppages is the reason for the strikes. There were more work stoppages in California during the first six months of the act's existence than in any previous six-month period. Why would strikes suddenly increase following the passage of

TABLE 5-3: Work Stoppages in California Public Education (1970-1977)

	70	71	72	73	74	75	76	to date 77 (May)
Number	4	3	1	8	22	10	8	11
Average duration (days)	10.7	21.6	5.0	4.7	2.5	8.5	7.5	5.3

Source: Jack W. Brittan, "The Implementation of Collective Negotiations under the Rodda Act," *California Public Employee Relations* 33 (June 1977), p. 10.

collective bargaining legislation? Significantly, in fifteen of the twenty stoppages, binding grievance arbitration was a key issue.[69] It was particularly crucial in work stoppages among certificated employees (teachers). Advisory arbitration was apparently the issue in the remaining cases. In essence, education employees were initiating job actions because they were seeking binding grievance arbitration as a technique for impasse resolution.

The failure of the Rodda Act to facilitate genuine bargaining in good faith is further evidenced by the failure of negotiation. For example, in every district that had experienced a certificated work stoppage, a mediator had been engaged at varying points during prestrike negotiations. Yet in no instance did the parties proceed entirely through the dispute process before work stoppage occurred.[70] Quite simply, the mediation process did not work; despite the fact that the state conciliation service's workload has apparently more than quadrupled in twenty-eight months (see table 5-4). The conciliation service also estimates that the average time per case has risen from twenty-five to fifty-one hours.[71]

One can conclude that mediation efforts to avoid work stoppages have apparently not been very successful. Rather than pursuing prestrike negotiation to completion, the employees would rather refer their case to the State Educational Employees Relation Board (EERB) for adjudication. There is evidently no compulsion for either employee organization or employer to agree on arbitration as a technique during the negotiation process.

A secondary impact of the Rodda Act was to allow public education employees to choose a proper unit for representation purposes.

TABLE 5-4: State Conciliation Service: Hours of Mediation Services Provided

1975	1976	1977 (first 4 months)
3,350	6,051	5,770

Source: Jack W. Brittan, "The Implementation of Collective Negotiations under the Rodda Act," *California Public Employee Relations* 33 (June 1977), p. 12.

Consequently, in elections throughout the state, the California Teachers' Association (CTA/NEA) and the American Federation of Teachers (AFL-CIO) waged intense campaigns to become designated as local bargaining units.[72] As expected CTA won a majority of elections, particularly outside the generally more militant San Francisco Bay region.

In summary, legislation in California to establish a collective bargaining system for public school employees has had both a short-term impact and long-term implications. The Rodda Act's short-term effects are as follows:

1. The act's failure to mandate a system of impasse resolution has resulted in a substantial increase in the number of work stoppages. One can reasonably conclude that this same conflict over impasse resolution techniques will repeatedly occur until a particular resolution technique is required.

2. Given the limited authority of EERB as an adjudicatory body that primarily interprets legislation and renders decisions, it cannot currently provide a comprehensive collective decision-making process. As a semijudicial commission, EERB can only settle disputes rather than facilitating the development of collective bargaining policymaking.

Following are the long-term implications of the Rodda Act, which are becoming increasingly apparent:

1. A collective bargaining act that fails to define a means of negotiating impasse resolution does not alleviate the sources of labor-management conflict or impasse.

2. Together with the Supreme Court's *Serrano* decision,* which effectively mandated that school financial bases be equalized

* The California Supreme Court ruled in *Serrano* v. *Priest* [4 Cal. 3d. 584 (1971)], that state legislation basing the financing of public schools primarily on property taxes discriminates against poorer districts and is thus unconstitutional.

throughout the state, the Rodda Act also exerts pressure toward raising teacher salaries statewide.

3. The scope of negotiation between teachers and educational administrators has been legally limited to salary and direct working conditions. In other words, collective bargaining can only include these issues. Broader policy issues, i.e., curriculum, class size, and administrative policies, are no longer within the scope of collective bargaining.

In conclusion, there is apparently no simple correlation between the existence of antistrike or collective bargaining legislation and the incidence of job actions. Similarly, regardless of the arguments for or against the legalization of strikes among states or at the federal level, strikes will be only implemented if they are efficacious in obtaining union objectives. Quite simply, if strikes, legal or illegal, prove ineffectual, they will not be employed as an impasse resolution technique.

Analyses of the effectiveness/ineffectiveness of legislative prohibitions against public employees strikes have proven thus far inconclusive. General hypotheses are frequently too superficial and thus overlook the selective impact of collective bargaining legislation. For example, Michigan, as one of the first states to promulgate collective bargaining legislation, has also been consistently near the top in the number of employee strikes. In fact, Congressman William Ford of Michigan claimed that his state has more strikes than any other state in the country.[73] (See table 5-5.)

However, in 1973 Michigan's original advisory arbitration statute was amended to provide final offer arbitration on economic issues related to firemen and police. The impact of the Michigan legislation is apparent in its effect upon police and firemen strikes since 1973. Although public employee strikes in Michigan have diminished only slightly, there was a complete absence of police and firemen strikes during the 1973-75 period.[74]

Other Antistrike Tactics: Court Injunctions, No-Strike Clauses, and Criminal Sanctions

State and local legislation attempts to prohibit public employee strikes by a variety of measures that include court injunctions against strikes, suspension or automatic dismissal of strikers, cancellation of promised salary increases or promotions for strikers, stiff fines levied against the offending union, fining and/or imprisonment of union leaders.

TABLE 5-5: Public Sector Work Stoppages in Michigan on Fiscal Year Basis

1965-66	11	1969-70	64
1966-67	15	1970-71	44
1967-68	52	1971-72	16
1968-69	39	1972-73	27

Source: Robert G. Howlett, *Federal Legislation for Public Sector Collective Bargaining*, ed. Thomas R. Colosi and Steven B. Rynecki (Chicago: International Personnel Management Association, 1975), p. 29.

Despite the vituperative implications of these antistrike tactics, their track record has been thus far inconclusive for several reasons according to Demetrios Caraley.[75] First, the realistic possibility of dismissing a large number of essential or highly skilled public employees is untenable; furthermore, it will not restore interrupted services. Second, the threat of legal action against striking employees is remote, since almost every eventual strike settlement includes an agreement that reprisals will not be taken and that limitations against pay increases will not be enacted. Third, short-term jail sentences or fines occasionally given to union leaders who defy court injunctions are seldom burdensome; often they confer a charismatic aura to those leaders who are so punished. As Caraley also points out:

> Fines imposed on the group's treasury have usually been moderate, relative to its total resources, and thus far from devastating in their impact. The United Federation of Teachers, for example, was fined $150,000 for its 1967 school strike in New York City and $220,000 for its 1968 strike. (The maximum that could have been imposed was $620,000). Since the U.F.T. had approximately 55,000 dues-paying members, the 1968 strike amounted to $4 for each member.[76]

In summary, the existing strike sanctions on the books have not been generally applied nor have those making public sector labor policy considered such sanctions as viable options.

Nonetheless, there is increasing evidence among our case studies and elsewhere that local governments are becoming less reticent to apply existing sanctions or to devise new punitive measures. For example, Atlanta used with some effectiveness the technique of suspending the union checkoff privileges (the automatic deduction by the

Part II: Politics of Collective Bargaining

city treasury of union dues from each employee's paycheck and forwarding it to the union) following the illegal city employee's strike in 1977.

With mounting public pressure to hold down budgetary increases, the ability of public managers to pubish unions who seek exorbitant economic demands may be strengthened. The public response to the illegal strike by San Francisco police and firemen in 1975 was vindictive. Not only were their recent wage concessions repudiated, but voters also revoked prior pension benefits, strengthened the Board of Supervisors' power to deal with strikes, and, perhaps most indicative of voter animosity, refused to allow firemen to work more than eight-hour shifts, thus depriving firemen of their traditional right to accumulate hours through working consecutive shifts.

The Injunction: An Uncertain Weapon

Historically, the federal courts felt unrestrained in halting peaceful strikes and picketing by utilizing a "labor injunction." This antilabor bias by the federal judiciary precipitated a congressional reaction in 1932—the passage of the Norris-LaGuardia Act,[77] which was a comprehensive antiinjunction statute. Essentially the act prohibited the federal courts from issuing injunctions against nonviolent labor disputes in interstate commerce; it also restricted the instances where federal courts could issue injunctions even in violent strikes.

With the Norris-LaGuardia limitations on federal court jurisdiction in labor disputes, employers have increasingly resorted to state courts for injunctive protection. Employers also prefer state courts for other reasons. First, under many state laws, injunctions based on violence and mass picketing can be issued very quickly on an *ex parte* basis. Secondly, many employers feel that state courts are generally more sympathetic to their cause than are federal courts.

Consequently, a number of more heavily unionized states have passed their own antiinjunction laws. These so-called baby Norris-LaGuardias are often as inclusive or even more inclusive than the federal law, a phenomenon that is an ironic reversal of the Taft-Hartley right-to-work section. A series of "preemption" case rulings by the Supreme Court has held that states are prohibited from regulating strikes, picketing, and other nonviolent conduct as sanctioned by the NLRA.[78] As a consequence, the latitude of state courts to issue injunctions against violence and mass picketing has been substantially curtailed.

Although the use of the labor injunction by either federal or state courts has been severely limited, its application to strikes that threaten the public interest is still unrestricted. In essence, the intent of Norris-

LaGuardia, its state level counterparts, and the Supreme Court's preemptive decisions is apparently to secure the rights of unions engaged in an essentially economic strike. However, any strike, public or private, that threatens the public safety, i.e., protective services, hospitals, etc., is subject to an injunction on that basis.

The Legality of No-Strike, Lockout Clauses

The assumption underlying a collective agreement, public or private, is that strikes and walkouts will not occur during the term of the contract. As a guarantee of that objective, the most common provision of any contract, therefore, is one binding the union not to call or condone a strike during the life of a contract and binding the employer not to lock out employees. However, the historical problem has been with strikes rather than lockouts.

A complex body of legislation and NLRB decisions covers the enforcement and interpretation of no-strike clauses. The salient issue is not whether such provisions *prevent* strikes; there is no evidence to indicate that they do. Rather, the question is whether an employer may sue for damages and/or secure an injunction against a strike. In a series of cases, the Supreme Court has ruled that an employer may seek a federal court injunction against an illegal work stoppage in breach of contract.[79] He may also sue a union for monetary damages resulting from an illegal strike in particular situations.*

Creation of a Separate Labor Court System

A system of labor courts has been proposed as a method to resolve disputes. Mayor Fiorello LaGuardia proposed such a system for New York in the 1940s. Judge Samuel I. Rosenman also outlined such a system; it would theoretically utilize all the techniques, such as arbitration, mediation, and fact-finding, to resolve impasses. In addition, it would create "a separate labor judiciary with the sole and exclusive function of deciding labor disputes that the parties cannot settle themselves."[80] Rosenman believed that if strikes are in conflict with the public interest, there must be "some form of final, compulsory decision provided."[81] The chairman of the New York State Mediation Board suggested that labor courts be established to rule on the justification for a public employee strike. If justified, "the court would issue an injunction pending the outcome of a jury trial on the issues."[82] If

---

* Suit may occur if the grievance-arbitration provision of the contract does not provide for arbitration of grievance impasse, in which case the employee must file a grievance over alleged violations.

unjustified, and a strike occurs, penalties would be brought against the strikers. However, Spero and Capozzola conclude that labor groups would ignore court rulings:

> *Having waged an enduring struggle to achieve bargaining rights, employee unions are likely to resist the imposition of judicial decrees and regard the labor court as a masquerade devised to protect the sovereign's rights to a privileged status.*[83]

The implementation of a separate labor court system has not seriously been considered by any of the states. Because of the extreme expense and implied delegation of power from other governmental branches, it is not likely to be tried, even on an experimental level.

In conclusion, the observer is free to accept or reject whichever arguments seem most logical and appropriate, whether pro or con. Regardless, several trends upon which there is relative consensus should be kept in mind concerning public employee strikes:

1. Such strikes show no signs of diminishing either at the work stoppage or overt strike level; the issue becomes whether or not to routinize and thereby control what is already occurring.
2. Neither their legislative prohibition nor judicial injunction has proven an effective deterrent to public employee strikes.
3. Strikes occur most frequently at a governmental level (local) that is most vulnerable, frequently over issues that are resolvable by effective collective bargaining.
4. Strike action is but the most dramatic means of resolving impasse resolution; it is too frequently considered the only means. Perhaps simplistically, the strike (like war as Clausewitz' ultimate weapon of statecraft) should only be emphasized as an ultimate solution after all other techniques of impasse resolution have failed.

Efforts to Avoid a Strike: Impasse Resolution Procedures

To the neutral party involved in collective bargaining impasse resolution, it is undoubtedly a challenge to successfully resolve any impasse in order to restore peaceful labor-management relations. Yet the third party is faced with the oftentimes unenviable task of persuading both management and labor not to employ their ultimate economic weapon, the strike/lockout. Unions in particular assume that the strike is an essential weapon, without which they are impotent in bargaining.

In California, almost all public employee organizations resolve their labor-management problems without impasse. For example, Department of Industrial Relations records statistics indicate that currently only 5 percent of all collective bargaining end in a labor dispute.[84] A CTA representative estimated that California, with over 1,100 school districts, had "less than half a dozen strikes, and they were not on economic issues."[85] However, this figure obscures the impact of a public sector strike. How does one measure the impact of over 822,000 work days lost due to public employee strikes in California alone during the 1974-76 period? Also indicative has been the geometric increase of public employee strikes during these three years. For example, the California Department of Industrial Relations figures show the following trend:

> *160,000 and 322,000 work days idle for fiscal years 1973-74 and 1974-75, respectively. Unofficial statistics from the same source and from the City and County of San Francisco show 340,000 work days idle for fiscal 1975-76.*[86]

There is no evidence that overall strike activity shows any indication of diminishing in California and the nation. The continuing increase in even the small overall number of public employee strikes only intensifies the need to develop impasse resolution alternatives for the public sector. To this end, the public sector is in a unique situation to both adopt impasse resolution procedures already developed in the private sector and to experiment with distinctive variations of its own. Although private sector techniques are somewhat limited to four traditionally employed methods, the public sector has thus far tested a variety of impasse resolution alternatives and variations.

Broad categories of impasse resolution options generally employed in the public sector include mediation, fact-finding, arbitration (advisory, binding, and nonbinding), a combination of mediation and arbitration (med-arb), and variations of final offer arbitration. Each of these techniques uses a neutral third party in the resolution process. Each technique also shifts, albeit to varying degrees, the decisions away from the public administrator who must face the taxpayers' criticism. A neutral party can also protect public employees from arbitrary managerial decisions. In any case, the objective of impasse resolution is the same: to prevent a strike. Obviously, it is more desirable for public management employees and the general public if an impasse dispute can be resolved rationally through negotiation rather than attempting resolution in an environment of work stoppage or management retaliation. Yet most impasse resolution procedures are hastily implemented in just such situations.

According to a 1973 survey by the Bureau of Labor Statistics of 318 collective bargaining agreements among state and local jurisdictions and employees, only 32, or 10 percent, included formal impasse procedures. In fact, three-fourths (23) of the agreements that included impasse procedures were from Los Angeles County, and 30 were from the county level (see table 5-6). The most frequently employed impasse resolution procedure proved to be mediation or fact-finding, provided by a state or county labor relations board. Fact-finding and/or mediation by a neutral was utilized in nine instances. Arbitration was included in only two bargaining agreements.

The low number of negotiation impasse procedures in bargaining agreements is partially attributable to legislatively dictated provisions, which prevail in approximately thirty-five states. Under such legislation, local or state bargaining units are required to notify a state mediation service upon reaching an impasse. In essence, negotiation impasse resolution is not a mutually agreed upon procedure to be included within a bargaining agreement. Rather, it is a procedure imposed by management, i.e., the state legislature.

Mediation

Professor Stahl optimistically believes that mediation has proven itself as a reliable impasse resolution technique: "Experience in government jurisdictions demonstrates that mediation is the most commonly used procedure and results in settlement in the majority of cases in which it is used."[87] The Intergovernmental Personnel Act has placed a major emphasis on strengthening impasse resolution by awarding over one hundred training grants to local jurisdictions. Some municipalities have used federally funded intergovernmental personnel act grants to provide cooperative union-management training programs.[88]

On the federal level, the Federal Mediation and Conciliation Service (FMCS) was established through the Taft-Hartley Act to supply carefully chosen and experienced mediators to assist parties in reaching an agreement. A former FMCS director, William Simkin, described the purposes of the Federal Mediation and Conciliation Service as threefold: first, to help avoid a strike; second, to shorten current strikes; and third, to assist the parties in improving their bargaining relationships to avoid future difficulties. Simkin defines two types of mediation: *crisis mediation*, which is "assistance in disputes settlement when a stalemate develops just prior to a strike deadline or after a strike starts"; and *preventive mediation*, which is "assistance in the development of ways and means to avoid a crisis or make productive the crisis elements that must remain."[89] In 1971, FMCS "handled" sixty-eight disputes and participated in over one hundred mediation cases.[90] By comparison and as an indication "of where the action is," the California State Conciliation Service provided mediation and conciliation for 600

TABLE 5-6: Impasse Procedures in State and County Collective Bargaining Agreements
(By Level of Government, 1972-73)

Provision	All Agreements		Level of Government			
			State		County	
	Agreements	Workers	Agreements	Workers	Agreements	Workers
Total	318	340,447	106	151,257	212	189,190
Total with impasse procedures	32	84,695	2	15,000	30	69,695
Fact-finding	9	28,423	1	5,000	8	23,423
Mediation	9	28,473	1	5,000	8	23,423
Arbitration	2	5,200	1	5,000	1	200
State or county labor relations board	24	57,393	1	10,000	23	47,393

Source: U.S., Department of Labor, Bureau of Labor Statistics, Bulletin 1920, pp. 75-76.

Note: Nonadditive. An agreement may contain more than one impasse procedure.

private and 800 public sector cases in 1975-76 (of the public sector caseload, approximately 122 were school districts).[91]

Mediation or conciliation, terms which are used synonymously, refer to assistance by a third party intermediary given to both parties in settling a dispute. Thus, "the primary function of a mediator is to keep the parties talking and to suggest possible solutions to those issues where the parties remain apart."[92] Theoretically, a good mediator serves only in an advisory capacity and cannot dictate the terms of an agreement. The mediator's objective is to progressively narrow the differences between the parties, relying on his abilities to persuade and cajole both parties to compromise.

Importantly, a mediator continues to function only as long as both parties agree to his presence and will withdraw from a case in the following circumstances: (1) agreement is reached, (2) one of two parties requests his departure, (3) the agreed upon time comes for appeal to the next step in the procedure, i.e., fact-finding or arbitration, or (4) he feels his acceptability or effectiveness is exhausted.[93] It is crucial to understand both the limitations and the potentiality of mediation as an impasse resolution technique. Mediation can be a viable and timely tool in continuing a stalled collective bargaining process. It may improve communication between entrenched adversaries. It may provide the invaluable perspective of a neutral and trusted counselor. In effect, a capable mediator may become the catalyst producing agreement.

However, the mediation technique has limited applicability and is inadequate as the single tool in resolving all negotiation obstructions. Ultimately, the mediator cannot force a settlement on any party. He can provide counsel but he cannot coerce. Finally, mediation is significantly affected by two variables that limit (or enhance) its applicability: (1) mutual confidence in the mediator, (2) the timing of its implementation. Both factors have been frequently unappreciated.

1. Mediation: A Matter of Trust Both labor and management must have emotional faith and confidence in the mediator's integrity in order to

> confide their position to the mediator without fear of it being revealed, and the mediator must be able to expect the parties to be truthful in their discussions with him.[94]

A mediator's success is ultimately dependent on both parties' willingness to be open and honest on all bargaining issues. Successful mediation is improbable if either party retains hidden agendas or attempts to undermine the mediator at the bargaining table.

2. Mediation: A Matter of Timing Obviously, mediation has more probability of success if employed before bargaining positions have become irreconcilable. Also, mediation should not be used when it would "allow the opposition to delay or avoid what may be an imminent settlement."[95] In essence, yet somewhat simplistically stated, mediation is problematic if either party is not genuinely interested in reaching a mediated settlement. If this is so, other more binding stages of impasse resolution must be employed. Mediation is also often untenable in a situation wherein one party cannot negotiate particular issues unless compelled to do so by alternative impasse resolution techniques. In such instances, it may be politically prudent to refuse mediation in favor of fact-finding, med-arb, or arbitration. As an example of mediation's inadvisability: in 1977 over forty bargaining units, representing about 65,000 employees in Los Angeles County, filed a formal notice of impasse. The county employee unions did so solely to obtain mediation assistance from the state mediation service. In this situation, the potential for a mediated settlement was bleak. The Los Angeles County Board of Supervisors had mandated its negotiators to be limited to a maximum 3 percent pay increase with ½ percent fringe benefits. In addition

> the supervisors ordered tight bargaining, as they sought to maintain or decrease the county tax rate of $4.46 per $100 of assessed value. The county's bargaining position included a roll-back of retirement and pension benefits for all future employees and removal of step increases for many existing jobs.[96]

However, the 1976 contract settlement with county employees, based on a 5 percent increase, complicated management's position. As an additional management pressure, the county charter required that pay be equitable with comparable rates in the private sector, which a county survey found to have increased by 7 percent the previous year.

The prospects for a negotiated settlement lessened as various county employees responded to the county's hard line position by staging rolling sickouts, which were particularly effective at county hospitals. The county personnel office retaliated by automatically docking pay of any employee who called in sick. In effect, the personnel office presumed automatic guilt on the basis of a one-day sick leave:

> Doctors' notes are going to be scrutinized. We're going to want specifics and a statement that in the doctor's professional judgment the employee should stay off the job for the entire day.[97]

It would be an understatement to suggest that simple mediation would have sufficed in resolving an impasse in such a rancorous environment. The Los Angeles County Personnel Office and the Board of Supervisors could not politically accept mediation as an impasse resolution technique. The supervisors would rather defend their actions as having been coerced or compelled by either fact-finding or arbitration to compromise, in acceding somewhat to union demands.

Fact-Finding

Some labor relations observers believe that fact-finding should not be an automatic or compulsory process, but that parties should try to reach agreement on their own.[98] Fact-finding is receiving more and more attention as an alternative to work stoppages and strikes and is seen as a method of resolving impasses. It has been used regularly, and generally successfully, in New York, Connecticut, Michigan, and Wisconsin. One study of fact-finding in these states found that the major problems encountered were the expense of the procedure and the desire of the parties to negotiate privately rather than submit to the publicity accompanying the fact-finder's report.[99] However, the fear of the results of publishing the fact-finder's report and recommendations—causing adverse public opinion—might cause the parties to be more receptive to reaching an agreement.[100] Most of the respondents to the survey felt that the fact-finding procedure was not a substitute but a complement to collective bargaining.[101] The study concluded:

> *The absence of good faith negotiation, the lack of significant negotiation progress, and the inability of public opinion to influence the negotiating parties are so frequent as to indicate that fact-finding will, perhaps, be only a temporary solution in the resolution of public disputes.*[102]

Several in-depth studies of the fact-finding experience in Wisconsin[103] and Michigan suggest that "most unions and employers indicated that fact-finding was effective in resolving their impasses. . . . "[104]

Some labor-management experts believe that the result of the use of this method of impasse resolution has been to minimize collective bargaining. There is a tendency for both sides to take polarized positions and go straight to fact-finding with confidence that the decision will be to their advantage.[105] This prospect is sometimes eliminated by limiting the fact-finder to a choice between the last counterproposal made by the union or by management. Such a provision leads to serious negotiation for settlement prior to the implementation of fact-finding.[106] However, even this may not result in a successful resolution of the dispute, and some more binding procedures may be implemented to resolve the negotiation impasse.

Once fact-finding or advisory arbitration recommendations are submitted, it is the role of the legislature, or its local equivalent, to either reject or to make these proposals binding. It may be argued that this is a violation of the fact-finding concept and makes it a form of arbitration.[107] This is, to a certain extent, true, but does not obviate the value of fact-finding as the proposals may be accepted by both parties.

If no settlement results from fact-finding, the next stage in order to avoid a strike is some form of binding arbitration.

Fact-finding may be separate and distinct from mediation or a stage following the failure of mediation. Like mediation, it involves a third party who analyzes relevant information and prepares a report to serve as the basis for further negotiation. The theory of fact-finding is that if the findings and subsequent recommendations of the fact-finder are well reasoned, they will be persuasive and accepted in whole or, at least, in part. Fact-finding actually consists of an impartial tribunal of neutrals or a tripartite body representing both of the disputing parties and the public. This group looks into the issues, hears the various representatives, considers the problems, and issues a report of facts or facts along with recommendations, depending on its authority. Fact-finding was designed in recognition of the urgent need to be reasonable on the part of management and employee unions.

It is crucial to realize that fact-finding may occur with or without accompanying recommendations. As Arnold Zack and others contend, fact-finding without recommendations is identical to "advisory arbitration." Ironically, both fact-finding and advisory arbitration are misleading terms. Fact-finding's impact is primarily dependent on the fact-finders' recommendations rather than the accumulation of facts; advisory arbitration "is in reality fact-finding, arbitration by definition being final and binding, not advisory." In fact, fact-finding with recommendations is proposed as a viable alternative for management to the feared evils of compulsory arbitration.[108]

Arbitration

True arbitration is binding on both parties and may be categorized in the following three types: (1) *voluntary* arbitration in which an arbitrator, selected jointly by the disputing parties, is called in to settle an impasse and both parties agree in advance to abide by the arbitrator's decision; (2) *compulsory* arbitration, required by law, when an arbitrator or arbitration panel is authorized to develop a solution binding on the disputing parties; and (3) *final offer* arbitration or "one-or-the-other" arbitration,[109] in which each party submits a final offer to the arbitrator for his final decision. There are important evolutionary variations of each basic technique.

Arbitration is employed in two types of impasse resolution negotiation: *interest* arbitration, which hears both parties' interests in order to reach a contract with mutually acceptable terms and conditions of employment; and *rights* arbitration, wherein a grievance is lodged within an existing contract as the focus of negotiation. It is the breakdown of interest or contract arbitration that presently concerns us because of its more frequent consequence—strike and work stoppage.

Critics offer a number of concerns regarding the utility of compulsory arbitration. Among these is that compulsory arbitration provides a poor substitute for collective bargaining, because the disputing parties often do not try to reach an agreement on their own and make unreasonable demands with which the arbitrators must deal.[110] Benjamin Rubenstein states that both labor and management fear compulsory arbitration because they feel that it would minimize the effect of collective bargaining.[111] However, a 1976 survey of 370 local fire fighter units (IAFF) and persons representing local municipalities concluded that union negotiators preferred compulsory arbitration to any other alternative. By comparison, municipal negotiators ranked mediation, fact-finding, and voluntary arbitration about equally.[112]

Secondly, compulsory arbitration has been criticized because surveys, such as one of Michigan fire fighters and police, indicate no appreciable differences in size of salary increases resulting from compulsory arbitration in comparison to those gained from alternate forms of dispute settlement.[113]

Arbitration critics indicate concern that labor and management may become dependent upon arbitration to settle a dispute. They are also concerned about the ability of the arbitrator to be familiar with "all or substantially all the elements that will produce a result which is fair to management and the workers as well as to the consuming public."[114]

Opponents of binding and compulsory arbitration believe that the arbitrator's task in settling wage disputes is inherently prejudiced by the necessity of relying on governmentally furnished wage rates. Furthermore, because relatively few jobs have comparable equivalents in the private sector, critics believe prevailing wage rates for private and public sectors are suspect.[115]

Beyond the mere difficulty of obtaining reliable and mutually acceptable data, critics also argue that arbitration removes the public officials' accountability for decision making. In effect, public officials could escape responsibility for the greatest cost in government—wages. Critics argue that all pay setting determination by both union and political representatives would be obscured. Advocates, however, respond that arbitration is no different than delegating the power of postal regulation to the postmaster general.[116]

Finally, critics of binding and compulsory arbitration as a technique for public sector negotiation impasse resolution contend that it represents a threat to the present state of private sector labor relations. If such arbitration becomes predominant in the public sector it will then present an irresistible trend for the private sector. Consequently, this could lead to business trying to preserve a fixed profit margin and, ultimately, governmental control of business policymaking.[117]

Proponents of interest arbitration justify its increasing use as the last step in public sector impasse resolution on these grounds:

1. Arbitration allows the arbitrator to separate superfluous but highly symbolic demands from the important issues to both parties. As indicated, both public management and labor are often compelled by external political forces and internal organizational objectives to present a variety of demands of vastly differing priorities. The arbitrator allows both parties to save face by eliminating symbolic demands.

2. The public nature of the final arbitration award allows an opportunity for both parties to reconsider their positions before its final issuance. In other words, both parties have the opportunity to reconsider and perhaps develop more acceptable trade-offs. However, as others observe, final offers that are not considered final by both parties become merely a continuation of the negotiation process.[118] Unless final offers are authentically final, they are not a distinctive tool in impasse resolution.

3. Interest arbitration imposes an effective deadline to the negotiating process. Frequently, public sector negotiations tend to drag on much longer than those in the private sector, which are governed by the contract expiration date. In the private sector, both management and labor negotiate within a "no contract, no work" framework. Arbitration advocates argue that negotiations in the public sector go on endlessly without the prod of an arbitration deadline. In effect, arbitration would provide a realistic deadline to public sector bargaining.

   Arbitration opponents feel the public sector impasse resolution should be linked to the annual budgetary process as a viable deadline to the negotiating process. However, they contend that the past willingness of the public officials to ignore budgetary deadlines by issuing interim memoranda of agreement has nullified the effectiveness of such deadlines.

4. Arbitration resolves those issues which are not genuinely soluble through negotiations. Those who support interest arbitration as an impasse resolution technique view it as the only means other than strike or work stoppage whereby an irresistible force can be forced to compromise with an immovable object.

5. Interest arbitration is the only effective means of preventing public employee strikes. Admittedly, interest arbitration severely restricts continued collective bargaining, but it does protect

labor peace. Particularly in protective services, it guarantees "the supply of vital services"[119] and prevents "the exercise of irresponsible power."[120] In fact, many proponents believe that compulsory arbitration should be legislated as a means of preserving the public protective services.

Several midwestern states employ a variety of impasse resolution techniques among police and firemen (see table 5-7).[121] Arbitration ranges from advisory status on all issues in municipal disputes in Illinois to final offer arbitration as mandated by state legislation in Minnesota and Wisconsin. In yet another variation, Nevada grants its governor authority, at the request of either party, to order binding arbitration.[122]

Two of the more important variations of interest arbitration are *final offer selection* and *med-arb*. In final offer arbitration, the arbitrator selects the last offer of one of the parties. In theory, both parties are motivated to bargain in good faith so that their final offer will appear most rational to the arbitrator.

A number of observers[123] feel that the major benefit of last best offer arbitration is that the process encourages "realistic bargaining positions." Wellington and Winter also point out: "Employer and union, realizing that the arbitrators' power is limited to accepting the entire proposed contract of one or the other party, will each bargain in good faith and in great earnestness to reach an agreement."[124] It is a device to pressure parties to negotiate in good faith.

The major criticism of the last best offer process is that the parties may make unreasonable demands since only one proposal will be accepted. The negotiated solution to the dispute probably would be mutual compromise, but this is unattainable under this process. A variation of the last best offer is for each side in the dispute to present its final stand on each issue and for the arbitrator to make his decisions on an issue-by-issue basis. This has obvious advantages in that both sides would be represented in the final agreement, but the problem of one or both of the parties making unreasonable demands is still available.

A variety of final offer systems has developed that vary according to the number of offers allowed, the method of selection, the selection criteria, payment of costs, and other variables.[125] The record of final offer arbitration has been profound if somewhat mixed in consequences. Results apparently range from "relatively successful" in jurisdictions such as Eugene, Oregon,[126] to Indianapolis, where observers believed that arbitrators' decisions were generally inferior and too inflexible.[127] Despite several problems, many experts believe that final offer arbitration, "may prove to be the most satisfactory alternative to the strike in

TABLE 5-7: Police and Fire Impasse Resolution Techniques in Midwest Labor Legislation

State	Coverage	Strike	Initiating Method	Status of Awards	Type of Arbitration	If Final Offer					Who Arbitrated	Who Pays
						Type	When Made	No. of Offers	Scope	Criteria		
Illinois	Fire fighters	No	Compulsory	Advisory		No provisions			All issues	None	Panel	Municipality
Indiana						No provisions						
Michigan	Police and fire fighters	No	Compulsory	Binding	Final offer	Issue by issue	At or before end of hearing	No provisions	Economic issues	Yes	Panel	Parties and state share
Minnesota	Police and fire fighters	No[1]	Compulsory	Binding	Final offer[2]	No provisions			All issues	None	Panel	Parties share
Ohio	All employees	No				No provisions						
Wisconsin	Police and fire fighters	No	Compulsory	Binding	Final offer[3]	Whole package	At time arb. requested[4]		All issues	Yes	Single	Parties share

Source: *Midwest Monitor: A Digest of Current Literature and Developments in Public Sector Labor Relations* (Bloomington, Ind.: Indiana University, (March/April 1977), p. 4.

[1] Limited right to strike under certain conditons.

[2] Parties are required to submit final offer but the arbitrator's decision is not limited to one or the other.

[3] Parties may agree to conventional arbitration.

[4] Final offer may be amended within five days of the date of the hearing.

the public sector,"[128] and should be made available as an option to conventional arbitration.[129]

The med-arb technique is supposedly a merging of mediation and arbitration in which both parties request a neutral third party to mediate impasse issues. If unsuccessful in his efforts at conciliation the mediator becomes an arbitrator with binding authority over impasse issues. Proponents argue that med-arb gives both parties an incentive to complete the negotiation process.

> The incentive is for the parties to settle their own agreement through direct negotiations, and the med-arbiter is really a threat to keep the parties honest and move them to a settlement.[130]

In effect, med-arb is a much less formal process than arbitration when those few remaining irreducible issues are isolated. At that point, the med-arb process becomes highly informal. One participant said, "We don't have records, we don't take a transcript, and we take up each issue whatever it might be."[131]

Med-arb proponents are generally enthusiastic about its innovative potential, which has been termed "the most creative and most flexible"[132] technique in recent years. Even so, one advocate cautions that med-arb "should not be used as a substitute for orthodox collective bargaining in routine cases, strike threats notwithstanding."[133] Rather, med-arb is proposed in particular situations:

> (1) It is a delicate mechanism which should be undertaken primarily in situations where the issues truly are difficult or complex; (2) it should be used where an impasse in negotiations could result in a strike that would have a serious impact upon the community. . . . [134]

Med-arb's primary assest as an alternative to traditional arbitration is its promise to reduce the number of issues that finally go into arbitration.[135]

Seemingly, med-arb is "accepted with greater reluctance by employers than by unions."[136] Their reluctance stems primarily from a potential loss of decision-making autonomy to the med-arbiter. The employer's fear is of any binding and compulsory arbitration process; that the neutral party will inevitably tend "to compromise, to split the difference, and to go beyond what the employers believe is good business judgment."[137]

Med-Arb in Practice: The California Nurses Association (CNA)

In 1970, over 4,000 nurses were organized by CNA in thirty-six hospitals throughout the San Francisco Bay Area. These CNA nurses were opening contract negotiations with three employer associations that included Kaiser Foundation and two independent hospital associations.

As background, there had been a nurses' strike in 1968, that was finally settled by direct mediation. Both CNA and the employer associations agreed to med-arb and thereby promised not to strike or lockout respectively.

The advantages of med-arb were seemingly useful in this situation. The nurses, in an increased mood of militancy, presented over ninety proposals. Many of these proposals were symbolic or bargaining pawns. Consequently, the med-arbiter was able to persuade CNA to drop many of these issues, which would have been submitted in orthodox or formal arbitration. However, a number of substantive or policy issues remained: "patient-care matters, such as staffing patterns, the ratio of Registered Nurses to patients, and the ratio of Registered Nurses to other paramedical personnel."[138] Initially hospital representatives were appalled that CNA sought to bargain on perceived management prerogatives. They were also dismayed that their fate rested in the hands of a third party. The generally agreed success of med-arb in this hostile situation is attributable to the mediator-arbitrator, who:

> by his very presence, forced the negotiators to respond to the issues with facts, statistics, and intelligent arguments. They could not resort to repetitious platitudes, bluff, or exaggeration in justifying positions. The presence of the mediator arbitrator kept the negotiators honest and created a new atmosphere.[139]

As a consequence, both parties were forced to be more flexible and innovative than in mediation or straight arbitration. It required forty-five days of utilizing the med-arb process to resolve the remaining sixty-eight issues (the prolonged period was due to differences between Kaiser and independent hospital representatives). Only two issues were ultimately decided by the med-arbiter. For example, the mediation-arbitration process was utilized in solving the refusal of primarily Catholic nurses to participate in therapeutic abortions:

> The parties worked out this problem by the way of the med-arb process. They drew up what they called a statement of conscience, which is actually a part of the collective bargaining agreement, in which a nurse in a non-Catholic hospital who does not wish to participate in this procedure notifies the employer in writing.[140]

Conclusion

We have presented an overview of the legal environment associated with contemporary labor relations in the public sector. Our analysis has focused specifically on the legal framework of impasse resolution and job action. We have attempted to assess the efficacy of various legal techniques, including state and federal legislation, executive orders, and judicial decisions, on public sector labor relations.

In order to understand the emerging nature of collective bargaining in the public sector, we have examined the evolutionary nature of its formulation in the private sector. Basic legal precedents and collective bargaining procedures were developed from 1932 to the present in private sector industrial relations. This development took place in the following phases: (1) the formation of private sector policymaking as indicated in the National Labor Relations Act (including its important amendments) and the function of the National Labor Relations Board; (2) the permeation of private sector concepts and procedures among public employees, at the federal level and among the states and municipalities.

We have noted the extent to which public sector collective bargaining is based on the private sector experience. Consequently, we have observed the degree to which public sector labor and management rely on legal formulas previously developed in the private sector, rather than developing unique techniques in impasse resolution or as strike remedies.

In general, our analysis has not found conclusive evidence that legislation, at either the federal level or among the states, has been effective in preventing strikes. Nor can we find overwhelmingly support for the contention that legalizing either the strike or collective bargaining will reduce the incidence of strikes or job actions. Instead, the evidence suggests that the incidence of strikes has been more dependent on increasing socioeconomic variables among the various states, i.e., wealth, industrialization, public expenditures, etc., than on types of legislation. There is evidence which suggests that specific types of legislation may affect the causes of strikes. For example, in a case study of California's Rodda Act, which authorized limited collective bargaining for public education employees, we observed a significant increase in labor unrest during the initial year of the act's existence. This, we hypothesized, was possibly due to the act's recognition of limited collective bargaining without authorizing a technique for impasse resolution. Consequently, a number of work stoppages over impasse techniques occurred. The California case study supports Theodore Lowi's contention that interest group liberalism's general failure to be specific in legislation undermines policy implementation.

Finally, we examined some evidence which indicates that one impasse resolution technique, binding and compulsory arbitration, may reduce the number of grievance related strikes. However, there are also indications that this impasse resolution technique may subvert the collective bargaining process, i.e., the intent of both parties to reach a resolution before impasse.

In summary, a simple correlation between antistrike legislation with a reduction of strikes or work stoppages does not apparently exist. Yet legislation may be effective in shaping the *causes* of work stoppages. Similarly, the mere promulgation of collective bargaining legislation will not automatically ensure peaceful labor-management relations. One can generalize that the more specific collective bargaining legislation becomes, the more predictable are its policy consequences.

Notes to Chapter 5

1. Harold W. Davey, *Contemporary Collective Bargaining*, 3rd ed. (Englewood Cliffs, N.J.: Prentice-Hall, 1972), p. 56.
2. Ibid.
3. For a study of the formation, organization, and procedures surrounding the NRLB, see Frank W. McCulloch and Tim Borstein, *The National Labor Relations Board* (New York, Praeger Pubs., 1974).
4. Bureau of National Affairs, *Major Labor Law Principles Established by the NLRB and the Courts, December, 1963-February, 1968* (Washington, D.C.: The Bureau of National Affairs, 1968).
5. Davey, op. cit., pp. 58-59.
6. Ibid.
7. Harry H. Wellington, *Labor and the Legal Process* (New Haven: Yale Univ. Press, 1968).
8. Edwin F. Beal, Edward Wickersham, Philip K. Kienast, *The Practice of Collective Bargaining*, 5th ed. (Homewood, Ill.: Richard D. Irwin, 1976), p. 150.
9. Robert Presthus, *Public Administration*, 6th ed. (New York: Ronald Press Co., 1975), p. 252.
10. Ibid.; Kenneth O. Warner, ed., *Management Relations With Organized Public Employees* (Chicago: Public Personnel Association, 1963).
11. Felix A. Nigro, *Management-Employee Relations in the Public Service* (Chicago: Public Personnel Association, 1969), p. 80.
12. Sterling D. Spero and John M. Capozzola, *The Urban Community and Its Unionized Bureaucracies* (New York: Dunellen Publishing Co., 1973), p. 139.
13. Report of Cornell University Conference, May 1970. *Labor Relations Yearbook* (Washington, D.C.: Bureau of National Affairs, 1971), p. 200. Cited hereafter as *Labor Relations Yearbook*.
14. Beal, Wickersham, Kienast, op. cit., pp. 479-480.
15. Richard J. Murphy, "The Difference of a Decade: The Federal Government," *Public Administration Review* 32 (March/April 1972), p. 110.
16. Theodore J. Lowi, *The End of Liberalism: Ideology, Policy and the Crisis of Public Authority* (New York: W.W. Norton & Co., 1969).
17. *Labor Relations Yearbook*, op. cit., p. 200.
18. Richard M. Nixon, *Public Papers of the President: 1971*, (Washington, D.C.: U.S. Government Printing Office, 1972).
19. Gerald R. Ford, *Public Papers of the President: 1975* (Washington, D.C.: U.S. Government Printing Office, 1976).
20. Beal, Wickersham, Kienast, op. cit., pp. 480-481.
21. Felicitas Hinman, ed., *The Rodda Act—One Year Later* (Los Angeles: Univ. of California, Institute of Industrial Relations, 1977), p. C-6.

22. Steven J. Andelson, "NLRB Procedures and Practices With Reference to the Rodda Act," *California Public Employee Relations* (Berkeley: Institute of Industrial Relations, University of California, September 1976), no. 30.

23. Spero and Capozzola, op. cit., p. 240.

24. California, State Senate, S.B. 164, 1977.

25. Al Bilik, "Toward Public Sector Equality: Extending the Strike Privilege," *Labor Law Journal* 20 (June 1970), pp. 338-356.

26. Lewis Coser, *The Functions of Social Conflict* (New York: Free Press, 1956).

27. E. Wright Bakke, Clark Kerr, and Charles Anrod, eds., *Unions, Management and the Public* (Chicago: Harcourt, Brace, and World, 1967), p. 295.

28. Ibid., p. 270.

29. Ibid.

30. Michael H. Moskow, Joseph Loewenberg, and Edward C. Kozaria, *Collective Bargaining in Public Employment* (New York: Random House, 1970), p. 73.

31. U.S., Bureau of Labor Statistics, *Handbook of Labor Statistics 1976*, p. 308.

32. Ralph J. Flynn in *Federal Legislation for Public Sector Collective Bargaining*, ed. Thomas Colosi and Steven Rynecki (Chicago: International Personnel Management Assn., 1975), p. 3. Cited hereafter as Colosi and Rynecki.

33. Bakke, Kerr, Anrod, op. cit., p. 247.

34. John F.J. Burton, "Can Public Employees Be Given the Right to Strike?" *Labor Law Journal* 21 (August 1970), pp. 472-78; Jerome T. Barrett and Ira B. Lobel, "Public Sector Strikes: Legislative and Court Treatment," *Monthly Labor Review*, 97 (September 1974), pp. 19-22; Antone Aboud and Grace Sterrett Aboud, *The Right to Strike in Public Employment* (Ithaca, N.Y.: Cornell Univ. Press, 1974).

35. "Public Sector Bargaining and Strikes: Text of Report by Public Service Research Council," (Washington, D.C.: Bureau of National Affairs, 1976), p. F-2.

36. Paul D. Staudohar, "Organization, Bargaining and Work Stoppages in California Public Employment," *California Public Employee Relations* 29 (January 1975), pp. 19-24.

37. U.S., Congress, House, Hearings before Special Subcommittee on Labor, "Labor-Management Relations in the Public Sector" (Washington, D.C.: U.S. Government Printing Office, 1972). Cited hereafter as "Labor-Management Relations in the Public Sector." Hearings before the Subcommittee on Labor Management Relations, "Public Employee Labor-Management Relations" (Washington, D.C.: U.S. Government Printing Office, 1976).

38. Jerry Wurf in *Federal Legislation for Public Sector Collective Bargaining*, Colosi and Rynecki, op. cit., p. 38.

39. John Ryor, testimony in "Public Employee Labor-Management Relations," U.S., Congress, House Committee on Education and Labor, Subcommittee on Labor-Management Relations, 94th Cong., 1st sess. (Washington, D.C.: U.S. Government Printing Office, 1976), pp. 5-6. Cited hereafter as "Public Employee Labor-Management Relations."

40. Ibid., p. 6.

41. U.S., Congress, Committee on Education and Labor, Subcommittee on Labor-Management Relations, 97th Cong. H.R. 1589, (1977).

42. *Federal Times*, 16 May 1977, p. 19.

43. "Labor-Management Relations in the Public Sector," op. cit., p. 1.

44. Robert W. Houghton, "What the Federal Government Proposes," Colosi and Rynecki, op. cit., p. 66-75.

45. Ryor, op. cit., pp. 8-9.

46. Peter Henle, "Reverse Collective Bargaining? A Look at Some Union Concession Situations," *Industrial and Labor Relations Review* 26 (April 1973), p. 956.

47. Kenneth Clark, "Public Employee Strikes: Some Proposed Solutions," *Labor Law Journal* 23 (March 1972), p. 115.

48. Walter J. Gershenfeld, J. Joseph Loewenberg, Bernard Ingster, *The Scope of Collective Bargaining* (Lexington, Mass.: D.C. Heath and Co., 1977).

49. Nigro, op. cit., p. 26.

50. Spero and Capozzola, op. cit., p. 265.

51. Ibid.

52. Derek C. Bok and John T. Dunlop, *Labor and the American Community*, (New York: Simon and Schuster, 1970), p. 322.

53. A.H. Ruskin, "A Strike Ban Is Essential," *Collective Bargaining for Public Employees*, ed. Herbert L. Marx, Jr. (New York: H. W. Wilson, 1969), p. 101. Cited hereafter as Marx.

54. Roch Bolduc, "The Framework of Collective Bargaining," *Collective Bargaining in the Public Service: Theory and Practice*, ed. Kenneth O. Warner (Chicago: Public Personnel Association, 1969), p. 15.

55. Keith Cottam, "Unionization Is Not Inevitable," Marx, op. cit., p. 88.

56. Michael J. O'Larny, "Unstrike Unsuccessful for Culver Teachers," *Fox Hills-Raintree Today*, 19 May 1977, p. 1.

57. Keppel, op. cit., p. 1.

58. Bok and Dunlop, op. cit., p. 285.

59. Ibid.

60. Ibid., p. 288.

61. Ibid., p. 232.

62. Ibid., p. 285.

63. Staudohar.

64. Thomas R. Dye, *Understanding Public Policy* (Englewood Cliffs, N.J.: Prentice-Hall, 1975).

65. California, Government Code, Section 3540-3549 (1975).

66. Hinman, *The Rodda Act*, op. cit., p. B.

67. Ibid., p. A-2.

68. California, Government Code, Section 3540.1 (1975).

69. Jack W. Brittan, "At the Table: The Implementation of the Collective Negotiations under the Rodda Act," *California Public Employees Relations* 33 (1977), p. 12.

70. Richard J. Currier, "A Case Study: Sixteen Public School Job Actions and the Use of Impasse Procedures," *California Public Employee Relations* 33 (1977), pp. 16-20.

71. Brittan, op. cit., p. 12.

72. One may consult the official California Teachers' Association publication, *CTA Action*, throughout 1976-77 for an overview of the CTA-AFT struggle.

73. William D. Ford, "Public Employee Labor-Management Relations," op. cit., p. 40.

74. James L. Stern, et al., *Final-Offer Arbitration* (Lexington, Mass.: D.C. Heath and Co., 1975).

75. Demetrios Caraley, *City Governments and Urban Problems*, (Englewood Cliffs, N.J.: Prentice-Hall, 1977), p. 259.

76. Ibid.

77. Beal, Wickersham, Kienast, op. cit., p. 138.

78. Alvin L. Goldman, *The Supreme Court and Labor Management Relations Law* (Lexington, Mass.: D.C. Heath and Co., 1975); San Diego Building Trades Council v. Garmon, 359 U.S. 236, 43 L.R.R.M. 2838 (1959).

79. Charles J. Morris, ed. *The Developing Labor Law* (Washington, D.C.: Bureau of National Affairs, 1971), pp. 495-496.

80. Spero and Capozzola, op. cit., p. 306.

81. Ibid.

82. Ibid.

83. Ibid., p. 308.

84. M.J. Fox, Jr. and L.B. McDonald, "The Need for Compulsory Arbitration, *Journal of Collective Negotiations in the Public Sector* 3, no. 4 (Fall 1974), pp. 327-337.

85. Hinman, *The Rodda Act*, op. cit., p. C-6.

86. *Impasse Resolution in Public Sector Interest Disputes,* (Los Angeles: Univ. of California, Institute of Industrial Relations, 1976), p. A-1.

87. Stahl, op. cit., p. 365.

88. *Network News*, Spring 1977 (Washington, D.C.: Newsletter of the National Training & Development Service for State and Local Government) 5, no. 2, p. 1.

89. William Simkin, quoted in Bakke, Kerr, and Anrod, op. cit., p. 320.

90. William Simkin, *Mediation and the Dynamics of Collective Bargaining* (Washington, D.C.: Bureau of National Affairs, 1971), p. 498.

91. Hinman, Felicitas, ed. *Impasse Resolution in Public Sector Interest Disputes* (Los Angeles: Univ. of California, Institute of Industrial Relations, 1976), p. B-3.

92. R. Theodore Clark, Jr., "Public Employee Strikes: Some Proposed Solutions," *Labor Law Journal* 23 (February 1972), p. 118.

93. Arnold Zack, *Understanding Fact Finding and Arbitration in the Public Sector* (Washington, D.C.: U.S. Department of Labor, 1974).

94. Hinman, *Impasse Resolution*, op. cit., p. B-13.

95. Ibid., p. B-7.

96. Bruce Keppel, "County Employees Resume Protest on Pay Offer," *Los Angeles Times*, 27 May 1977, pt. I, p. 3.

97. Bruce Keppel, "County Taking a Closer Look at 'Sick-Outs,'" *Los Angeles Times*, 28 May 1977, pt. II, p. 1.

98. Clark, *Labor Law Journal*, op. cit., p. 118.

99. William R. Word, "Fact-finding in Public Employee Negotiations," *Monthly Labor Review* 95 (February 1975), p. 63.

100. Zack, *Understanding Fact Finding*, op. cit.

101. Word, op. cit., p. 63.

102. Word, op. cit., p. 64.

103. Jacob Finkelman, "When Bargaining Fails," *Collective Bargaining in the Public Sector*, ed., Kenneth O. Warner (Chicago: Public Personnel Association, 1969), p. 130.

104. James L. Stern, "The Wisconsin Public Employee Fact-finding Procedure," *Industrial and Labor Relations Review* 20 (October 1966), pp. 3-29. Benjamin W. Wolkinson and Jack Stieber, "Michigan Fact-Finding Experience in Public Sector Disputes," *The Arbitration Journal* 31, no. 4 (December 1976), pp. 225-247.

105. Arnold M. Zack, "Improving Mediation and Fact-Finding in the Public Sector," *Labor Law Journal* 30 (1970), pp. 259-273.

106. Joseph J. Loewenberg and Michael H. Moskow, eds., *Collective Bargaining in Government: Readings and Cases,* (Englewood Cliffs, N.J.: Prentice-Hall, 1972), p. 315.

107. Rustin, A. H., op. cit., p. 59.

108. R. Theodore Clark, Jr., *Compulsory Arbitration in Public Employment* (Chicago: Public Personnel Association, 1972).

109. Harry H. Wellington and Ralph K. Winter, *The Unions and the Cities* (Washington, D.C.: Brookings Institution, 1971).

110. Clark, *Labor Law Journal*, op. cit.

111. Benjamin Rubenstein, "The Bugaboo of Compulsory Arbitration," *Labor Law Journal* 23 (February 1972), p. 168.

112. Hoyt N. Wheeler, and Frank Owen, "Impasse Resolution Preferences of Firefighters and Municipal Negotiators," *Journal of Collective Negotiations in the Public Sector* 5, no. 3 (1976), pp. 215-224.

113. Robert H. Bezdek and David W. Ripley, "Compulsory Arbitration versus Negotiations for Public Safety Employees: The Michigan Experience," *Journal of Collective Negotiations in the Public Sector* 3, no. 2 (Spring 1974), pp. 167-176.

114. Bakke, Kerr, Anrod, op. cit., p. 327.

115. James D. Brown, "No Strikes for Government Employees, But. . . ," *Collective Bargaining for Public and Professional Employees,* ed. Robert T. Woodworth and Richard B. Peterson (Glenview, Ill.: Scott Foresman, 1969), p. 38.

116. David G. Shenton, "Compulsory Arbitration in the Public Sector," *Collective Bargaining in the Public Service,* ed. Daniel H. Kruger and Charles T. Schmidt, Jr. (New York: Random House, 1969), p. 191.

117. Finkelman, op. cit., pp. 118-119.

118. Charles M. Rehmus, "Is a 'Final Offer' Ever Final?" *Monthly Labor Review* 97, no. 9 (September 1974), pp. 43-45.

119. *Midwest Monitor: A Digest of Current Literature and Developments in Public Sector Labor Relations* (Bloomington, Ind.: Indiana Univ. Press, March/April 1977), p. 4.

120. Bakke, Kerr, Anrod, op. cit.

121. *Midwest Monitor*, op. cit.

122. Joseph R. Grodin, "Arbitration of Public Sector Labor Disputes: The Nevada Experiment," *Industrial and Labor Relations Review* 28 (October 1974), pp. 89-102.

123. James L. Stern, Charles M. Rehmus, J. Joseph Loewenberg, Hirschel Kasper, Barbara Dennis, *Final-Offer Arbitration: The Effects of Public Safety Employee Bargaining* (Lexington, Mass.: D.C. Heath and Co. 1975).

124. Wellington and Winter, op. cit., p. 180.

125. See: Peter Feuille and Gary Long, "The Public Administrator and Final Offer Arbitration," *Public Administration Review* 34, no. 6 (November/December 1974), pp. 575-583.

126. Gary Long and Peter Feuille, "Final-Offer Arbitration: 'Sudden Death' in Eugene," *Industrial and Labor Relations Review* 27 (January 1974), pp. 186-203.

127. Fred Whitney, "Final Offer Arbitration: The Indianapolis Experience," *Monthly Labor Review* 96, no. 5 (May 1973), pp. 20-25.

128. Nels Nelson, "Final-Offer Arbitration: Some Problems," *The Arbitration Journal* 30, no. 1 (March 1975), p. 50.

129. Joseph R. Grodin, "Either/Or Arbitration for Public Employee Disputes," *Industrial Relations* 77 (May 1972), pp. 260-266.

130. Sam Kagel, "Combining Mediation and Arbitration," *Monthly Labor Review* 96, no. 9 (September 1973).

131. Ibid.

132. Harry Polland, "Mediation-Arbitration: A Trade Union View, *Monthly Labor Review,* 96, no. 9 (September 1973).

133. Ibid.

134. Ibid.

135. Peter Feuille, *Final Offer Arbitration* (Chicago: International Personnel Management Assn. 1975).

136. Laurence P. Corbett, "Mediation-Arbitration, from the Employer's Standpoint," *Monthly Labor Review* 96, no. 12 (December 1973).

137. Ibid.

138. Ibid.

139. Ibid.

140. Kagel, op. cit.

6 Role of Public Employee Unions in Public Policymaking

The potential impact of public employee organizations on traditional patterns of public policymaking is only now being felt. The brief history of collective bargaining in the public sector suggests the initiation of policymaking changes that are both pervasive and significant. Our analysis examines three major areas of public policymaking in assessing the nature of these changes.

First, the advent of collective bargaining in the public sector indicates an expansion and restructuring of the interest group policymaking process through the introduction of yet another political interest group—the public employee union. Second, public sector unionism represents a challenge to traditional methods of exclusive decision making by key bureaucrats within bureaucratic oligarchies. Third, public employee unions, through collective bargaining, are becoming important participants in the politics of the budgetary process. Public employee unions are also factors in the proposed implementation by public management of various budgetary reform systems. Finally, it is essential to appreciate whose interests public employee unions are actually representing through the internal decision-making process by which union members determine their own policymaking agenda.

Role of Public Employee Unions in the Analysis of Public Policy

There are many dimensions and perspectives in public policymaking analysis. Many observers would agree with Robert Salisbury's trichotomy of policymaking as (1) the substance of what government does, (2) the processes by which decisions are made, and (3) the outcomes or outputs of governmental processes.[1] In other words, policy analysis may either focus separately on legal content, process of decision making, the consequences of policy adoption, or the total analysis of all three categories.

Public policymaking analysis has historically focused on institutional activity, specifically on governmental rulings and legislation. Early policy analysts, such as Woodrow Wilson, believed that only governmental policies could be considered legitimate, hence morally and legally binding on citizens. Nongovernmental or interest group participation was considered by policy analysts as illegitimate, therefore not to be included in policy studies. In other words, only decisions made within recognized political institutions by public authorities could be categorized as public policy. Consequently, interest groups such as trade associations or unions were ignored as policy participants. Such groups were seen as involved in private policymaking outside the public policymaking arena.

A delineation between public and private policies, or between political and nonpolitical issues is somewhat unrealistic. Only if one considers policy decisions at the microcosmic or individual level can policymaking be classified as either exclusively public governmental or private. For example, the individual union member who calls for an investigation into corrupt union leadership through either the NLRB or the Labor Department's Government Regulations and Labor Section, is initiating a purely public or governmental decision.

However, in most policy issues, private sector organizations or pressure groups participate in clarifying public policies by competing for the allocation of public values and resources. For example, Robert Dahl argues that private corporations must be treated as political entities: "It is a delusion to consider [the corporation] a private enterprise. General Motors is as much a public enterprise as the U.S. Post Office."[2] One may also consider various postal workers' unions and other public employee unions as active public policymaking participants. As a consequence, the once clear dichotomy between public and private policymaking has been generally replaced by a continuum of public policymaking variables.[3] If, as Patrick Moynihan suggests, there are no social interests about which government does not make policy, then even private decisions have public consequences.[4]

As Mark Nadel suggests, the blurring of boundaries between public and private policymaking, i.e., the interaction between governmental and corporate elites, has important ramifications.[5] First, the extensive policy communication between public and private elites means that no single all-powerful elite dominates every area of public policymaking. The effect is a cooperative elite that formulates most public policies.

Consequently, as Seymour Melman states, "it is no longer meaningful to speak of [the] elites of industrial management, the elites of finance, and the elites of government and how they relate to each other. The elites have been merged in the new state-management."[6] In fact, Morton Grodzins believes that this public-private policymaking subsystem of elite rule is actually more entrenched at the local than at the federal level.[7] He argues that in many municipalities, private businesses and trade associations perform a variety of political functions in cooperation with local governments, e.g., the Chamber of Commerce, the Better Business Bureau, and various civic clubs.

Secondly, the intertwined public-private policymaking subsystem of elites has delegated to particular nongovernmental organizations the right of unilateral or exclusive policymaking on certain policy issues. In some issue arenas the exercises of public policymaking power has been co-opted by nongovernmental organizations; in others the power was specifically assumed by private groups.[8] Another instance of delegation is that of collective bargaining policymaking to independent regulatory commissions such as the NLRB or state regulatory commissions. The comparable domination of public policymaking by private organizations was exemplified by the actions of the major petroleum corporations during the supposed gasoline shortage of 1973. As Thomas Dye and Harmon Zeigler point out, the six major oil corporations successfully exercised a monopoly of critical information in manipulating policymaking priorities during the supposed "energy crisis."[9]

Less susceptible to easy policy classification are those organizations which perform a public service function yet are neither governmental nor profit-oriented private organizations. Peter Drucker feels that these public service or not-for-profit institutions are the real growth sector of modern society.[10] Public service organizations such as school and university staff, public utilities, hospitals and health care facilities are neither purely public or private. Although legally not-for-profit and frequently funded by public sources, such institutions are oftentimes profit-oriented in order to survive.[11] Like governmental bureaucracies, public service agencies participate in public policymaking issues such as health, education, and welfare. The inclusion of such public services or not-for-profit organizations under the NLRB's aegis in 1974 marked the first expansion of national collective bargaining rights beyond the exclusively private sector.

Perhaps the greatest obstacle to public policy analysis is the value-laden nature of many policy issues. The issue of collective bargaining by public employees only adds to existing controversy surrounding other policy issues such as poverty, crime, education, or criminal justice. Most such public policy issues have been emotionally perceived, and, therefore, debated from fixed ideological positions. Consequently, public policy advocacy is frequently confused with policy analysis. The public policy arena, for better or worse, is one in which all public-minded citizens, in the heritage of Jacksonian Democracy, consider themselves policy experts. Intense pressure group activity and polarized public opinion already exist on key national issues such as crime, health education, and poverty. The introduction of collective bargaining by public employees groups in each of these issue arenas only injects further controversy and confusion. Yet, the entrance of police unions into criminal justice policymaking or teachers' unions into education policymaking is a seemingly irreversible trend.

In order to develop a theoretical policymaking framework for analysis, public sector unionism is approached on three levels: (1) policy content, (2) the policymaking process, and (3) the policymaking environment. The policymaking framework will then be applied in assessing the evolution of public sector collective bargaining. Hopefully, this policymaking framework for analysis will make the activities of public employee organizations less mysterious and more predictable.

In summary, rather than assuming that public policymaking occurs primarily in governmental institutions, whether by elected or appointed officials, public policymaking analysis focuses on the decision-making process wherever it occurs. This process may occur anywhere: board rooms, council chambers, the proverbial smoke-filled rooms, or the golf course. Any decision that affects the lives of citizens, often by compelling them to take specific actions, is a component of the public policymaking system. Consequently, analysis of public policymaking may often include unexpected political actors.[12] It is our contention that public employee unions are newly emergent actors who are significantly altering the public policymaking system.

Policy Content of Public Sector Collective Bargaining

Policy studies focusing on the content of public policies emphasize formal-legal results' (output). Content studies are based on what policymakers intend to happen through official policy statements.[13] Analysis of the policymaking process and social consequences are secondary. For example, the Executive Orders of Presidents Kennedy and Nixon defining limited collective bargaining for federal employees are important policy content. As such, this policy content is not only legally binding but is also important as symbolic content in the evolution of federal personnel policy for federal employees.

The content of federal policymaking for collective bargaining includes the following areas for policy analysis and research:

1. A group of employees to whom policy content is directed,[14] e.g., GS level employees.
2. The calculated strategies precipitating the content, e.g., the co-optation by management of union organizing efforts. Content includes Henry Riecken's definition of strategy as a "deliberate allocation of resources . . . intended to achieve a chosen end."[15]
3. Line of action or consequences intended by particular content, e.g., to alleviate public employee labor unrest. Vernon Van Dyke defines this action as a "deliberate selection of one line of action from among several possible ones."[16]
4. A public declaration, e.g., the official legitimization of collective bargaining for federal employees.
5. Line of action or consequences actually taken, e.g., an attempt to limit rather than expand the scope of federal employee collective bargaining.

These content categories for public policy analysis have been utilized in several excellent case studies of specific decisions.[17] However, their utility is somewhat narrow and problem-oriented for the analysis of more comprehensive policymaking such as public employee collective bargaining.[18]

The experience of those supporting antistrike legislation and referenda for public employees among the states illustrates the complex nature of policy content analysis. In a 1977 California initiative, which is somewhat typical of such antistrike prohibitions, proponents introduced a clause that theoretically would have made public employee strikes unconstitutional. The initiative was introduced even though strikes were already illegal in California and collective bargaining only legally guaranteed on specific issues for public school teachers. Although the initiative was ostensibly aimed at public employee strikes, the actual policy content was intended to compel public officials to punish strikers through existing laws. Critics argued that the initiative's language would severely restrict collective bargaining and reopen the dormant right-to-work issue in the state.[19] In essence, policy content or formal policy output is multi-dimensional and, therefore, best analyzed along with the policymaking process and policy consequences.

The formal content or output of public policymaking is usually considered to include the following statements: *ex cathedra* statements, statutes and constitutional law, administrative regulations, judicial decisions, and other recognized policy guidelines. Specifically, the policy output or content of public sector labor relations is still developing. Consequently, it is often highly fragmentary and transitory in nature. As such, public sector policy output has been more procedural than substantive, although this is rapidly changing as more pervasive legislative responses to collective bargaining emerge among the states.

From another dimension, policy outputs or contents are reflective of hoped for behavior change in clientele groups. For example, collective bargaining legislation with the stated intention of improving public sector labor relations, i.e., the Rodda Act in California or the Taylor Act in New York, achieved entirely unforeseen consequences of increasing job actions by public employees. Consequently, policy analysis must also separate intended policy outputs from actual outcomes. In other words, the intent of legislation, judicial or regulatory decisions, and administrative guidelines should not be confused with resultant policy consequences for society. It is the impact of policy outcomes, rather than the outputs themselves, that are causal factors in policy change or development. In our case study of the Rodda Act, the unintended and unanticipated policy consequences of this legislation for teachers motivated numerous legislative bills designed to both redefine collective bargaining and expand it to include a policy for all California public employees.

Although the intent of public sector collective bargaining legislation is officially to regulate labor-management behavior, policymaking orientations among public employees are seldom derived from formal rules or procedures. Their behavior is more often affected by the decision-making process and the political environment encompassing this process. For example, issues relating to safety and security were among the chief causes of strikes by prison employees during the late 1960s and 1970s.[20] Organizations representing prison employees were particularly opposed to efforts giving prisoners adequate due process rights in disciplinary and classification matters, programs increasing community and family involvement in institutional activities, and programs granting community furloughs to prisoners for educational or work purposes. Prison employee unions opposed such programs because they felt the programs would result in increased smuggling-in of contraband and a breakdown in authority; hence these programs were considered a threat to prison employees.[21]

The corrections policymaking process occurs in state capitols, far from the environs of correctional facilities. Prison employees have historically been excluded from this process, with no influence on policy outcomes. In effect, prison employee unions have emerged not so much to change correctional policy content; rather they have emerged because of employee beliefs that their own security is not being considered and that final correctional policy content does not protect their own security interests.

Finally, the analysis of public policymaking contents and formal outcomes, although an important approach in policy analysis, cannot be completely utilized as the only approach to policy analysis. However, this is not to disparage the number of excellent, descriptive case study and problem-oriented approaches.[22] Although essential for policy research and theory building, such studies provide the bases for more explanatory models of public employee policymaking yet to be developed. As Yehezkel Dror contends, a significant gap exists between the theoretical models of public policymaking and the experimental realities of how policies are generally formulated.[23] Only by developing theoretical models of public employee unionism can the true nature of this phenomenon be properly understood. Only by placing policy content within the framework of decision-making processes and policy consequences can generalizations be tested.[24]

Process of Making Public Policy for Collective Bargaining

The prevailing model of the public policymaking process is quite simple in its essential components. (See figures 6-1 and 6-2. Figure 6-2 is essentially the same policymaking process approached from a systems perspective.) As with any systems model, each component is interrelated and affected by the functions of every other systemic variable. Therefore, a change in existing components or the introduction of new variables theoretically causes a restructuring of the (policymaking) system. Accordingly, emergence of public employee unions as participants in the public policymaking system has important consequences throughout the system. The impact of public employee unions on public policymaking can be analyzed from various subsystem perspectives: the legislative process, i.e., collective bargaining legislation among the states; public personnel systems; elite interaction; political groups, i.e., parties; interest groups; movements; and public opinion trends, i.e., public opinion, electoral results. Each of these approaches, combined with other analytical tools, is important in providing data and generalizations concerning the participation of public employee unions in the public policymaking system.[25]

The public policymaking process should also be distinguished from the related decision-making process, which it includes.[26] Although utilizing many of the same analytical methodologies as policy studies, decision-making studies focus on specific case studies. In contrast, policymaking studies are longitudinally developed over a period of time and usually include many critical decisions. Too frequently, policies are approached as a decisional "slice in time" rather than as evolutionary phenomena. For example, the political struggle among various groups that resulted in the compromise Rodda Act can be fruitfully

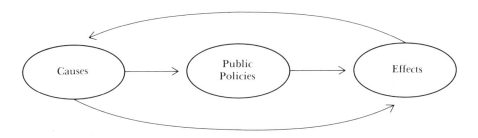

FIGURE 6-1: The Policymaking System

Source: Cover diagram of all issues of *The Journal of the Policy Studies Organization*, Policy Studies Organization, Urbana, Illinois.

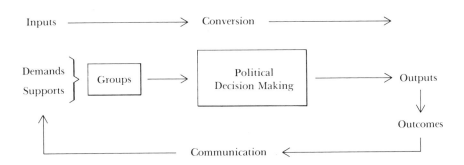

FIGURE 6-2: The Political System

Source: Gabriel Almond and Bingham Powell, *Comparative Politics: A Developmental Approach* (Boston: Little, Brown & Co.).

approached as a significant decision-making case study of interest group politics. However, it is also an evolutionary development of public sector policymaking in California.

As an evolutionary process, public policymaking usually proceeds through the following sequential phases or developmental stages:

1. *Problem formation*, which occurs when a social problem formerly dormant is perceived as a political issue requiring a policy response. For example, a comprehensive policy analysis might begin with the recognition of poverty as a political issue in the early '60s, or pollution and environment in the late '60s, or energy during the early '70s. Analysis of problem formation directs particular attention to possible linkages with varying perceptions of the problem held by bureaucratic elites, elected officials, clientele groups, property owners, constituent groups, pressure groups, media, and others.

   The problem formation stage with public employee unionization begins with their "proletarianization," or loss of professional identity. This was particularly evident during the '60s. Other variables in the formation of public policy toward public employee collective bargaining include: public opinion toward civil servants, loss of economic security and parity with private employees, decline of unionization in the private sector, reluctant role of civil service commissions, and media (electronic and printed) coverage of public employee activities.

2. *Policy formulation*, which occurs when various alternatives or options for dealing with the problem are developed within the political arena. Specific attention is given to key participants (actors) in the decision-making process. On a theoretical level, policy options are supposedly debated within a representative framework of legislative and executive compromise. On an informal basis, comprehensive policy analysis includes both elected officials and any other participants who are involved in the consideration of policy options.

   This phase considers how policymakers receive information; how they are presented with possible policymaking options, and how they decide upon an eventual policy. The policy formulation process has a dual impact on public employees. First, an increasing number of collective bargaining demands include policy issues or conditions of employment, i.e., classroom size, case load size, patrol methods, etc. Second, public policymakers unilaterally consider a variety of options in formulating collective bargaining policy for public employees. Consequently, the very nature of collective bargaining may become a bilateral decision-making process in which employees demand to be included in the entire gamut of policy issues.

3. *Policy adoption*, which occurs when a particular policy alternative is selected and legitimized as public policy. It is important to note which symbolic and material considerations have been "satisfied" by this particular policy adoption. Since most policymaking is responsive to interest group pressures, the policymaking process essentially suffices by particularly satisfying the key interest groups invovled.

Most public policymaking, unless key participants disagree, involves only a few participants. Only infrequently are crucial policy priorities set by parliamentary procedures, roll call vote, or an open forum of elected representatives. Although political actors may vary, depending on the specific issue involved, the policy adoption process is usually decided by the same policy participants. Typically, the process of policy adoption is conducted by an informal subsystem of policy-makers (see figure 6-3) who function as surrogate policymakers for government. In other words, the formal or constitutional prescription for the making of policies is not often descriptive of the reality of representative democracy. Although legislatures have authority for formulating collective bargaining legislation for public employees, such policy issues are usually developed informally by pressure group conflict and compromise.

Most policy analysts would agree with Randall Ripley and Grace Franklin in defining this policymaking subsystem to include "clusters of individuals that effectively make most of the routine decisions in a given substantive area of policy."[27] As Ripley and Franklin point out, generally decision making is "routine most of the time,"[28] consequently a patterned subsystem. Therefore, the critical participants in major policy decisions display a familiar pattern of interaction between executive, legislative committees, bureaucratic elites, and pressure groups (as shown in figure 6-3). The most important participants in the policymaking subsystem include key committe members in Congress, top-level bureaucrats, and relevant pressure groups.

The participation of pressure groups in policymaking processes is particularly important. Although private sector labor groups have been influential in policymaking, most public employee organizations have been traditionally excluded from participation in the policy adoption stage of public policymaking. Public employee groups were seldom consulted by bureaucratic elites, infrequently summoned before substantive congressional committees, and considered illegitimate participants in the policymaking process. This policy adoption stage has provided most private sector groups with their primary access for affecting

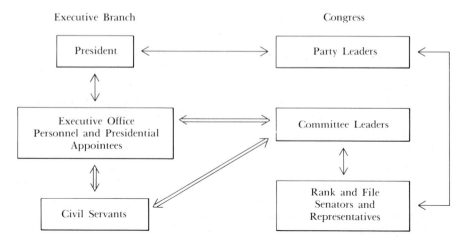

Executive Branch   Congress

| President | ←——————————→ | Party Leaders |

| Executive Office Personnel and Presidential Appointees | ⇔ | Committee Leaders |

| Civil Servants |

| Rank and File Senators and Representatives |

FIGURE 6-3: Critical Relationships for Policymaking in the National Government

Source: Randall B. Ripley and Grace A. Franklin, *Congress, the Bureaucracy, and Public Policy* (Homewood, Ill.: Dorsey Press Inc., 1976), p. 2.

Note: Double lines have been added to emphasize primary relationships.

policy decisions. Yet public employee unions have historically been prevented from participating in this policymaking process.

The public policymaking process concludes with the following two stages:

4. *Program implementation*, which occurs with the actual programmatic implementation of avowed policy statements into policy outputs. As Theodore Lowi observes, the compromise process inherent within contemporary interest group liberalism often fails to accomplish stated policy objectives. Vague policy goals often make the implementation of specific programmatic objectives difficult. For example, the pronouncement of liberal sentiments against poverty, as embodied within the Economic Opportunity Act of 1964, resulted in confusion regarding the purposes of community action programs. No one really knew whether community action programs were supposed to provide social services, accomplish political reform, or seek economic prosperity. Consequently, program implementation often attempted all three objectives simultaneously.

5. *Policy evaluation*, which concerns the consequences or impact of public policymaking. As Drucker, Lowi, and others have observed, programmatic *efficiency* in public agencies is often confused with program *effectiveness*.[29] For example, cost ef-

fectiveness is oftentimes utilized as a measurement of policy effectiveness. True policy evaluation focuses on the extent to which programmatic activities accomplish policy objectives. In other words, do programs do what they say they do? If objectives are intangible, valid programmatic evaluation is impossible.

Policy evaluation as the measurement of actual outcomes against original objectives is seldom implemented in public agencies. Most frequently, authorizing legislation basically calls for specified functions to be performed, i.e., street maintenance, recreation programs, police patrol, teaching, probation, or a seemingly infinite number of other public services. There are few motivational incentives, along with numerous political disincentives, to legislatively clarify social priorities, quantify objectives, or evaluate programs by tangible objectives. For example, antipoverty or welfare programs do not generally articulate the reduction of poverty as a quantifiable objective nor do criminal justice programs include a reduction in crime as an evaluation criterion. In neither case would agency administrators propose that programmatic evaluation be based on demonstrable success in accomplishing an objective.

The consequences of this reluctance or inability to effectively evaluate public policymaking outcomes significantly affects public employee morale. Without clearly defined goals, objectives, and evaluation, public organizations often fail to develop a sense of purpose or mission. They become a "bureaucracy without culture."[30] Bureaucratic activity oftentimes seems to the employee to be purposeless and meaningless. More specifically, police departments, schools, and other public agencies are frequently expected to "be all things to all men" by performing an increasingly wide range of activities or tasks. Consequently, the policeman is forced to spend the majority of his time dealing with noncrime related activities, i.e., traffic control, family disputes, or court appearances. Teachers are frustrated by spending time on such diverse topics as sex education, physical education, civics, and geography, rather than focusing on reading, composition, and quantitative skills.

Judging Collective Bargaining Policymaking Outcomes by Independent and Dependent Variables

A variety of factors influence public policy development in each policy issue, e.g., criminal justice, education, housing, etc. These factors are crucial either in the usual policymaking subsystem developed for settling that issue or in causing nonconsensual policies to be settled in the larger conflict arena. Policy outcomes are affected by both (1) independent environmental variables, and (2) dependent variables, commonly held attitudes or values of key policymakers. In other words, certain policies are more generally affected by environmental, usually socioeconomic, variables, while other policies are apparently more influenced by the values and attitudes ("orientations") held by the subsystem policymakers themselves.

There are a number of studies which indicate that socioeconomic, political, and cultural variables significantly affect the outcomes of public policymaking.[31] Thomas Dye, for example, argues that the level of economic development among the states and cities exercises a prevailing influence on policies.[32] Dye indicates that the "total level of resources," as measured by per capita income, urbanism, industrialization, and educational level, has a direct correlation with the level of public policy expenditure. Ira Sharkansky essentially agrees with Dye's thesis but feels that economic variables are more explanatory at the local policymaking level than at the federal level.[33]

Despite Dye's related conclusions, scant effort has occurred in testing public sector collective bargaining with these socioeconomic and political variables. An exception is the pioneering work done in this area by Alan Bent and George Noblit, who sought to provide predictive models of environmental conditions that affect collective bargaining in municipalities.[34] Their study isolated the demographic character, political culture, and service orientation of a city and measured the impact of these variables on the ability of public sector unions to negotiate gains. The data for this investigation were obtained from thirty-nine cities with populations of 250,000 or more.

The measure of union "strength" was determined by the unions' ability to negotiate for union security and control over promotion, as well as the number of agreements each city had with public employee unions. Their first independent variable, the demographic characteristics of a city, consisted of measures of median education, median income, percent white-collar, and percent black citizens in each of the cities surveyed. Political culture was defined as governmental organization, i.e., mayor-council form, council-manager form, and commission form. The remaining variables were measures of political party competition and the service orientation of a city. The latter was determined by examining the monthly payroll of each city and each city's per capita outlay.

The data in this study revealed that the "best" environmental indicators explaining union "gains" were the city's political character and especially its public policy orientation in terms of a service commitment. But, the authors admit to inconclusive findings. The highly politicized city, and the city's degree of "consumer welfare-orientation" seemed to incur a large degree of collective bargaining activity, "yet did not, as often, include provisions of union security thereby obscuring, in this case, a valid assessment of the true nature of union strength." Bent and Noblit concluded their analysis by cautioning that collective bargaining may be affected by a host of variables:

> *[It] must not be overlooked that a number of other variables play a major role in municipal collective bargaining outcomes. The ability of the city or any other governmental organization to grant union demands in view of legislative and budgetary restrictions is an essential consideration. Relative skills, [the timing of negotiations], and political support that each side can muster in the collective bargaining process undoubtedly have a bearing on the final outcome.*

Although there have been few comprehensive efforts to test collective bargaining among public employees with economic indicators, several preliminary trends suggest a relationship with general economic prosperity. For example, although apparently a cross section of communities permit some form of collective bargaining, such communities tend to be primarily in urban areas nationally and in smaller communities in the North and West. The greatest incidence of public employee job actions generally occurs in the eight most industrialized states.* However, there is no readily apparent pattern in the states that have legalized the strike or collective bargaining. Nor does such legislation affect union organizing efforts. For example, over half of AFSCME members are located in five affluent states—New York, Ohio, Wisconsin, Michigan, and Massachusetts.[35] Yet these states vary significantly in their recognition of collective bargaining for public employees. In essence, although the nature of public employee collective bargaining cannot be linked to particular economic variables, it will predictably be an issue in those states which are economically prosperous and socially diverse.

The political culture among each of the states is also viewed by several observers as a major variable in public policymaking. Daniel Elazar finds significant state-to-state differences, particularly regional differences, that affect public policies.[36] He categorized three types of political culture: (1) moralism, (2) individualism, (3) and traditiona- alism, which were believed to be major influences in public policy- making. Ira Sharkansky, in a similar conclusion, found a pattern of public policies among states with similar regional historical experiences and cultural norms.[37] Such culturally influenced policymaking patterns persisted over time, despite various levels of economic development in each region.

* New York, Massachusetts, Ohio, Pennsylvania, Illinois, Michigan, New Jersey, and California.

Political culture analysis attempts to isolate particular political values held in common by a community of people. For example, cross-national studies[38] of various societies indicate that Americans generally accept the following values: efficacy in their own ability to change the political system, individualism and self-reliance, liberalism and equalitarianism, and a propensity for voluntary action. Such values do not predispose one to join a union. Therefore, environmental variables may be highly significant in shaping public opinion attitudes toward union activities. It can probably be assumed that English, Italian, and American cultures, for instance, vary significantly in their political orientations toward public employee unionism. Similarly, attitudes in heavily unionized (private sector) states and cities are more receptive to extending collective bargaining rights to public employees.

Finally, institutional structures as environmental variables also have a significant effect on the evolution of public policymaking. For example, the unique institutional arrangement in the American political system has probably shaped public sector unionism in two ways. First, state sovereignty within federalism undoubtedly focused the struggle for public sector collective bargaining legislation at the state level. Second, the concept of judicial review was introduced as a basic principle of labor-management relations in both the private and public sectors. Courts and regulatory bodies such as the NLRB and appellate courts review lower decisions for constitutionality. Consequently, private sector labor-management decisions are protected as a basic right rather than a mere legal concession by government.

On a local level, the structure of government frequently affects public policymaking, particularly collective bargaining policies, in a variety of ways. Briefly, the type of local government organization shapes the nature of policy outcomes as follows:

1. *City manager, who although possessing administrative authority, is hired by a city council that has final authority for public policy. In reality, whenever a strong manager makes policy, the policy-making distinction is blurred both by his administrative style and his recommendations to the council. The city manager, usually lacks the stronger job security of other executives at the state and federal levels. Consequently, managers often attempt to serve as mediators in conflict or impasse situations between the council and public employee unions. Quite simply, if the manager possesses the council's confidence, he will be a key policymaker. If not, the council will assume a more direct policymaking role.*

2. *Mayor, whose power may be defined in either a strong or weak organizational structure. The strong-mayor form of government concentrates administrative responsibility in the mayor and*

requires him to share policymaking power with the council. The
weak-mayor role restricts his administrative authority generally
to limited policymaking powers. Obviously, a weak-mayor form
of government is highly fragmented with mayor, council, and
commissions often seeking to maximize their own policymaking
powers. However, even these generalizations do not always hold
true in analyzing the role of symbolic policymaking. For example,
although Los Angeles is an excellent example of a weak-mayor
form of government, several mayors, such as Tom Bradley, have
been quite powerful as symbolic policymakers. Mayor Bradley
has used such factors as his national reputation as a leading black
politician, his long-time background as a councilman, and his
experience as a politically adroit deputy mayor, in maintaining a
highly symbolic image to enhance his policymaking power.

In reform-oriented states where municipal elections are nonpartisan, policymaking power is often somewhat fragmented. Yet, "although the chief executive [local] may play many different roles, he will probably be the one individual who, in the public mind, represents the position of the jurisdiction."[33]

As exemplified in the San Francisco police and firemen's strike (1975), local legislative bodies, such as the San Francisco County Board of Supervisors, are frequently most susceptible to political pressures from community pressure groups. Although certain councilmen or supervisors may be prounion in orientation, they are often subjected to intense pressure from economy-minded constituents. The fragmented nature of many councils or supervisory boards combined with their range of attitudes toward collective bargaining issues frequently result in opposition to at least some public employee union demands.

Clientele interest groups, composed of specific groups affected by particular policies, are primarily interested in protecting their resource allocation through the maintenance of agency budgetary allocations. For example, the National Welfare Rights Organization (NWRO) has been quite protective of welfare budget allocations and public policymaking on welfare issues. As Lawrence Bailis points out, the Massachusetts Welfare Rights Organization (MWRO) has quite aggressively participated in state policymaking.[40] MWRO actively mobilized other interest groups, including social workers, in opposing (unsuccessfully) the governor's effort to institute flat grants for all welfare recipients (without consideration for special needs).

A similarly close liaison with clientele groups was developed very early by the Department of Labor, which actively encouraged the development of trade unions. Francis Rourke has underscored the Labor Department's support of labor organizations:

> *The reason the department gave for this support was that the growth of labor union membership would facilitate collective bargaining and promote industrial peace. "The absence of organization," the department stated, "means the absence of a medium through which the workers* en masse *can discuss their problems with employers."*[41]

Policymakers within the Department of Labor viewed the strengthening of wage-earner organizations as a means of increasing clientele support for the department. However, the department, along with other agencies such as the Veterans' Administration, the Defense Department, and the Department of Agriculture, became clientele agencies of vested interests. As such, these interest groups exercised considerable influence over departmental decision making, including the selection of assistant and under secretaries. For example, the Department of Labor was suspected by other groups of being a spokesman for labor, incapable of objectively mediating between opposing labor-management factions.

Not all public policies are primarily determined by social, economic, or political variables. Certain social policies are more fruitfully approached as independent policymaking variables so that internal or nonrational (psychological) models are more explanatory for policy analysis. In general, independent policies are those where existent policymaker attitudes and values rather than socioeconomic variables play a determining role in formulating public policy issues. Our analysis provides several examples of the considerable extent to which policymaking participants, through preconceived attitudes and values, have shaped the nature of collective bargaining in the public sector.

In essence, public policies are independently influenced as the policymaking process varies depending on the issue, or when there is a relationship between decision-making structures and types of public policies.[42] In other words, the value orientations of key policymakers, particularly bureaucratic or group elites, often shapes policymaking quite independently of environmental pressures. Theoretically, one must assume that the emotional nature of a public issue, such as public employee unionization, exercises an independent impact upon the policymaking process. Participants entering these policymaking subsystems for the first time will predictively perceive policymaking options in accordance with preset orientations defined by the policy issue at stake.

The essence of a policy's independent influence concerns how a particular policy issue is perceived by both the public and the policymakers. For example, Murray Edelman categories public policies as producing either material or symbolic satisfactions, according to public perceptions.[43] By applying Edelman's criterion the Nixon and Kennedy

Executive Orders regarding collective bargaining for public employees produced primarily symbolic rather than substantial material policy consequences. From another perspective, Lewis Froman dichotomizes urban policy outputs as either areal (total) or segmental, according to their perceived impact by the public.[44] By both the Froman and Edelman models, policies may be categorized by their scope and consequences. For example, public employee unions frequently pursue policy objectives on both symbolic and economic levels.

Symbolic and Redistributive Policymaking

Both private and public sector unions have long been symbolically identified with the plight of the poor, particularly the urban poor. Many unions began by organizing the urban unemployed or under-employed. Traditionally, private sector unions were an important pressure group in forcing up the minimum wages, lowering interest rates, and expanding the economy in order to produce more jobs. Some public sector unions, particularly AFSCME, as typified by its organizing campaigns in Memphis and Atlanta, have cultivated their image as an advocate for the urban poor.

However, analysis of policymaking consequences indicates that despite a symbolic commitment to the urban poor, union policies are often obstacles to urban development. As Neal Pierce has suggested, the successful union-backed effort of increasing the minimum wage to $2.65 in 1978 and to $3.35 by 1981 would seemingly aid the urban poor.[45] Yet many economists, such as Leonard Greene, would argue that such increases will cause many teenagers, particularly among unemployed black youth (comprising 40 percent of those unemployed), to lose hundreds of thousands of jobs.[46] Unions also lobbied against a proposed 15 percent lowering of the minimum wage for teenagers during the first six months on entry level jobs because it would supposedly cause employers to fire older workers and employ less expensive teenagers.

On one level, private sector unions are symbolically supportive of an economically viable and livable central city environment. On another level, a material level, such unions also advocate those policy decisions which are economically in their own self-interest. For example, construction trade unions have frequently been in conflict with local neighborhood associations and cities over a prevailing wage clause of the Davis-Bacon Act, which requires that union construction wages be paid on federally supported projects, (usually 50 to 100 percent above nonunion contractors' pay). Consequently, the use of federal man-power or interest rate subsidy to rehabilitate substandard housing is often made economically prohibitive. Philip St. George of the Urban Homestead Assistance Board in New York accused unions of also "destroying neighborhoods" by their opposition to the "sweat equity" approach in rehabilitation, which allows poor people to develop job skills while fixing up their own housing.[47] *Sweat equity* means that poor people are encouraged to refurbish their own dwellings without having to pay union-scale wages to those assisting them in this work. Unions traditionally oppose this concept because it is not in their best economic interest.

One should not assume that unions and neighborhood groups will inevitably be in conflict. Milton Kotler, director of the National Association of Neighborhoods, believes that many labor-neighborhood conflicts can be overcome through local neighborhood-union task forces.[48] Regardless, one should not assume that unions have necessarily been deceptive in their policymaking priorities. Rather, one must appreciate that the analysis of policy consequences occurs on both symbolic and material levels. Both public and private sector unions advocate policy outputs on a symbolic level in which the union's role within the larger social framework is defined. For example, it is a symbolic union commitment to provide employment for the unemployed and to generally support means that uplift the socially disadvantaged. For instance, the rhetoric and actions of AFSCME in the Memphis and Atlanta sanitation strikes exemplify this concern. Yet unions also seek policy consequences, usually economically beneficial to the union itself, that strengthen the union's own organizing and collective bargaining capabilities. That such policy advocacy may occasionally be contradictory to symbolic commitment is usually not problematical. Only policy options that compel the union to actually choose between various economic and social alternatives produce real conflict.

The impact of policymaker orientations on policymaking can also be categorized by Theodore Lowi's trichotomy of issue typologies.[49] By Lowi's criteria, public policies are viewed by participants and the public as either distributive, redistributive, or regulatory. *Distributive* policies are generally subsidies over which particular actors/groups compete for their slice of the budgetary pie, i.e., welfare recipients, farmer subsidies, and so on. In other words, distributive policies do not require policymakers to reallocate societal resources. Those clientele groups that are direct recipients of the particular policy outputs do not see themselves in competition with other pressure groups for an increased share in the allocation of scarce resources. In many instances public employee groups have probably approached collective bargaining as a distributive policymaking process in which the objective is primarily to increase their fair share of the public resources. Claims by public managers or taxpayer groups that increased allocations for employee demands will result in decreased spending for public programs are usually rejected as poppycock. Employee groups generally contend that their economic demands constitute distributive justice rather than a forced redistribution of public resources.

Redistributive policies occur within a highly competitive policymaking arena in which various groups are often highly resourceful and ideological in seeking to effect governmental restructuring of the public pie. There is generally the acute realization by both policymakers and clientele groups that a reallocation of resources is intended as a policy objective. Certain interest groups will gain, inevitably at the expense of others. Redistributive policymaking almost always occurs with energy versus environmental groups or in the distribution of scarce resources such as water among consumer groups. As suggested, it is probable that public managers often view employee unionization as an attempt to force a redistribution of public funds and approach the prospect of collective bargaining from that perspective.

Lowi's *regulatory* policies extend governmental control over particular behavior of private individuals or businesses by establishing a general rule or law that requires a certain segment of the population to conform in their behavior. Obviously, the NLRB performs a regulatory function in private sector labor relations. Independent regulatory commissions such as the NLRB have frequently been accused of representing the interests that they supposedly are to regulate. Consequently, commissioners appointed to regulatory agencies have generally been scrutinized for possible bias or representational interests. For example, the Eisenhower Administration narrowly won confirmation for an NLRB nominee who had a business management background that senate Democrats believed inappropriate.[50] Subsequent presidential nominations to the NLRB have not included candidates with such backgrounds.

The conflicting perceptions by policymakers and public employee unions of the same policy is illustrated by correctional policymaking. On one level, policymakers intended correctional policies to, in fact, be regulatory policies, to regulate the behavior of prisoners. On another level, prison employees viewed the same policies as redistributive policies that threatened their own security. The issue was seemingly polarized by a recommendation of the National Advisory Commission of Criminal Justice Standards and Goals in 1973 to shift correctional policy emphasis away from institutional incarceration to community-based rehabilitation programs.[51]

Although a long-standing policy debate among correctional policymakers, such policy experts have now been forced to contend with prison employee unions. For example, at its 1976 convention, AFS-CME, which represents more state prison personnel than any other union, passed a resolution opposing the "contracting out" of any public work that had traditionally been performed by public employees.[52] The same union has long been against deinstitutionalization and the development of community-based programs.[53] In numerous instances, prison employees have carried out job actions against a proposed implementation of new rehabilitative programs. These prison employee actions occur because such programs are perceived as potentially reducing the number of correctional employees.[54]

In essence, policy classification is usually dependent on the policymakers' intentions or outcomes. However, one must also add the dimension of policy consequences, which are frequently assessed by the outside observer.[55] For example, labor leaders might view collective bargaining as a distributive policy, public management, as redistributive, while the policy analyst determines it to be symbolic in its consequences. Consequently, comprehensive policy analysis must necessarily include the psychological perspective of the policymaker, not solely that of the policy analyst.[56]

Independent ideological orientations of policymakers and program administrators often define the shape of public policy whenever they are insulated from environmental policy pressures. It is important to note that such policymaking orientations are neither exclusively Democratic nor Republican. Rather, as James Sunquist has noted, each party since the New Deal era has contained a cleavage between activist and conservative factions.[57] An activist was defined by Sunquist as an individual with a positive commitment to "take action through the national political and governmental processes" in order to achieve policy priorities. Activists, who dominated the presidential Democratic party throughout the Kennedy-Johnson years, believed in utilizing the bureaucracy to solve major social problems, i.e., poverty, racism, etc. Conversely, conservatives in both parties were defined as those who disliked federal intervention and looked to local institutions, particularly in the private sector, for policy solutions. Conservative policy orientations dominated public policymaking approaches in the presidency during the Nixon and Ford Administrations.[58]

In a similar vein, in a study of city councilmen and policy outcomes, Robert Eyestone and Heinz Eulau discovered that policymaking orientations were relatively unrelated to socioeconomic variables.[59] Councilmanic policy preferences become independent variables in policymaking reality. Significant correlations did, however, exist between social policies and (1) the *social* development of the city, irrespective of size, and (2) the *scope* of municipal government activities. However, the authors attributed the willingness of policymakers to tap available resources as the most important variable affecting policy development. In his earlier, related analysis, Aaron Wildavsky examined the nature of adversary group attitudes during the Dixon-Yates controversy concerning the role of public electrical power in supplying energy needs. Wildavsky's study indicates that existing policymaking orientations had influenced policymakers significantly:

> *The public versus the private power issue [has been a longstanding controversy]. . . participants on both sides have long since developed a fairly complete set of attitudes on this issue. . . . They have in reserve a number of prepared responses ready to be activated in the direction indicated by their set of attitudes whenever the occasion demands.*[60]

Public and private orientations, like collective bargaining orientations, often form the framework for decision making.

Public Employee Unions and Budgetary Policymaking

It is highly important to understand what a budget is and what it is not. Public budgets, whether at the municipal or federal level, are no longer simply line-item documents intended to keep graft-ridden politicians honest. Neither should the budgetary process be confused with techniques of public finance.

Public budgets are perhaps the most political of all documents. As one observer has noted, they represent "a series of goals with price tags attached";[61] budgets are the outcome of the allocation of scarce resources. Public budgets separate monetary fact from political fantasy. Quite literally, public budgets represent the bottom line of public priorities. If those priorities are perverted, as Duane Lockard and others declare,[62] then the budget serves as a litmus test. For it is in the budget that policymaking priorities are allocated—defense, criminal justice, education, and the myriad other budgetary demands.

What, then, is the importance of the budgetary process to public sector collective bargaining, aside from the obvious possible increase in salaries and wages? Clyde Summers suggests the possible impact:

> *Collective bargaining significantly changes the role of public employees in the budget-making process, providing them with a special procedure through which they can participate which is not available to other interest groups.*[63]

Collective bargaining for public employees may potentially change the budgetary process as it commonly occurs in governments at every level throughout the United States. In addition, the nature of public employee unionism looms as a major variable to the implementation of various budgetary control systems such as Planning-Programming Budgeting, Management by Objectives, and Zero-Base Budgeting.

The budgetary process, whether at the state, local, or federal level, is a highly political one that reflects the larger struggle among competing interests in society. In other words, the incremental process of budget-making is somewhat derivative of the pluralistic competition among groups in the political arena.

Essentially, the budgetary process is a bargaining process, despite its rational procedures. It has been dryly described by Charles Lindblom as "the science of muddling through."[64] Aaron Wildavsky describes it as *incrementalism*. Budgetary managers generally seek to increase their previous year's allocation by small increments. According to Wildavsky, designated budget managers frequently utilize a variety of strategies and calculations to increase their budget allocation.[65] By whatever appellation, the budgetary process includes participant/recipients who utilize strategies in a seemingly never ending quest to increase their slice of the budgetary pie.

Several features of the incremental budgetary process should be emphasized as pertinent to collective bargaining. First, budgetary bargaining and negotiation occur almost entirely at the managerial level. Department heads submit budgetary proposals to agency directors, who prepare agency budgets for submission to the legislature. Only infrequently are public employees included in the process of budget preparation. Secondly, as Peter Drucker and others have indicated, there is little incentive for budgetary managers to resist the incremental process.[66] Prevailing career incentives for the career civil servant often necessitate his having to increase staff, programs, and budgetary allocation. Quite simply, there is little incentive to decrease one's budget, reduce one's staff, or return unexpended funds. Consequently, although elective officials and even some top-level bureaucrats may be pressured to resist budgetary expansion, it has not generally been in the career interests of those who prepare the budget to do so. Only such tactics as the 1978 passage of the Jarvis-Gann initiative in California ("Proposition 13") have seriously threatened to alter the traditional budgetary process.

Public budgets also reflect the compromise that governments have worked out with all the multiple and competing interest groups. The budgetary allocation of resources is generally insufficient to meet the demands of any one group, particularly in many fiscally plagued cities. Public employee organizations are but one group entering an already overcrowded budgetary arena. The question then becomes to what extent does the emergence of public employee unions change the budgetary process and the larger pluralistic group arena?

Public employee defenders argue that public sector unions essentially add to pluralistic democracy by representing another interest, which had been suppressed. Far from being against the public interest, their representation in the policymaking process is healthy for the system. Others argue that public employee collective bargaining includes a secret weapon that other interest groups lack: "collective bargaining provides the union a closed two-sided [policy] process within what is otherwise an open multi-sided [policy] process."[67]

The crux of the issue is that there are essentially two budgetary processes in governmental jurisdictions where public employees have been unionized. On one level, the programmatic budgetary process allocates resources to various policymaking priorities. On another level, public employees bargain separately in closed bilateral negotiations. In many instances, a collective bargaining contract may be concluded even prior to budgetary negotiations with other interest groups.

Clyde Summers believes that the public employee claim to separate budgetary procedures has three major elements.[68] First, "payroll costs in most cities constitute 60 to 70 percent of the total operating budget." Since any significant wage increase frequently results in a budgetary increase, there should be a special bargaining procedure for wages. Second, public employee organizations do not see themselves as "just another interest group." Rather, any public employee economic demands necessitate the diminution of funds for other interest groups. Therefore, the unions believe that their demands should not be linked to those of other interest groups. Third, public employee unions argue that they have few natural allies and are therefore limited in their ability to form coalitions with other interest groups.

It is certainly not circumstantial that many job actions, such as the Atlanta sanitation workers' strike (1977) and the San Francisco police and firemen strike (1975) coincided with the end of the municipal fiscal year. Frequently public employee unions exert pressure on local officials at budget review time by such tactics as declaring a state of impasse, job slowdowns, and strikes. These practices have both a tactical and legal purpose. Technically and legally, public budgets are not effective until approved. Therefore, public employee job security is tenuous until the budget is finally approved. However, memoranda of understanding between labor and management or interim agreements effectively preclude the possibility of job layoffs or job insecurity. Tactically, the coordination of public union pressure with the budgetary process supposedly impacts on policymakers who are considering both collective bargaining and budgetary allocation priorities simultaneously. As the mixed results of the San Francisco strike and the failure of the Atlanta strike suggest, such tactics do not always end up successfully.

In addition to bilateral participation in the budgetary process on an annual basis, public employee unions have utilized a second weapon that is unavailable to other interest groups—a fixed remuneration set by public referendum. This tactic circumvents public policymakers by submitting salaries, wages, pensions, and even working conditions to a public vote. Throughout the '60s and early '70s in charter mandated cities, proposed raises for groups such as firemen and police were submitted and approved by public referenda. However, as salaries were improved and homeowners became more vociferous in their opposition to any increased public spending (thereby necessitating increased taxes), proposed salary and wage increases were frequently rejected, e.g., the San Francisco referendum in 1975.

Consequently, public employee unions, wherever possible, have attempted to have guaranteed minimum salary, wage, and pension benefits as nonnegotiable items in collective bargaining. Furthermore, emphasis in some cases has been placed on fringe benefits or deferred benefits, i.e., pension plans rather than direct salaries and wages. In effect, the union strategy is to guarantee irrevocable acceptance of any previous remunerative base at the polls while keeping only proposed increases as a subject for collective bargaining or public policymaking.

A study of Los Angeles city employees illustrates union efforts to constitutionally (by charter) guarantee both the fire and police pension systems and a prevailing wage clause. Both examples indicate efforts to exclude these issues from the purview of public policymakers. Both attempts were aggressively resisted by legislative policymakers.

Los Angeles Municipal Employees: Case Study of Budgetary Policymaking

Even a superficial overview of the expenditures for the Los Angeles Fire and Police Pension System (LAFPPS) reveals a fundamental problem. It is a pension system financed by $110.7 million in county property taxes a year.[69] Approximately, one-third of each city property tax dollar is expended for police and fire pensions alone. By comparison, an additional $81.1 million in property tax dollars was contributed by the city toward other municipal employee pension plans, resulting in a total of $192.5 million paid toward municipal pensions. This amount is approximately 20 percent of the total city budget or 28 percent of the total payroll account in Los Angeles.

If city pensions were merely a financial problem of consuming current tax revenues, the problem would still be complex. However, even the pension system itself is controversial. For example, LAFPPS had an unfunded liability of $1.5 billion. This unfunded liability is the debts owed that are not backed by assets; or the difference between the total value of the system's assets (in the form of cash, bonds, stocks, real estate, member and city contributions) and its current and future obligations. By comparison, the pension plan's unfunded liability in 1959 was $309.8 million. This growth occurred even though the city began the process of amortization, i.e., paying off its unfunded liability by building up its assets.

The limited public interest in the pension issue contrasts sharply with the issue prevalent in the public consciousness—public employee pay raises. Each is formulated differently as a public policy issue; pensions and most public employee fringe benefits are indirect costs, while salaries and wages are highly visible, direct expenditures in municipal budgets. As an example, the city of Los Angeles pays a fixed amount, 17.5 percent of each member's salary, into the pension fund; the employee contributes 7 percent.

However, the political controversy surrounding the fire and police pension system does not concern the amount of the pension payments. Rather, the debate revolves around the method of financing the pension plan. The mayor and a former fire commissioner running for city comptroller argued that the unfunded liability was fiscally sound. Both candidates were heavily supported by fire and police unions; both won. Critics argued that the system was actuarially unsound. Yet, opponents were unsuccessful in mobilizing public or media attention on the fire and police pension issue.

By contrast, the issue of direct salary and wage increases was highly volatile during the same time period. Consequently, the public policy-making process was quite different from the concurrent pension issue. For over fifty years the Los Angeles City Charter had a section which required that city employees be paid a wage "at least equal to" that earned by their counterparts elsewhere. In 1956, the city council passed a law that rejected the method of calculating salary increases based on neighboring municipal jurisdictions. Instead, the council voted to base its decision on a "wage trend" survey of the local economy, that is, the average overall rate of wage increase in local industry. This calculation, determined annually by a joint wage and salary survey, surveyed selected jobs in local industry, none of them government related. A councilman who was critical of the effects of the prevailing wage clause for municipal employees stated his case this way:

> For example, you cannot do much about city expenses without tackling police and fire fighter pay, which alone constitutes some 27.5% of the total budget. Our city police officers and fire-fighters are the highest paid in the nation—probably, for that matter, in the world. This year, a police lieutenant at the top of

*the pay scale will make more than $31,000 (not counting bene-
fits). In addition, his pension allows him to retire after 20 years,
still young enough to start a new career. His monthly pension?
More than $1,000 a month.[70]*

Specifically, the city spent more than $700 million of its total budget
($1 billion) on municipal salaries and wages. The more far-ranging
implication of the prevailing wage clause is reflected in the fact that
striking San Francisco police and firemen in 1975 used the Los Angeles
pay scale as rationale for increased wages.

The courts have held that the prevailing wage clause is a mandatory
standard rather than a guideline. Therefore, the city is compelled to
pay at least the amount of the increase in the private sector. For example, the 1977-78 fiscal year survey revealed that police and firemen
qualified for a 7.27 percent raise increase. The implication for collective bargaining is that this amount usually serves as a base from
which to bargain upward. The implication for the budgetary process
is that the expansion cannot be diminished.

Fearful of a fiscal crisis if the prevailing wage clause continued, the
mayor's ad hoc committee on city finances, the city administrative
officer, the county committee on economy and efficiency, and the
county grand jury all recommended that the prevailing wage clause
be repealed. Subsequently two city councilmen running for reelection,
Ernani Bernardi and Marvin Braude, persuaded their colleagues to
place the prevailing wage issue before a voter referendum. However,
following intensive lobbying by public employee unions, the council
reversed itself by rescinding its ballot initiative. The two councilmen
retaliated by launching a movement to obtain a sufficient number of
voter signatures to place the issue before the electorate.

In a dramatic break with its traditional stance of backing incumbents, the county federation of labor's Committee on Political Education (COPE) targeted Councilman Braude for defeat. The United Firefighters of Los Angeles City listed Councilman Bernardi for defeat
because of his opposition to the prevailing wage clause. The public
employee unions hoped "to instill some fear into other elected officials
tempted to tinker with the wage setting process."[71] Accordingly, the
AFL-CIO federation and the firefighters' union poured considerable
resources into the primary campaign to defeat the two incumbents.
However, both candidates were elected by majorities sufficient to
prevent runoffs.

The prevailing wage controversy will undoubtedly persist. It is unlikely to dissipate as long as budgetary interest groups continue their
opposition to automatic or nonnegotiable salary increases. Attempts by
public employee unions to protect their bugetary base face a difficult

struggle. As one observer noted of the struggle between unions and voters:

> *The voters who share the voter's economic concerns far out-number those who share the employee's economic interest. This does not mean that public employees are politically helpless, but it does mean that, to the extent that people vote their pocket-books, public employees are at a significant disadvantage when their terms and conditions of employment are decided through a process responsible to majority will.*[72]

The 1975 referenda in San Francisco and the prevailing wage issue in Los Angeles suggest that submitting proposed salary and wage increases to the voters will usually result in their defeat. However, the experience of the Los Angeles Fire and Police Pension System indicates that less obtrusive expenditures may fare more favorably. In other words, increases in salary and wages have an immediate effect on public budgets and thus arouse the public interest; pensions and other fringe benefits lack the sense of immediacy, thereby vitiating the public interest in this issue as a policy concern.

Budgeting Reforms and Collective Bargaining

In order to appreciate the various budgetary reform proposals as well as their implications for public employee collective bargaining, one can reflect on a 1977 study of the Los Angeles County budgeting process conducted by Price, Waterhouse, a major management consulting firm. Five of its eleven recommendations are important in appreciating the supposed inadequacies of prevailing policymaking and budgetary planning processes:

> 1. *County budgeting is performed without a functioning policy and objectives-setting framework. We recommend that the county develop a policy and objectives -setting framework. (They would be stated in "measurable terms.")*
> 2. *Present budgetary information is not decision-oriented, e.g., it does not offer choices or alternatives.*
> 3. *The present "incremental" aproach does not penetrate into the budget "base" carried forward from year to year.*
> 4. *The county does not conduct formal county-wide long-range financial planning, i.e., a three-year financial forecast.*
> 5. *The county might achieve improved efficiencies if the county charter were amended to provide for private contracting of services.*[73]

Other criticisms of budgetary incrementalism would generally concur with the Price, Waterhouse assessment of incrementalism. In essence, the prevailing incremental process does not encourage long-range planning or rational allocation of resources. Furthermore, incrementalism does not allow for even a consideration of programmatic alternatives. Perhaps most critical is that incrementalism as a compromise approach does not facilitate the establishment of social priorities nor the implementation of measurable objectives. In sum, critics argue that incrementalism subverts creativity and authoritative policymaking in the public interest. Of course, Wildavsky and Lindblom defend incrementalism as a means of reducing conflict and promoting policymaking consensus among multiple competing interests.[74] Consequently, since the Lyndon Johnson Administration, three key budgetary reform systems have been applied in public agencies, initially at the federal level and filtering down to local jurisdictions. These budgetary control systems, Planning-Programming Budgeting (PPB),[75] Management by Objectives (MBO), Zero-Base Budgeting (ZBB)[76] each offer an alternative to incrementalism. Again, each budgetary control system must be viewed not as a new technique in public finance. Rather, such systems are a means for implementing public policy priorities. Each theoretically assumes that such priorities should be determined by legitimate policymakers, rather than in the marketplace of incrementalism.

Planning-Programming Budgeting (PPB), legitimized by President Johnson, was most controversial in its attempted implementation at the Department of Defense by Secretary Robert McNamara (PPB was also implemented in a number of state and local settings).[77] In essence, PPB attempts to bring about bureaucratic control by placing ultimate planning responsibility with a group of independent systems analysts answerable only to the director. The approach is that comprehensive agency planning should be managed by programmatic objectives and budgetary control systems. In its strictest application, budgetary managers do not determine objectives or set priorities.[78]

Zero-Base Budgeting (ZBB), implemented by the Carter Administration after its controversial experience in the state of Georgia and in Texas Instruments, combines aspects of both PPB and MBO systems.[79] Public budget managers are required to submit decision packages for budgetary input. In essence, each budgetary package contains various levels of funding options that include performance levels. Each manager projects possible consequences of funding at various percentages of the previous year's base. For example, a manager might project the performance consequences of funding only 50 or 75 percent of last year's figure. Theoretically, each manager begins with a zero-base and justifies each funding level upward. In theory too, final budgetary decisions are made by agency executives.

Management by Objectives (MBO) focuses on the identification and implementation of objectives as a prerequisite for program management. Theoretically, objectives are made explicit or quantifiable whenever possible. The MBO process is particularly concerned with identifying two types of conflict: (1) vertically between top level managers and subordinates, and (2) horizontally between competing organizational units. Perhaps most importantly, MBO attempts to provide a forum for participatory management through the process of setting objectives. By participating in the setting of priorities, managers will supposedly accept responsibility for the results. More specifically, managers can be evaluated by their contribution in attaining organizational objectives.

Although an integral component in most schools of business and management, MBO has only sporadically been attempted in the public sector, primarily in the Nixon Administration's Office of Budgeting and Management (OMB). The problem in implementing MBO in an amorphous agency such as HEW was stymied by the difficulty of setting priorities from within the organization. Furthermore, public sector managers, under the aegis of civil service, were not eager participants in managerial performance evaluation.

What is the future and significance of these three techniques for systematic budgeting? Regardless of whether ZBB, MBO, PPB, or yet another budgetary system is implemented, the persistency of systematic or management budgeting is seemingly inevitable. Many versions of each budgetary techinque have been implemented in federal, state, and local agencies as well as in numerous private corporations. It is apparent that some form of management budgetary systems is preferable to having managers faced with the usual incremental or political demands. Each budgetary system, although different in approach, emphasizes characteristics which are antithetical to incremental budgeting: MBO stresses participatory management with performance evaluation of managers; ZBB also emphasizes manager participation, but primarily in the preparation of decision options; and PPB focuses on long-range planning and budgetary control.

It must be underscored that the collective bargaining process is inextricably linked with incremental budgeting as the politics of the budgetary process. Incrementalism assumes that the previous year's budget constitutes a base from which incremental increases are negotiable. Collective bargaining frequently focuses on an increase in wages and fringe benefits, not their decrease. Furthermore, PPB, ZBB, and MBO are management-oriented; each technique responds, albeit differently, to the need for more effective reallocation of increasingly scarce resources. Incrementalism's approach to budgeting is to satisfy sufficiently the competing interests in society by granting each a piece of the pie. Management approaches are synoptic and comprehensive; each claimant must be examined from the framework of total budgetary priorities.

Systematic or rational approaches to budgeting such as MBO, ZBB, or PPB also utilize participatory management principles. Such approaches do not include a "participatory labor" component. In sum, although the incremental budgetary process does not involve nonmanagement public employees in the determination of budgetary priorities, public employee unions are at least policy participants in the pressure group process. By contrast, the management approaches to budgeting attempt to remove the budgetary process from political pressure and compromise. Systematic budgeting seeks managerial accountability, bureaucratic control, and responsibility. Incrementalism stresses accommodation through politics as usual.

In essence, public employees may pursue either of two options: (1) to demand participation in the budgetary reform process, or (2) to resist such techniques by seeking to maintain the politics of the budgetary process. Although not likely to occur, participation in the management decision-making process encourages professionalism and works against the proletarianization of white-collar workers. By contrast, incrementalism allows public employee unions a role in affecting budgetary priorities through a new avenue, the pressure group process.

Analysis of Union Democracy

Our analysis has often discussed the role of public employee unions analytically, as if such organizations were generic or homogeneous entities. However, one must also consider an internal issue. Whom do public employee organizations represent when they participate in public policymaking—the collective will of the rank-and-file or that of a small union elite? Are union decisions made in a democratic fashion, i.e., by obtaining the consent of the governed? Finally, to what extent do public employee unions function in the pluralistic interest group model? Rather than answer each issue compartmentally, we will treat the overall perspective using three examples of union democracy in America; then we will offer final conclusions.

Two seemingly opposite concepts should be introduced first: democracy and elitism. Democracy as a "general will" or majoritarian rule has rarely existed in reality. In only a few historical instances might one claim that the masses have prevailed, and then only for brief periods and, in the main, with undesirable consequences. Whether one examines the primitive governments at one end of the organizational continuum or the complex postindustrial, predominantly Western societies at the other end, societies have been ruled by various elite groups.

The impetus toward majoritarian (democratic) rule, either in society or in social groups has been handicapped by a persistent phenomenon—the antiliberal orientation of the masses. Attitudinal surveys indicate that organizational leaders (elites) are frequently more committed to such liberal values as individual liberty, toleration of diversity, and freedom of expression than are the masses. Some observers have found this to be ironic; others believe it inevitable. The framers of the American Constitution had as their task the making of government democratic in principle capable of promoting the virtues of liberalism. However, in practice, the procedure of democratic government has not always guaranteed the substance of liberalism.

One assumption is commonly made—that democratic procedures and institutions constitute *prima facie* evidence of the substance of democracy. For example, observers frequently assume that if open, secret elections are held, the subsequent results must be good or just. Or, if representatives are freely elected, then the constituents must be represented. More specifically, in order for elections to be at least procedurally democratic, criteria similar to the following would be necessary:

1. A general will or common agreement (consensus) existed among voters regarding the issue being voted upon.
2. An election represented a choice between alternatives.
3. The election results represented a clear preference by the voters for one of the options.
4. The voting results represented a mandate for programmatic action and, if the mandate were ignored, those elected could be easily removed.

Regardless of whether one examines elections within organizations, i.e., unions, parties, lodges, etc., or within society for political office, these or similar conditions would need to be approximated if elections are to be termed *democratic*. And, even if these conditions are met (the means) it does not mean that the policy outcome will be substantively democratic (the ends).

Elections as measurements of mass or rank-and-file preferences only occasionally meet even procedural democratic criteria. First, only occasionally do group members have consensus, a clear majority preference about election issues. More often, issues are blurred or perceived as inconsequential. Just as frequently, only a minority of eligible voters even bothers to vote, thereby leaving the majority's view unknown. Second, only rarely do elections represent a clear choice between option A and option B. Usually elections present a choice between candidates (two) who do not differ significantly, rather than a choice between policy alternatives, i.e., referenda issues. Third, election results, rather than reflecting policy preferences, are often a tribute to one candidate's ability to receive one more vote than his opponent. Simply, the individual casts his ballot for a variety of rational and nonrational motivations. Finally, elections are seldom a clear mandate for action; those elected are usually not held accountable until the next fixed time for elections.

Elections, such as in public employee organization unions, do not usually conform to the classical democratic model. Yet, elections serve a highly symbolic role of relating the individual to the group. Group boundaries are reinforced as the individual is given identity or group consciousness. The loss of professional identity on the job may be replaced by union consciousness. As Anthony Downs, William Domhoff, and Mancur Olson have noted, individuals often join voluntary associations such as unions for social rather economic reasons.[80] Hence, participation in the group through the act of voting becomes highly symbolic to the individual.

Consequently, if union democracy is a rare phenomenon and if elections are unreliable indicators of democracy, how can one know who rules the public sector union? This is not to ask who should govern public employee organizations? Rather, it is asking what has thus far been the experience of such organizations? Not facetiously, the answer is the same as for almost every other large organized group—an elite.

The fields of comparative politics, anthropology, and history have repeatedly revealed a consistent pattern—domination of groups and societies by elites. The elite may be a military officer class in one society, tribal elders in another, or the key business leaders in yet another. Our analysis does not inevitably presume, like Roberto Michels in "Iron Law of Oligarchy,[81] that an elite will always emerge in even the most avowedly democratic organizations. But, the overwhelming pattern in society and its social groups is that elites eventually emerge:

> In all societies—primitive and advanced, totalitarian and democratic, capitalist and socialist—only a few men exercise great power. This is true whether the power is exercised in the name of "the people" or not.[82]

Theoretically, Pareto, Mosca, and numerous other theorists tell us that elites emerge due to society's need for equilibrium and order. In effect, the loss of elite control is equated with *anomie*, or the loss of social order.

Unfortunately, the term *elite* and the concept of *elitism* are highly pejorative and value-laden. Both are frequently defined with a nondefinition: the antithesis of democracy. The concept of elitism refers to roles rather than to individuals per se. Elite analysis assumes that certain roles in every society will carry with them a degree of decision-making power. In most complex societies these key roles will be carried out by the leaders of the major social institutions. Political power is, therefore, attributable to anyone who fulfills a particular role. For example, the leaders of business in many American communities will also be important members of the community elite. This is because successful business entrepreneurs are valued in American society. Major union leaders in America may be considered elites by virtue of the reverse role they potentially serve by threatening prevailing business interests. Hence, the leadership of major public employee unions may also be considered elites because of their threatening role to prevailing elites.

Public policy analysis is not directly concerned with elite interaction beyond the scope of a particular policy issue. The larger issues of elite analysis cannot be resolved here. For instance, is there one power elite, i.e., the military-industrial complex of C. Wright Mills, who conspiratorially rules America, or are there a plurality of competing elites (pluralism) who coalesce and compromise in public policymaking? Or is there a ruling class that still wields political power even though it may not choose to exercise it?

These are questions beyond the scope of this analysis. Our analysis focuses on elite activity within public employee unions. We are concerned with the representational role of union elites as participants in public policymaking. Specifically, to what extent do public union member attitudes differ from nonunion members of the same occupation? In other words, can we assume that public unions represent the cutting edge of professional concerns and group interests? We will analyze this issue through case studies of two public teacher unions in California. Also, what are the existing models of union democracy, and to what degree is majoritarian rule possible in public employee unions? Our analysis focuses on two public employee unions and one private union in order to demonstrate the varieties of union decision-making models.

Teacher Unions and Membership Concerns

According to traditional interest group theory, those teachers who are most militant and most concerned with the erosion of their professional prerogatives join interest groups in order to express their collective concerns. In effect, the unions supposedly become the collective voice of the professionally concerned rank-and-file teacher. In our California case study, NEA affiliated California Teachers' Association (CTA) and AFL-CIO affiliated American Federation of Teachers (AFT) are usually assumed to be the professional consciousness of public school teachers. AFT's image has generally been more militant with its proclaimed principal concern "to protect teachers' rights and to assure adequate compensation through collective bargaining."[83] However, in recent years, NEA has increasingly become more like AFT with respect to teachers' rights.[84] In fact, NEA has expanded beyond the educational arena by advocating gun control legislation and supporting Jimmy Carter for president.[85]

Despite their ideological differences, both NEA and AFT are supposedly comprised of the more professionally concerned teachers. Again, according to group theory, those professionals with a more developed sense of their common interest would form or join interest groups. For example, in her study of teacher attitudes Nancy Gilgannon found that "professional educators desire a part in the decision making while employee educators are satisfied to be controlled by the bureaucratic and public situation."[86] However, two assumptions must be subjected to closer examination. First, that either teacher union accurately represents the views of most teachers, second, that either organization's leadership reflects the views of its own rank-and-file.

There are a number of studies indicating that contemporary public school teachers are somewhat more dissatisfied than their previous counterparts. According to one study by Samuel Lambert, "there is a new breed of teacher. . . . He is younger, better educated, more active, and more courageous."[87] In effect, he is more concerned about his overall role as a professional educator. A similar study by Theodore Bienenstok and William Sayres found that "certain teacher characteristics tend to be associated with dissatisfaction. . . a strong academic orientation, a relatively high valuation of professional status and prestige."[88] In general, similar disaffection with professional status and prestige by teachers are corroborated by several other studies.[89]

Consequently, the increasingly militant stance of teacher organizations, primarily the National Education Association (NEA) and the American Federation of Teachers (AFT), has generally been attributed by observers to changing teacher attitudes. This new militancy (defined as "group-based challenges to authority; an ideologically couched confrontation between groups")[90] can be generally linked to two core issues: (1) professional control, and (2) educational bureaucratization. Many studies of these two issues as underlying explanations for why teachers organize collectively are summed up by James Anderson:

Realizing their (teachers) limited power as individuals to effect changes in personnel policies, salary schedules, instructional procedures, and so on, they are turning to group action.[91]

Supposedly, group action is most frequently translated into joining either NEA or AFT. The issue of professional control by teachers of the educational process as a precipitating factor in educational unionization is easily misunderstood. Public education has always been controlled by elites or by institutions who are not professionals (teachers). Teachers, unlike the more prestigeous professionals, i.e., physicians and attorneys, have not controlled certification, licensing, or accreditation of professional training programs. Rather, control of education has rested firmly with various levels of public bureaucracies: local, district, state, and finally the federal government. Again, this lack of involvement in educational policymaking and the quest for job autonomy are major causes of teacher militancy.[92] In essence, teacher unions claim not to seek control of education; rather they want more participation in policymaking.

Bureaucratization of public school systems is often presented as a second causal factor in teacher unionization. Paradoxically, it is seemingly both too much bureaucratization and too little bureaucratization that have aggravated teacher frustration. Needless routinization and policy inflexibility prevent teacher decision-making authority; teachers lose "their sense of personal participation in the process of formulating school policy."[93] Both NEA and AFT have actively opposed this perceived bureaucratic rigidity by

insisting on the right of teachers to participate with boards of education in determining the policies of common concern, including salary and other conditions of professional service.... [94]

Teacher organizations claim not to be opposed to the bureaucratic process, merely to bureaucracy that inhibits their own professionalism.

Surprisingly, too little bureaucratization or undefined exercise of authority by school administrators are frequently given as factors in unionization. Teachers have complained that principals improperly used authority in loose and ill-defined situations.[95] A study by Edwin Bridges found that many teachers resent "being consulted on decisions which they felt the principal was to make."[96] One study by several University of Oregon researchers indicated that, in general, school superintendents quite capably utilized their expertise and experience in either diffusing or diverting educational interest groups. In effect, community interest groups were either ignored or co-opted by superintendents. The researchers found

that the matrix of pressure group activity, presumed under an early "group theory" orientation to be definitive in decision-

making, explains little of the usual allocations of resources and values in schools."[97]

It is perhaps indicative of the successful insulation of superintendents from pressure group activity that only 27 percent of the sample in the Oregon study listed teachers' organizations as important interest groups in their communities.[98]

In a sense, teachers are on the horns of a dilemma between perceived administrative authoritarianism and their own professional authority role. On one hand, rationally derived rules and procedures are at the essence of bureaucratic authority. Hence the professional's expectation of compliance and deference. On the other hand, the professional's authority is also derived from a set of expectations that include responsibility, self-determination, and professional autonomy.[99] The consequences are that while theoretically union militancy may advance teacher goals, the polarization between educational administrators and teachers is frequently an accompanying factor.[100] Why then do teachers become active in professional teachers' associations? Do those who do not become active in professional organizations have less concern for policymaking and professional recognition than union members? Finally, do teacher unions have an effect on teacher attitudes regarding their decision-making roles?

According to prevailing group theory, "teachers join professional associations because they are interested and because of the responsibility they feel as members of their profession."[101] Several empirical studies of teacher motivations for joining or not joining professional/union groups indicate that such assumptions are too simplistic. For example, Ronald Corwin found that faculty members who had a high employer orientation and a low professional orientation were more active in their professional associations.[102] If the professional associations are filled with "company men," to use Corwin's term, then where does that leave teachers who are not members or formally active in professional associations? Are they more complacent than active teachers, or are they possibly involved in other efforts to secure teacher professionalization? The Corwin study found that on most faculties there is a group of "informal leaders" who are not active in professional associations, but who are widely respected by their colleagues for their positions on professionalism and educational concerns. "Much of the actual leadership for the broad gauge problems of professionalism in education seems to be coming from the behind-the-scenes informal leaders."[103] These informal leaders "have not been officers in either organization, but are by far more militant than either group's official leaders."[104]

Ralph Kimbrough corroborates the Corwin findings by discovering that in some school settings there is an informal power structure among teachers that strongly affects teachers in decision making—even to the point of indicating to them how to teach their classes.[105] Furthermore, "without an analysis of the informal activity and relative power of persons involved one can never really know the nature of participation in school decisions."[106] Peter Hennessy's comparative study of Ontario, New York, and Quebec teachers found "that the New York teachers were the most professionally active. . . by a substantial margin, yet in total they are the least militant.[107] There appears the possibility that more teachers than just the visibly "active" teachers in professional associations are concerned about educational issues. Perhaps, public teachers are more unified on the basic issues of professionalism and policymaking than has often been believed. In essence, one cannot automatically assume that a public employee union, particularly one that represents recognized professionals, represents primarily those professionals who are truly concerned with educational policymaking issues. Rather, it may well be that such profession-oriented unions are somewhat in the mainstream of professional consciousness.

Union Democracy: Three Examples from the Crafts, Not-for-Profit, and Public Sectors

A classic example of internal union democracy is frequently presented through a private sector example—the International Typographical Union (ITU). ITU's supposed democratic framework is derived from historical factors and the legitimized nature of the two-party system in the American political system. In an important analysis of ITU, Seymour Martin Lipset attributes much of its internal democratic process to historical persecution and the closely knit occupational identity of the printers. These stemmed primarily from the irregularity of their hours and the elevated social status that printers had originally as members of guilds.[108]

Unlike other associations that organized as unions, the printers did not organize various locals into one organization. Rather, the printers brought together two separate, equal printer groups. Consequently, ITU became more like a federation than a centralized union. These two separate groups evolved during the late nineteenth century in reaction to secret societies that had emerged among printers to combat employer persecution. Both groups formed to debate the secret society's tactics and were instrumental in accomplishing a high degree of member politicization on the issues. The emergence of these two groups as a "fortuitous reaction to a crisis"[109] was the antecedent of the modern two-party system within the union.

Because ITU members were concerned with threats to the union, both internally and externally, constitutional provisions were made for (1) a popular election of all ITU leadership rather than reliance on the traditional election-by-convention method, and (2) the institution of popular referenda by the rank-and-file to resolve internal disputes. Furthermore, the ITU ruling party has always relinquished power peacefully when voted out of office. Usually the competition between the opposing administration and progressive parties has been quite intense with the executive's role generally secondary to the legislative.

Critics argue that the ITU example is a highly visible yet atypical example of union democracy; certainly not one that could be duplicated in a public sector that emphasizes the political neutrality of the public servant. However, in a study of a public employee union in a public hospital, Stanley Sloan found evidence to the contrary.[110] The Sloan study attempted to assess the union members' perception of the degree of union democracy and to determine why nonmembers did not join the union. Responses to democratic values were compared to certain arbitrary standards of union democracy as follows:

1. Degree of member participation in selection of union government.
2. Clear lines of responsibility by officers to rank-and-file.
3. Degree of member participation on critical policy issues.
4. The right to criticize without reprisal.

The responses to various questionnaire items were grouped as follows:

1. *Representation* Ninety-five percent of *all* employees (union and nonunion) felt free to join the union. Hence no coercion to join the union existed.
2. *Majority rule* Almost seventy-five percent of union members recognize no strong power groups. However, this case was almost exactly reversed for nonunion members, two-thirds of whom recognized a ruling clique.
3. *Participation* Seventy-five percent of the union members felt their opinions did matter in union affairs. Fifty-four percent of the nonunion members were undecided about the degree of rank-and-file participation in unions.
4. *Protection* Seventy-five percent of the union members felt the union defends them "fearlessly"; sisty-six percent of the non-union members agreed.
5. *Responsibility* Eighty percent of the union members felt their officers were responsible.
6. *Individual and minority rights* Eighty percent of the union members felt free to express themselves on any subject; ninety percent of the nonunion members felt this was the case in the union.

At least in this particular example, evidently a significant number of union members and nonmembers perceived this public employee union to be democratic.

The largest union comprised solely of public employees is the AFL-CIO affiliated American Federation of State, County, and Municipal Employees (AFSCME), which is open to all state and local employees except teachers and fire fighters (although employees of not-for-profit organizations also belong). Although its homogeneous membership is derived primarily from public employees, AFSCME members are still representative of a range of employer and occupational types.

Constitutionally, AFSCME is organized on four levels: the international president, the international executive leadership, the international convention, the councils and the local unions (see figure 6-4). Policymaking power is highly concentrated in the president and the international executive board, which determines national policy priorities and objectives. Essentially, district councils coordinate local activity while locals are responsible for negotiating contracts and handling grievances. Locals tend to be somewhat smaller than, and therefore more controlled by, the district and international levels.

The primary allocation of resources and professional staff focus is directed toward organizing campaigns such as the Memphis (1968) and Atlanta (1977) sanitation efforts. The union's secondary interest has been concentrated on lobbying at the national level, particularly in an effort to secure federal legislation for public employee collective bargaining. Until AFSCME called the strike against Mayor Jackson, a black, in Atlanta (1977), the union sustained the image of an affirmative action oriented union. The union has also directed a considerable effort in Democratic party politics, particularly in supporting Jimmy Carter's primary efforts to defeat George Wallace. Finally, AFSCME has also expended considerable resources since 1968 in attempting to repeal or liberalize the Hatch Act's limitation on public employee involvement in politics.[111]

The AFSCME organizational structure, as with most unions, offers an interesting structural duality of internal government.[112] In effect, unions usually are a dual government, which performs two separate functions. The constitutionally defined union structure (see figure 6-4) is designed to serve an intraunion function. On another level, a separate union structure operates to deal with employers. For example, stewards, grievance committees, and even officials of the local represent the union to the public agency or organization. Yet it is often the internal power structure of the union that plays the primary role in collective bargaining.

Although not as hierarchically controlled as the Teamsters' Union, AFSCME nonetheless represents an organizational model that is highly centralized in decision making. Traditionally, the union's executive leadership (convention) has primarily exercised a ratifying or legitimizing

Internal Organization of AFSCME

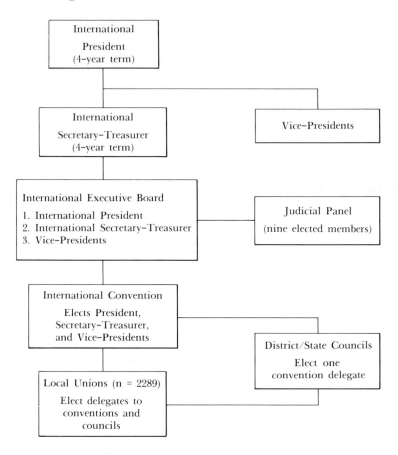

FIGURE 6-4: Internal Organization of AFSCME

function. In AFSCME's case, this executive leadership role has been identified with its controversial president, Jerry Wurf. In other words, AFSCME is a highly organized, aggressive union that has utilized this fact as an asset in expanding so rapidly in recent years.

Three particular aspects of union democracy have been examined to show several possible variations in decision-making style and approach. Again, it must be emphasized that democracy's existence is not determined by assessing the existence of constitutional procedures within the union. Such formal procedures may contribute to an open organization environment, yet they are not the essence of union democracy. In

Part II: Politics of Collective Bargaining

its essentials, union democracy hinges on the degree of active participation by rank-and-file in ongoing union decisions. Democracy also includes the representational method by which the majoritarian interests are included in conscious decision making by union elites.

Representation of the rank-and-file interests is not always easy to demonstrate, yet it has several important dimensions. In an over simplistic analogy, one can envision the California teacher unions, ITU, and AFSCME resembling some aspects of classical democratic theory. For example, the studies of teacher union members and nonmembers suggests an attempt at Rousseau's "general will," whereby underlying consensus exists, regardless of organizational structure. ITU embodies a Madisonian representation of the masses through political factions. Finally, the centralized AFSCME, by seeking to make policies that are in the best interests of the masses, although not necessarily representing them directly, approximates a political framework preferred by the founders of this republic. In essence, models of union democracy are neither always obvious nor unidimensional. Yet regardless of the approach, union democracy is perhaps best indicated in the union's policy outcomes—to what degree are the policy consequences in the best interests of the public employee? As public sector unions become legitimized as a policymaking influence, their internal decision-making process will be critically analyzed. Claims of internal union democracy will undoubtedly become a focus of this scrutiny. Unlike the private organizations and public bureaucracies whom they supposedly oppose, unions have actively portrayed themselves as models of democratic decision making. Unions, all unions, champion themselves as protectors of the underprivileged. Many intellectuals see the idealistic union movement as a powerful vehicle to form a better society. The laws that condone unions, that were enacted by democratic statutory process, almost dictate that unions themselves be democratic. And the fact that when a majority of the members of a government unit organize, they represent all members in that occupation and/or unit, means they must operate democratically to protect the rights of the minority.[113]

The only recourse in challenging autocratic or undemocratic union leadership rule is either through criminal or civil litigation. However, correction by law of suppressive union procedures is often stifled by the acute inadequacy of the channels of dissent. For example:

1. Union members many times do not know or understand the legal ramifications of their unions' actions, internally or externally. Also in unions that tend to be autocratic, not only will ignorance of a potentially liberating law inhibit individual member action, but the backlash of the power structure is a contending factor.

2. If litigation is pursued, it is expensive. Even the American Civil Liberties Union has a strong affinity for constitutional issues rather than union "squabbles."
3. One peculiar problem in the public labor union field is the unfamiliarity of the court with the entire issue of public sector labor relations. The courts do not know how a public labor union conducts its internal affairs and are often unfamiliar with the origin or purposes of the unions in a historical context.
4. An additional factor is that courts are quite reluctant to give precedent setting rulings in an emerging field. Therefore, the negative edicts they produce are easily by-passed by the union, and the expensive litigation is obviated.
5. In every union all litigation challenging union procedures comes under "the exhaustion of remedies" doctrine which means quite lengthy case duration. This automatically gives the union leadership the upper hand in most cases because of the costs involved.[114]

Again, the essence of union democracy is not dependent on the degree to which the rank-and-file can block policymaking by the union's elite. The ability to oppose policy outcomes should not be confused with a participatory role in the union's policymaking process itself.

Finally, one may speculate on what degree real union democracy is a feasible objective at this initial stage of unionization among public employees. In other words, union democracy or majoritarian rule within public sector unions may be viewed by union leaders as undesirable for this particular developmental stage. One theory holds that the democratic tendencies of public unions are somewhat suppressed because the concentration and intensity of power usage by the unions' elite is necessary in order to effectively bargain within a system that does not fully recognize their right to exist. This oligarchical rule is justified by government's sovereignty thesis: "In the public sector, the sovereignty doctrine makes it impossible for labor and management to bargain as equals."[115] The supreme power that the political system contains supposedly encourages public unions to become organizationally solid and power-oriented in order to be countervailing. In effect, the supposed inequity of the bargaining system influences the internal politics of public unions.

The bargaining process confronting public unions makes the attainment of union democracy problematic. Resulting authoritarian rule by labor leaders could become comparable to that of public management, which unions frequently criticize. As the organized public labor sector expands in an era of cohesive national public unions, the notion of control and power necessary for success in local labor-management confrontation may become obsolete.[116] One might compare union intentions to eventually become more democratic to the intentions of many military regimes. Almost invariably, power is first seized by the military in order to preserve order, with the assurance that eventually constitutional government will be restored. However, once in power the ruling elites often feel the return to democracy is less important.

Conclusion

Public employee unions have emerged as a new and highly important variable in contemporary American public policymaking. Their impact in policymaking has already been significant in scope and depth. Public sector unions now affect all phases of public policymaking from issue formation to policy outcomes and consequences. Of particular interest is the increasing role that they are exercising at the policy adoption stage, wherein policymakers perceive a range of options and adopt one particular alternative. In effect, public employee unions have generally focused on becoming participants in the process of formulating public policies rather than on simply reacting to policymaking outcomes.

Public employee unions have perceived the reality of the governmental subsystem that determines most public policymaking. This subsystem of participants, which has primarily included the bureaucratic elites, pressure groups, and key legislative committees, has historically excluded public employee groups. This exclusion is particularly significant in view of the increasing "bureaucratization of the policymaking process," i.e., the dominant role frequently played by the bureaucracy in subsystem policymaking. Consequently, the unique position of public sector employees within these public bureaucracies has meant that they were frequently a part of the policymaking subsystem without being participants in it.

Public sector unions have become particularly important in influencing the policymakers' allocation of resources through the budgetary process. In effect, public employee unions influence budgetary decision making through a separate process, collective bargaining—a means unavailable to other interest groups. Because of their distinctive access to policymakers in determining budgetary allocations, the traditional subsystem model based on a triad between bureaucrats, groups, and committeemen, is outdated. In effect, the triangular policymaking model is more aptly perceived as a square:

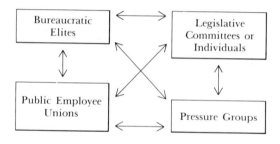

FIGURE 6-5: The Policymaking Process

This model of policymaking interaction is increasingly prevalent in redistributive policies where public employee unions become participants. For example, one can observe similar subsystem relationships in the prevailing wage issue for Los Angeles municipal employees: the public employee unions, taxation reform groups, key councilmen, and city administrators.

Finally, an appraisal of the role of public sector unions in public policymaking must inevitably include an analysis of who, within the union, really participates in public policymaking? In other words, do policy positions taken by union leaders represent rank-and-file attitudes, attitudes of nonunion professionals generally, or only the perspective of union elites? After examining the available data, our analysis finds no conclusive evidence that union and nonunion members of the same occupation possess significantly different occupational viewpoints. The evidence also indicates that powerful elites function as policymakers in most unions, public or private, as is true in any complex social organization. Union democracy is symbolically important, but rank-and-file members do not generally make policy through the mechanisms of democratic procedure. Consequently, union policy priorities are usually determined by union elites. Such decisions may be affected by the elite's assessment of the union's best interest, or they may be expressions of their own self-interest.

Thus, public employee unions are similar to other interest group participants in the policymaking process in one respect—in both those types of organizations, decision making is done by elites. Yet, public employee unions are different from other pressure groups because of their exclusive access to those who formulate policy and those who implement budgets. Consequently, public labor-management relations may have irretrievably altered the process of public policymaking.

Notes to Chapter 6

1. Robert Salisbury, "The Analysis of Public Policy: A Search for Theories and Roles," *Political Science and Public Policy*, ed. Austin Ranney (Chicago: Markham Publishing Co., 1968), p. 152.
2. Robert A. Dahl, *After the Revolution?* (New Haven: Yale Univ. Press, 1970), p. 120.
3. Robert A. Dahl and Charles A. Lindblom, *Politics, Economics and Welfare* (New York: Harper & Row, 1953), p. 9.
4. Patrick Moynihan, "Policy vs. Program in the '70's," *The Public Interest* 20 (Summer 1970), p. 91.
5. Mark V. Nadel, *Corporations and Public Accountability* (Lexington, Mass.: D.C. Heath and Co., 1976), p. 109.
6. Seymour Melman, *Pentagon Capitalism* (New York: McGraw-Hill Book Co., 1970), pp. 13-14.
7. Morton Grodzins, "Local Strength in the American Federal System: The Mobilization of Public-Private Influence," *Continuing Crises in American Politics,* ed. Marion D. Irish (Englewood Cliffs, N.J.: Prentice-Hall, 1963).
8. Mark V. Nadel, "The Hidden Dimension of Public Policy: Private Governments and the Policy-Making Process," *The Journal of Politics*, 32, no. 1 (February 1975), p. 7.
9. Thomas R. Dye and Harmon Zeigler, *The Irony of Democracy* 3rd ed. (Belmont, Cal.: Wadsworth, 1975), pp. 268-274
10. Peter F. Drucker, "On Managing the Public Service Institution," *The Public Interest* (Fall 1973), pp. 43-60.
11. Amitai Etzioni and Pamela Doty, "Profit in the Not-For-Profit Corporation: The Example of Health," *Political Science Quarterly* 91, no. 3 (Fall 1976), pp. 433-453.
12. Mark V. Nadel, *Corporations and Political Accountability*, op. cit.
13. Austin Ranney, "The Study of Policy Content: A Framework for Choice," *Political Science and Public Policy*, ed. Austin Ranney (Chicago: Markham Publishing Co., 1968), p. 8.
14. Ibid.
15. Henry W. Riecken, "The Federal Government and Social Science Policy," *Annals of the American Academy of Social and Political Sciences* 394 (March 1971), p. 101.
16. Vernon Van Dyke, "Process and Policy as Focal Concepts in Political Research," *Political Science and Public Policy*, op. cit., p. 27.
17. An example of the former is Sar Levitan, *The Design of Federal Antipoverty Strategy* (Ann Arbor: Univ. of Michigan Press, 1967); the latter, Clyde E. Jacobs and John F. Gallagher, *The Selective Service Act: A Case Study of the Governmental Process* (New York: Dodd, Mead & Co., 1967).
18. Lewis A. Froman, Jr., "Public Policy," *International Encyclopedia of the Social Sciences* 13 (New York: Crowell Collier & Macmillan, 1968), p. 204.
19. Charles T. Kerchner, *Los Angeles Times*, 27 October 1977, pt. II, p. 7.
20. John M. Wynne, Jr., *Prison Employee Unionism: The Impact on Correctional Administration and Programs* (Sacramento: American Justice Institute, 1977), p. 218.
21. Ibid., p. 228.
22. An early example is Stephen Bailey, *Congress Makes a Law: The Story Behind the Employment Act of 1946*, (New York: Columbia Univ. Press, 1950).

23. Yehezkel Dror, *Public Policymaking Reexamined* (San Francisco: Chandler Publishing Co., 1968), p. xi.

24. Van Dyke, op. cit., p. 28.

25. For an excellent overview of prescriptive theories of policymaking in complex organizations, see Alexander L. George, "The Case for Multiple Advocacy in Making Foreign Policy," *American Political Science Review* 66 no. 3 (September 1972), pp. 751-785.

26. Theodore J. Lowi, "Decision Making vs. Policymaking: Toward an Antidote for Technocracy," *Public Administration Review* 30 (May/June 1970), pp. 314-325.

27. Randall B. Ripley and Grace A. Franklin, *Congress, The Bureaucracy and Public Policy* (Homewood, Ill.: Dorsey Press, 1976), p. 5.

28. Ibid.

29. Drucker, "Public Service Institution," op. cit.

30. Ralph P. Hummel, *The Bureaucratic Experience* (New York: St. Martin's Press, 1977), p. 83.

31. Harold D. Lasswell, *A Preview of Policy Sciences* (New York: Elsevier-North Holland Pub. Co., 1971), p. 4.

32. Thomas R. Dye, *Politics in States and Communities* (Englewood Cliffs, N.J.: Prentice-Hall, 1969), pp. 439-444.

33. Ira Sharkansky, *The Politics of Taxing and Spending* (Indianapolis: Bobbs-Merrill Co., 1970).

34. Alan Edward Bent and George W. Noblit, "Collective Bargaining in Local Government: Effects of Urban Political Culture on Public Labor-Management Relations" *Urban Administration: Management, Politics, and Change*, ed. Alan E. Bent and Ralph A. Rossum (Port Washington, N.Y.: Kennikat-Dunellen, 1976), pp. 46-61.

35. Karen De Young, "Public Employee Militancy," *Editorial Research Reports* 2 (19 September 1975), p. 695.

36. Daniel Elazar, *American Federalism: A View From the States,* (New York: Thomas Y. Crowell, 1966).

37. Sharkansky, op. cit.

38. Gabriel Almond and Sidney Verba, *The Civic Culture* (Boston: Little, Brown & Co., 1965).

39. Felicitas Hinman, ed., *Building Your Management Team: A Framework for Public Sector Labor Relations* (Los Angeles: Institute of Industrial Relations, Univ. of California, 1976), p. A-19.

40. Lawrence Neil Bailis, *Bread or Justice: Grassroots Organizing in the Welfare Rights Movement* (Lexington, Mass.: D.C. Heath and Co., 1974).

41. Francis E. Rourke, "The Department of Labor and Trade Unions," *The Western Political Science Quarterly* 7 (December 1954), pp. 661-662.

42. Theodore J. Lowi, *The End of Liberalism: Ideology, Policy and the Crisis of Public Authority* (New York: W.W. Norton & Co., 1969).

43. Murray Edelman, *The Symbolic Uses of Politics* (Urbana, Ill.: Univ. of Illinois Press, 1964).

44. Lewis Froman, Jr., "An Analysis of Public Policies in Cities," *Journal of Politics* 29 (February 1967), pp. 94-108.

45. Neal R. Pierce, *Los Angeles Times*, 6 November 1977, pt. IV, p. 5.

46. Leonard M. Greene, "Who Benefits From the Minimum Wage," *The Socio-Economic Newsletter* 11, no. 10 (October 1977), p. 2.

47. Pierce, op. cit.

48. Ibid.

49. Lowi, *The End of Liberalism*, op. cit.

50. James E. Anderson, ed., *Politics and Economic Policymaking*, (Reading, Mass.: Addison-Wesley Pub. Co., 1970), pp. 373-376.

51. National Advisory Commission on Criminal Justice Standards and Goals, *Corrections* (Washington, D.C.: U.S. Department of Justice, 1973), pp. 609-614.

52. *Labor-Management Relations Service Newsletter* 7 (September 1976), p. 1.

53. Henry Santiestevan, *Deinstitutionalization: Out of Their Beds and into the Streets* (Washington, D.C.: American Federation of State, County and Municipal Employees, 1975).

54. Wynne, op. cit.

55. Froman, "An Analysis of Public Policies in Cities," op. cit., p. 20.

56. Eugene J. Meehan, *Value Judgement and Social Science* (Homewood, Ill.: Dorsey Press, 1969), p. 43.

57. James L. Sunquist, *Politics and Policy: The Eisenhower, Kennedy and Johnson Years* (Washington, D.C.: Brookings Institution).

58. Thomas Zane Reeves, "The Influence of Partisan Orientations Upon the Role of Voluntary Action in Anti-Poverty Programs," *Journal of Voluntary Action Research* 5, no. 2 (Spring 1976), pp. 75-81.

59. Robert Eyestone and Heinz Eulau, "City Councils and Policy Outcomes: Developmental Profiles," *City Politics and Public Policy*, ed. James Q. Wilson (New York: John Wiley & Sons, 1968), pp. 37-65.

60. Aaron Wildavsky, "The Analysis of Issue-Contexts in the Study of Decision-Making," *Journal of Politics* 24 (1962), pp. 717, 732.

61. Aaron Wildavsky, *The Politics of the Budgetary Process* (Boston: Little, Brown & Co., 1964).

62. Duane Lockard, *The Perverted Priorities of American Politics* (New York: Macmillan Publishing Co., 1971).

63. Clyde W. Summers, "Public Employee Bargaining: A Political Perspective," *Yale Law Review* 83 (1974), pp. 1156, 1164-68.

64. Charles Lindblom, "The Science of Muddling Through," *Public Administration Review* 19 (Spring 1959), pp. 79-88.

65. Wildavsky, *Politics of Budgetary Process*, op. cit., chap. 2.

66. Peter F. Drucker, "On Managing Public Service Institutions," op. cit.

67. Summers, op. cit., p. 1165-1166.

68. Ibid.

69. Douglas Shuit, *Los Angeles Times*, 7 March 1977, pt. I, p. 3.

70. Marvin Braude, *Los Angeles Times*, 10 July 1977, pt. IV, p. 5.

71. Sid Bernstein, *Los Angeles Times*, 3 April 1977, pt. II, p. 1.

72. Summers, op. cit.

73. Price, Waterhouse and Company, "County Budgetary Process" Report no. 2 (1976-77 Grand Jury, County of Los Angeles, 1977), Los Angeles.

74. Aaron Wildavksy and Arthur Hammond, "Comprehensive Versus Incremental Budgeting in the Department of Agriculture," *Administrative Science Quarterly* 10 (December 1965), pp. 321-46.

75. Dwight Waldo, ed., "Planning-Programming-Budgeting System Reexamined: Development, Analysis and Criticism: A Symposium," *Public Administration Review* 29 (March/April 1969), pp. 111-202.

76. Rodney H. Brady, "MBO Goes to Work in the Public Sector," *Harvard*

Business Review (May-June 1965), pp. 63-74; Peter Phyrr, *Zero-Base Budgeting: A Practical Management Tool for Evaluating Expenses* (New York: Wiley, 1973).

77. Allen Schick, "The Road to PPB, the Stages of Budget Reform," *Public Administration Review* (July-August 1975), pp. 387-395.

78. Bruce H. DeWoolfson, Jr., "Public Sector MBO and PPB: Cross Fertilization in Management Systems," *Public Administration Review* (July-August 1975), pp. 387-395.

79. U.S., Office of Management and Budget, "Zero-Base Budgeting" Bulletin no. 77-9, (19 April 1977); U.S., Office of Management and Budget, "Zero-Base Budgeting," *Federal Register* 42, no. 84, pt. VII, (2 May 1977).

80. Mancur Olson Jr., *The Logic of Collective Action* (New York: Schocken Books, 1971), pp. 135-136.

81. Roberto Michels, *Political Parties: A Sociological Study of the Oligarchical Tendencies of Modern Democracy* (1915) (Glencoe, Ill.: Free Press, 1962).

82. Thomas R. Dye, *Who's Running America? Institutional Leadership in the United States* (Englewood Cliffs, N.J.: Prentice-Hall, 1973), p. 3.

83. *The American Teacher* (January 1977).

84. Peter H. Hennessy, "Teacher Militancy: A Comparative Study of Ontario, Quebec and New York Teachers," (Ottawa: Canadian Teachers Federation, July 1975).

85. *The NEA Reporter* (February 1977).

86. Nancy Green Gilgannon, "A Study to Determine the Perceptions of Vocational Educators Regarding a Professional Association," Ed.D. Dissertation, Pennsylvania State Univ. (August 1975).

87. Samuel M. Lambert, "Current Problems with the Teaching Profession," Annual Meeting, Council of Chief State School Officers, San Juan, Puerto Rico (November 1967).

88. Theodore Bienenstok and William C. Sayres, "Problems in Job Satisfaction Among Junior High School Teachers," New York State Education Department, Albany, New York (June 1963).

89. James Haehn, "Collective Bargaining in Higher Education: An Empirical Analysis in the California State Colleges," (April 1971); James Belasco and Joseph Alutto, "Determinants of Attitudinal Militancy Among Nurses and Teachers," Paper presented to American Educational Research Association Annual Meeting, Chicago, Illinois (April 1972); James Belasco, "Commitment and Attitudes," American Educational Research Association (1970) Annual Meeting, Minneapolis, Minnesoto.

90. Ronald G. Corwin, *Militant Professionalism* (New York: Appleton-Century-Croft, 1970).

91. James G. Anderson, *Bureaucracy in Education* (Baltimore: Johns Hopkins Press, 1968), p. 171.

92. Belasco and Alutto, op. cit.; George B. Redfern, "Will Teacher Militancy Make Evaluation of Teacher Performance Obsolete?" Paper presented at the Annual Meeting of the American Association of School Administrators, Atlantic City, N.J. (February 1969).

93. Thomas G. Gans, "Teacher Militancy, The Potential for It and Perceptions of School Organizational Stucture," Paper presented to the American Educational Research Association (1972) Annual Meeting, Chicago, Ill.

94. Corwin, op. cit., p. 48.

95. Gans, op. cit.

96. Edwin Bridges, "A Model for Shared Decision-making in the School Principalship," (1967), St. Ann, Missouri: Central Midwestern Educational Laboratory.

97. Michael O. Boss, Harmon Zeigler, Harvey Tucker, and L.A. Wilson, "Professionalism, Community Structures, and Decision-Making: School Superintendents and Interest Groups," *Policy Studies Journal* 4, no. 4 (Summer 1976), pp. 351-362.

98. Fred G. Berke, "Comment," *Policy Studies Journal* 4, no. 4 (Summer 1976), p. 365.

99. Anderson, op. cit., p. 116.

100. John Stucky, "Views and Feelings of Superintendents who are Disturbed About Teacher Militancy," (Eugene, Oregon: School Study Council, September 1970).

101. Barton W. Welsh, "Camouflage and Professionalism Don't Mix: Observations from the Local Level," *American Vocational Journal*, 1972.

102. Corwin, op. cit., p. 214.

103. Ibid., p. 195.

104. Corwin, op. cit., p. 328.

105. Ralph B. Kimbrough, *Political Power and Educational Decision-Making* (Chicago: Rand McNally & Co., 1964), p. 240.

106. Ibid., p. 241.

107. Hennessey, op. cit.

108. Seymour M. Lipset, et al., *Union Democracy* (Glencoe, Ill.: Free Press, 1956), p. 394.

109. Ibid., pp. 396-397.

110. Stanley Sloan, "Democracy in a Public Employee Union," *Public Personnel Review* (October 1969), pp. 194-198.

111. Jack Steiber, *Public Employee Unionism: Structure, Growth, Policy* (Washington, D.C.: Brookings Institution, 1973), p. 194.

112. Alice H. Cook, "Dual Government in Unions: A Tool for Analysis," *Industrial and Labor Relations Review* (April 1962), pp. 323-331.

113. Seymour M. Lipset in *Private Government*, ed. Sanford A. Lakoff (Glenview, Ill.: Scott, Foresman & Co., 1973), pp. 89-111.

114. Ibid.

115. Louis V. Imundo, "Some Comparisons Between Public Sector and Private Sector Collective Bargainings," *Labor Law Journal* (December 1973), p. 811.

116. William E. Leiserson, in *Unions, Management and the Public*, ed. E.W. Bakke, et al. (New York: Harcourt, Brace, World, 1960), pp. 146-147.

PART **III**

Conclusion

The first six chapters have presented a descriptive framework and analysis of the political and economic contexts of public sector collective bargaining. The last chapter summarizes the short- and long-term effects of collective bargaining on government organization, the civil service system, and public policymaking. The chapter also deals with the two issues of affirmative action and tri-lateral bargaining. These items have been left to the last because of their relative uncertainty in these contexts. Ultimately, this part assesses the present position of public sector unions and raises certain questions about their future.

Conflict, Power, and the Public Interest

Unique Features of Public Sector Bargaining

Although it has become commonplace to speak of the distinction between the private and public sectors in matters of economics as "blurred," in matters of collective bargaining the distinction is, to a large extent, persistent. Unlike the private sector, where industrial relations operate in a systematic way and with a set of rules and principles, labor-management relations in governmental jurisdictions have experienced casual and undirected growth with a limited effort at codifying this practice. In the federal service, Executive Orders 10988 and 11491 created a tentative bargaining format for the classified civil service, but these only affect a portion of the federal employees and restrict negotiation to personnel policies and grievances. They have entirely left out financial issues and major benefits. In the states and municipalities, there has been a great variance in collective bargaining experiences according to existent (or nonexistent) statutes, the mood of lawmakers, or, crucially, the relative political strength of the involved actors.

Prior to the Second World War, the issue of managerial prerogative was a major source of contention in private sector bargaining. Corporate officials repeatedly invoked the sanctity of their obligation to stockholders—to discharge the interest of stockholders by managing the corporation's assets. This relationship precluded negotiation with an "outside group responsible to nonstockholder interests" over matters that had a direct implication for the profitability of the corporation.[1] The principle of managerial prerogative was resolved in the private sector as a matter of relative bargaining powers. Management did not surrender the principle of prerogative; it simply became a matter for settlement in collective bargaining.

In the public sector the issue of managerial prerogative operates under the guise of sovereignty, and it continues to exist. Although the sovereignty argument has been explored earlier, we will briefly restate the principle: government is said to be the holder of ultimate power since it responds to the interests of all of its constituents. Under this rubric collective bargaining is opposed because it is a concession of the right to bargain with a special interest group. Thus it may result in terms that violate the public interest, thereby obviating government's primary responsibility. The argument maintains that for the good of all, government must retain the singular responsibility for public policy. In this case, control over policy means that government shall be the sole determinant of allocation of tax revenues for the discharging of such public services as teaching, sanitation, and police protection, among others.

Other obstacles unique to public sector collective bargaining concern the questions of union recognition and exclusive recognition. The former issue is exemplified by the Memphis sanitation strike of 1968 caused by the refusal of a white city government to recognize a union made up primarily of black workers. The latter issue rears up because governments are generally opposed to such union security conditions as the union shop, a provision that is common in private sector labor contracts.

In the 1930s, labor negotiators were sometimes faced with an obfuscating of true corporate authority when they wished to negotiate. Contracts were negotiated and signed with lesser corporate officials, e.g., plant managers, who would cast doubt on the validity of the contract by claiming a lack of sufficient authority to truly commit the corporation to it. Whether this was a tactic of gameplaying or simply a matter of inexpertise in collective bargaining is now irrelevant; it is presently a rare occurrence in the private sector.

However, in the public sector, the question of locating the real source of authority for collective bargaining is a persistent issue. In the public sector, bargaining is complicated by the separation of powers between the legislative, executive, and judicial branches of government. Indeed, a key question is whether public sector collective bargaining can be reconciled with the existing structural and functional separation of governmental entitities.[2]

In the private firm the cost of a new labor contract package can be covered by one or more of the following sources: a reduction in profits, an increase in productivity, or a higher price on the product. The bargaining stance of a firm will be directly related to the availability or permissibility of these sources. The firm will be more generous if these

316

sources are feasible, less generous if they are not. Government, however, operates in a different context. It makes no profit and, since it deals mainly in services, its potential for productivity increases is limited. Its major source of revenue for meeting higher costs is in raising prices, which in this context means raising taxes. Because raising taxes is a volatile political act, government will only undertake it with reluctance. Thus, government will frequently pursue a tougher bargaining stance in labor negotiations than will private firms. "The consequence is that, on the whole, the incomes of public employees have shared less in the general prosperity than have private incomes. It simply takes more pressure to raise the public remuneration level, given the different nature of the public employer."[3] Yet, despite conditions forcing "more pressure," public employees are legally denied their most telling pressure capability—the strike. Although the doctrine that workers cannot strike against government still stands, the high incidence of walkouts by public employees suggests that no amount of legislation has removed the application of labor's most potent weapon in the public sector.

Finally, a crucial variable unique to the public sector is the role that collective bargaining plays in the determination of public policy. A question vexing to many observers is whether it is appropriate and in the public interest for public policy matters—often going beyond the scope of the labor-management relationship—to be shaped by the outcome of collective bargaining. "For example, should the level of benefits of welfare recipients or the quest of school desegregation be determined primarily by collective bargaining? Or, are such issues really the primary responsibility of the executive and legislative function with the employer and employees affected having a voice, but not being the sole determinants in deciding such policy questions?"[4]

Collective Bargaining and the Civil Service System

Most civil service systems, as presently constituted and conceived, restrict what a public employer can agree upon in a negotiated contract. Collective bargaining agreements cannot alter statutory rights created by a civil service system. For instance, a statutory requirement that entrance into the civil service is to be governed by competitive written examination cannot be altered by a collective bargaining contract. However, in the absence of expressed statutory prohibition, bargaining may take place so long as the negotiated contracts are consistent with the civil service system. Therefore, the content of civil service examinations and the definition of satisfactory performance are potentially negotiable. But, there is a catch. Since, as a rule, a civil service system is governed by a board or an independent commission, any labor-management agreement concerning the nature of competitive examinations would merely serve as a joint recommendation to the governing body.[5]

Realistically, the existence and growth of collective bargaining is circumscribing the traditional role of civil service commissions as the personnel arms of government. This is especially true when new agencies are created for carrying out labor relations duties. It is likely that the functions of civil service commissions will be confined to prescribing hiring criteria, administering entrance and promotion examinations where they are required, and protecting the merit system. At the extreme, collective bargaining may make the commissions altogether superfluous; then, they will either remain as mere appendages in labor-management relations or wither away.

It is now clear that personnel policies and their implementation will increasingly become the subject matter of collective bargaining rather than being unilateral decrees by agency heads. Additionally, the pressure for increased wages by employee organizations will have an impact on traditional budget-making processes. Anticipated wage demands will have to be included in budget submittals. Undoubtedly, new ways may have to be devised for moving the budget through legislative bodies.[6] These concerns will have the greatest impact upon local governments, because it is here that financial resources are the most tenuous; and, it is here that the relative power balance between the negotiating sides is often weighted in favor of public employee organizations.

Affirmative Action and Collective Bargaining

The Civil Rights Act of 1964 marked a legal milestone in the struggle against discriminatory practices in education, housing, voting rights, and employment. Its Title VII prohibits all types of employment discrimination that violate the equal protection clause of the fourteenth amendment. In an effort to go beyond prohibiting discriminatory practices, Title VII was expanded by the Equal Employment Opportunity Act of 1972 to provide added employment opportunities. The Civil Rights Act and the *Brown* v. *Board of Education* decision are indicators of a policy commitment to prohibit discrimination against any individual because of race, creed, color, sex, national origin, or age.

However, the commitment to end discrimination was not limited to changing the law of the land. Programs and agencies were created with the mandate of making the equal opportunity ideal a reality. In addition to compensatory programs, one approach consisted of affirmative action programs.

In theory, affirmative action in employment simply means to take "positive or active steps to accomplish the public policy goal of equal employment opportunity."[7] Both President Kennedy's Executive Order 10925 and President Johnson's Executive Orders 11246 and 11375 required an active program that was intended to go one step beyond nondiscrimination by publicizing employment opportunities and by removing any obviously discriminatory barriers to employment. However, affirmative action quickly became enmeshed in an imbroglio of quotas, reverse discrimination, and tokenism.

The affirmative action debate focuses on whether goals and timetables are, in reality, quotas in disguise. Clearly, statistical quotas for ethnic minorities, women, or any other group have been consistently prohibited by the U.S. Constitution, legislation, Executive Orders, and judicial precedent. Such quotas are seen as an illegal form of preferential treatment or reverse discrimination. However, an increasing number of observers argue that affirmative action goals and timetables are really quotas—a rose called by another name. In essence, affirmative action now requires quantifiable results, not merely equal employment opportunity or nondiscriminatory procedures.

Statistical parity or affirmative action quotas have been proposed as a solution to the problem of historical racial and sexist discrimination. The objective is supposedly "justice"—equality of opportunity in education, housing, and employment. Advocates argue that affirmative action quotas will result in equal employment opportunity:

> It is a question of reparations. . . . Restoring to these [minority] communities what they have been robbed of for years—equal opportunity.[8]

Affirmative action proponents claim that the historical denial of equal employment opportunities to women and ethnic minorities has resulted in the contemporary imbalance of Caucasian males in better employment and educational positions. In order to rectify this unequal situation, they propose a narrowing of the imbalance:

> Imagine a 100-yard dash in which one of the two runners has his legs shackled together. He has progressed 10 yards, while the unshackled runner has gone 50 yards. At that point the judges decide that the race is unfair. How do they rectify the situation? Do they merely remove the shackles and allow the race to proceed? Then they could say that equal opportunity now prevailed.

But one of the runners would still be 40 yards ahead of the other. Would it not be the better part of justice to allow the previously shackled runner to make up the 40-yard gap; or to start the race all over again? That would be affirmative action towards equality?

Initially, affirmative action was intended to prepare individuals, not groups en masse, so that they might have equal opportunity. The race would still be run according to one set of rules, not two. Each participant was to be trained and treated the same. Affirmative action programs included goals and timetables for a variety of personnel practices—recruitment, hiring, upgrading, demotion, transfer, layoff or termination, wages and fringe benefits, selection and conduct of training (apprenticeships), and upward mobility. Those who defend contemporary affirmative action programs maintain that such goals and timetables do not constitute preferential treatment for certain minorities against others. The U.S. Commission on Civil Rights insists that such programs

> *are designed not to establish preferential treatment for minorities and women. Rather the purpose of such programs is to eliminate institutional barriers that women and minorities now encounter in seeking employment and thereby to redress the historic imbalance favoring white males in the job market.*[10]

The commission acknowledges that to discriminate against white males on the basis of their sex or race would be as unconstitutional as past discriminatory practices.

However, because quantifiable quotas are illegal, no bureaucratically imposed affirmative action objectives can be legally mandated. For example, employers are not required to hire a specific number or percentage of minorities or women. Rather, the employer learns through a somewhat unofficial process to either give preferential treatment to minorities in all hiring or to utilize regional census figures to justify a particular prescriptive quota. The employer is required to conduct a self-analysis of:

> *all major classifications at the facility, with explanations if minorities or women are currently being underutilized in any one or more job classifications. . . . "Underutilization" is defined as having fewer minorities or women in a particular job classification than would reasonably be expected by their availability.*[11]

Again, affirmative action compliance is no longer defined as equal employment opportunity. Rather it is an active effort to achieve statistical parity for minorities and women in all job classifications. Specifically, statistical parity is an objective or at least determined within each department and for each occupational category.

Critics charge that statistical quotas can only provide opportunity for minorities and women by limiting the rights of other citizens. In other words, equal employment opportunity can only exist for all citizens, not just for a few. Justice does not discriminate in favor of certain social groups or against other groups. Nor is it served by justifying current discrimination by past injustices. Nathan Glazer is representative of an increasing number of observers who contend that affirmative action programs no longer create true equal employment opportunities.[12] Rather, Glazer feels that affirmative action has become a concept that unjustly provides preferential treatment for particular ethnic minorities. Thus, affirmative action has provided a form of "reverse discrimination" against yet other ethnic and social groups. In addition, affirmative action evolved from a *de jure* focus against discriminatory legislation to the bureaucratic "setting of statistical requirements, based on race color and national origin for employers and educational institutions."

The Affirmative Action Program of Los Angeles County (AAPLA) provides an excellent case study of the difficulty that an acknowledged equal opportunity employer has in achieving the multi-dimensions of statistical parity. The program set as an objective the increase of numbers of ethnic minorities and women at all salary levels, within each department, and in each occupational category. An evaluation by Price, Waterhouse indicates that the program was dramatically successful (table 7-1).

TABLE 7-1: Los Angeles County Employee Ethnic Mix (by percent)

Race/Ethnic Group	1970	1975	1976	Change 1970-76	Change 1975-76
White	64.3	54.2	52.5	-11.8	- .3
Black	25.1	28.2	28.7	+ 3.6	+ .3
Hispanic	6.0	11.4	12.3	+ 6.3	+ .9
American Indian	. . . .	0.3	0.3	. . .	. . .
Asian American	2.8	4.4	4.7	+ 1.9	+ .3
Other non-White	1.8	1.4	1.5	- 0.3	+ .1

Source: *Personnel Organization, Policies and Practices Review*, Report no. 3 (Los Angeles: Price, Waterhouse and Company, 2 May 1977), p. 11-13.

The county's affirmative action program was a major variable in expanding the number of minority employees from 33.5 percent in 1968 to 47.8 percent in 1976.

In comparison to overall population percentages for the county's major ethnic groups, several interesting trends emerge. First, affirmative action succeeded in overrepresenting certain groups while others remained below the general census parity. For example, blacks comprised 10.85 percent of the county's population in 1976, 28.7 percent of the county employees. By comparison, Hispanics comprised 18.33 percent of the county population, 12.3 percent of the county employees. Caucasians comprised 67.8 percent of the general population, 52.5 percent of the county employees.

The county's affirmative action plan also includes goals for increasing the number of women and ethnic minorities at all salary levels and occupational classifications on a parity with regional census figures. A 1976 progress report particularly laments the inbalance of minorities and women at the plus $25,000 level (table 7-2).

However, an analysis of ethnic minorities in all salary categories indicates an impressive level of upward career mobility (table 7-2). Within only one year (1975-76), at almost all levels the number of minorities increased. These statistics strongly suggest that equality of employment opportunity is best measured through indicators of upward mobility rather than statistical parity. Moreover, because the expansion of employment opportunities for ethnic minorities is a relatively recent phenomenon, the data for the plus $25,000 category is not surprising. It can be assumed that longevity and experience are key factors in salary determinations.

The major impact of affirmative action upon collective bargaining has been in the area of seniority. Seniority, the length of continuous service accumulated by an employee, has long been the protective mechanism for job security. Unions have historically insisted that a seniority system be utilized in determining such personnel practices as promotion and layoffs. Seniority in the plant provides an objective standard for ascertaining retention and release of employees whenever reduction in the work force occurs. Seniority has finally found widespread acceptance among management as an effective tool in reducing employee tension and conflict. However, the seniority system has been frequently attacked by affirmative action proponents because of its failure to protect the job security of ethnic minorities and women during layoffs. Often hired because of affirmative action programs, these workers claim to be the "last hired, first fired" during layoffs. Critics argued that seniority systems which were existent before passage of Title VII often reflected discriminatory personnel practices.[13]

In a number of important test cases, minorities demanded affirmative action restitution for past discriminatory seniority systems. Court rulings have been mixed. On one hand, the courts rejected the continuance of departmental seniority systems wherein previously segre-

322   Part III: Conclusion

TABLE 7-2: Los Angeles County Employees Ethnic Compostition by Salary

Annual Salary	White (percent) 75	76	Black (percent) 75	76	Hispanic (percent) 75	76
25,000+	86.4	88.2	6.1	5.8	2.2	2.6
16,000-24,999	79.5	75.5	10.3	12.3	5.0	5.5
13,000-15,999	65.6	58.1	17.5	22.8	7.2	9.9
10,000-12,999	46.6	42.6	35.8	36.9	12.0	14.6
8,000-9,999	39.0	32.0	42.1	44.2	13.8	17.8
Below 8,000	26.6	20.3	42.1	41.9	25.2	31.3

Source: *Progress Report on Los Angeles County: Affirmative Action Program,* 26 November 1976.

gated employees lost seniority benefits upon transferring to other departments.[14] However, the courts also rejected the notion that minority employees be awarded "fictional" seniority or be permitted to bump white employees with more seniority. In essence, the courts have stressed a forward rather than a retroactive emphasis of Title VII.[15] In a 1977 decision, the Supreme Court ruled seven to two that minority truck drivers contending that they had been victims of discrimination before the Civil Rights Act's passage were not entitled to retroactive job seniority.[16] Retroactive seniority may only be awarded to those identifiable victims of discrimination since the enactment of Title VII.

The future of affirmative action and equal employment opportunity is problematical. Both public opinion polls and recent court decisions portend a retreat from quotas and parity formulas.

In an exhaustive analysis of every available public opinion poll that assessed attitudes toward affirmative action programs and equal employment opportunity, Seymour Martin Lipset and William Schneider underscored the consistency of the opposition to such efforts. The surveys revealed that while a majority favored equal opportunities for ethnic minorities and women, they nonetheless "overwhelmingly rejected" the use of affirmative action and preferential treatment to achieve such equality. Typical of these public opinion polls was a 1976 Cambridge Survey Research poll that asked respondents the following question:

> Some large corporations are required to practice what is called
> affirmative action. This sometimes requires employers to give

TABLE 7-3: Should Women and Miniorities Receive Preference in Jobs and Education? The issue of affirmative action was presented in broad terms, as follows:

Some people say that to make up for past discrimination, women and members of minority groups should be given preferential treatment in getting jobs and places in college. Others say that ability, as determined by test scores, should be the main consideration. Which point of view comes closest to how you feel on this matter?

	Should	Should Not	No Opinion
NATIONAL	11%	81%	8%
Men	10%	82%	8%
Women	12%	80%	8%
Whites	9%	84%	7%
Nonwhites	30%	55%	15%
College	15%	81%	4%
High School	9%	84%	7%
Grade School	11%	70%	19%
East	13%	77%	10%
Midwest	8%	87%	5%
South	9%	79%	12%
West	15%	82%	3%
18-29 years	11%	81%	8%
30-49 years	10%	84%	6%
50 years and older	9%	81%	10%

Source: Gallup Report, George Gallup, "Public Favors College Entry by Ability," *The Cincinnati Enquirer*, 20 November 1977, p. J-5.

special preference to minorities or women when hiring. Do you approve or disapprove of affirmative action?[17]
A majority of the respondents—51 percent—disapproved of affirmative action. In an even more recent poll (Gallup Report, November 1977), the American public overwhelmingly chose ability, as determined by examination, and not preferential treatment, in selecting applicants for jobs or students for college admission. In this poll eight out of ten of the respondents opposed preferential treatment (see table 7-3). Even most nonwhites and women, persons who would benefit from affirmative action, voted in favor of ability as the criterion for entry into industry and college.

Part III: Conclusion

It is possible that the future of affirmative action programs in the field of employment may be determined by a court case concerning the twice denial of admission to a medical school to a white engineer. Allan Bakke sued the University of California at Davis on the basis of reverse discrimination, claiming to have been denied admission while the university admitted minority applicants who were less qualified.[18] The California Supreme Court concurred that Bakke's equal opportunity rights had been abridged. The university's Board of Regents subsequently appealed the case to the U.S. Supreme Court. Although the nature of equal educational opportunity is somewhat different than equal opportunity, the Bakke precedent affects the definition of equal rights in both areas. It is conceivable that equal educational opportunity and affirmative action will continue as unresolved sources of judicial policymaking. However, it is evident that Bakke has permanently laid to rest the use of statistical quotas in employment.

Management has had a difficult task in trying to reconcile the pressure to adhere to affirmative action and the pressure from unions when affirmative action threatens individual worker security. Most unions in both the private and public sectors are numerically dominated by whites, and a majority of the workers enjoying seniority are white. Despite the rhetoric of some labor leaders professing to support the principle of affirmative action, the action of most unions, when directly confronted with the issue in collective bargaining, has been negative. Clearly, affirmative action is not in the best interest of the majority of the rank-and-file union members. Although, there is no statistical data on the attitudes of union rank-and-file toward affirmative action, it can be assumed that they hold the majoritarian view opposing affirmative action.

AFSCME is a major exception; it proudly proclaims itself an "affirmative action union." AFSCME, over the years, has been successful in organizing and representing minority group workers. However, it has encountered difficulties where white workers are numerically greater. For instance, AFSCME has not captured a contested representational election involving police since April 1966.[19] Assuredly, AFSCME has several handicaps in competing for police members. The union strictly forbids police "to strike or take strong positions or demonstrate" and has suspended striking police locals. Another obstacle to AFSCME's potential as a police representative is the industrial nature of the union, which organizes workers by employer rather than by occupation or craft. Policemen view this eclecticism with disfavor because they believe that an organization exclusively identified with the police suits them better than an organization representing a wide variety of workers. However, the liberal social viewpoint of AFSCME has proved to be its greatest handicap in police unionization:

AFSCME is probably the most politically liberal trade union, having been praised for its liberal stands on civil rights, and domestic and foreign policy. (AFSCME was the union involved in the Memphis sanitation strike in 1968.) If they joined the AFSCME, policemen would no doubt find themselves aligned against their union as well as their employer on political issues.[20]

Constraints on Local Governments

The handicaps that beset local jurisdictions in their collective bargaining activities are, in the main, caused by the restrictions imposed on them by state legislatures. Most of them are caused by a jealously guarded taxing power and a lack of confidence that local officials would be responsive to standards of "good government," as defined by state legislatures. Certain constraints have also been maintained in order to preclude some subjects from local collective bargaining altogether.[21]

The fiscal dilemma confronting local governing units is that while there is generally a state-imposed obligation (or insurmountable pressure from employee groups) to negotiate wages and fringe benefits with inevitable increases in budget expenditures, the state nonetheless retains existing limitations on the taxing capabilities of local jurisdictions. Local government officials are thus unenviably trapped between employee group demands and pressure; the state legislature's reluctance to permit local jurisdictions the flexibility to levy income, sales, or excise taxes; and a public resistance to increased millage levied on property.

Local governments encounter complications in the actual process of collective bargaining as well. They face problems in meeting budget deadlines because of the inadequate coordination between collective bargaining and budget making. Public sector budgets and accounts are not secret documents; thus, operating reserves or contingency funds are open targets for employee groups. It is difficult for management to hide its collective bargaining strategy and tactics from the employees; unions can infiltrate management's decision-making structure through friendly elected officials.

State legislation urging collective bargaining covering "terms and conditions of employment" is usually thrust upon an existing civil service merit structure. While the original concept of a merit system had a beneficial effect on city government, it now has a questionable role in a personnel system featuring bilaterally negotiated settlements. Having the merit system simultaneous with collective bargaining suggests that either state legislatures have not given enough thought to the problem that an adherence to merit guidelines or rules would reduce appreciably the extent of bargainable issues, thus diminishing the flexibility of management negotiations, or, it is another way of limiting the authority of local governments in managing their own personnel systems.

Rational collective bargaining takes place when both sides enjoy freedom and flexibility. For government it is the freedom to trade one proposal for another and to trade increased costs in one area for cost reductions in another; it is also the freedom to raise the funds needed to meet employee demands or to be able to withstand the consequences of a refusal. Because many of these freedoms are unavailable to local governments, their flexibility at the bargaining table is seriously impaired. Without benefit of flexibility, local government bargaining has suffered from impasses and employee pressure tactics, which, in many cases, could have been avoided.*

The Strike

Strikes and other forms of work disruptions are not necessary outcomes of collective bargaining. A major cause of public employee

* There is the potential that the "taxpayers' revolt of 1978" may have a direct impact on collective bargaining relationships in the public sector. Local governments and states will be the first affected; but, it has the potential to affect all levels of government eventually. On 7 March voters in Tennessee by a 2-1 majority approved a state constitutional amendment to limit the "rate of growth" of state spending to the "estimated rate of growth of the state's economy." Even more politically significant was the approval on 6 June by the citizens of the largest state, of the Jarvis-Gann amendment, Proposition 13, a tax-limitation amendment to the California Constitution. This was achieved over the opposition of public employee groups, a number of politicians—including the governor—and some large business corporations. Proposition 13 will limit property taxes in California to 1 percent of assessed valuation. It will restrict increases in assessed valuation to a maximum of 2 percent a year except when property changes hands. Moreover, it will require a two-thirds vote of the legislature to raise other taxes. Similar amendments are expected to be on the ballot in a number of other states this year (1978). And the prospects for passage appear to be good.

What Proposition 13, and similar legislation, does is cut taxes and raise obstacles to further increases in government spending. These tax-limitation amendments appear to be an expression of a rising public opinion—especially among the middle-classes, who bear the major brunt of taxes—to stop the growth in government spending. If this is indeed a move in the direction of limiting government and government spending it will have a major effect on public employee unions' ability to obtain resources through collective bargaining. The bargaining posture will be altered as unions attempt to hold the line against losses, rather than try to obtain no-longer-available gains. Shrinking public fiscal resources would force unions to a greater accommodation with management as both sides collaborate to protect public services from worker layoffs, program elimination, and other reductions.

strikes has been government's inflexibility at the bargaining table; another major cause has been the refusal of public employers to recognize employee organizations for purposes of collective bargaining. Theoretically, the issue of collective bargaining and the issue of strikes are separable; the legitimization of the former does not necessarily require the legitimization of the latter.[22] But, as a practical matter, the frequency of strikes in the public sector demonstrates that the *power* to strike is more relevant than the *right* to strike.[23] As long as strikes are seen as a useful way of obtaining gains, they will continue to take place as a method of bargaining by other means.

Whether or not the availability of the strike to public employees is essential to legitimate collective bargaining is the subject of a lively contemporary debate among scholars and practitioners. John Burton, Jr., and Charles Krider argue on behalf of the right of public employees to strike.[24] Their rationale for legitimizing the strike is that it is a necessary weapon for a union in order to obtain recognition by the employer, and the potential for work interruption forces serious bargaining by both sides. They feel that there are comparable environmental restraints in both the private and public sectors which ensure prudence in the collective bargaining process. In the public sector the concern over taxes parallels the market restraints in the private sector. They feel that in the public sector both parties are sensitive to the economic implications of bargaining and to their attendant political consequences. This awareness thus serves as a check on excessive behavior in labor-management relations. Moreover, they point out, there are alternatives to essential public services that are withheld. For instance, when Warren, Michigan, negotiators reached an impasse with an AFSCME local, the municipality subcontracted to the private sector for its sanitation service. Finally, they downgrade the importance that political pressure, in reaction to a strike, has in distorting the decision-making process of government. Among their examples, they refer to Kalamazoo, Michigan's ability to withstand a forty-eight day strike by sanitationmen and laborers, and Sacramento County, California's surviving an eighty-seven day strike by welfare workers.

In their conclusion, Burton and Krider provide guidelines with the effect of rationalizing the treatment of strikes in public employment. They divide public services into three categories (with strikes in each

---

Public antipathy to government spending, vividly manifested in the passage of California's Proposition 13 and similar amendments, could force a labor-management *rapproachment*, the likes of which has been nonexistent since the advent of collective bargaining in the public sector. For an expanded analysis of tax limitation actions by the public and their measured consequences on government, see Milton Friedman, "The Limitations of Tax Limitation," appearing in the summer 1978 issue of *Policy Review*, a quarterly publication of the Heritage Foundation.

separately regulated): essential services, intermediate services, and nonessential services. Police and fire are deemed essential services; strikes here would be prohibited since they would immediately endanger public health and safety. Sanitation, medical care, transit, water, and sewage are called intermediate services. With the exception of sewage, which is an essential service for large cities but not as critical in smaller communities "where there are meaningful alternatives to governmental operation of sanitation services," strikes of short duration may be "tolerated." However, Burton and Krider specify that injunctive relief from a strike should be available if the health and safety of a community is threatened. The last category, called the nonessential services, consist of streets, parks, education, housing, welfare, and general administration; here strikes of indefinite duration may be tolerated.

Jack Stieber takes issue with the proposal to grant the right to strike to only a portion of public employees. He points out that the distribution of public employment at the local level has only a small minority of the workers in nonessential occupations—"nonessential in the sense that interruption of service could be endured for an extended period without posing a threat to the health, safety, or welfare of the populace." He concludes: "A law which extended the right to strike only to a small minority of all public employees, most of them unorganized and without the power to carry out a successful strike, would be a hoax."[25]

Robert Booth Fowler presents an interesting analysis of the right to strike by public employees from the standpoint of political theory. He rejects the "natural" right of government employees to strike, as "someone's private value reified into an absolute claim."[26] He posits that this claim is not part of the traditional notion of natural rights; it is a decision to be made by the political community. Moreover, to dismiss the argument of sovereignty because of the growing recourse to strikes is "to accept the implication that whatever is, ought to be."

He states that the legalization of strikes as a means necessarily sacrifices the "basic authority of the political community or its governmental agents." With some government functions, a strike by public employees would place government at a serious bargaining disadvantage because of pressure to end the strike and restore an essential service. "The result might be a fatal delegation of final authority out of the hands of the political community, or its responsible governmental agents, into some irresponsible part of it, such as a public employee union.... Democratic values require that in the end the will of the community must not be thwarted by self-seeking minorities, as long as minorities have equal political rights." But, in the end, Fowler shows a sensitivity to political realities: "It is very possible that simply dismissing any efforts to legalize the right to strike by public employees will lead only to increasingly divisive and uncontrolled splits within the political community as strikes occur."

Harry Wellington and Ralph Winter, Jr., compared the claims of unions in the private and public sectors. While they found common ground in most cases, they submit that there is a crucial distinction. The areas of commonality are claims to industrial peace, industrial democracy, and effective political representation. The first claim is made possible through collective bargaining, which enables each side to gain a better understanding of the other and of the actual state of the enterprise. The second claim is the industrial counterpart of community participation; it is the achievement of industrial democracy by having workers participating in their own governance through collective bargaining. The third claim—effective political representation—is made possible by having unions represent workers in the political arena, and "political representation through interest groups is one of the most important types of political representation that the individual can have."[27]

There is a fourth claim made for collective bargaining—that collective bargaining is required in order to counteract the unequal power of employer and employee in individual bargaining. "Monopsony—a buyer's monopoly, in this case a buyer of labor—is alleged to exist in many situations and to create unfair contracts of labor as a result of individual bargaining." Wellington and Winter hold that this is a legitimate claim in the private sector. But, their thesis is that the unequal bargaining argument of public employee unions is less clearly analogous to the private model. They cite the political nature of governmental decisions, with economic considerations being one of several criteria, as uniquely characteristic of the public sector.

In public sector bargaining the costs are primarily political; in the private sector they are economic. "It further seems to us that, to the extent union power is delimited by market or other forces in the public sector, these constraints do not come into play nearly as quickly as in the private." A public sector decision maker is inevitably faced with a political dilemma during the course of collective bargaining.

> What he gives to the union must be taken from some other interest group or from taxpayers. His is the job of coordinating these competing claims while remaining politically viable. And that coordination will be governed by the relative power of the competing interest groups.

On the question of the relative power of competing interest groups, Wellington and Winter hold that public employee unions "possess a disproportionate share of effective power" because, in addition to the usual methods of political pressure, they are able to withhold labor—

to strike. Thus, public sector collective bargaining, with its accompanying pressure methods, is able to "skew the results of the 'normal' American political process" of countervailing interest groups competing for allocations from government.

They argue that strikes by public employees are more damaging not because public services are any less or any more essential than private ones (they admit that this is an arguable point), but because the disruption of these services "may seriously injure a city's economy and occasionally the physical welfare of its citizens."

> What is wrong with strikes in public employment is that because they disrupt essential services, a large part of a mayor's political constituency will press for a quick end to the strike with little concern for the cost of settlement. The problem is that because market restraints are attenuated and because public employee strikes cause inconvenience to voters, such strikes too often succeed. Since other interest groups with conflicting claims on municipal government do not, as a general proposition, have anything approaching the effectiveness of this union technique—or at least cannot maintain this relative degree of power over the long run—they are put at a significant competitive disadvantage in the political process.[28]

The authors conclude that what sovereignty really means in this field is not the source of ultimate authority, "but the right of government, through its laws, to ensure the survival of the 'normal' American political process. As hard as it may be for some to accept, strikes by public employees may, as a long run proposition, threaten that process."[29]

Our own analysis indicates public employee strikes to be a much more varied and complex tactic than has generally been appreciated, either by management or by labor. Quite simply, public employee strikes are not always a predictable phenomenon nor do they inevitably secure labor's short- and long-term objectives. Neither is the strike an action that public management can take lightly. Public employee strikes are implemented in hopes of attaining both short-term and long-range objectives. Generally, public employee unions initiate a strike to obtain an immediate end, i.e., recognition, immediate security, grievance, or interest impasse resolution. In addition, there are certain long-range goals, although indirectly related to the job action, that are equally important, i.e., favorable public opinion, legalization of collective bargaining and the right to strike, and increased union security.

The public employee strike, as a political weapon, may typically result in three consequences: (1) a gain in both short- and long-term objectives, such as occurred with the postal workers in 1970; (2) the attaining of immediate goals while suffering the pyrrhic consequences of losing long-term goals, such as happened in the 1975 San Francisco firemen and police strike; (3) or the humiliating loss of both primary and secondary objectives, as befell the Atlanta sanitation workers in 1977. The effectiveness of public employee strikes or job actions, in general, is not dependent solely on one variable. Rather, the efficacy of such employee tactics can be more closely correlated with variables of group (union) organization, resources, leadership, and strategy. In addition, external factors, such as public opinion, media relations, and solidarity with other groups are important to the successful attainment of objectives on both levels.

In summary, both labor and management have viewed the public employee strike in absolute terms. For public sector unions, the strike has often been perceived as the irresistible force that would accomplish any objective. At times, the strike has even been employed as a panacea for sagging union fortunes. In Canada, public employee unions were permitted to choose between binding arbitration or the right to strike, provided the strike was not injurious to the general public. Increasingly Canadian unions were choosing the right to strike option, with the consequence that the courts in that country were clogged with cases determining which particular employee strikes were detrimental to the public interest.[30] Apparently, the lure of the strike as a political weapon is still overwhelming to public employee unions, in this country or elsewhere.

For public sector management, the strike was frequently envisioned as an overwhelming juggernaut to which one must inevitably capitulate. In many cases, the public sector strike did wreak havoc as unions forced management to grant immediate concessions. Yet, in an apparently increasing number of situations, the public strike has failed as a political weapon. Seemingly, public management has discovered new allies among taxpayers and the media. Perhaps the most effective ally has been the poorly conceived strike action, which seeks to gain economic objectives by seeming to hold the city for ransom.

Reorganizing Government for Labor Relations

Harold Davey, a noted labor-management relations authority, calls public sector collective bargaining "underdeveloped."[31] He proposes some major corrections to aid in creating "developed" bargaining. A major priority is the clarification of the identity and authority of management at the bargaining table. Another requirement is logical coherence for the maze of differentiated laws addressing state and local public sector bargaining. Finally, Davey believes that constructive

Part III: Conclusion

bargaining can only take place if governmental units are realigned to accommodate effective labor-management relations.

> *Over time, the requirements for constructive labor relations may prove to be a more powerful factor in bringing about state and local governmental reorganization than all the many studies by public administration experts stressing the merits of county consolidation, statewide school organization instead of autonomous local districts and the like.*[32]

Not the least of the reasons for governmental reorganization for collective bargaining is the need for government to develop effective structures capable of confronting the power capabilities of public employee unions.

The problem of identifying the employer would be alleviated if the appropriate legislative body (Congress, state legislature, city council, and so on) clearly established the identity and the authority of the operating agency as the employer with whom public employee groups must bargain. Moreover, legislation must be explicit that fiscal control is not vested with the "employer" at the bargaining table, unlike the practice in the private sector.

> *The enabling legislative enactment can and should establish the parameters of discretionary authority for the government agencies who do the actual bargaining. It can also relate the timing of negotiations to the legislative year in terms of appropriation. Both the government agency and the employee organization must know what can (and cannot) be done on economic (labor cost) issues.*[33]

Public sector bargaining at the state and local government level occurs under a wide variety of legislative controls and authorization. In some jurisdictions, bargaining takes place on a *de facto* basis, because there are no laws on the matter. The consequence is that the bargaining experience at the state and local level is uneven and often inequitable. Where government is adamantly opposed to collective bargaining, the employees' only recourse is to strike or to employ the "economic force subterfuges of mass resignations, sick-ins, 'blu flu' and so on."[34] An alternative to this unhappy condition is for the states to recognize collective bargaining and to adopt uniform laws. Another alternative is for the federal government to pass legislation on collective bargaining covering public employees at all levels of government.

The restructuring of some governmental units to accommodate collective bargaining is to provide economics of scale and to equalize the power wielded by organized employees. For instance, Davey believes that centralized and consolidated bargaining structures are probably "unavoidable" in public education, "if equity is to be achieved for all teachers while achieving and then maintaining comparable educational opportunities for all pupils, wherever situated."[35] He states that small districts are uneconomical; collective bargaining urges the development of a larger financial base. In public education, this could mean having statewide bargaining of minimal economic standards between a "multi-employer" school board association and an NEA or AFT bargaining team. The same requirement holds for other units of local government as well. As presently constituted, many governmental structures are unsuitable for collective bargaining. An example of a governmental structure suitable for collective bargaining is that of Philadelphia, discussed in chapter 2. Our analysis suggested that because of that city's initiative in restructuring its government in order to clearly establish public management authority, its collective bargaining process was a "developed" one. Unfortunately, this condition has not often been attained—or even attempted—elsewhere.

Collective Bargaining: New Dimensions in Public Policymaking

The impact of public sector collective bargaining on public policymaking has already begun to change the essential characteristics of that process. Traditionally in American politics, public policies have been made by a subsystem of government at all levels that has included bureaucratic elites, pressure groups, and key legislative committees. Within this subsystem of government, key bureaucratic elites have performed an increasingly important role in "the bureaucratization of the policymaking process."[36] The introduction of public employee unions into this policymaking process has frequently resulted in a realignment of the subsystem—particularly when challenging the dominance of policy adoption by public bureaucratic elites. In essence, bureaucratic elites are now being confronted by public employees within public bureaucracies. Increasingly, this struggle within public agencies concerns not just the conditions of employment but public policy priorities as well.

Specifically, our analysis indicates two major trends that have resulted from public employee collective bargaining. First, collective bargaining increasingly includes quality of work/life issues in addition to the usual economic concerns. Second, the bargaining process itself is being urged to become "trilateral" if not multilateral in practice. This is occurring because policymaking priorities are frequently decided at the negotiating table, thus affected interest groups are making efforts to be included. We will examine the implications of these trends in more detail.

334   Part III: Conclusion

Employee Behavior: Economic versus Psychological Incentives

Thus far, most public employee unions, like their private sector counterparts, have stressed the primacy of economic issues in collective bargaining. Social issues (employee work satisfaction) and political matters (equal employee opportunities) have seemingly not been major policy objectives. (An exception is the concern over working conditions held by professional worker groups, discussed earlier.) However, there are some indications that social and political matters may become more important as collective bargaining issues; if for no other reason than that they might become negotiable issues for trade-off.

The increasing importance of social and political policy concerns is indicated in one survey of nonprofessional union activists in upstate New York (see table 7-4); nonetheless, the primary concerns were still economic.[37] However, it is significant that so many activists also rated as "very important" such issues as safety; control of work, i.e., "having more to say about how the work is done"; adequate resources, i.e., "improving conditions that interfere with getting the job done"; and interesting work. Union activists in this study apparently believed that although an improved working environment is secondary, it is still a highly important consideration.

Historically, American private and public labor unions have focused on a few key tangible issues on which there has been a high degree of membership consensus:[38]

> *American unions have bargained successfully and contributed significantly... by achieving economic gains, grievance procedures, better general working conditions, and job security for their members. The overwhelming, consensus of workers' views of these tangible quality of work/life issues has made them ideal for a collective bargaining process that relies on support of rank-and-file and the threat of strike for gains.*[39]

Consequently, intangible or nonquantifiable issues have only recently become important as minimal economic standards were obtained for both public and private sector employees. Jerry Wurf, AFSCME president, even asserts that public employees do not join a union for primarily economic reasons:

> *Every competent union organizer understands this: workers don't join a union merely for the right to get a nickel or dime an hour or an extra week's vacation; they join the union for the same reason that men lust for freedom and democracy. They join a union because they want to obtain dignity by participating in the process that decides their social and economic well-being.*[40]

Whether or not Wurf is correct, the economic versus social priorities

TABLE 7-4: Attitudes of Union Officers toward Selected Issues

	Issue "very important"[a] (percent)	Issue Integrative [b] (percent)	Issue Appropriate for Joint Programs (percent)
Earnings	92	26	6
Fringe benefits	79	48	4
Safety	75	68	41
Job security	68	44	12
Control of work	47	34	54
Adequate resources	46	46	61
Interesting work	41	39	68
Productivity	30	30	51
Workload	22	29	44

Source: J. Richard Hackman and J. Lloyd Suttle, eds., *Improving Life at Work: Behavioral Science Approaches to Organizational Change* (Santa Monica, Ca.: Goodyear, 1977), p. 355.

[a] Percent rating issue "very important."

[b] Percent reporting that with regard to any given issue "my union and company want to accomplish completely the same thing" or "my company and union want to accomplish somewhat the same thing."

[c] Percent feeling that the "best way" to deal with the issue is to "set up a joint program with management outside collective bargaining."

debate is central to explanations about the development of public employee collective bargaining. In an analogous case, Theodore Roszak's study of the counterculture movement found that its proponents are torn between those who emphasize economic liberation and those who seek the psychic or cultural liberation of individuals.[41] In other words, certain critics such as Karl Marx and Herbert Marcuse argue that the attainment of economic security is the highest human priority. Others, such as psychologists and religious leaders, believe that economic materialism co-opted real liberation; therefore a group movement should focus on helping individuals to self-actualize or develop their human capabilities. They strongly believe that work should not become alienating, but an experience that provides employees with creativity and challenge.

Finally, it is important to assess the causes of public employee unionism from the perspective of organizational behavior. For years many behavioral scientists accepted Douglas McGregor's assumption that employees were either Theory X or Theory Y motivated: that employees disliked work, needed to be coerced and avoided responsibility; or that employees could find work creative, sought responsibility, and could integrate intrinsic with organizational goals. An approach that avoids the X-Y dichotomy is John Morse and Jay Lorsch's "contingency theory—the fit between task, organization, and people," which assumes:

> that the appropriate pattern of organization is contingent on the nature of the work to be done and on the particular needs of the people involved.[42]

Stated another way, decision makers should not simply attempt to match tasks with organization, but also tasks with people and people with organizations. If this occurs, employees will supposedly perform well through acquired feeling of competence that are in turn reinforced through successful performance. The results, claim Morse and Lorsch, "can be a more consistent and reliable motivator than salary and benefits."[43]

The implications of contingency theory for public employee collective bargaining are twofold. In those public organizations where individuals do not attain feelings of competence, the appeal of unionization if often overwhelming. For example, frustrated employees within an alienating work environment will be attracted to a union that articulates their collective frustrations. On the other hand, public managers who were previously supportive of contingency theory approaches may abandon such approaches when suddenly confronted with organized employees.

In effect, contingency theory generally assumes the psychological needs of man to be significantly more important than purely economic incentives. Although some private sector unions have given indications of change, much of public sector collective bargaining insofar as it concerns nonprofessional employees, still frequently stresses the tangible issues of economic rewards. Consequently, in cases where economics constitute the only real issues in collective bargaining, the managerial incentive to promote "quality of work" programs for employees might be greatly diminished.

Trilateral Collective Bargaining

Increasingly, interest groups that are affected by public policies are seeking to participate in collective bargaining and thereby attempt to make the process trilateral rather than bilateral in nature. This occurs whenever policymaking is perceived by such groups as happening in collective bargaining rather than in the pluralistic political arena. Our analysis will focus on the trilateral phenomenon in a specific case study of efforts to pass a comprehensive collective bargaining bill in California.

For California's 1.2 million public employees, 1975 was to be the year Democratic Governor Jerry Brown delivered on his campaign pledge to push a comprehensive collective bargaining measure through the state legislature. Its certainty was seemingly guaranteed by Democratic majorities in both Houses of the legislature and an expected favorable report by an Assembly-appointed council on public employee relations. Although opposition to public sector collective bargaining was vocal, the governor's recent successful compromise in bringing together divergent groups in the State Farm Labor Relations Act seemed to assure similar results.

The mechanism for implementing public employee collective bargaining appeared to be a State Senate bill (S.B. 275) known as the Dills-Berman bill. In essence, the Dills-Berman measure would provide collective bargaining for all public employees. Introduced concurrently, although not given much chance of success was the much weaker Rodda bill (S.B. 160), which only provided for public education collective bargaining (affecting teachers in elementary and secondary schools and two-year colleges). The Dills-Berman bill was actively lobbied for by the California Labor Federation (AFL-CIO) and the California Teachers' Association, while its primary opposition stemmed from the California League of Cities and Republican leaders.

However, the Dills-Berman bill was ultimately to be defeated in committees of the Assembly and Senate by the unanticipated intervention of student pressure groups; they wished to be included in bargaining with faculties of institutions of higher education. The governor, caught in a crossfire between student and labor groups that had both backed him in the campaign, was unable to thwart the student opposition.

Student opposition to bilateral collective bargaining for public employees (specifically, for college and university faculties) was led by the California student lobby, representing the University of California students, and the state university and colleges lobby, which lobbied on behalf of all other students in public four-year institutions. Both student groups wanted to be nonvoting participants in the collective bargaining process on the rationale that "students pay for services and are also the product of these services and therefore have an interest in what happens to their money at the bargaining table."[44]

In fact, student insistence on a third-party role in collective bargaining in institutions of higher learning was so intense that one spokesman claimed students would rather relinquish their nonvoting seat on

Part III: Conclusion

the University Board of Regents if compelled to choose between it and a role in collective bargaining.[45]

It must be emphasized that the student lobbies wanted to participate as a third party in the process, not as management or labor. Only by participating in collective bargaining did student representatives believe that they could affect such issues as student-faculty ratios and curriculum; otherwise "they would lose input in these areas gained during the '60s."[46] Public employee unions felt that any third party in collective bargaining would only serve to "confuse, disrupt and undermine the negotiating process."[47] The very essence of collective bargaining had always been defined bilaterally, not tri- or multilaterally. One union leader protested:

> You cannot bargain on wages and working conditions on Main Street, and if the students come in, then every other interested group should be able to, also, including minorities and women, and collective bargaining just doesn't work like that.[48]

Even the governor's office seemed opposed to the inclusion of students on all collective bargaining issues.

> If students are permitted into collective bargaining then social welfare workers and parents of kids in elementary school should be given similar access to the negotiation table.[49]

The labor unions argued that students were actually "management" in a bargaining situation because their fees and tuitions paid for employee services and personnel.[50] Student lobby leaders declared that they were neither since in the world of academe, students, faculty, and administrators supposedly shared many administrative responsibilities.[51] The student lobby claimed that students were already involved in academic policymaking throughout the university system:

> Students now sit on committees which decide how registration fees should be used, which programs should be funded and the number of hours a week faculty members should teach.[52]

According to the logic of the students' argument, since collective bargaining implied a shift in academic policymaking to the negotiating table, and given that students were recognized participants in the present policymaking system, then they should also be included in collective bargaining. Although opposing such logic, the governor dispatched a staff aide to meet with student representatives in order "to decide what role students should play in the collective bargaining process."[53]

Finally, an amendment to the Dills-Berman bill before the Senate Finance Committee was passed; it provided for student representation in public employee collective bargaining. Immediately, AFL-CIO dropped its support of the bill and the measure was ultimately defeated on the Senate floor. Later, in the session, the much weaker Rodda Act, without student representation provisions, was enacted.

The implications of the student lobby effort in California extend far beyond the scope of a single case study. The demand by third parties to be included as participants within the collective bargaining process suggests some assumptions and trends:

1. Unlike the private sector, where collective bargaining is perceived as legitimately occurring in bilateral negotiations, public sector negotiations are viewed as directly affecting many other groups.

2. Other pressure groups believe that policymaking often occurs in collective bargaining rather than in the pluralistic political arena. It is seemingly a political axiom that interest groups will apply pressure at the point where policy decisions are actually made, not where they are legitimately "supposed" to be made.

3. It is possible that other interest groups, particularly consumer and taxpayer groups, will follow the student lobby lead and seek to create trilateral collective bargaining.

4. It is not likely that the demand for trilateral collective bargaining by other groups will always be strenuously resisted by public management. Seemingly, such additional participants would function as management allies in a consensual effort to hold budgetary spending, increase productivity, and maintain managerial prerogatives.

Conclusion

The field of public labor-management relations is a fertile one for scholars and practitioners. It is a relatively young field and because of its youth it is undergoing growth pains fraught with uncertainties, trial-and-error experiences, and recklessness. But, because of its youth, it is also a vigorous, dynamic, and growing field. The action in unionization today is in the public sector, and it promises to remain so for years to come. Thus, it affords scholars with ample and challenging research, consulting and teaching opportunities; and, it offers practitioners a challenging and promising career field, no matter on which side of the negotiation table they sit.

As this book is being completed, news of new strikes by public employees, new developments in public labor-management relations—legal, political, and practical—stream in. In view of the dynamic and changing nature of the field, one is continually tempted to rewrite portions of the book, to delay its completion in order to await "definitive" resolutions of conflicts, "definitive" judgments and legislation. This would be the cautious approach. We have chosen to boldly venture forth with our analysis of the contemporary state of public sector labor-relations. Even though this is the last page of our last chapter, we know that this cannot be the final chapter.

Notes to Chapter 7

1. Neil W. Chamberlain, "Public versus Private Sector Bargaining," *Collective Bargaining in Government: Readings and Cases*, eds. J. Joseph Loewenberg and Michael H. Moskow (Englewood Cliffs, N.J.: Prentice-Hall, 1972,), p. 12. Cited hereafter as Loewenberg and Moskow.
2. Richard F. Dole, Jr., "State and Local Public Employee Collective Bargaining in the Absence of Explicit Legislative Authorization," in Loewenberg and Moskow, op. cit., pp. 46-47.
3. Chamberlain, op. cit., p. 15.
4. Arvid Anderson, "The Structure of Public Sector Bargaining," in Loewenberg and Moskow, op. cit., pp. 48-49.
5. Dole, op. cit., pp. 49-50.
6. Harry P. Cohany and Lucretia M. Dewey, "Union Membership among Government Employees," in Loewenberg and Moskow, op. cit., p. 11.
7. Felicitas Hinman, ed., *Equal Employment Opportunity and Affirmative Action in Labor-Management Relations, A Primer* (Los Angeles: Univ. of California, Institute of Industrial Relations, 1976), p. H-I.
8. Henry Disuvero, quoted in the *Los Angeles Times*, 16 September 1977, pt. I, p. 22.
9. Seymour Martin Lipset and William Schneider, *Los Angeles Times*, 31 July 1977, pt. IV, pp. 1:6.
10. *Statement on Affirmative Action for Equal Employment Opportunities*, Clearinghouse Publication No. 41, (Washington, D.C.), February 1973.
11. Nathan Glazer, *Affirmative Discrimination: Ethnic Inequality and Public Policy* (New York: Basic Books, 1975).
12. Ibid.
13. Hinman, op. cit.
14. *Quarles* v. *Philip Morris, Inc.*, 279 F. Supp. 505, E. D. Va. 1968.
15. *Papermakers, Local 189*, v. *United States*, 416 F. 2d 980 (CA 5), 1969; *Waters* v. *Wisconsin Steel Works*, 502 F. 2d 1309 (CA 7), 1974; *Watkins* v. *Steelworkers, Local 2369, and Continental Can Co.*, 369 F. Supp 1221 (E.D. La), 1974; *Jersey Central Power and Light Co.* v. *IBEW Locals 327*, et al., 9 FEP Cases 117 (CA 3) 1975.
16. *Teamsters* v. *U.S.* 75 - 636.
17. Lipset and Schneider, op. cit.
18. *Bakke* v. *The Regents of the University of California*, 1974.
19. Alan Edward Bent, *The Politics of Law Enforcement: Conflict and Power in Urban Communities* (Lexington, Mass.: D.C. Heath & Co., 1974), pp. 79-80.
20. M.W. Aussieker, Jr., *Police Collective Bargaining* (Chicago, Ill.: Public Employee Relations Library, 1969), p. 12.
21. Charles M. Rehmus, "Constraints on Local Governments in Public Employee Bargaining," in Loewenberg and Moskow, op. cit., pp. 135-141.
22. Dole, op. cit., p. 51.
23. Arnold M. Zack, "Impasses, Strikes, and Resolutions," *Public Workers and Public Unions*, ed. Sam Zagoria (Englewood Cliffs, N.J.: Prentice-Hall, 1972), p. 102.
24. John F. Burton, Jr., and Charles Krider, "The Role and Consequences of Strikes by Public Employees," in Loewenberg and Moskow, op. cit., 275-289.

25. Jack Stieber, "A New Approach to Strikes in Public Employment," in Loewenberg and Moskow, op. cit., pp. 298-299.

26. Robert Booth Fowler, "Public Employee Strikes and Political Theory," in Lowenberg and Moskow, op. cit., pp. 291-294.

27. Harry H. Wellington and Ralph K. Winter, Jr., "The Limits of Collective Bargaining in Public Employment," and Harry W. Wellington and Ralph K. Winter, Jr., "More on Strikes by Public Employees," in Lowenberg and Moskow, op. cit., pp. 264-273, and pp. 289-290.

28. Wellington and Winter, "The Limits of Collective Bargaining in Public Employment," ibid., p. 271.

29. Ibid., pp. 272-273.

30. U.S., Civil Service Commission, *Civil Service Journal* (Washington, D.C.: U.S. Government Printing Office), January-March, 1977.

31. Harold W. Davey, *Contemporary Collective Bargaining*, 3rd ed., (Englewood Cliffs, N.J.: Prentice-Hall, 1972), p. 345.

32. Ibid., p. 348.

33. Ibid., p. 349.

34. Ibid., p. 354.

35. Ibid., p. 373.

36. Frances E. Rourke, *Bureaucracy, Politics and Public Policy* (Boston: Little, Brown and Co., 1969).

37. T.A. Kochan, D.B. Lipsky, and L. Dyer, "Collective Bargaining and the Quality of Work," in *Proceedings of the Twenty-Seventh Annual Winter Meeting of the Industrial Relations Research Association*, San Francisco, December, 28-29, 1974.

38. A. Salpukas, "Unions: A New Role?" in *The Worker and the Job: Coping with Change*, ed. J. M. Rosnew (Englewood Cliffs, N.J.: Prentice-Hall, 1974), pp. 99-117.

39. J. Richard Hackman and J. Lloyd Suttle, ed., *Improving Life at Work: Behavioral Science Approachers to Organizational Change* (Santa Monica, Cal., Goodyear Publishing Co., 1977), p. 404.

40. Jerry Wurf in *"Labor-Management Relations in the Public Sector,"* Hearings before the Special Subcommittee on Labor, House of Representatives, 92nd Cong. 2nd sess., (Washington, D.C.: U.S. Government Printing Office, 1972), p. 44.

41. Theodore Roszak, *The Making of a Counter Culture* (Garden City, N.Y.: Doubleday & Co., 1969).

42. John J. Morse and Jay W. Lorsch, "Beyond Theory Y," *Tomorrow's Organizations: Challenges and Strategies*, eds. Jongs S. Jun and William B. Storm (Glenview, Ill.: Scott, Foresman & Co., 1973), p. 42.

43. Ibid., p. 48.

44. Harry Bernstein, *Los Angeles Times*, 26 June 1975, pt. II, p. 1.

45. Ibid.

46. Don Speich, *Los Angeles Times*, 1 July 1975, pt. I, p. 28.

47. Ibid.

48. Bernstein, op. cit., p. 8.

49. Speich, op. cit., p. 28.

50. Ibid., p. 3.

51. Ibid.

52. Ibid.

53. Ibid.

Index

Abood v. *Detroit Board of Education,*
  70
ACTION agency
  political patronage, 27, 29
Affirmative Action, 318-326
  affirmative action programs, 319-323
  compliance, 320
  quotas, 319, 325
  reverse discrimination, 321
AFSCME
  attitudes toward
    public, 323-324
    union rank-and-file, 325
  civil service advocacy, 32
  discrimination, *de facto,* 34, 321
  regional census parity, 322
Agency shop. *See* Collective Bargaining:
  issues
Alaska, 222
Albuquerque
  police strike (1975), 180
Alioto, Joseph, 197-205
Almond, Gabriel and Bingham Powell,
  269n
Amalgamated Transit Union.
  See Transit Workers Union
American Arbitration Association, 125
American Association of Classified
  School Employees, 20
American Association of University
  Professors (AAUP), 48
American Civil Liberties Union, 304
American Federation of Government
  Employees (AFGE)
  civil service reform, 45
  collective bargaining
    fringe benefits, 121
  membership
    organizing efforts, 16
  organizing efforts
    interunion rivalry, 5, 16
American Federation of Labor (AFL)

Great Schism (1936), 157
  political activities, 145, 153
  presidential campaign of 1924, 157
American Federation of Labor-Congress
  of Industrial Organizations
  (AFL-CIO)
  affiliated unions
    AFGE, 16
    AFSCME, 18
    Amalgamated Transit Union, 20
    American Federation of Teachers,
      21
    International Association of
      Machinists and Aerospace
      Workers (IAMAW), 17
    International Brotherhood of
      Electrical Workers, 20
    Metal Trades Council, 17
    Postal Clerks and Letter Carriers,
      17
  merger (1955), 158
  organization
    public employees division, 23
  political activities, 144
    Committee on Political Education
      (COPE), 144, 158, 171-174, 288
American Federation of State, County
  and Municipal Employees
  (AFSCME)
  collective bargaining
    Atlanta, 190-196, 301
    Cincinnati, 94-96, 167
    Memphis, 135
  dual organizational structure, 301-302
  historical development, 56, 325
  membership, 18, 196, 279, 325
  organizing efforts, 335
    interunion rivalry, 5
  Philadelphia, 89
  policy positions, 301
    affirmative action, 325
    contracting out, 282, 328